IF GOD MEANT TO INTERFERE

IF GOD MEANT
TO INTERFERE

AMERICAN LITERATURE AND THE
RISE OF THE CHRISTIAN RIGHT

CHRISTOPHER DOUGLAS

CORNELL UNIVERSITY PRESS

Ithaca and London

First published 2016 by Cornell University Press

Printed in the United States of America

Library of Congress Cataloging-in-Publication Data

Names: Douglas, Christopher, 1968– author.
Title: If God meant to interfere : American literature and
   the rise of the Christian right / Christopher Douglas.
Description: Ithaca : Cornell University Press, 2016. |
   Includes bibliographical references and index.
Identifiers: LCCN 2015043533 | ISBN 9781501702112
   (cloth : alk. paper)
Subjects: LCSH: American fiction—20th century—
   History and criticism. | American fiction—21st century—
   History and criticism. | Christianity in literature. |
   Fundamentalism in literature. | Evangelicalism in
   literature. | Christianity and literature—United States—
   History. | Christian conservatism—United States—
   History. | Religious right—United States—History.
Classification: LCC PS374.R47 D68 2016 |
   DDC 813/.5409382—dc23
LC record available at http://lccn.loc.gov/2015043533

Cloth printing   10 9 8 7 6 5 4 3 2 1

Contents

ACKNOWLEDGMENTS

I would like to thank my many colleagues and students at the University of Victoria who, over the years, have suggested ideas and provided feedback to sections of this work, including Shamma Boyarin, Paul Bramadat, Luke Carson, Alison Chapman, Gaelan Gilbert, Mikka Jacobsen, Magda Kay, Erin Kelly, Gary Kuchar, Allan Mitchell, Stephen Ross, Lincoln Shlensky, Madeline Walker, Adrienne Williams-Boyarin, and Adam Yaghi. My graduate student research assistants Vivian Binnema, Leah Ellingwood, Brittany Muffet, Max Olesen (at the University of Victoria), and Krista Thompson (at the University of Texas–San Marcos) provided invaluable help in tracking down some of the material for this book.

I would like to thank the publishers of *American Literary History*, *NOVEL*, *Modern Fiction Studies*, and *Religion & Literature* for permission to reprint articles of mine as sections of this book. I am especially indebted to the anonymous readers at these journals for their valuable and timely criticisms, and for challenging my thinking and pointing me in new directions. Portions of chapter 2 were previously published as *"The Poisonwood Bible's* Multicultural Graft: American Literature during the Contemporary Christian Resurgence," *American Literary History* 26.1 (2014): 132–153, by permission of Oxford University Press; portions of chapter 3 as "Christian Multiculturalism and Unlearned History in Marilynne Robinson's *Gilead*," *Novel* 44.3 (2011): 333–353, by permission of Duke University; portions of chapter 4 as "'Something That Has Already Happened': Recapitulation and Religious Indifference in *The Plot against America*," *Modern Fiction Studies* 59.4 (2013), 784–810, copyright 2013 The Johns Hopkins University, by permission; and portions of chapter 7 as "If God Meant to Interfere": Evolution and Theodicy in *Blood Meridian*," *Religion & Literature* 45.2 (2013), 83-107, by permission of the University of Notre Dame.

I'm grateful to Tracy Fessenden, Susan Harding, Michael Lackey, John McClure, Walter Benn Michaels, and Chris Teuton, among others, for conversations, critiques, and other support during the course of this project.

I thank the Social Sciences and Humanities Research Council of Canada for supporting this work with a research grant. I thank the Center for the Study of Religion and Society at the University of Victoria, as well as its members and its director, Paul Bramadat, for many conversations and for the additional time to write in the form of a Faculty Fellowship. I'm grateful for the continued support of Peter Potter and the editorial and production staff at Cornell University Press.

I thank the West Point Museum Collection, United States Military Academy, for permission to reprint an image from Samuel Chamberlain's *My Confession*.

My greatest thanks go to my family, Lynnette, Kaela, and Nathalie, for listening to me talk for years about American literature and religion.

I dedicate this book to all the Americans in my extended family: you know who you are.

Introduction
Fiction in the God Gap

The end of Don DeLillo's *White Noise* sees its protagonist, Jack Gladney, seeking solace in religion, but not in a traditional way. Treated in a Catholic hospital for a gunshot wound to his wrist—strange stigmata—Gladney seeks assurance about not his own faith, but the faith of others. "What does the Church say about heaven today?" he asks the elderly nun bandaging his wrist. He is surprised when she denies believing in angels, remarking about him in her German immigrant speech, "This is a dumb head" (302). Gladney protests: "You must believe in tradition. The old heaven and hell, the Latin mass. The Pope is infallible, God created the world in six days. The great old beliefs. Hell is burning lakes, winged demons." But the nun mocks these beliefs beyond belief, including "armies that would fight in the sky at the end of the world," and lets Gladney in on a secret: that a "tiny minority" merely pretends "to believe things no one else takes seriously. . . . To embody old things, old beliefs. The devil, the angels, heaven, hell. If we did not pretend to believe these things, the world would collapse" (303). As though overcome by enthusiasm, the distinctly German immigrant idiom patterns characterizing the nun's earlier speech are displaced by DeLillean flights of oratory:

> Our pretense is a dedication. Someone must appear to believe. Our lives are no less serious than if we professed real faith, real belief. As belief

shrinks from the world, people find it more necessary than ever that *someone* believe. . . . There must always be believers. Fools, idiots, those who hear voices, those who speak in tongues. We are your lunatics. We surrender our lives to make your nonbelief possible. You are sure that you are right but you don't want everyone to think as you do. There is no truth without fools. We are your fools, your madwomen, rising at dawn to pray, lighting candles, asking statues for good health, long life. (304)

Recasting religious belief in terms of pretense, the nun portrays religion in the final stages of secular decline, a portrayal heightened by the notion that a postmodern remnant simulates belief so that we secular moderns can remain comfortably superior, knowing who we are.

It was a vivid literary snapshot of American religion in the 1980s, but one that was spectacularly wrong. Perhaps caught in her own parochial enclave ("Germantown"), the nun seems unaware that many Americans continued to believe strongly in many of the ideas she derides, including God, the devil, angels, hell, heaven, and even the final battle between the heavenly host and Satan's forces. Indeed, according to survey research conducted in 2010, "roughly half (48%) of Christians in the U.S. say they believe that Christ will definitely (27%) or probably (20%) return to earth in the next 40 years."[1] Almost twenty years after DeLillo's novel, Tim LaHaye and Jerry Jenkins published *Glorious Appearing: The End of Days* (2004), the twelfth and concluding volume of the fundamentalist *Left Behind* series, which features Jesus leading the armies of heaven against the Antichrist's forces in the final Armageddon, modeled directly on the prophecies in the biblical book of Revelation. When Jesus sentences the Antichrist, his followers, and Lucifer to a thousand years of bathing in an actual lake of fire at the end of the book, the novel reflects the ongoing relevance of many of the beliefs DeLillo's nun mocks. Sixty-five million copies of this twelve-part series have sold since they began publication in 1995, suggesting the continuing appetite for strong, doctrinally specific, Christian belief.[2] What if such belief was not near the end of a long-suffering decline, as the nun suggests, but was surprisingly reemerging in a form that was somehow difficult to recognize?

If God Meant to Interfere is about that new form, and the difficulty post-1970s American writers faced in recognizing and responding to the most important national development in religion in that period: the social and political empowerment of conservative Christianity. Part of their difficulty lay in the type of secularization thesis articulated by DeLillo's nun, which imagined—and continues to imagine—that insofar as societies grow more modern they become more secular, discarding outmoded religious traditions and beliefs.[3] This classic "subtraction story" underlies the "master narrative of secularization," critiqued by Charles Taylor in *A Secular Age*, in which a progressive diminishment of religious authority and experience in the West results from the challenges of science and the Enlightenment (530). Liberal intellectuals, including many writers and literary critics, have been only slowly and painfully pulled away from this article of faith in recent years, as we gradually responded to evidence that, while secularization stories might apply in part to Western Europe or Canada, they don't at all accord with the facts on the ground in the United States. Indeed, Lawrence Buell wondered a few years ago whether American literary studies was "in danger of being 'left behind'" like the characters in LaHaye and Jenkins's series, noting the contrast between an increasingly "evangelical" Christian public sphere and the fact that "during the same period, literary studies by and large has moved decisively *away* from religiocentric explanations of the dynamics of cultural history," often preferring to see religion as an epiphenomenon of some deeper movement (32). It was as though literary history had merely traced the forward momentum of the *Scopes* "monkey trial" in 1925, which exposed fundamentalist Christian belief to ridicule, without noticing that strong, conservative Christian belief reemerged half a century later from a period of relative hibernation as a vibrant social force that staked crucial ground in the culture wars and forged alliances that realigned domestic politics. This resurgence has been the unrecognized religious context for US literary production since the 1970s. Writers had difficulty conceptually processing it at first, in part because the secularization thesis was so ingrained in American culture, but there were other reasons as well.

To be sure, DeLillo's nun is not a spokesperson for her author—although the analytic lyricism she achieves may reflect an authorial sympathy for her views. *White Noise* may suggest that "the most intense religious experiences in contemporary American culture may be those that derive their mysterious power from the communication loops that humans have themselves created" (Modern 198). However, other critics see it as an exception to DeLillo's work, which is generally interested in religion and has religious sensibilities; the novel "now seems an aberration within DeLillo's oeuvre," suggests Amy Hungerford, who argues that DeLillo should be understood "as a religious writer" (xx). But, notes John McClure, DeLillo tends to imagine religious energy—its "enthusiasm, irrationality, exclusivity and mindless obedience"—as foreign and exotic, and to "identify the rise of fundamentalist militancy in the United States . . . with the 'conversion of the white-skinned by the dark'" (*Partial* 71), as in the mass Unification Church wedding that opens

Mao II. Religious enthusiasts in DeLillo's fiction tend to be non-American or nonwhite, a remarkable inattention to the indigenous religious energy around him during his career. Indeed, what's striking about *White Noise*'s disbelief in the traditional articles of Christian faith is its contrasting willingness to believe in the unusual and the surprising. Characters believe all kinds of strange things throughout the book, which takes as its theme that a postmodern uncertainty about the state of knowledge seems to permit belief in all things, belief without limits once reason has collapsed. How strange it seems for DeLillo to have excluded traditional Christian belief from the smorgasbord of options available in contemporary America.

This book examines fiction that takes the conservative Christian resurgence's public presence and political issues as its occasion—especially when that public presence is addressed indirectly or evasively. The reasons for indirection and evasion were not just the unanticipated reversal of the master narrative of secularization, though that did play a part. I argue that the very coincidence of the resurgence with the post-1970s literary paradigms of multiculturalism and postmodernism resulted in a strange, and initially confusing, rearrangement of the cultural field. It wasn't, it turned out, that progressive multiculturalism and relativistic postmodernism couldn't get along with conservative Christianity (which had, after all, been there all along). It was rather, as I shall show, that multiculturalism and postmodernism became complexly intertwined with the resurgence. Indeed, two emergent nodes of complex entanglement, which I call "Christian multiculturalism" and "Christian postmodernism," forestalled simplistic oppositions in the literary and cultural fields wherein, perhaps, a multiculturalism unsullied by religious commitments might have faced a Christian religious tradition that was only universalist, and a postmodernism confident in its secular methods and conclusions might have confronted rigid Christian theological certainties. This strange trinity of the multicultural, the postmodern, and the resurgent was entangled from the beginning, I contend, all under the aegis of our supposedly growing secularization.

The chapters that follow examine selected literary novels (and some nonliterary popular ones) that attempted to grapple with the political and social implications of the conservative Christian resurgence, even as their authors proceeded with caution and hesitation, in roundabout ways and by indirect address. I argue that the resurgence was the specific religious context for American fiction in the postwar years, even when that context was not explicitly announced. While the resurgence itself was unexpected, and difficult for both novelists and critics to conceptually apprehend, some of our fiction nonetheless registered its advances and exposed its tensions as the resurgence reshaped the political and social landscape. *If God Meant to Interfere* is about learning to listen to our literature for its sometimes subterranean attention to the religious upheaval that was going on around it.

The Conservative Christian Resurgence

Christian belief and practice had, of course, never really gone away in the United States. What occurred, rather, was a decline in public religiosity in the 1930s, marked both by the legislative overturning of Prohibition (which had had considerable Christian support) and by the public ridicule fundamentalist Christians faced during the *State of Tennessee v. Scopes* trial. After the trial, writes José Casanova, fundamentalism "collapsed and, once banished from public view, most intellectuals assumed that it had been relegated to the dustbin of history" (143). We often forget, of course, that John Scopes, the high school teacher who challenged the Tennessee ban on teaching evolution, actually lost his case, and that the ban on teaching evolution there and in other states was upheld by the courts, widely and judicially supported until Cold War anxieties about science education led to curricular changes decades later. What did happen during those years was a calculated withdrawal from public political life by many American fundamentalists following these two public defeats, as evangelicalism "ceased being the public civil religion of American society" (143). But public withdrawal did not entail the diminishment of private Christian belief and practice.

Sociologists and historians of religion have different ways of describing the very public return of conservative Christianity in the years following the Second World War. One of the most compelling explanations, pursued by Robert Putnam and David Campbell in *American Grace*, is that it began as a reaction to the sexual revolution of the "long Sixties." Their examination of historical public survey data shows that the "civil religion," Cold War, anticommunist upturn in religiosity in the 1950s was politically uncorrelated, as "liberals and conservatives were equally represented among those thronging the pews" (85). But the younger generation's shifting attitudes toward sexual morality—especially premarital sex—constituted a cultural "shock" in the 1960s and early 1970s, a "seismic" and long-lasting generational shift in attitudes. What followed in the 1970s and 1980s was a "first aftershock" of rising religious conservatism. A "real and statistically significant" rise in (mostly conservative) evangelical Christian affiliation was enabled by better evangelical "retention" of children and by outside conversion to conservative evangelical denominations (104, 110). But a "second aftershock" produced a seeming backlash against politically muscular religious conservatism, as the

1990s and 2000s saw a substantial rise in Americans claiming "none" as their religious affiliation. Importantly, as Putnam and Campbell show, what began in the first aftershock and continued through the second was a demographic sorting, as political liberals became less religious and political conservatives more religious. This eventually produced a "God gap" (119) between liberals and conservatives and encouraged the polarization we experience today (132). "Religiosity has partisan overtones now that it did not have in the past," say Putnam and Campbell (369), and in this sense, the resurgence is not over.[4]

Historian Daniel Williams makes clear that the sorting Putnam and Campbell found in the survey data helped to produce the Christianization of the Republican Party, as the Religious Right, along with elements of movement conservatism, succeeded in determining much of the GOP's policy platform in recent decades. The Religious Right is an alliance of conservative evangelicals and post-separatist fundamentalists, eventually joined by conservative (Anglo-) Catholics and Mormons. While scholars do not always agree on a single term to describe this movement, I use the term "conservative Christian resurgence" to refer to the political and social empowerment of the Religious Right since the 1970s.[5]

Conservative Christians reshaped the political and moral landscape of the nation in recent decades by making universal claims within the culture wars, from questions of gender roles and sexuality, the Cold War and the War on Terror, science and health education, race and immigration, economic policy and the welfare state, and indeed the meaning of America and America in the world. Conservative Christians in general believed that communism, pornography, abortion, premarital sex, evolution, homosexual acts and homosexual marriage, and anthropogenic climate change were wrong or untrue. Conversely, they argued that school prayer, traditional gender roles, creationism, abstinence-only sex education, and the untold Christian history of the nation were morally right and factually correct. Their universalism entailed the belief that people who believed in evolution or who had abortions or engaged in homosexual sex were not just culturally different, but were in error and were morally wrong. To anticipate, by paraphrase, a character in Barbara Kingsolver's *The Poisonwood Bible* to whom I will return, what made conservative Christians' universalism universal was their willingness to assume that what was right or wrong for them was also right or wrong for other Americans—and then to push for legislation and judicial review that would make what they thought was right and true, right and true for all.

But to imagine the social and political resurgence of conservative Christianity in the postwar period as an unprovoked movement misses the way in which conservative Christians themselves experienced modernity as a secular, aggressive intrusion making claims on them and their children and destroying the nation's moral fabric. It was not just the society's fairly rapid changes in sexual mores that caught them off-guard. They also viewed a series of Supreme Court decisions and federal legislation as threatening traditional values and destroying a conventional accord between church and state. *Roe v. Wade* (1973) became a particular rallying cry because it combined the ways in which judicial overreach, lax sexual morality, and a society that placed more value on individual liberty than human life seemed to characterize a changing America. Similarly, the Supreme Court's *Epperson v. Arkansas* decision in 1968 voided state laws and local school board regulations prohibiting the teaching of evolution because they violated the Establishment Clause; it doubled down on that decision in *Edwards v. Aguillard* (1987), which struck down newer regulations requiring an "equal time" approach in which "creation science" was taught alongside evolution. Previous rulings in 1962 (*Engel v. Vitale*) and 1963 (*Abington v. Schempp*) had banned school prayer and mandatory Bible reading. These federal rulings overturned a more traditional respect and place for religious belief in the educational system. Reaction against them, especially by many conservative Christians in the South, built on earlier resentments stemming from the 1954 *Brown v. Board of Education* decision and the desegregation directives that changed American society in the following decade.

As we shall see, many conservative Christians who were previously opposed to the mixing of religion and politics changed their tune once they saw the great success of African American Christians and their allies during the civil rights movement; it is not an exaggeration to say that the conservative Christian resurgence begun in the 1970s was both a tribute to and a reaction against that success. While liberals, secularists, and progressives may have experienced the unexpected resurgence as an intrusion of religion into a properly secular public sphere, conservative Christians had already experienced postwar changes in America that they deemed an intrusive pulling apart of traditional values and an external limitation on their religious freedoms.

The life and career of Michelle Bachmann provides an instructive synecdoche for the conservative Christian resurgence, allowing us to grasp its shape and complexity. A four-term Republican Congresswoman from Minnesota and a candidate for the Republican nomination in the 2012 Presidential campaign, Bachmann's trajectory allows me to offer a thumbnail sketch of some of the qualities and history of the resurgence, in an admittedly schematic way.

Born in 1956 in Iowa to a family of Lutherans who voted Democratic, Bachmann, like many Christians, doubled her childhood religious upbringing with teenage and then adult commitment. Bachmann's father abandoned the family in 1970. Two years later, his daughter joined a high-school prayer group. There, she became a "born-again Christian" at age sixteen, as she recounted in a speech in 2006:

> I didn't know I wasn't a believer. But they knew I wasn't a believer, and they started praying for me. And all of a sudden the holy spirit started knocking on my heart's door and I could hear the Lord tug me and call me to Himself, and I responded on November 1st of 1972, and I knew that I knew that I knew [sic] that I had received Jesus Christ as my lord and savior and that my life would never be the same after I made that commitment, because I knew what darkness looked like. I knew it from my home life. I absolutely understood sin, and I wanted no part of it. When Jesus Christ came in and cleaned out this dark heart, that was light. That was rest. That was peace. It was refreshment. Why would I ever want the world? I knew what that had to offer. This was great. That didn't mean that I woke and all of a sudden I had money, all of a sudden I had position, all of a sudden I had education. It didn't. But what it meant was that all of a sudden I had a father. (quoted in Lizza)[6]

Coming of age during the sexual revolution of the "long Sixties," Bachmann's religious experience reminds us that that revolution was unevenly experienced by young people of her generation, a great many of whom turned to traditional moral values amidst the upheaval.

Bachmann's politics underwent a sea change in the late 1970s. After meeting her future husband in 1975 they campaigned for Carter, the first evangelical, "born-again" president, in 1976, and attended his inauguration the next year. During his term in office, the Bachmanns married and became disillusioned with Carter's liberal politics, eventually becoming fundamentalist supporters of Ronald Reagan—Reagan Democrats on their way to becoming Republicans—and working for his 1980 campaign. Reagan attracted a large number of conservative Christians to his cause, telling one group in Dallas that year, "You may not endorse me, but I endorse you" (quoted in Wilentz 122). The 1980 presidential election represented an important milestone in the development of the "God gap," wherein increasing numbers of evangelical and fundamentalist Christians voted Republican.

Part of that shift, for the Bachmanns and many others, was the role that abortion played once it had been politically activated in the late 1970s. When *Roe v. Wade* was announced in 1973, Catholics responded immediately but Protestants, who had not been greatly interested in abortion, took a range of positions on the issue (Harding 189–90). Conservative Protestant opposition to abortion changed only slowly in the 1970s, and was significantly galvanized by Francis Schaeffer's documentary *How Should We Then Live?* in 1977. The film played the crucial roles of mobilizing a generation of previously separatist fundamentalists and radicalizing previously moderate evangelicals. Bachmann and her future husband saw Schaeffer's documentary in 1977, and by 1980 were praying outside abortion clinics.

Because Bachman was a Midwesterner, her story allows us to see the way in which the rise of the Religious Right was a national, not regional, phenomenon. To be sure, the "Bible Belt" in the South was the core constituency in the political realignment, as many states-rights Democrats became Dixiecrats and then Republicans, especially following the civil rights movement. The South continued to be an intellectual and organizational base for the Religious Right—Jerry Falwell's founding of the Moral Majority in 1979 from his church in Virginia is a good example. But the political and social resurgence of conservative Christians was occurring in suburbs and cities across the country, often beginning in local school board politics, as with the Bachmanns.

Bachmann attended the law school of fundamentalist Oral Roberts University beginning in 1979, and there became exposed to some of the currents in conservative Christian thought. She worked as a research assistant for a professor who influenced her interest in both the home-schooling movement and his scholarly work on how America "'was and to a large extent still is a Christian nation,' and that 'our culture should be permeated with a distinctively Christian flavoring'" (Lizza). Oral Roberts University was one of a network of hundreds of sectarian conservative Christian postsecondary institutions, a parallel academic system that, with churches, publishers, and media broadcasters, provided the intellectual, social, and political ground for the resurgence to come.

Bachmann's skepticism of evolution as "a theory that has 'never been proven'" (Lizza) and her willingness to see Intelligent Design taught in public schools represents another intellectual current of the resurgence. Over the last four or five decades, political activism for the resurgence at local school boards and state legislatures has focused on opposition to teaching evolution and promotion of either young-earth creationist or old-earth creationist "alternatives."

After high school Bachmann worked briefly on a kibbutz in Israel, an experience that has given her, according to Ryan Lizza, an emotional connection to the country. The historical influence of premillennial dispensationalism on fundamentalist thought (Harding 228–46)—that is, the theological expectation that we are currently in the last human era, during which Christ will return to set up his thousand-year kingdom on earth—has lent the conservative Christian resurgence a strong current of what Jonathan Freedman, in his discussion of the *Left Behind* series, calls "philosemitism" (142) and reflects ways the resurgence affects international as well as domestic politics, with Israel playing a central role.

That the Bachmanns opened their home to twenty-three foster children over the years, "all of whom were teen-age girls and many of whom had eating disorders" (Lizza), reflects the general fact that Americans who are more religious tend to be more charitable and generous than less-religious Americans, as Putnam and Campbell show (443–79). Indeed, focusing on the conservative cultural politics of the resurgence—as this book does—risks occluding the way in which conservative Christianity often maintains an emphasis on "good works," whether it be foster care by individuals or the evangelical president George W. Bush's sustained support of HIV prevention in Africa, where he continues to enjoy approval ratings in the 70s and 80s.[7] Although it is easier for liberals to remember the good works of progressive Christians like Martin Luther King, Jr., doing so risks losing sight of the ways in which many conservative Christians have also pushed, and continue to push, social gospel concerns.

Michelle Bachmann's career is also an indicator of the way in which conservative Christian families have adopted some of the gender role changes in American society (see Harding 166–76; Griffith). Public political figures such as Bachmann, or Phyllis Schlafly heading opposition to the Equal Rights Amendment, or erstwhile vice-presidential candidate Sarah Palin, would still affirm their husbands as the spiritual heads of their households. Yet at the same time, the revolution in gender roles in recent decades has affected conservative Christianity as well. The conservative Christian resurgence has not been merely reactionary, in simple opposition to modernity, but is, rather, sometimes selective and adaptive. At the same time, Bachmann is a good example of what conservative newspaper columnist David Brooks has called the "alternative-reality right—those who don't believe in global warming, evolution or that Obama was born in the U.S."[8] As I will develop in the coming chapters, the conservative Christian resurgence often turns its back on human knowledge in favor of its sectarian understanding of divine revelation.

Bachmann is "the archetypal Tea Party politician" (Putnam and Campbell 574), a movement that is, contrary to occasional rhetoric and reputation, strongly linked to the conservative Christian resurgence. Putnam and Campbell conclude from their survey data that "what really distinguishes rank-and-file Tea Party supporters from other Americans and even other Republicans is their desire to bring more God into government" (571)—a priority ranking even higher than "less government" in general (573). In this sense, the Tea Party is an intensification of the conservative Christian resurgence, one seemingly caused by both the 2007–2008 financial crisis and the election of the nation's first African American president. The continued relevance of race for this core constituency of the Republican Party is seen in the data presented by Putnam and Campbell, who conclude that "even compared with other white conservative Republicans, [Tea Party supporters] had a low regard for minorities when we first interviewed them [in 2006], and they still did in 2011" (573).

Michelle Bachmann's decision not to seek reelection in 2014—as well as the mention of the Tea Party and politics in the 2010s—brings us to the question of whether the social and political resurgence of conservative Christians is already receding or is transitioning to a new phase. The political apex of the resurgence (so far) was the administration of President George W. Bush (2001–2009); the election and then reelection of President Barack Obama appears to have thrown the resurgence off-balance. Americans remain very culturally and politically divided: reviewing 2014 data, the Pew Research Center reports that "Since 1992, the share of white evangelical Protestants who align with the GOP has never been higher. About two-thirds (68%) of white evangelicals either identify as Republicans or lean Republican, while just 22% affiliate with the Democratic Party or lean Democratic."[9] The God gap remains vast, and the next decade will tell whether the resurgence is entering a new phase, or whether its social and political power is beginning to recede from a height reached in the first decade of the new millennium.

American Literature and the Resurgence

How did American literature respond to the radically altered social and political landscape characterized by the postwar reemergence of conservative Christianity? Strangely, the most famous literary response was a Canadian novel, Margaret Atwood's *The Handmaid's Tale*. Published a year after *White Noise*, it lay at the other end of the spectrum: if DeLillo imagined American Christianity as a waning energy, Atwood crafted a near-future dystopia in which fundamentalist Christians had overthrown the United States government and established a totalitarian theocracy named Gilead. Modeled in some ways after George Orwell's Oceania, Gilead ordains conformity of belief, rigidly controlled sexual practices and gender roles, and networks of spies to seek out traitors within. Taking their cue from the biblical story of Abram's "handmaid" Hagar who bears him a child in the place of his barren wife Sarai in Genesis 16, the leaders of the new republic combat an infertility epidemic by employing surrogates like the novel's protagonist. This arrangement, the handmaid's Commander explains, fixes the social ills characterizing pre-revolution America:

> This way they all get a man, nobody's left out. And then if they did marry, they could be left with a kid, two kids, the husband might just get fed up and take off, disappear, they'd have to go on welfare. Or else he'd stay around and beat them up. Or if they had a job, the children in daycare or left with some brutal ignorant woman, and they'd have to pay for that themselves, out of their wretched little paychecks. Money was the only measure of worth, for everyone, they got no respect as mothers. No wonder they were giving up on the whole business. This way they're protected, they can fulfill their biological destinies in peace. (219–20)

At the handmaid indoctrination center, she hears a lunchtime prayer, "*Blessed are the meek. Blessed are the silent*," and reflects, "I knew they made that up, I knew it was wrong, and they left things out too" (89). Atwood's metaphor suggests how conservative theology, even among biblical literalists, rests on selection and emphasis that transform potentially progressive hermeneutics ("Blessed are the meek, for they will inherit the earth" in Matt 5:5) into justifications of current social relations, a new beatitude for silent acquiescence.

Aside from occasional conception ceremonies, the handmaid spends her days in household prayer sessions, the communal witnessing of the executions of traitors, homosexuals, or Jews who will not convert, and in boredom, without access to print or television. She eventually recognizes her Commander's wife as someone from the previous era: Serena Joy had been a gospel singer on television when the narrator was a child, and later became famous for "making speeches. She was good at it. Her speeches were about the sanctity of the home, about how women should stay home. Serena Joy didn't do this herself, she made speeches instead, but she presented this failure of hers as a sacrifice she was making for the good of all," even in the face of assassination attempts (45). She is now consigned to her home and garden by the strict gender roles established by the new Christian theocracy she helped create. At the novel's end the narrator attempts an escape to Canada, and its epilogue suggests she gets at least partway, with enough time to record her experience on audiotape before disappearing from the historical record. Taking its cue from the 1980s culture wars on abortion, sexual morality, and gender roles, in which conservative Christians played a large part—Serena Joy seems modelled on both the mascara-laden, tearful televangelist Tammy

Faye Bakker and the speech-making, Equal Rights Amendment–opposing Schlafly—Atwood's novel was the most direct (and obviously critical) literary reaction to the conservative Christian resurgence. Indeed, Gilead was "a dystopian state that the novel hypothesizes as the logical extension . . . of the agenda articulated during the 1980s by America's fundamentalist Christian Right" (Neuman 857).[10]

If American literature produced anything as obviously registering and responding to the social and political empowerment of conservative Christianity, it would perhaps be Tom Perrotta's *The Abstinence Teacher* (2007), a character drama featuring a protagonist who has "been reborn in Christ" (81), a conversion that helps the sinner reorder a life disordered by alcoholism, drug use, and divorce. But offering a brief, unpremeditated prayer of thanksgiving following a win by the soccer team of ten-year-old girls Tim coaches puts him on a collision course with the novel's other protagonist, Ruth, a secular high-school teacher who faces her own battle against offended Christian students when she happens to mention in a sex-education class that some people like oral sex. In both cases, the question becomes the role of public religiosity and public pedagogy that offends religious sentiments, as focused through the prism of parents worried about their children being exposed to the "other side" of the conservative Christian / secular divide. (Ruth and Tim both have daughters on the soccer team Tim coaches.) Ruth is coerced into teaching a new school board–approved curriculum on abstinence as a result, and thus *The Abstinence Teacher* has for its setting the new political muscle of conservative Christianity in the first decade of the new millennium. Perrotta, indeed, wrote the novel in the wake of the 2004 Presidential election. Best known for his 1998 novel *Election* (adapted into a TV movie the next year), Perrotta is perhaps representative of bewildered liberals who didn't understand the source and nature of this resurgent power. As he put it in an interview, "I did feel somewhat inadequate as a novelist, just like I'd missed something huge happening in this country. I really did set out to kind of investigate that world" (quoted in M. Rich), and so his question became "Is it going to be possible for me to write a believable version of contemporary American evangelical Christianity? Because it really is a little bit outside of my daily life. I mean, [*ominous voice*] they're all around us. [*Laughter*]" ("Tom," 365–66). Perrotta may have felt like his born-again character Tim, who reflects about his new Christian wife that "he and Carrie had effectively grown up in different countries" (101), but eventually realizes that "*he* was the immigrant, a tourist who'd gone to a foreign country, met a local woman, and decided to stay" (102).

Earlier novelists in what appeared to be an era of receding religious enthusiasm were often aware of evangelical energy, even if they were not so topical as Perrotta. At the end of Sylvia Plath's *The Bell Jar* (1963), as the rehabilitated (or culturally brainwashed) Esther Greenwood prepares to leave the mental health facility where she has been receiving treatment, she reflects that it was as if she were preparing to be married: "But I wasn't getting married. There ought, I thought, to be a ritual for being born twice—patched, retreaded and approved for the road" (233). Of course, there was a ritual for being born twice: baptism, as practiced since early Christian times to signify the need for adult transformation and commitment, suggested by Jesus's instructions that to see the Kingdom of God one had to be "born again" (John 3:3). Plath's vocabulary was Christian traditional, but it was also language central to the conservative Christian resurgence that was yet to come as she was writing her novel in the early 1960s.

Indeed, while the phrase "born again" would not really enter popular parlance until presidential nominee Jimmy Carter used it to describe himself in 1976 (M. Taylor 257), evangelical energy was already afoot—as with Billy Graham, the nation's chief evangelist and pastor to presidents since Eisenhower. Preaching during this time and into the resurgence, Graham "ended every sermon by asking people to let Christ enter their lives and inviting them to approach the altar to receive God's blessing. For the Evangelical Christian, what is most important is his or her *individual* decision in response to the forgiveness offered by the *transcendent personal* God made present in the person of Jesus Christ," notes Mark Taylor. "As this message has become attractive to more and more people over the past four decades, what has occurred can only be described as the Fourth Great Awakening" (258).[11] For Plath, then, evangelical energy is apprehensible as metaphor, not quite as its own phenomenon, available for her ironic description of the supposed progression of her protagonist.

In a more religiously aware novelist like John Updike, a similar phrase retains its more directly religious meaning. When Rabbit Angstrom is asked by his Episcopal pastor's wife, in the first Rabbit novel, if he has been "born anew," Updike crafts his response in terms of a Dantean echo: "Last night driving home I got this feeling of a straight road ahead of me; before that I was sort of in the bushes and it didn't matter which way I went" (180). That Rabbit does not quite stay on the straight road in *Rabbit, Run* or the rest of the tetralogy does not disqualify Updike's appeal to the evangelically charged language in his 1960 novel. The Rabbit series was conceived in part as a chronicle of a character through the decades of the 1950s, '60s, '70s, and '80s, and it is a good example of how American fiction began to register the religious transformation the nation was undergoing. This is especially true of the last novel, *Rabbit at Rest* (1990), set in 1989. Rabbit's mistress is newly fundamentalist ("One of these new denominations that goes back to fundamentals. You know—we're lost, and we're saved" [1236]), whose church is "just a plain raw building, a warehouse" (1388). The presence of "evangelical fundamentalists" (1064) in communities and in the media has percolated its way into Rabbit's consciousness. A local suburb has been developed on farmland previously owned by an "old spinster who lived there so many years and had wanted to leave it to some television evangelist as a kind of salvation park, a holy-roller retreat" (1223). Rabbit hears a radio report on the trial of the televangelist "Jim Bakker . . . on twenty-four counts of fraud in connection with his scandal-ridden PTL television ministry," and on his wife Tammy who "prayed with him and they agreed that they would trust in the Lord," as well as from his accuser "Jessica Hahn, the former PTL secretary whose sexual encounter with Bakker in 1980 led to his downfall," and who calls him "a master manipulator. I think this is a sympathy stunt just like it is every time Tammy gets on TV and starts crying and saying how abused they are" (1448–49). The Rabbit novels were said to give "the fullest scope to [Updike's] remarkable gifts as an observer and describer. What they amount to is a social and, so to speak, emotional history of the United States" (Quinton)—even when, in this passage and elsewhere, their attention to current events is somewhat awkwardly incorporated.

The Rabbit tetralogy is a good example of how contemporary American fiction registered the renewed public presence of conservative Protestants in the postwar years, confirming Updike's status as a chronicler of Middle America. But Updike's interest is not really in the resurgence itself, or its crucial cultural politics. The topic of abortion is briefly debated at the car lot Rabbit runs (1370–72), for example, but Updike's project is not really to examine the religious cultural politics of that issue, or other issues. The deepest religious questions these novels raise tend to be more personal and metaphysical. In the last novel they take the form of Rabbit musing on his mortality, and the fate of his soul in a material body experiencing worsening heart disease. When a friend asks him, regarding the procedures of one surgical option, "What's wrong with running your blood through a machine? What else you think you are, champ?" Rabbit's anxiety occasions an answer in Updike's religious lyricism:

A God-made one-of-a-kind with an immortal soul breathed in. A vehicle of grace. A battlefield of good and evil. An apprentice angel. All those things they tried to teach you in Sunday school, or really didn't try very hard to teach you, just let them drift in out of the pamphlets, back there in that church basement buried deeper in his mind than an air-raid shelter. (1265)

Attending to the cultural politics of the conservative Christian resurgence is not Updike's project—nor should it be, in a tetralogy for which religious belief is a largely private affair—and its passing presence alerts us to how contemporary American fiction often registered the phenomenon, however briefly.

Evangelical language lingers in Plath's "born twice" Esther as an empty vehicle available for ironic metaphor, exists for Updike's "born anew" Rabbit as the deeply private marker of a personal struggle with faith, and ultimately remains for Perrotta's "reborn" sinner the realm of a "foreign country." For all its research into that alien territory of resurgent cultural politics, however, *The Abstinence Teacher* remains a witty, insightful character drama; its setting and plot revolve around two resurgent flashpoints—public prayer and sex education—but it is less interested in investigating the complexities and nuances of that conflict than in presenting sympathetic portraits of two characters who came of age in the wake of the sexual revolution (one a bewildered and ambushed liberal, the other a saved and temporarily-empowered substance abuser) and then experienced the resurgent reaction in different ways. *If God Meant to Interfere* examines texts that are, in contrast, more centrally concerned with the cultural politics of the resurgence, especially in their moments of complex entanglement with multiculturalism and postmodernism, even if and when such issues are less directly registered than in Updike's Rabbit tetralogy or Perrotta's novel.

Scholarly Context

No account of contemporary American fiction within the context of the conservative Christian resurgence yet exists, even amidst the valuable scholarship on the religious dimensions of contemporary literary production. Scholars have dwelt in particular on two possibly related phenomena: first, the redirection, emerging from contemporary religious studies scholarship, from questions of theological history to questions of everyday religious practice and experience, associated with work by Robert Orsi and others; and second, the literary effects of that other great tectonic shift in contemporary American religion, the proliferation of pluralist religious identities and numbers since American immigration law ceased in 1965 to give preference to Europeans.

That the importance of religious experience has reemerged simultaneous with a disavowal of religious dogma and certainties has been the general conclusion of two recent (and excellent) studies of religion in contemporary American literature by John McClure and Amy Hungerford. In *Partial*

Faiths: Postsecular Fiction in the Age of Pynchon and Morrison, McClure characterizes "postsecular" fictions as those in which characters turn "back toward the religious," though in a mode of experience that is partial, unresolved, and generally not traditionally doctrinal (3–6). Drawing on Gianni Vattimo's notion of "weak religion," McClure sees authors such as Toni Morrison, DeLillo, Thomas Pynchon, and Louise Erdrich as evading historical institutionalizations of power and certainty by inscribing in their "spiritual comedies" (16) impiety, extravagance, and excess. Pynchon's world, then, is one that is reenchanted but ontologically pluralist (33–35); conversion in Pynchon, as in other works of postsecular fiction, is often to "some only faintly affirmed, or weakly articulated, or dramatically marginal form of spirituality" (41). In a similar vein, McClure writes of Morrison's tactic in *Paradise* that "by creolizing the cosmos, she affirms the supernatural while rendering any specific mapping of its population, laws, and terrain manifestly partial" (106). Analogously, says McClure, in works by Native American writers like N. Scott Momaday, Leslie Silko, and Erdrich, "characters disenchanted with secularization stumble back toward religiously inflected modes of being that are marked by key features of postsecular spirituality: polytheistic pluralism, attention to the Earth, an emphasis on spiritual practice, and a distrust at once of sweeping claims for salvation and dogmatic rigidities" (133). While attentive to the many differences among these authors—including Tony Kushner and Michael Ondaatje—McClure argues that postsecular fiction "presses back" against the false dichotomy of fundamentalism/secularism, opening spaces for forms of spiritual experience that are often plural, noninstitutional, and shy of rigid doctrines or systems of certain knowledge (196).

Hungerford's analysis is different from McClure's, but its account of belief in contemporary American literature complements it. *Postmodern Belief: American Literature and Religion Since 1960* examines the will to believe in contemporary American literature, culture, and academic discourse. Facing squarely the all-important conundrum of the state of belief in contemporary America—its centrality to our national discourse, but its simultaneous pluralist practice and diversity in public life—Hungerford argues that these different fields have tended to arrive at a common solution: belief in belief itself, a kind of contentless religious experience where doctrine is disavowed in favor of meaninglessness, incommunicable thoughts and practices, and religious language as style and material signifier. Her contentions that "belief in meaninglessness confers religious authority upon the literary" and that "such belief, and its literary vehicles, becomes important to the practice of religion in America" (xv) are central to her analysis that establishes religious longing at the heart of a reenchanted postmodern formalism.

She contextualizes DeLillo among American Catholic writers, including key figures such as Flannery O'Connor and Walker Percy (54–55) and reminds us of the debates about the Latin mass and the vernacular that characterized DeLillo's upbringing; this too, Hungerford suggests, was part of a larger cultural fascination with the possibility of language's nonreferential spiritual or psychological effects, as she demonstrates in Allen Ginsberg's chant-inspired poetry and Marshall McLuhan's oft-cited gospel that the medium was the message. While Ginsberg, McLuhan, and DeLillo might arrive at some of the same sensibilities, the Jewish Ginsberg does so through training in Indian chanting and a disturbing encounter with William S. Burroughs' creative method, while it is by virtue of childhood training that the latter two come to their notions that form can be a kind of spiritual experience that stands outside of—and may even be superior to—doctrinal instruction. Hungerford sees these different social strands converging onto this will to believe she diagnoses in contemporary culture and literature, even as she disentangles the different roles of belief in Jewish, Protestant, and Catholic understandings, amid rival values centered on practice, performance, and ritual.

If God Meant to Interfere concurs with McClure and Hungerford about the retreat of doctrine in much of the literary work they examine, and seeks to build on their groundbreaking studies in a couple of ways. Most important, of course, I concentrate on the conservative Christian resurgence characterizing the contemporary religious context for American literature—a context in which, crucially, doctrine is not at all in retreat and the religion offered is the "strong" variety in contradistinction to which Vattimo proposed the "weak." But I also wish to situate the resurgence within the context of a developing multiculturalism alongside which it emerged. While both McClure and Hungerford see postmodernism as the key frame for the reemergence of public religious expression in the contemporary period, I include multiculturalism as an important third term of analysis. I wish to offer a more complex critical genealogy of the resurgence and multiculturalism, one that sees the two operating in a dialectic of response and interrogation. The literary history of the period, in other words, is not just one in which religious experience and contemporary literature share homological qualities of a disinterest in beliefs and doctrines, but one in which that disinterest itself is understood to be a manifestation of religion's quasi-secularized status as a culture granted the same virtues of pluralism and relativism as other cultures. As we shall see, it is the conservative Christian resurgence's continual switching of registers between cultural tradition held by private individuals who have the right to be protected from intrusive, secular modernity on the one hand, and the universal basis for public policy on the other, that begins to sketch the complex ways in which the resurgence at times opposes and at other times dovetails with multiculturalism. My term "Christian multiculturalism" begins to name this site of complex entanglement and mutual engagement.

The other way I build on these studies is by elaborating on the ways in which the "postsecular" (McClure) "faith in faith" (Hungerford) is postmodern not just in terms of the genealogy of modern secularization. Taking up Charles Taylor's provocative thesis in *A Secular Age* that we need to get past the "subtraction story" that forms the dominant account of secularization, I see the conservative Christian resurgence not so much as a postsecular "weak" movement as the social emergence of a renewed set of "strong" authorities and experiences that had never really gone away. It was a movement of what José Casanova calls "the deprivatization of modern religion" (220), but one that could productively be understood as a phenomenon of the postmodern leveling of discourses of authority, expertise, and mastery, the effect of which was to recreate the religious choices of everyday life in public space. I want to extend this sense of the postmodern to look at how knowledge and modes of expertise came to be seen as suffering from a crisis of legitimation in both literature and society during the contemporary period. Once our modes of expert evaluation begin to be seen as rhetorical conventions along the lines outlined by Jean-François Lyotard in *The Postmodern Condition*, another unusual dovetailing of the conservative Christian resurgence and postmodernism emerges, with the expert accounts of the biological origins of species and the historical authoring of the Bible becoming merely sets of "language games" that can be placed against others not necessarily any worse or less true on a now properly leveled playing field. I call this site of complex entanglement "Christian postmodernism."

Although it is temptingly easy to think of the conservative Christian resurgence since the 1970s as being naturally oppositional to the two social and literary paradigms of postmodernism and multiculturalism that were contemporaneous with it, I argue for a more complex (and, hopefully, truer) story of their entanglement. I also argue that, insofar as the conservative Christian resurgence sometimes strangely shared logics and vocabularies with postmodernism and multiculturalism, it was that very coincidence that made it difficult for literary writers to conceptually apprehend what the resurgence was and how it operated. The resurgence, in other words, sometimes looked like a species of multiculturalism or postmodernism—and, in fact, it often was, in substantial and nontrivial ways. My aim here is to think through the coincidences of the resurgence with multiculturalism and postmodernism: what it means for our literature that these movements emerged alongside one another in the contemporary period. In doing so, I follow Taylor's invitation to move beyond the "subtraction story" and see the way in which secularization has not banished religion, but led to a proliferation of possible positions of belief and unbelief. Taylor calls these alternatives the "nova," and suggests that their increased proliferation, especially following World War Two, constitutes a kind of "super-nova" of potential belief and unbelief subjectivities (377). I see the nodes of Christian multiculturalism and Christian postmodernism as being sites of just such nova. Likewise, I offer these possibilities as a potential answer to Tracy Fessenden's recent and provocative question as to "what's *American* about postsecular claims made in, around, or on behalf of American literature" ("Problem" 165). These entangled sites of Christian multiculturalism and Christian postmodernism, I contend, depend on historically American cultural and religious genealogies; they could not have happened anywhere else.

Accordingly, this book is divided into two parts, with the first unravelling the coemergence of the conservative Christian resurgence with multiculturalism, and the second doing so in terms of the state of postmodern knowledge. Chapter 1 establishes the mutually entangled developments of canonical multiculturalism and the resurgence in terms of their shared rejection of an assimilationist civil rights consensus. Chapter 2 examines Barbara Kingsolver's attention to missionary work, race, and the antecedents of the conservative Christian resurgence in *The Poisonwood Bible*. In contrast to Kingsolver's outsider status, chapter 3 looks at a liberal Christian response to the resurgence, Marilynne Robinson's *Gilead*, in terms of its imagining of family and history in a time before the resurgence had taken hold. Chapter 4 turns to Philip Roth's rendering of resurgent politics in *The Plot Against America*.

Part 2 turns to the interweavings of the resurgence with postmodernism. Because postmodern religion is a better-understood intersection than literary multiculturalism and Christianity—thanks to critics such as Hungerford and McClure—I focus my analysis on the postmodern state of knowledge and its ways of "reading" the world. Chapter 5 begins with Thomas Pynchon's *The Crying of Lot 49*, whose sociopolitical terrain, I argue, is prophetic of the paranoid style emergent at the time of its composition. In chapter 6 I examine Carl Sagan's science fiction novel *Contact*, which imagines a virulent fundamentalist reaction to a message received from extraterrestrials. Chapter 7 rereads Cormac McCarthy's *Blood Meridian* in terms of the most famous science-religion debate of its moment of composition—that between evolution and "creation science." Chapter 8 looks at the status of expert knowledge of religion in Dan Brown's *The Da Vinci Code*, a novel that has had an outsized effect on American belief. These four novels turn on the question of what it means to read design in nature and in history.

Throughout both parts, I intersperse my examination of contemporary American fiction and the conservative Christian resurgence by looking briefly at the texts of the resurgence itself, including the *Left Behind* series, sensational Christian fiction like *The Shack*, and nonfiction resurgent Christian texts such as Schaeffer's *How Should We Then Live?* and Tim LaHaye's *Faith of Our Founding Fathers*. Each chapter is a snapshot of the literary reaction to the conservative Christian resurgence, together encompassing a wide range of angles, from canonical multiculturalists through a progressive pantheist, a liberal Christian, a secular Jew, an early postmodern master, a working scientist, a late modern master, and a bestselling pop fiction author. The title of my book borrows a line from a character in McCarthy's novel who asks, "If God meant to interfere in the degeneracy of mankind would he not have done so by now?" (153). The novelists here under study, Christians and non-Christians alike, answer that question differently, and proceed to wonder what the shape of God's intervention is, and how we are to read its signs. *If God Meant to Interfere: American Fiction and the Rise of the Christian Right*'s goal is to map the strange, unanticipated return of resurgent, conservative Christianity, as well as the strangeness of what its encounter with multiculturalism and postmodernism means for a literary history of the present.

PART ONE

Multicultural Entanglements

CHAPTER 1

Multiculturalism, Secularization, Resurgence

A spectre is haunting america—the spectre of neo-hoodooism. all the powers of old america have entered into a holy alliance to exorcise this spectre: allen ginsberg timothy leary richard nixon edward teller billy graham time magazine the new york review of books and the underground press. may the best church win. shake hands now and come out conjuring.

Ishmael Reed, "Black Power Poem"

But if Christianity is truth and God is really there, we don't need to do this stuff to make ourselves feel Christian. . . . So I think that's a good example of the kind of baggage that we brought along. It's a cultural, it's like a, sort of our own form of jive if you like. . . . Then we go around and say, well, why doesn't the world understand anything we're saying, or whatever. Because we're speaking a foreign language!

Frank Schaeffer, "Christianity Is Truth Rather Than Religion"

This pair of epigraphs begins to tell the story of how the revitalization of religion in post-1970 America was premised on the mutual attention with which emergent multiculturalism and the conservative Christian resurgence regarded one another. Though we might be tempted to regard progressive multiculturalism and the conservative resurgence in simple oppositional terms, both were reactions against the vaguely religious liberal consensus on civil rights that preceded them and both sought to reenergize specific religious traditions, with consequences for their communities and for the question of how those communities should live. Their religious activations took form through a shared rejection of the tepid, conformist religiosity of the 1950s, and also through a mutual attentiveness, multiculturalism's eye on the resurgence no less than the resurgence's eye on multiculturalism.

One gets a sense of that attentiveness in the shape of Black Arts Movement writer Ishmael Reed's 1970 clash of civilizations, wherein one side is characterized by pairs such as Leary *and* Nixon, Ginsberg *and* the famous Baptist evangelist Billy Graham. Reed's formulation of this essential opposition as being between churches, with Graham as one of the leaders, bespeaks the way he constructed his multicultural counter-project in terms of the evangelical Christianity that would soon be politically energized and increasingly conservative, as the arc from Ronald Reagan to George W. Bush suggests. Thinking of hoodoo—the voodoo-inspired African American religious tradition—as an alternative church, he imagines it opposing not the dry, proper Episcopalian church down the road (Updike's literary territory), but rather America's chief evangelist, counselor of presidents, who fills football stadiums with born-again crowds. The flipside of Reed's attention is nicely captured in Frank Schaeffer's argument in his 1982 guest sermon to the chapel congregation at Jerry Falwell's Liberty University. In his view, separatist fundamentalism, which had withdrawn from public life since the *Scopes* trial decades before, had developed into a kind of marginal culture. In this milestone sermon, Schaeffer—speaking for his father, Francis Schaeffer IV, author of *How Should We Then Live?*—likened the private evangelical discourse fundamentalists spoke to one another to "jive," African American vernacular difference. Schaeffer's sermon shook up Falwell's transitioning congregation, calling it to reenter the public sphere and stop being a marginal, private culture on the sidelines of American society. The university provided counseling for some disturbed listeners (Harding 142). Reed and Schaeffer issued their calls to religious activation not simply by eschewing the dry religiosity of the preceding decades, but by each polemical spokesman bearing witness to the other's important religious movement alongside which their own coemerged.

In this chapter I argue that multiculturalism and the conservative Christian resurgence were mutually entangled responses to the civil rights consensus of the 1950s and 1960s. These co-implicated movements emerged almost simultaneously in the late 1960s and the 1970s with an eye on each other. Just as important, both emerged as reactions to—and in some important ways, against—the civil rights period and its successes. These movements insisted that the United States was far more sectarian than the consensus imagined; they likewise understood older religious traditions to be available for reactivation, as current resources for identity communities and daily living. John McClure's account of the postsecular in American literature demonstrates a postmodern ontological pluralism, as he particularly shows is true of Pynchon, DeLillo, Kushner, and Morrison. But he also shows that for Morrison and several Native American novelists, the postsecular turn entails a multicultural "creolizing [of] the cosmos" (*Partial* 106), insofar as metaphysical incommensurability or plurality often includes a reclaiming of non-Christian spiritualities. This is true, crucially, for many of the writers I examine in this chapter. As multicultural writers reclaimed ancestral spiritual resources, they emerged from secularization's shadow, contesting it in complicated ways that challenged it and yet continued some of its understandings about religious cultures.

This chapter has three related goals. First, it sets the stage for my analysis of the literary response to the conservative Christian resurgence by looking at the conventional wisdom about religion that directly preceded it. I outline how a midcentury social science model explained religion as prioritizing community, not belief. Second, I argue that the reason progressive multiculturalism and the conservative Christian resurgence were entangled movements is that they were motivated responses to a liberal consensus about religion and civil rights after the 1960s. Third, I show that the reclamation of ancestral religious traditions was constitutive of the multicultural turn. If, as Tracy Fessenden has illuminated, "American civil religion, a devotion to the nation's sacred ideals that allegedly transcends denominational alliance, emerges from the Protestant-secular continuum and renders it coextensive with American identity" (*Culture* 140), the multicultural turn articulated its project by contesting both the invisible Protestantism of civil religion and its disenchanted banishing of the gods.

Religion and/as Culture

> A careful study of Negro churches, *as conducted by Negroes*, will show, I think, that the Negro is not a christian, but a pagan still.
>
> Zora Neale Hurston, "The Florida Expedition"

When Norman Mailer was released after spending a night in jail following the March on the Pentagon in 1967, he gave a remarkable speech declaring his wife's love for Jesus Christ. With cameras rolling (Mailer was the subject of a documentary) and feeling a spiritual contentment that he imagined akin to what "Christians . . . must signify when they spoke of Christ within them," Mailer decided to "pick up some of the Chaplain's language" (referring to John Boyle, the Presbyterian Chaplain at Yale and fellow antiwar protestor). Referring to himself in the third person, he announced:

> "Today is Sunday, and while I am not a Christian, I happen to be married to one. And there are times when I think the loveliest thing about my dear wife is her unspoken love for Jesus Christ." Unspoken

it was, most certainly. She would wonder if he was mad when she read this, for outside of her profound observance of Christmas Eve and her dedication to decorating a Christmas tree, they never talked about such matters. As a child, she had rarely gone to church, but he knew what he meant—some old pagan spirit of her part Swedish blood must have carried Christ through all the Southern exposures of her mixed part Indian blood, crazy American lass . . . yes the loveliest thing about his dear wife was her unspoken love for Jesus Christ. . . .

"You see, dear fellow Americans, it is Sunday, and we are burning the body and blood of Christ in Vietnam. Yes, we are burning him there, and as we do, we destroy the foundation of this Republic, which is its love and trust in Christ." (213–14)

His wife wasn't the only person who thought Mailer mad—Boyle "gave him a sidelong look, as if to say, 'Watch it, old buddy, they put junior reverends in the cuckoo house for carrying on'" (214).

One aspect of the speech that was not very remarkable was its invocation of a national religious foundation. The year before, in 1966, sociologist Robert Bellah had defined "American civil religion" as a "public religious dimension . . . expressed in a set of beliefs, symbols, and rituals" available especially for ceremonial events such as Presidential inaugurations (n.p.). American civil religion, Bellah explained, is Judeo-Christian but more or less nondoctrinal. It is an unspoken accord about public religiosity that gives "religious legitimation" to certain national celebrations: "The principle of separation of church and state guarantees the freedom of religious belief and association, but at the same time clearly segregates the religious sphere, which is considered to be essentially private, from the political one." Bellah drew on Rousseau for his definition of civil religion as entailing the "simple dogmas" of "the existence of God, the life to come, the reward of virtue and the punishment of vice, and the exclusion of religious intolerance. All other religious opinions are outside the cognizance of the state and may be freely held by citizens." Part of the mythic self-imagining of the nation, civil religion discourse is available to be drawn on in times of crisis—particularly in Lincoln's Gettysburg Address, Bellah notes, but also President Johnson's campaign in favor of the Voting Rights Act of 1965. We might read Mailer's invocation of the national religious mission as a similarly political plea: here, to cease the Vietnam War.

On the other hand, Mailer's oratory goes beyond the general sanction Bellah found in the civil religion consensus, which referenced God but was only vaguely Christian, owing more to natural theology than to the Bible

or any specific church tradition. Inaugural addresses and civil religion discourse, Bellah noted, tend to reference God, but never Christ; thus: "This
religion—there seems no other word for it—while not antithetical to and
indeed sharing much in common with Christianity, was neither sectarian
nor in any specific sense Christian." In describing his wife's "love for Jesus
Christ," Mailer goes beyond the civil religion consensus, and insofar as he
"pick[s] up some of the Chaplain's language," he evokes phrasing more resonant with evangelical Christianity's emphasis on one's love for Jesus, but
also one's sensation of having Christ inside. The fact that Boyle plays only
a minor role in the story—their brief talk after their arrests lacks any mention of religion (154–55)—suggests that Mailer isn't really picking up the
Chaplain's language at all; rather, he's channelling evangelical rhetoric that
had begun to work its way into public culture.[1]

Mailer's religious evocation wavers between civil religion and the more
specifically sectarian love for Jesus as "the foundation of this Republic,"
whose national public expression Bellah believed was receding. Indeed, conservative Christianity looked like a residual culture, to borrow Raymond
Williams's term: Bellah suggests that the attempt by some Christians to claim
America as a specifically sectarian Christian nation was an echo from a
bygone era. "From the earliest years of the nineteenth century," he remarked,
"conservative religious and political groups have argued that Christianity is,
in fact, the national religion. Some of them from time to time and as recently
as the 1950s proposed constitutional amendments that would explicitly recognize the sovereignty of Christ." The past-oriented analysis of a relatively
current group betrays the secularization thesis that theoretically underpins
Bellah's analysis of American civil religion: here, a 1950s political gesture is
understood to be a remainder of a political energy that properly belongs to
history, not to the future—a diminishing remnant of a bygone era. In truth,
it was, to return to Williams's terms, both a residual culture and an emergent one.

While Mailer's speech comes at the beginning of the first decade of
American literary multiculturalism (1965–1975), Mailer himself was no multiculturalist. Nonetheless, he, like the multiculturalists to come, believed that
the nation was characterized by a historical, cultural Christianity—a belief
system perhaps akin to his own Jewish cultural formation, which was not for
him a lived religious experience. We can see the tension caused by these two
different religious registers—civil religion as the nation's foundation and the
love of Jesus as an experience a Christian feels within herself—in Mailer's
strange portrait of his wife's religious devotions. Her love for Jesus (he imagines) is not expressed through a profession of belief but by decorating a

Christmas tree. Mailer's wife, it seems, is religious in an ethnic sense: this act is a lingering trace of her ancestors' perhaps more meaningful (and originally pagan) religious practices. He imagines her devotion not so much as learned as transmitted in the "blood" from (strangely) her Swedish and Indian ancestors. She is not born again, having asked Jesus into her heart and thus having "Christ within." Mailer declares his wife's centrality by describing the nation as culturally Christian, but the wobbliness of the passage comes from his use of evangelically charged language. He recognizes the Christian "heritage" of the United States using the emergent language of evangelical experience, language that had begun to be rejuvenated by nationally popular ministers such as Billy Graham.

Thinking about religion primarily in terms of identity and social community was integral to the secularization thesis that dominated the understanding of what happens to religion in modernity. This connection was famously suggested by Will Herberg in *Protestant-Catholic-Jew* in 1955, in a decade of increased religiosity well before Mailer's speech. Herberg answered the paradox of how an increasingly secular nation could simultaneously have rising church and synagogue attendance and construction by arguing that religion had become the site of social identification amid watered-down Judeo-Christian thought—an insight largely corroborated by Bellah's delineation of America's "civil religion" a decade later (see Putnam and Campbell 518). Without metaphysical, transcendent, and universal claims, Herberg reasoned, increased church activities were signs of communal belonging and identity formation.

But that sense of community came at a cost, as it became "only too evident that the religiousness characteristic of America today is very often a religiousness without religion, a religiousness with almost any kind of content or none, a way of sociability or 'belonging' rather than a way of reorienting life to God" (260). Herberg continues, "Insofar as the 'Americanness' of religion in America blunts this sense of uniqueness and universality, and converts the three religious communions into variant expressions of American spirituality . . . the authentic character of Jewish–Christian faith is falsified, and the faith itself reduced to the status of an American culture-religion" (262). The new religious dispensation allowed for the civic inclusion of previously marginalized religious communities like Catholics and Jews, Herberg saw, but it did so by draining their metaphysical, spiritual, and universal dimensions. Thus, to use his examples, bar mitzvahs might be more common, but are "usually nothing but a lavish and expensive party, with the religious aspect reduced to insignificance, if not altogether ignored" (196). As a consequence, "much of the institutional life of the synagogue has become . . . secularized and drained of religious content precisely at the time when religion is becoming more and more acknowledged as the meaning of Jewishness" (196–97). Similarly, Herberg suggests that statements by Jewish leaders at Passover that do not mention God or the Exodus but mark instead freedom and democracy, and are occasions for family reunions, indicate that the *"religious* significance of Passover has entirely disappeared" (209n65). In other words, when Passover no longer memorializes God's historical miracle in the Exodus, it becomes mere communal belonging without transcendent, spiritual, metaphysical meaning.

The answer to Herberg's research question of how a nation of vibrant religious communities could simultaneously be growing more secular was Bellah's civil religion—a vague national consensus on the existence of a deity and his blessing that permitted different flavors because those traditions were sources of ethnic identity and cultural belonging rather than metaphysical, universal claims or required religious practices. The distinction I am developing (following Herberg) helps us begin to understand 1950s religiosity as the dialectical precursor to both the conservative Christian resurgence and multiculturalism. We might take, in this regard, the alliance between President Eisenhower and Billy Graham in the 1950s as a signal development. Eisenhower's widely-quoted tenet, "Our government makes no sense unless it is founded on a deeply felt religious faith . . . and I don't care what it is" (quoted in D. Williams 27) is a classic expression of both Bellah's American civil religion and Herbergian indifferent "American culture-religion." Contemporary social science affirms Herberg's eyewitness account of 1950s religiosity as a time of "exceptional religious observance" (Putnam and Campbell 83) led by a generation of GIs and their young families. It was ecumenical and patriotic and did not emphasize "fine theological distinctions," as Eisenhower's principle reflects; furthermore, "this surge had no partisan political cast" (Putnam and Campbell 88, 85). Graham, meanwhile, continued his series of national evangelical crusades begun in the late 1940s; his Cold War anticommunist message was bipartisan, but he was also the precursor to the evangelical awakening that was much more doctrinally sectarian and political than the consensus allowed. Indeed, though the Eisenhower-Graham alliance characterized the bipartisan religiosity of the 1950s, Kevin M. Kruse has recently shown that Graham became explicitly partisan and pro-Republican in the decades ahead, as his "words and deeds helped make piety and patriotism seem the sole property of the right" during the Nixon administration (243).

This flavor of widespread but theologically indistinct religiosity was available to the civil rights movement. As Bellah notes, President Johnson invoked civil religion on behalf of the Voting Rights Act of 1965. Another classic example is Martin Luther King's 1963 "I have a dream" speech, which invoked God four times, but Jesus or Christ not once. The rise of civil religion coincided with a liberal civil rights consensus emerging in the decade following *Brown v. Board of Education* in 1954 and culminating in Johnson's 1965 Act—a connection suggested by Mailer's recollection that William Sloane Coffin "had been arrested in the South on one civil rights affair or another, perhaps in Selma" (67). This is not to say that King and Coffin and Jimmy Carter and Graham—as opposed, perhaps, to Johnson and Eisenhower—did not have deeply felt religious commitments and quite doctrinally specific beliefs. It is only to note that an alliance emerged in the decade of advances (1955–1965) between the civil rights movement and the generalized civil religion that it mobilized in its support. Recognizing this alliance is crucial for understanding the literary history of the conservative Christian resurgence that followed.

American literary history has yet to comprehend the extent to which US multiculturalism after 1965 articulated itself in religious terms, as a break with a mainstream but (Fessenden reminds us) "unmarked category" of Protestant Christianity (*Culture* 6). In *A Genealogy of Literary Multiculturalism*, I argue that our current paradigm of literary multiculturalism took shape through a break with an assimilationist consensus phase of literature and culture that occurred in the middle of the twentieth century. The inaugural decade of literary multiculturalism, 1965 to 1975, saw some of our most famous writers across several minority traditions (Toni Morrison, Alice Walker, Ishmael Reed, N. Scott Momaday, Frank Chin, Oscar Zeta Acosta, and others) develop a critique of mainstream culture and its assimilative pressures. They returned to an earlier anthropological model of cultural pluralism developed by Zora Neale Hurston and Franz Boas and reconceptualized culture as something that survived over long periods, sometimes in submerged ways, and to which minority communities could return for psychological, social, and, indeed, spiritual nourishment. Unlike Richard Wright, John Okada, Jade Snow Wong, and the other integrationist, liberal assimilationist writers who preceded them, these multicultural writers affirmed the health and relative worth of minority cultures. They traced their longstanding cultural presence in America and questioned the relative and universal grounds on which the preceding liberal consensus expected them to give up their cultural traditions. The civil rights liberal assimilationist consensus asserted equality of race, but not equality of culture; the multiculturalist turn was to retain the former principle but reject the latter.

I want to build on this analysis by examining more closely how newly culturalized religious traditions became a pivot for this multicultural revolution in the post-1965 era. While it will come as no surprise that multicultural writers discovered religion as a site of profound social difference, I want to explore how they were not content just to articulate their difference from the civil religion consensus that Bellah described, but how their multicultural break implied that his account of the consensus was itself wrong—that the national cultural norm was far more sectarianly Christian than the wan nondoctrinal form he identified. One of the polemics strangely shared by multicultural-ists and the conservative Christian resurgence during this period, then, was a rejection of Bellah's nondoctrinal civil religion, with both groups insisting that America had historically been and continued to be, in essence, much more specifically Christian in its values, spirit, and beliefs.

Pagans Still: Morrison, Reed, Walker, Wideman

One of the most vivid early multicultural indictments of the assimilationism of the civil rights / civil religion consensus can be found in *The Bluest Eye*. Published in 1970, Toni Morrison's first novel took aim at the assimilationist social science that undergirded *Brown v. Board of Education* and pathologized African American cultural distinctiveness.[2] Her portrait of Geraldine and her son Junior, as well as the category of "brown girls" (82) Geraldine rep-resents, is a devastating critique of the expectation that black people should properly seek to adopt the bodily and material culture of white, Protestant, middle-class society. The white culture into which Geraldine has assimilated includes desexing herself, but also suppressing what the novel calls the natu-ral "funkiness" of human nature and emotion (83). Her suppression of the body—of her own and of her son's—produces in him a rage that he directs outward toward the novel's scapegoat, Pecola, who represents for Geraldine the epitome of the "nigger" against which she has carefully constructed the difference of "colored" (87).

The Bluest Eye is an important inaugural novel in American literary multi-culturalism due to its critique of Geraldine's assimilation into white culture, but the novel also suggests that religious assimilation is an important aspect of middle-class black aspiration to white propriety. One of the WASP-y trappings that Pecola notices in Geraldine's house, beside the lace doilies she admires, is "a big red-and-gold Bible on the dining-room table" (89). Deco-rative rather than dog-eared, her Bible, we sense, is not often read: Morrison's portrait is not of a Bible-believing or -reading Christian but, rather, a par-ticipant in civil religion culture. The "color picture of Jesus Christ [that] hung on a wall with the prettiest paper flowers fastened on the frame" (89) is similarly decorative rather than devotional, and when Pecola is exiled from the home by Geraldine, who calls her a "nasty little black bitch," Pecola sees

"Jesus looking down at her with sad and unsurprised eyes, his long brown hair parted in the middle, the gay paper flowers twisted around his face" (92–93). The effect is to emphasize the white Jesus's approval for the colored, assimilated Geraldine, but not the black Pecola. Rather than expressing a religiously vibrant personal faith, Geraldine's Christianity is characterized as part of the white, middle-class aspiration Morrison critiques. Morrison thus tries to make visible the "particular strand of post-Calvinist Protestantism whose popularization renders it so pervasive as to become invisible to many observers," as Fessenden puts it (*Culture* 249n41)—to make visible, that is, the submerged Protestant tradition in which originates the bland, secularized sense of civil religion. While Morrison surely would not have quarreled with King's (or Johnson's) invocation of God in pursuing civil rights, *The Bluest Eye* nonetheless marks the alliance between official, national Christianity and the white culture that was the unquestioned norm in the novel's early 1940s setting.

While Morrison's first novel contains only a peripheral nod to the relation between religious identity and assimilation, that connection became hugely important to another African American novelist beginning his career at the same time: Ishmael Reed. Indeed, the mythology Reed developed in his novels and essays of the late 1960s and into the 1970s was one of the most spectacular and fully-conceived examples of multicultural insistence on the Christian nation. While critics have long recognized the centrality of voodoo to Reed's aesthetic and historical sense of the "black Atlantic" (see, for instance, Patrick McGee), I am more interested in naming the pagan-Christian religious dynamic that animates his multiculturalism. Its most realized form is his 1972 novel *Mumbo Jumbo*, which reconceptualizes American and Western history in terms of a millennia-old struggle between monotheism and polytheistic paganism. Set in the Harlem Renaissance, *Mumbo Jumbo* imagines a plot by the forces of "Atonism"—named after Aton, the first Egyptian deity declared to be the only god—to crush the burgeoning African American artistic movement, which traces its aesthetic inspiration through the Caribbean back to pagan Africa.

Reed offers universalist and relativist critiques of "Judeo-Christian culture, Christianity, Atonism whatever you want to call it" as one character puts it (114). The universal aspect of the critique is that Christianity represses the body, whether in terms of dance, sensuality, or sexuality. Unlike the fertility rituals in many pagan practices, Christianity fears human sexuality and subordinates the body to mind and rigid doctrine. The novel also critiques Christianity (and monotheism in general) for its insistence on "interpret[ing] the world by using a single loa. Somewhat like filling a milk bottle with an ocean" (24). Using the Haitian word for deity, Reed

compares the Christian insistence on the singular God unfavorably to polytheistic pagan pantheons that accommodate plurality. Reed means by this not
just plurality of gods, but also more broadly pluralism: that the "Jes Grew"
epidemic in the 1920s embraces different art, music, and dance forms and
validates continuing human creativity and innovation, and also that it avoids
programmatic certainties and dogmas in any human endeavor. Thus, when
Hinckle Von Vampton, head of the newly empowered Knights Templar and
"Wallflower Order" ("those to whom no 1 ever asked, 'May I have this 1?'"
[132]) charged with defending Atonism, discovers Woodrow Wilson Jefferson, a Negro who has "read all the 487 articles written by Karl Marx and
Friedrich Engels," Von Vampton decides he is the "perfect candidate" to
undermine black creativity because "he doesn't mind the shape of the idol:
sexuality, economics, whatever, as long as it is limited to 1" (76). Whether
Christianity, Marxism, Islam or doctrinaire Freudianism, any single-lensed
worldview will do for Von Vampton's plan of creating a "Talking Android,"
the Negro critic who will help forestall the Harlem Renaissance by insisting
on a programmatic univocality of expression. Reed's universalist critique of
Christianity takes aim at its doctrinaire rigidity, which makes it incapable of
adequately responding to the messiness and chaos of nature, human cultural
and artistic diversity, and the body's sexuality and sensuality. It is a universalist
critique in that, according to the book's logic, Christianity (or any monotheism) is bad for everybody, having these effects of repression regardless of
race or culture.

Reed's relativist critique of Christianity, on the other hand, suggests that
Atonism and Christianity are especially bad for what the novel calls "Jes
Grew Carriers" or J.G.C.s: African Americans who are descended from
historical slave populations in the New World. The novel is productively
ambivalent about whether J.G.C.s carry Jes Grew as a cultural survival (of
the kind identified by Zora Neale Hurston, whom Reed studied deeply
during this period, calling her "our theoretician") or a racial essence transmitted in the blood. (Intriguingly, those characters who have mismatched
their racial cultures, including a black Muslim, end up dead by the end of
the novel.[3]) In either account, the origin is pagan, polytheistic Africa. As
the Pope explains in Reed's 1967 novel *Yellow Back Radio Broke-Down*, the
United States is experiencing "the Hoo-Doo, an American version of the
Ju-Ju religion that originated in Africa. . . . When Vodun arrived in America,
the authorities became so paranoid they banned it for a dozen or so years,
even to the extent of discontinuing the importation of slaves from Haiti and
Santa [sic] Domingo. . . . It's important that we wipe it out because it can
always become a revolutionary force" (152, 154).

According to this mythology, which is simultaneously parodic and serious, Christianity shapes the history of the New World and the United States in particular. As in the work of other key multiculturalist writers during this time period, Reed insists on the Christian history of the nation, but also on its enduring cultural presence. The rage for order, dominance, and control is at the center of white culture, race, and religion—a mix we might call Euro-American Christian identity. This force is responsible for slavery and colonialism, but also racial hierarchies, the suppression of indigenous religious traditions worldwide, and the transformation of living indigenous art and sacred objects into dead, vanished cultures collected in Western museums. The Wallflower order's task in America is to ensure continued white, Christian supremacy, to beat back aesthetic challenges to Western culture that go beyond mimicry (challenges such as the Harlem Renaissance and, in the time of Reed's writing, the Black Arts Movement), and to preserve the Christian suppression of human sexuality and bodily pleasure. This struggle involves Christian opposition to black music forms such as ragtime, the blues, and jazz, but also to new dance forms attending the "epidemic" of Jes Grew—which can be contracted by white Christians, as happens in the opening pages to a priest: "It seized him too. He was shouting and carrying on like any old coon wench with a bass drum" (5). In *Mumbo Jumbo* and other novels, essays, and poems from this inaugural period of American literary multiculturalism, Reed locates Christianity at the heart of a millennia-old historical conspiracy suppressing polytheistic rivals and pagan practices, a conspiracy linked to specific practices of bodily repression and aesthetic values. Importantly, his multicultural critique was attentive to the emerging evangelical energy: thus, he says of the ancient Atonist followers, using a playful anachronism, "His legislators and their wives resembled a Billy Graham audience at Oakland Coliseum" (173). Reed portrays America as far more particularly Christian in doctrine and practice than Bellah's consensus allows. In doing so, he not only politically breaks free from the liberal, assimilationist, civil rights and civil religion consensus through a multicultural return to pagan hoodoo traditions: he also offers a historical corrective refuting the consensus's purported liberality, benevolence, and doctrinal flexibility.

If that correction is part of Reed's universalist critique of Christianity, his understanding of religious traditions is simultaneously framed by formulations of cultural pluralism and relativism that he learned from his "theoretician" working decades before. Voodoo, Hurston wrote in her ethnography of Haitian religion (cited in *Mumbo Jumbo*'s bibliography), is "no more venal, no more impractical than any other" religion (*Horse* 204). In her Boasian, anthropological pose, Hurston does not judge the universal worth or truth of religious traditions. Writing of her confrontation with a zombie (whose photo she snapped), Hurston suggested that the interface between the mundane world and metaphysical reality was different in Haiti than it is "in the shadow of the Empire State Building" (179). Hurston accepted anthropology's relativist, descriptive methodological approach to religious traditions: thus hoodoo in America burns "with all the intensity of a suppressed religion. It has its thousands of secret adherents. It adapts itself like Christianity to its locale" (*Mules* 183). The adaptability of hoodoo is the essence of Reed's novel, and Reed was deeply shaped by Hurston's cultural understanding of religious traditions.[4]

Thus, in *Mumbo Jumbo*, even when Thor Wintergreen forsakes his European heritage to join the *Mu'tafikah* guerillas intent on liberating indigenous art from the Centers for Art Detention "so that we could see the gods return and the spirits aroused" (88) and "await the rise of Shango, Shiva, and Quetzalcoatl" (89), this is not so much understood to be a kind of religious conversion to paganism as it is an intellectual and ethical decision about aesthetics and politics. When Charlotte, a white woman apprenticed to the hoodoo doctor PaPa LaBas, leaves the Kathedral for Broadway, LaBas is dubious about whether "the Haitian aspects of The Work can be translated here" in Manhattan, echoing Hurston's sentiments about the incommensurable metaphysics of Haiti and New York (52). Importantly, LaBas's verb recasts the rival religions as languages, a crucially important component of cultures. And strangely, even the Atonists themselves seem to concede the factual truth that there are many gods. Abdul, a Muslim, debates LaBas and his associate Black Herman on what first seem to be theological grounds. He warns them, citing the Quran, "He that worships other gods besides Allah shall be forbidden to Paradise and shall be cast into the fires of Hell" (35).[5] LaBas and Herman, meanwhile, articulate the novel's point that Abdul is "no different from the Christians you imitate" (34), and that he has "picked up the old Plymouth Rock bug and are calling it Mecca" (36). But when Abdul's audience disappears during the debate, he concedes much of his theological ground, admitting, "I believe that you 2 have something. Something that is basic, something that has been tested and something that all our people have" (38). Abdul's conviction is pragmatic and tactical rather than metaphysical or doctrinal: "It's the 1920s, not 8000 B.C." (38). "This is the country where something is successful in direct proportion to how it's put over; how it's gamed. Look at the Mormons," Abdul continues, hoping to mimic their success because after all "the Mormons got Utah, didn't they?" (38). Like the Pope in *Yellow Back Radio Broke-Down* (164), this monotheist concedes the metaphysical truth of many gods and powers, but both characters adhere to monotheism for the tactical and cultural advantages it supplies.

The vision of African American identity in Reed's early work, then, has a religious dimension to it, but its vocabulary has been significantly culturalized: conversions are tactical and political rather than spiritual, and theoretically exclusive doctrinal conventions (are there many gods or just one?) coexist within a frame of a relativism and pluralism that will not push the issue to resolution. McClure argues that we should understand "the postmodern moment as one in which such voices challenge the hegemony of secular rational discourse with unprecedented power," allowing us to better witness in Pynchon, DeLillo, Reed, Morrison, Silko, and Erdrich "the untidy resurgence of magical, sacred, pre-modern and non-western constructions of reality" ("Postmodern" 148). This is certainly true, and my argument is that there is a multicultural as well as a postmodern genealogy to this "untidy resurgence," especially in Reed's work. In this scheme of postwar religious revivals, deeply felt cultural traditions organize societies and individual behaviors; repressed ones can be recovered by ethnic minorities for the politics of anti-assimilation and for psychological and spiritual nourishment. Thus when Earline at the end of the novel declares to LaBas that she wants to "learn more" about The Work, the model Reed has in mind is cultural anthropology rather than monastic commitment or religious conversion: "Yes, I want to learn more, pop. I'm thinking about going to New Orleans and Haiti, Brazil and all over the South studying our ancient cultures, our HooDoo cultures. Maybe by and by some future artists 30 to 40 years from now will benefit from my research" (206).[6] So while Reed, like Bellah, sees religion as an enduring cultural presence in the nation, his work argues that a more sectarian version of Christian culture has historically helped suppress other religious traditions, which he also conceives as cultures vulnerable (but resistant) to American Christian imperialism.

Despite the mutual disdain between Zora Neale Hurston's two most important literary and intellectual descendants, Ishmael Reed and Alice Walker, Reed's term for Hurston in the 1970s—"our theoretician"—was no less apt for her relation to Walker, who discovered Hurston's work in 1970 while doing research for a story about "voodoo practices among rural southern blacks of the thirties" (Walker, Foreword xi). Both Reed and Walker discovered in Hurston the pagan cultural survivals in African America that might stand against Christian America as a source of multicultural resistance. In Walker's 1982 novel *The Color Purple*, that resistance partly takes the form of Shug's critique of Celie's notion of the Christian God as "big and old and tall and graybearded and white" with "white robes" and "bluish-gray" eyes (201). Shug suggests that this God comes from "the white folks' white bible" (201) and recommends to Celie a pantheism wherein God "ain't something you can look at apart from anything else, including yourself. I believe God is everything" (202). This pantheism is complemented by the novel's critique of Christian missionary activity in Africa in the form of Celie's sister Nettie, and is completed, in Walker's life, in her own spiritual practice, as we shall see in the next chapter.

But the lingering presence of ancient pagan religious practices was a widely used trope in African American multicultural fiction beyond Reed and Walker, who stand as its most obvious and programmatic practitioners. John Edgar Wideman's *Homewood* trilogy, for instance, frames its fictional project about African American lives in twentieth-century Pittsburgh—the first volume of which is titled *Damballah*, after the chief loa of the Haitian pantheon, termed by Hurston to be "the highest and most powerful of all the gods" (*Horse* 118)—as descending from the African slave Orion, who remembers African religious traditions (12). Orion, himself a "heathen" (15) who resists the "Christianizing project" of his slave-owner (16), transmits the name Damballah to a young slave in whom it takes hold, "a sound measuring his heartbeat then one with the pumping surge of his blood" (15). Having learned Damballah's name, the boy is implied to be an ancestor of the characters who follow in the short-story cycle and the other two novels, even though the trilogy in general attests to the success of the "Christianizing project" in that his descendants are Christians attending the local Homewood AME Zion Church, and who pray, sing in the choir, invoke God, and go to revivals.

Damballah is thus a story cycle about different generations of Christians in Homewood, but, strangely, their descriptive religious practices and beliefs are framed by this pagan presence. In the rest of the trilogy there is not really any submerged paganism in characters' worship experiences—as there is, momentarily at least, in Hurston's *Jonah's Gourd Vine*—but rather the representation of culturally specific African American Christianity. Nonetheless, the framing of the trilogy serves as a religious trace within a distinct African American cultural community (162), an account of origin and a ground for identity that is alluded to in the opening epigraph from anthropologist Maya Deren's *Divine Horsemen: The Voodoo Gods of Haiti*: "Precisely because these divinities are, to a certain extent, vestigial, they give, like Damballah's detachment, a sense of historical extension, of the ancient origin of the race. To invoke them today is to stretch one's hand back to that time and to gather up all history into a solid, contemporary ground beneath one's feet" (5). Thus, in one scene in the second novel, *Hiding Place*, a character seems judged instead of aided by a picture of Jesus with "long, soft, blond hair like a woman's, a cutie-pie beard, blue eyes painted in a tricky way to stare at you" (280)—a scene reminiscent of Pecola's encounter. He does, however, find a "hiding place" with the "Hoodoo Woman" Mother Bess (312), who is not a Christian (218), a religious dynamic that remains in the background. In the *Homewood* trilogy, pagan religion lingers not so much as a lived distinctiveness in the African American community as a residual but largely unclaimed identity. Wideman's half-completed gesture suggests the powerful appeal of voodoo-inspired, non-Christian religious identities to African American writers of the last third of the twentieth century. Perhaps sensing that this appeal was in danger of becoming a too-standard trope in African American fiction, Morrison chose, in her 1997 novel *Paradise*, to portray a similar theme of discovering (or recovering) gods as a reclamation that hearkened back to a different African-derived religious tradition—Candomblé, the Afro-Brazilian cousin to Voodoo and Obeah.[7]

Outwaiting the Christian Invaders: Leslie Silko and N. Scott Momaday

> In these novels [by Momaday, Silko, and Erdrich] . . .
> characters disenchanted with secularization stumble
> back toward religiously inflected modes of being that
> are marked by key features of postsecular spirituality:
> polytheistic pluralism, attention to the Earth, an
> emphasis on spiritual practice, and a distrust at
> once of sweeping claims for salvation and dogmatic
> rigidities.
>
> John McClure, *Partial Faiths*

A generation of inaugural multicultural authors who began writing between 1965 and 1975 defined their cultural politics in religious terms, contesting Herberg's and Bellah's vision of religion's benign influence on American affairs, and outlining Christianity's historical role in oppression and assimilation. But they concurred with these scholars' larger sense that religion was an important source of social identity, even in the supposedly secularized contemporary period. The emerging multicultural understanding of religious social identity took shape not only through a dialectic with the civil religion consensus, but in what we might call a trialectic with the emerging religious energy of conservative sectarian Christianity. Multiculturalism and the resurgence were not always oppositional, as both contended that America was more specifically and sectarianly Christian than the previous civil religion consensus had conceded.

Two Native American contemporaries of Ishmael Reed focused their work during this time on the Christian character of the nation during its formation, and the role that Christianity played in American imperialism. N. Scott

Momaday (Kiowa) and Leslie Marmon Silko (Laguna Pueblo) are Southwest writers who were part of a self-conscious multicultural matrix in the late 1960s and 1970s linked to a West Coast literary axis developed between Reed and Chinese American author Frank Chin. Like Reed, Silko and Momaday developed both universalist and relativist critiques of American Christianity; their literary critiques named the Christian role played in the developing nation and they took part in a broader reconceptualization of religion in terms of culture.

Silko's well-known novels *Ceremony* (1977) and *Almanac of the Dead* (1991) indict Christian ideas and practices on theological and historical grounds. In *Ceremony*, Tayo returns to his Laguna Pueblo reservation after spending time in a Japanese prison camp during World War Two. His illness represents both his personal war trauma and the larger communal need for healing and proper alignment. One of the novel's lessons is that his illness is not separable from the social disorder of the Pueblo peoples; in fact, the spiritual separation of the individual is an aspect of the problem to be cured. Recounting the evils of colonialism, the novel explains: "Christianity separated the people from themselves; it tried to crush the single clan name, encouraging each person to stand alone, because Jesus Christ would save only the individual soul; Jesus Christ was not like the Mother who loved and cared for them as her children, as her family" (68). Tayo's Auntie has been seduced by this promise of personal salvation, and has for years gone to church alone, prompting Tayo to wonder "if she liked it that way, going to church by herself, where she could show the people that she was a devout Christian and not immoral or pagan like the rest of the family. When it came to saving her own soul, she wanted to be careful that there were no mistakes" (77). Rather than turn to Christianity, which historically worked to destroy Native communities by splitting off individuals for salvation, Tayo's healing takes place through a return to the stories and ceremonies of his Laguna Pueblo culture. Silko's universalist critique is that Christianity is part of the destructive valuing of individualism in Western culture, and is therefore bad even for white Christians; its relativist edge is that Christianity was (and is) especially destructive for Native communities, part of Tayo's problem, not healing solution.

Christianity's atomizing effect is linked in *Ceremony* to another nascent separation developed in *Almanac of the Dead*: that of people from the natural world. Like Reed, Silko develops a complex mythology that places white American imperialism within a larger metaphysical and religious context. The separation from the land encouraged by Christianity makes it part of the larger "witchery" afflicting human beings. As in *Almanac*, in *Ceremony* witchery is not (quite) synonymous with white people, but it uses whites to create "a nation built on stolen land," a nation of spiritual "emptiness" that must be filled by wealth, technology, and patriotism (191). As the wise

Betonie explains, "it was Indian witchery that made white people in the first place" (132),[8] an origin story that leads to the objectification of the world: *"white skin people / . . . / grow away from the earth / then they grow away from the sun / then they grow away from the plants and animals. / They see no life / When they look / they see only objects"* (135). The white fascination with dead objects like plastic, neon, concrete, and steel ends with the atomic bomb—and so part of what afflicts the Laguna community is local uranium mines, sourced for the first of these weapons. Influenced by witchery, some Native people also become "destroyers," a movement that Christianity, complicit in these processes of spiritual separation, cannot help arrest.

Almanac develops this portrait by suggesting that the Christian God's expulsion of Adam and Eve from Eden was the first forced migration, a separation of people from the land to which they had been spiritually linked. This ethos remains within Christianity, encouraging Europeans to leave the place their God resides to go to new places where they have no gods. In an important passage in which Silko grants African Americans indigeneity in the Americas because the African gods accompanied the kidnapped peoples to the New World, she distinguishes the Middle Passage from European migration:

> Slave masters had tried to strip the Africans of everything—their languages and histories. The slave masters thought Africans would be isolated from their African gods in the Americas because the slave masters themselves had left behind their God, Jesus, in Europe. The Europeans had been without a god since their arrival in the Americas. Of course the Europeans were terrified, but did not admit the truth. They had gone through the motions with their priests, holy water, and churches built with Indian slave labor. But their God had not accompanied them. The white man had sprinkled holy water and had prayed for almost five hundred years in the Americas, and still the Christian God was absent. Now Clinton [an African American character] understood why European philosophers had told their people God was dead: the white man's God had died about the time the Europeans had started sailing around the world. (416–17)

The absence of God is true of this specific geography of the Americas, Silko suggests, but is also intrinsic to basic Christian ideas. The separation from the creator and from their geography of mythic origin makes European Christians into migrants, thinks another character:

> He thought about what the ancestors had called Europeans: their God had created them but soon was furious with them, throwing them out of their birthplace, driving them away. The ancestors had called

Europeans "the orphan people" and had noted that as with orphans taken in by selfish or coldhearted clanspeople, few Europeans had remained whole. They failed to recognize the earth was their mother. Europeans were like their first parents, Adam and Eve, wandering aimlessly because the insane God who had sired them had abandoned them. (258)

Silko's works, like Reed's, are novels of ideas, and while characters in fictional plots are the ones voicing these ideas about Christianity, both Silko and Reed developed in interviews and essays their sense of the fundamentally religious sources of conflict in the American past and present, sources in which Christianity plays a central role.[9]

As is clear from these passages, Silko critiques Christianity on universal grounds for separating the individual from the land, the community, and the spiritual. But the critique is simultaneously relativist insofar as the supposedly universal monotheistic God is no longer the author of humanity, but (somewhat improbably, given Christianity's roots in ancient Palestine) only of Europeans. Silko treats the Christian origin story as the mythological account it clearly is by placing it implicitly alongside other accounts of origin. Each people—or rather, each cultural tradition—speaks of its origin in different ways. Thus the truthfulness of the Judeo-Christian account is no longer universal (as, we shall see in chapter 6, it was clearly understood to be by many Christians contesting evolution), but culturalized: each culture has its own origin story, a mythological polygenesis that is unresolvable and not to be critiqued by supposedly universal accounts (say, of the anthropology of human origins that has us all coming out of Africa). The European God creates Adam and Eve and then abandons their descendants, consigning them to spiritual restlessness and constant migration. Try as they might, five hundred years of Christianity in the Americas cannot make great inroads into Native communities, precisely because the religion is alien: one's proper religion is the religion of one's ancestors. Thus, thinks another character in *Almanac*, "Christianity might work on other continents and with other human beings; Yoeme did not dispute those possibilities. But from the beginning in the Americas, the outsiders had sensed their Christianity was somehow inadequate in the face of the immensely powerful and splendid spirit beings who inhabited the vastness of the Americas" (718). This acknowledgement that Christianity might be right for Europeans in Europe gives Silko's critique of the religion its relativist edge. In this account—and anticipating my argument about Barbara Kingsolver in chapter 2—imperialism and proselytization are the real problems with Christianity. Silko's multicultural fiction contests Christianity both on universal grounds, for its ideas and historical practices, and on relative grounds, that it is not right for the land and Indigenous peoples of the Americas.

The intertwining of Christianity and imperialism in America is likewise the historical backdrop of N. Scott Momaday's most famous work, *House Made of Dawn* (1968), a crucial text in the development of American literary multiculturalism and a novel said to have begun the so-called Native American Renaissance. It focuses on the religious practices of several characters, including Francisco, the protagonist's elderly grandfather, and three priests—two Catholic and one of the "Native American Church," which appears at first to be a hybridized creation mixing Christian and Indigenous beliefs and practices. The novel carefully contextualizes religion in terms of the region's history of imperialism and colonization, beginning with the vision of the first peoples' migration to the region thousands of years before. There are still traces in the surrounding hills of the ancestors of the Jemez Pueblo community that is the setting for much of the novel, traces that almost suggest the people had left briefly and will soon return, "and then everything would be restored to an older age, and . . . a bad dream of invasion and change would have been dissolved in an hour before the dawn. For man, too, has tenure in the land; he dwelt upon the land twenty-five thousand years ago, and his gods before him" (52). As Momaday's famous rendition of "tenure in the land" suggests, he, like Silko, links Indigenous peoples' belongingness to a specific landscape in terms of spiritual belonging.

Momaday imagines the history of European and American imperialism in religious terms that inflect the action. The Jemez Pueblo people whose ancestors left traces in the hills above, the novel asserts,

> do not hanker after progress and have never changed their essential way of life. Their invaders were a long time in conquering them; and now, after four centuries of Christianity, they still pray in Tanoan to the old deities of the earth and sky and make their living from the things that are and have always been within their reach; while in the discrimination of pride they acquire from their conquerors only the luxury of example. They have assumed the names and gestures of their enemies, but have held on to their own, secret souls; and in this there is a resistance and an overcoming, a long outwaiting. (52–53)

This historical long view is the key to unravelling the different religious practices, beliefs, and mixes at work in the novel. The town's Catholic priest Father Olguin should be read as one of the Christian "invaders" and "conquerors" whose presence is tolerated during the novel's setting of 1945–53. As the novel makes clear through several passages of free indirect discourse, Olguin imagines that he understands the town and its people far better than he really does. Momaday represents him as a spiritually inert local folklorist who resignedly recognizes "the matter of some old and final cleavage, of certain exclusion, the whole and subtle politics of estrangement" (170) from the town.

Olguin reads the journal and letters of a predecessor, Fray Nicolás, through which we gain a sharp sense of the religious struggle between Christianity and pagan practices that characterized European and American imperialism in the American Southwest. The journal's troubled entries of 1874 and 1875—addressed to God—reflect an older Christian interpretation of Native religious beliefs and practices as forms of devil worship, with Jemez Pueblo burial rites seen as a "dark custom" (42). An 1888 letter addressed to the priest's brother speaks of Francisco as a young boy, who the novel hints is Nicolás's illegitimate son. As a child, Francisco had been a "sacristan" in Nicolás's church, but years later the priest fears that he "is evil & desires to do me some injury . . . . He is one of them & goes often in the kiva & puts on their horns & hides & does worship that Serpent which even is the One our most ancient enemy" (46). *House Made of Dawn* renders Olguin and Nicolás as part of the ongoing Christian colonization of Native communities. The former character takes an almost secularized, disenchanted, quasi-anthropological stance, while the latter represents an older European interpretation of the metaphysical conflict between the unseen spiritual forces of the Christian God and what the novel portrays as the Tanoan deities who reside still in the land. Indeed, in Nicolás's belated "missionary despair"— Stephanie Kirk's phrase for the "fatigue and disenchantment" that Franciscan missionaries eventually felt in New Spain at their "inability to excavate the indigenous idolatrous practices" they linked to Satan (8)—Momaday traces the long arc of failed Christian imperialism. Both he and Olguin experience the silence of God in theologically troubling ways.[10]

Contrasting the two priests are the Jemez Pueblo Francisco and the Kiowa priest of the Native American Church, Tosamah, both of whom seem to incorporate Christianity into their religious lives. Critics sometimes read these two characters as instantiating a kind of hybridized or syncretic religious practice that mixes the two religious world views, with Francisco participating in both Catholic and Jemez rites and Tosamah embracing a theology reflecting different Native beliefs and assumptions. Lynn Domina, for example, argues that the Church "has absorbed and been absorbed by, rather than conquered, native traditions" (8), with Tosamah crafting a hybrid Kiowa-Christian theology ("Tai-me is the Word; John is a Kiowa" [23]) and Francisco's grandson, in the end, "acknowledg[ing] the presence of the Christian influence at Jemez" (24). In a more nuanced account, Alan Velie argues that "Indian religions in *House Made of Dawn*, Pueblo Catholicism and the Peyote Cult [of the Native American Church], are a blend of Christianity and the religions that the tribes had practiced before their contact with whites" (141). Velie also suggests that only Momaday's later novel, *Ancient Child* (1989), showed that "the Christian component in Indian religion has diminished substantially" (141). But I would like to suggest that this is true even of *House Made of Dawn* when we regard it in its context of colonization and its key component of multicultural resistance to assimilation. Velie suggests that "what Momaday shows is that in certain ways some Indians who became Christian did so without abandoning their previous religion" (136). But a better way to consider Francisco's participation in "Pueblo Catholicism" is that these religious practices are merely what the novel has previously termed the "luxury of example" and "the names and gestures of their enemies," even as his true spiritual home is with his Pueblo ceremonial practices. Rather than see Francisco's religious practice as a kind of "blend," in other words, we might see that practice as a way for him to hold on to his "secret soul," adopting with others the occasional outward gesture as a method of long-term resistance to colonization.

Tosamah is another good example of the superficiality of supposedly syncretic religious traditions in the novel. Velie shows that Christian imagery has penetrated both Pueblo and Native American Church practices and beliefs. But Tosamah preaches a remarkable sermon in *House Made of Dawn*, an exegesis of the first phrase of the gospel of John, "In the beginning was the Word." Tosamah sermonizes on the importance of language, suggesting that John had seized on a truth with this first phrase, but then perilously and erroneously went on in the entire rest of the Gospel to produce falsehood: "It was the Truth, all right, but it was more than the Truth. The Truth was overgrown with fat, and the fat was God. The fat was *John's* God, and God stood between John and the Truth" (82). In other words, the rest of the Gospel's sequence on the life, acts, words, death, and resurrection of Jesus is merely a kind of theological delusion that the gospel writer develops as he tries to move beyond his initial flash of insight that "in the beginning" was only language and its sacred power. It is difficult to consider this heretical theology to be a "blend" of Christianity and other traditions. I think we might more usefully consider it to be a case of outward trappings—here, the first line of John—being used to articulate and simultaneously conceal enduring Native religious survivals.

In chronologically backdating Velie's argument—in seeing *House* as the site of less Christianity, before the later *Ancient Child*—I am likewise locating Momaday's cultural politics in terms of its anti-assimilationist impulse. The occasion for part of its plot is the government policy of Relocation that sought to move young Native men off reservations and into urban centers where they might be culturally assimilated by virtue of separation from their homes, families, and communities. It is Francisco's grandson Abel who undergoes Relocation to Los Angeles, and the novel's tale of how he is lost and begins to become found again only once he returns to his dying grandfather and his Jemez Pueblo town is what makes *House Made of Dawn* a characteristic novel of the multicultural turn in the literary movement's first decade.[11] The novel's critique of assimilation and its counterethos of cultural pluralism and cultural relativism partly take shape through its suggestion that Christianity is part of the Western culture that needs to be outwaited and resisted. Momaday's model, I would like to suggest, is the palimpsest rather than the hybrid: Christianity furnishes the outward gestures of contemporary Native peoples, even as they hold on to their secret souls in a strategy of long outwaiting. As with Reed's voodoo, in which the loa might be iconographically represented by Catholic saints, the truth is what lies behind: the more vibrant, attuned, and proper pagan practices that "endure" and "outwait" the Christian "invaders" (as *House* puts it) precisely by taking up Christian disguises for old ways. This structure of religious identification makes it possible to return to one's ancestral religion, here conceived as the object of proper cultural identity from which one might be historically misaligned: to scrape away the surface of the historical palimpsest to reveal one's true ethnic religion lying beneath.

Aztec Resistance: Oscar Zeta Acosta and Gloria Anzaldúa

This dynamic of returning to one's ancestral religion animates the religious dimension of a Mexican American contemporary of Momaday's, Oscar Zeta Acosta. A lawyer and autobiographer involved in the "Brown Power" (*Autobiography* 196) movement of the late 1960s and 1970s, Acosta, like his contemporaries in this first multicultural, post–civil rights, anti-assimilationist generation, was a cultural pluralist who imagined resistance to the dominant culture through a rejection of Christianity and a return to the indigenous religion of his ancestors. Unlike Momaday, however (and more like Reed), Acosta has a great sense of humor. Thus at the end of his autobiography he imagines the cultural nationalist speech he intends to give to the other "brown buffaloes":

> They stole our land and made us half-slaves. They destroyed our gods and made us bow down to a dead man who's been strung up for 2000 years. . . . Now what we need is, first to give ourselves a new name. We need a new identity. A name and a language all our own. . . .

So I propose that we call ourselves . . . what's this, you don't want me
to attack our religion? Well, all right . . . . (198)

The complicated fact is that the Mexican American community is committed to Catholicism, and Acosta finds that this struggle against and within the
church makes ethnic revolution difficult. In these circumstances, there can
be no simple return to a pre-Catholic religious tradition, so Acosta struggles
to forge a suitable non-mainstream identity within an ethnicized Mexican
American Catholic tradition.

As Madeline Walker argues, religion is a question of communal belonging
in Acosta, and his autobiographical texts illustrate "the pitfalls of conversion qua assimilation," potential transformations that are "intensely social
and often prescriptive" (60). Acosta recounts that in 1954, before becoming a cultural nationalist, he intriguingly encountered early postwar evangelical energy in the form of religious discussions with a Baptist Air Force
enrollee that culminated in his conversion. For Walker, this change to Baptist
Christianity was compelled as much by Acosta's desire to be accepted by
white society (and found attractive by white women) as his proselytizer's
superior knowledge of the Bible. Duane Dunham is an anti-papist who
questions Catholic doctrine—"How about Purgatory. Where's that in the
Bible?" (*Autobiography* 131)—and Acosta is eventually persuaded, seemingly
for theological reasons, to give up his familial Catholicism:

> I finally gave up on Catholicism and admitted to Duane Dunham that
> he knew more about Jesus than I did. We went into the boiler room
> under the barracks and he called down the Holy Ghost to save me. I took
> Jesus as my savior and became a Baptist right on the spot. I talked Jesus
> morning, noon and night. I was a fanatic of the worst kind. (131)

Acosta becomes a "Mexican Billy Graham" in Panama, where he undertakes
missionary work to the local Indigenous peoples (132). But he realizes that
something is not right, a lack that Walker sees as Acosta's experience of the
limit of "assimilative conversion," wherein he is admired as an evangelist
but not accepted as a social equal by white Baptists. It is at this point that
Acosta undertakes a Bible study unusual for conservative evangelical Baptists:
a "comparative study of the Synoptic Gospels" that, among other things,
enumerates the "inconsistent" (133). Recapitulating the starting point of the
so-called higher biblical criticism begun in the nineteenth century (the demonstration and comparing of differences among Mark, Luke, and Matthew),
a subject I address in chapter 5, this amateur Bible scholar eventually seems
persuaded to abandon his faith, again for apparently theological reasons that
may conceal other social reasons of assimilative acceptance and rejection.

Acosta's deconversion, says Walker, is followed by a less hectic adherence to a more culturally appropriate religious tradition: "a Mexican American folk Catholicism lined richly with their pagan rituals, myths, gods, and goddesses" (87). This cultural nationalist struggle takes the form of challenging the class- and ethnic-based hierarchies of the Southwest's mainstream Catholic Church dominated by Irish Americans, as he describes in the companion volume / sequel to his autobiography. The *Católicos por la Raza* demonstrate at St. Basil's Church in 1969, and, in a passage Walker cites, Acosta witnesses a new Eucharist with "tortillas," "the buttered body of Huitzilopochtli," and "red wine" in "up-tilt earthen pottery": "It is a night of miracles: never before have the sons of the conquered *Aztecas* worshipped their dead gods on the doorstep of the living Christ" (*Revolt* 12–13). Acosta's "offhanded use of Aztec religion as cultural habit rather than belief"—he has an image of Huitzilopochtli, the Aztec hummingbird god, printed on his business cards—confirms his overall tone of flip satire (M. Walker 88). Nevertheless, this syncretic Catholicism is a crucial identity formation for the multicultural politics Acosta embraces. Hence the shape of his religious trajectory—from weak familial Catholicism to assimilationist evangelical Christianity to nationalist syncretic folk Catholicism—strongly suggests the way religious questions were always inextricable from those of social community.

It is after having been an evangelical Christian himself that Acosta embraces the folk Catholicism that seems to have continuities with the Aztec ways of his ancestors. This time there is no theological encounter or argument to talk him into a (re)turn to Aztec gods and syncretic Mexican Catholicism: he does not put Huitzilopochtli to the scriptural test that he put Jesus. But Acosta's experience of rejecting evangelical Christianity for a more natural and ancestral pluralist religious tradition encapsulates the dynamic I am trying to name in this chapter, of multiculturalism formulating its religious dynamism and pluralism against a backdrop of not only a vaguely Christian nation—Bellah's civil religion in the civil rights era—but more particularly a nation about to undergo the conservative Christian resurgence.

Acosta's difficulty in articulating a cultural nationalist position that did not outright reject the Catholicism to which most Mexican Americans were committed was conceptually solved fifteen years later by another multiculturalist with the same heritage, Gloria Anzaldúa. Anzaldúa's rather brilliant solution to the problem of continued Mexican American cultural commitment to Catholicism was to render that Christian formation as a disguised historical paganism, a solution hinted at in Momaday and explored in Reed. As I argue in *A Genealogy of Literary Multiculturalism*, her vision of identity is expressed in the language of hybridity and mestiza consciousness, but it is a deeply essentialist one that constructs the project of returning to her maternal ancestors' Aztec religious traditions, which are imagined to have been truly hers all along. In Anzaldúa's formulation, Mexican American folk Catholicism's chief icon, the Lady of Guadalupe, is a religious palimpsest, beneath which lies the ancient Aztec goddess Coatlalopeuh, the Snake Woman. As Anzaldúa explains, "My family, like most Chicanos, did not practice Roman Catholicism but a folk Catholicism with many pagan elements. *La Virgen de Guadalupe's* Indian name is *Coatlalopeuh*. She is the central deity connecting us to our Indian ancestry" (49). The return to this deity is, as with the other authors discussed here, couched in terms of resisting subordination to mainstream Christian culture, whether in terms of the oppression of the body and sexuality that Anzaldúa, like Reed, sees as intrinsic to the Catholic church, in terms of linguistic domination that sees her growing up in schools that enforce English (75), in a culture that expected silence from women, and among Latinos who made her ashamed of the linguistic specificities of her non-normative Chicano Spanish.

The historical palimpsest that interests Anzaldúa was occasioned by Christianity's role in colonizing the central Americas in the sixteenth century. According to Anzaldúa, a key event occurred when the Virgin Mary was iconically swapped in for an Aztec deity:

> *Guadalupe* appeared on December 9, 1531, on the spot where the Aztec goddess, *Tonantsi* ("Our Lady Mother"), had been worshipped by the Nahuas and where a temple to her had stood. Speaking Nahuatl, she told Juan Diego, a poor Indian crossing Tepeyác Hill, whose Indian name was *Cuautlaohuac* and who belonged to the *mazehual* class, the humblest within the Chichimeca tribe, that her name was *María Coatlalopeuh. Coatl* is the Nahuatl word for serpent. *Lopeuh* means "the one who has dominion over serpents." . . . Some say it means "she who crushed the serpent," with the serpent as the symbol of the indigenous religion, meaning that her religion was to take the place of the Aztec religion. Because *Coatlalopeuh* was homophonous to the Spanish *Guadalupe*, the Spanish identified her with the dark Virgin, *Guadalupe*, patroness of West Central Spain. (50–51)

This figure's ambiguity comes partly through the serpent's different meanings in different cultures. On the one hand, Coatlalopeuh "has dominion over serpents" because she is "descended from, or is an aspect of, earlier Mesoamerican fertility and Earth goddesses," one of which is "*Coatlicue*, the Serpent goddess" (49). On the other hand, Coatlalopeuh's purported "crush[ing of] the serpent" links her to the Christian symbolism of Mary, whose son Jesus achieved dominion over the devil in fulfillment of God's judgment on the serpent of Eden that there would be "enmity between you and the woman, and between your offspring and hers; he will strike your head, and you will strike his heel" (Gen 3:15). This ambiguity became further tilted toward traditional Christian theology when the Catholic Church ruled in 1660 that the *María Coatlalopeuh* seen by Juan Diego was in fact the "Mother of God, considering her synonymous with *la Virgen María*; she became *la Santa Patrona de los mexicanos*," to be invoked in later times of national struggle, whether during the Mexican Revolution or the formative Mexican American agricultural Delano strike in 1965 (Anzaldúa 51).

But while Anzaldúa terms *la Virgen de Guadalupe* "a synthesis of the old world and the new" (52) who might thus be a symbol of the hybridity the author is often identified as championing, the religious project in *Borderlands / La Frontera* can better be understood through the metaphor of the palimpsest rather than the hybrid. It is the Christianization of Coatlalopeuh—and before that, an intra-Aztec religious struggle between male warfaring deities and female agricultural ones—that separates this god's different aspects, rendering Guadalupe as "docile" and desexualized. But these deities continue to exist and be worshipped, much like the Tanoan deities of Momaday's novel. As Anzaldúa puts it, "In the U.S. Southwest, Mexico, Central and South America the *indio* and the *mestizo* continue to worship the old spirit entities (including *Guadalupe*) and their supernatural power, under the guise of Christian saints" (53). It is these older entities and deities to which she seeks to return because, Anzaldúa says, "In my own life, the Catholic Church fails to give meaning to my daily acts, to my continuing encounters with the 'other world'" (59).

Anzaldúa's religious return to Aztec deities and spirituality entails rejecting not just the Christian "fear and distrust of life and of the body" (59), but also modern views of pagan spirituality that render it superstitious. When younger, she, "an unbeliever, scoffed at these Mexican superstitions as I was taught in Anglo school" (58):

> Like many Indians and Mexicans, I did not deem my psychic experiences real. I denied the occurrences and let my inner senses atrophy. I allowed white rationality to tell me that the existence of the "other world" was mere pagan superstition. I accepted their reality, the "official" reality of the rational, reasoning mode . . . . In trying to become "objective," Western culture made "objects" of things and people when it distanced itself from them, thereby losing "touch" with them. This dichotomy is the root of all violence. (58–59)

Anzaldúa's critique of Western, Christian modernity thus proceeds along two tracks. As with Reed's account, the suppression of body to mind is premised on the fear of sexuality, a religious attitude damaging to people of all religions, cultures, and races: it is something universally wrong with Christianity. Furthermore, the cognitive mode of objectification entails instrumentalism, becoming "the root of all violence"—a universal ethical condemnation also made by Silko. At the same time, however, Christian modernity—in which one rationally scoffs at pagan superstition but finds structure and meaning within traditional institutions like the Church—is revealed itself to be not universal at all, but only another culturally relative position that exists beside others, even if it erroneously imagines itself to be universal. Once Western modernity and its apparatus of disenchantment are revealed to be not the logical end of all cultures, but rather a specific historical moment in one civilization's imperialist history, Anzaldúa's pluralist cultural politics allows for the reenchantment of the world, populated once more by ancient spirits and deities.[12]

Although Anzaldúa's spiritual life becomes recognizably religious at this point—specific ideas, histories, beliefs and practices associated with the Aztec spirit world beneath her folk Catholicism now serve to symbolically fuse her mundane world with a transcendentally meaningful one—it is equally akin to what has become termed in multiculturalism a "cultural memory." *Borderlands / La Frontera* tends, in other words, to construct this Aztec religion as a kind of natural identity. Guadalupe "is the symbol of the *mestizo* true to his or her Indian values," Anzaldúa says (52), imagining continued adherence to one's ancestors' gods through this goddess. Under these conditions, it is difficult to conceive of anyone converting to the Aztec religion championed in *Borderlands*, unless one was already a part of that racial-cultural group who was returning to "his or her Indian values." But the flip side of this impossibility of conversion—of changing one's religious culture in Anzaldúa—is that this Aztec religion has actually been her religion all along, even in unconscious ways while she was still an adherent to folk Catholicism.

In this second sense, Anzaldúa ultimately configures Aztec religion as an inalienable cultural identity because it is the true pantheon lying behind the saints of folk Catholicism. The Church tried to use Guadalupe "to placate the Indians and *mexicanos* and Chicanos" as part of an ongoing colonial "institutionalized oppression," but this failed because *indios* and *mexicanos* across the Americas "continue to worship the old spirit entities (including *Guadalupe*) and their supernatural power, under the guise of Christian saints" (53). What at first looks like a cultural survival turns out to be an ancestral memory; consequentially, even those who think they are revering the Virgin Mary are actually, unbeknownst to them, worshiping Coatlalopeuh. The spiritual struggle in *Borderlands / La Frontera*, then, promises not conversion to a new religion, but the discovery of who Anzaldúa already is, the religion she already has. "Like the ancients, I worship the rain god and the maize goddess, but unlike my father I have recovered their names," she explains (112). This project of recovery characterizes Anzaldúa's research into palimpsest religious structures.

Borderlands thus imagines a civilizational struggle between Christianity and Aztec pagan religion. Though that struggle begins with the Spanish conquest of the middle Americas and the Southwest, it continues today in the United States, where Mexican American children are taught to ridicule the pagan "superstition" of their forbears, a set of beliefs and intuitions that turn out to be remnants of ancestral religion to which they can return for spiritual strength and cultural healing. Anzaldúa's development of a palimpsest model of religion as a strategy to resist Christian America, akin to other ancestral returns discussed in this chapter, is a strain of contemporary American literature partly distinct from the postmodern "ontological pluralism" that McClure finds characteristic of "postsecular" fiction. The rival metaphyscial schemes developed by Anzaldúa and Reed (and Momaday and Silko) do not just coexist and sometimes overlap, but suggest that, in a real way, ancestral pagan spiritual pasts are truer and better than the Christian scheme characterizing the nation—at least for their multicultural protagonists. Anzaldúa's attention to the history of colonization and religious proselytization corrects the premise of Bellah's nondoctrinal civil religion; like the other multicultural authors examined in this chapter, her cultural pluralism entails diagnosing and then rejecting a more specifically Christian national history—or, given Anzaldúa's cross-border focus, specifically Christian national histories—than is recognized in the notional liberal consensus on American civil religion.

Writing Is Fighting: Frank Chin and Christian Assimilation

> ("Are you a Christian?" my mother asks periodically. "No, of course not." "That's good. Don't be a Christian. What *do* you believe in?" "No religion. Nothing." "Why don't you take the Chinese religion, then?" And then a few minutes later, "Yes, you do that," she'd say. "Sure, Mom. Okay.")
>
> Maxine Hong Kingston, *China Men*

Another influential multiculturalist who returned to ancestral gods in order to combat Christian America during this period was the playwright, critic, and novelist Frank Chin. The outspoken leader of the editorial group that published *Aiiieeeee!: An Anthology of Asian American Writers* in 1974 (which included Jeffery Paul Chan, Lawson Inada, and Shawn Wong), Chin helped develop a wide-ranging attack on the nation's marginalization of Asian Americans and their literatures (see Elaine Kim 124–25). Like his friend and fellow Californian Ishmael Reed, with whom he was in a literary and publishing alliance, Chin argued that the United States historically repressed its ethnic minorities through religious assimilation and literary form.[13] If *Mumbo Jumbo* imagines the demand for a monolithic black aesthetic as the Atonist Trojan Horse introduced to crush the messy creativity of the Harlem Renaissance, Chin suggests that America assimilated its most "model minority" through Christianization and the primary Christian literary form: confessional autobiography. He explored this theme in writings beginning with "Racist Love," an essay he coauthored with Jeffery Paul Chan in 1972, and continuing with "This Is Not an Autobiography" in 1985 and his overview of Asian American literary history, "Come All Ye Asian American Writers of the Real and the Fake" in 1991. While some critics have noticed a change in Chin's thinking in the late 1980s—from a nationalist emphasis on Chinese American vernacular to an interest in cultural survivals across the Pacific (see Kim 226)—one point of continuity is Chin's emphasis on the oppressive and assimilative dimensions of Christianity in America.

As with Reed, there is a legendary backstory to Christianity's conflict with its Other: for Chin, this begins with Marco Polo's visit to China and return to the Vatican with an excess of trade goods that disturbs the Pope, prompting him "to get China out of his system" ("Come All" 10) by demonizing this civilization that lay beyond the bounds of Christendom. Thus began a Western notion that saw China as being without morality, or, indeed, history, and a missionary project that imagined the Chinese as "'choice souls' ripe for salvation" (10). In the United States, Chin argues, conversion as assimilation had a literary dimension:

> A traditional tool of Christian conversion, the autobiography became the sole Chinese American form of writing. . . . Every Chinese American autobiography and work of autobiographical fiction since Yung Wing, from Leong Gor Yun and Jade Snow Wong to Maxine Hong Kingston and Amy Tan, has been written by Christian Chinese perpetuating and advancing the stereotype of a Chinese culture so foul, so cruel to women, so perverse, that good Chinese are driven by the moral imperative to kill it. Christian salvation demands the destruction of all Chinese history: that's the Second Commandment, children. (11)

In Chin's literary history, autobiography is "not a Chinese form," but is rather imported by Westernizing Christian Chinese in the twentieth century; it is a particularly Christian genre "descended from confession" and including St. Augustine's *The Confessions* (11). In Chin's formulation, Christian conversion need not be a topic of a Chinese American autobiography because the form itself already contains the ethos and worldview of the religion. The genre and act of confession entails "admission of guilt, submission of my self to others for judgment" and as such is a "humiliating declaration of betrayal of your self," as Chin has the hero/god Kwan Kung declare in "This Is Not an Autobiography" (121). As such, confession is intrinsically assimilationist because it seeks the acceptance of the listener, the "conversion from an object of contempt to an object of acceptance" (122). This literary history of Christianization first applied to Indigenous peoples, explains Kwan Kung: "The autobiography did not exist among American Indians til the Christians came. And the Christians taught them to write in a white man's language, and began converting them with their autobiographies" (124).

Like Momaday, Reed, Silko, and Anzaldúa, Chin's critique of Christian America has an implicit universal dimension. For him, guilt and confession constitute a betrayal of the self. The individual should be his or her own law-maker and judge. This criterion in Chin's work is Confucian-derived, which does not deactivate its implicit universalist ethos, but does suggest the ultimately pluralist—multicultural—ground of Chin's critique. The primary problem he sees with Christianity is that it is a proselytizing religion that has historically been tied to imperialism, racism, stereotypes, and enforced assimilation. "Christian conversion is cultural extinction and behavior modification," says Chin: "The social scientists call it 'acculturation'" ("Come All" 18). Chin's understanding of conversion as assimilation into the American way of life is thus a relativist critique: Christianity is fine for the Pope, for Marco Polo, and for white Americans, but not for Chinese or Americans of Chinese descent.

Chin's opposition between Christianity and Chinese American culture bespeaks their equal status as cultures, but it was not as obvious what the religious component of Chinese culture could be. To cite an instance from one of the main authors Chin sees as writing Christian autobiography, Maxine Hong Kingston (cited in this section's epigraph, and whose work is neither Christian nor quite autobiographical), in *China Men* the narrator wonders what "religion" she should identify with:

For the Korean War, we wore dog tags and had Preparedness Drill in the school basement. We had to fill out a form for what to engrave on the dog tags. I looked up "religion" in the *American-Chinese Dictionary* and asked my mother what religion we were. "Our religion is Chinese," she said. "But that's not a religion," I said. "Yes, it is," she said. "We believe in the Chinese religion." "Chinese is our race," I said. "Well, tell the teacher demon it's Kung Fu Tse, then," she said. (276)

While this is another instance of proclaimed nonauthoritative knowledge in Kingston's work,[14] it also suggests the blurring between ethnicity and religion, as she parodies both the central slippage of Chin's cultural politics and his answer in Kung Fu Tse—also known as Confucius.

Part of Chin's scheme entails Confucianism and the possibilities for Confucian cultural survivals in Chinese America as a suitable pluralist opposing force to Christian America. But this search for survivals occurs in a more limited degree and in a different form than those of his friend Ishmael Reed, who influenced him, and in Chin's criticism Confucian survivals never quite blossom into a full-fledged oppositional *religious* resource for Chinese Americans.[15] Indeed, Chin's thinking on religion and religious survivals developed considerably between the 1970s and the 1990s. In the earlier "Racist Love" essay, for example, Chin and Chan refute the idea that the lack of juvenile delinquency in Chinese American families was because "Confucianist Chinese culture was making law-abiding citizens of us." On the contrary, the reason "has less to do with Confucian mumbo-jumbo than with that law against the birth of Chinese kids" (72): the Chinese immigration laws, that is, preventing Chinese women from accompanying men to the United States. In this early indictment of Christian America there is no opposing religious or philosophical force: Confucianism and Chinese folk religion have not yet turned into a source of resistance and cultural endurance. In fact, in this year of the publication of *Mumbo Jumbo* by Ishmael Reed (whose poem "catechism of d neoamerican hoodoo church" directly follows "Racist Love" in Richard Kostelanetz's *Seeing Through Shuck*), Chin and Chan's "mumbo-jumbo" signifies not so much Reed's sense of religious resistance and incommensurability between the white and minority worlds as it does the previous generation's assimilationist sensibility, as expressed in John Okada's *No-No Boy*, whose protagonist is alienated from the Buddhist "mumbo jumbo" of his mother's funeral (191). For Okada in 1957 and Chin and Chan in 1972, Asian American religious survivals—whether Buddhist mumbo jumbo or Confucian mumbo jumbo—cannot be sources of legitimate cultural distinction.

Perhaps learning from his ally's search for religious survivals, Chin eventually discovered in the earlier, eschewed Confucianism an analogous cultural retention with which to resist Christian America. But this was not so much a religious tradition because, as Chin later perceived, Confucianism—what he calls "Confuciandom" ("Come All" 34)—is not really a religion but rather a moral-philosophical tradition expressed in canonical Chinese literary and historical texts. Nevertheless, it serves as a belief system encoded in a set of precepts and stories, especially the Chinese classic *The Romance of the Three Kingdoms*, which upholds the ethic of the oath of brotherhood among three strangers who are loyal not only to one another, but who together reflect the Confucian "mandate of heaven" that allows for the overthrow of the corrupt state. This Confucian ethos is a cultural survival that endures in America's Chinatowns, in its literature, celebrations, and public art. It does have a conventionally religious component in that one of the heroes of *Three Kingdoms*, Kuan Yu, would later become in Chinese folk religion the god Kwan Kung, whom Chin calls "the god of war, plunder, and literature" ("Come All" 38) and who in slightly different forms enters Taoist and Buddhist traditions. This god arrived with Cantonese immigrants to America in the nineteenth century and was instantiated in the fraternal organizations of the tongs, which took oaths of mutual alliance and aid modeled on the "peach garden" oath famous in *Three Kingdoms*. Kwan Kung continues to be available as a divine resource for Chinese America. His importance is reflected in his status as the god of war and literature, making him an excellent symbol of Chin's distilled Confucian precepts that all "life is war," and that "writing is fighting," as he says many times (34–35; see also "This Is Not" 129). This god of the literary battle, Christopher Shinn suggests, is perhaps the most obvious example of Chin's influence on Reed, insofar as he is "conjuring a Neo-Chinese muse, or what Reed himself calls a 'Chinese loa,' in the form of Kwan Kung, the Chinese folk god of art and literature and a 'symbol of plunder, revenge, drama and literature'" (65). Like Silko extending indigeneity to African gods, so too does Reed extend indigeneity to a Chinese god, with both instances indicating a self-consciously pan-ethnic multicultural alliance against Christian imperialism and assimilationism. For Chin, Kwan Kung is the proper deity, uniting literature and cultural warfare, to be called on by Chinese Americans opposed to Christian autobiography and assimilation.

But Chin "believes" in the supernatural presence of Kwan Kung no more than he believes in the Christian God. Both are cultural artifacts with immense importance for the psychology of the civilizations that articulated them. It doesn't matter for Chin—or Reed, or Bellah—whether one really believes in certain supernatural deities; the important thing about these religious oppositions is that they articulate deeply held cultural presuppositions informed by historically dynamic traditions. To return to an earlier quotation above, while Chin might reasonably construe Jade Snow Wong as a

Christian writer (she talks about her father's Christian ethos in her autobiography), Kingston is most certainly not Christian in any relevant sense.[16] That doesn't matter for Chin, for whom Christianity stands as a cultural alliance entailing no necessary metaphysics. Whether Confucianism is a religion or not—and most commentators would agree with Chin that it is not, that it is a moral and philosophical system that disrupts traditional Western notions of what counts as a religion[17]—it is primarily on the terrain of cultural and psychological difference that Confucian Chinese America confronts and resists assimilationist Christian America. Thus, when Chin opens his manifesto by comparing how Chinese Americans grow up chanting "The Ballad of Fa Mu Lan" to how European Americans grow up knowing the Bible ("Come All" 3–4), the comparison does not so much imagine Mu Lan as a religious resource as it does the Bible as a secularized cultural one, texts manifesting Herbergian culture-religions.

Chin's critiques reference centuries of Christian belief and practice, but also, perhaps, the more immediate context in the 1980s of the arrival of the Moral Majority, televangelism, and the rise of a strenuously evangelical Christian confessional mode that had less to do with the Pope and more with the revival of born-again Protestantism and its growing popular culture presence and influence on politics. We get the hint of this presence in Chin's conceptualization of Christianity and its modes of guilt, confession, self-abasement, and the submission to a higher law. Such dramas became the stuff of American popular culture in the 1980s, most spectacularly with the rise (and sometimes fall) of television ministries by those such as Jim and Tammy Faye Bakker, Jimmy Swaggart, Pat Robertson, Jerry Falwell, and others—as was registered in novel form, we saw in the introduction, by John Updike in 1990 and 1985 by Margaret Atwood. Televangelism made a spectacle of ritual confession and self-abasement, and 1987–88 witnessed the very public implosion of two important televangelical empires, those of the Bakkers and Swaggart. One of the iconic photos of the 1980s remains Swaggart's tearful, upheld face as he confessed before a rapt congregation and television audience his rendezvous with a New Orleans prostitute. While sinfulness, confession, and forgiveness are standard aspects of Christian theology and practice, Chin's characterization of Christian America resonates more with this particular resurgent Protestantism than with, say, medieval Catholicism, Luther's Reformation, or twentieth-century Episcopalianism.

These canonical multicultural writers suggest the complex ways contemporary American multiculturalism formulated its programmatic pluralism in a dialogue with both the concurrent conservative Christian resurgence, sometimes borrowing its language and ideas, and the civil religion liberal consensus of the preceding decades. As shown in the Frank Schaeffer epigraph to this chapter—the plea that fundamentalists cease speaking in private "jive" and instead reengage in the public square—the conservative Christian resurgence attended to multicultural challenges in much the same way. While we might be tempted to imagine multiculturalism and the conservative Christian resurgence in simple oppositional terms, the facts suggest a more complex and interesting story of contestation and convergence. In the next few chapters, I show that both movements accepted the civil religion understanding of religion's role in social belonging and identity. If multiculturalism and the resurgence agreed that America had been a Christian nation, the former saw that fact as a point of departure for its antiassimilationist cultural politics of pluralism and relativism, while the latter saw in it the basis for American social morality, law, and education policy. In other words, both used the definition of America as Christian as the basis for articulating a call to return to the faith of one's imagined ancestors. Their shared rejection of the bland, liberal, civil religion, assimilationist consensus would decisively shape the culture wars in the decades to come.

CHAPTER 2

The Poisonwood Bible's Multicultural Graft

> There is no longer Jew or Greek, there is no longer
> slave or free, there is no longer male and female; for
> all of you are one in Christ Jesus.
>
> Galatians 3:28
>
> For if the Pauline move had within it the possibility
> of breaking out of the tribal allegiances and commit-
> ments to one's own family, as it were, it also contained
> the seeds of an imperialist and colonizing missionary
> practice.
>
> Daniel Boyarin, *A Radical Jew*

When Alice Walker wrote in 1996 that "It is my habit as a born-again pagan to lie on the earth in worship" (*Same* 25), her language suggested the complicated blend of contestation and convergence marking the intersection of multiculturalism and the social and political resurgence of conservative Christianity in the United States since the 1970s. Explaining how she caught Lyme disease after *The Color Purple* (1982) was published, Walker observed, "I imagine I am like my pagan African and Native American ancestors, who were sustained by their conscious inseparability from Nature prior to being forced by missionaries to focus all their attention on a God 'up there' in 'heaven'" (25). Walker's self-identification as a "born-again pagan" established a contrast between Christianity and the ancestral religious traditions to which she turned—but it did so by drawing on the very vocabulary and religious experience of conversion and redemption at the heart of the Christian resurgence. Though we might wish to imagine post-1970s multiculturalism and the conservative Christian resurgence in simple oppositional terms, Walker's vocabulary suggests a more complicated and surprising story of mutual influence and response in which the movements sometimes shared a way of thinking and talking about religious practice and religious cultures—as we began to see in the previous chapter.

Walker's religious self-description was one 1990s node of multicultural response to the conservative Christian resurgence. In this chapter I examine another, Barbara Kingsolver's *The Poisonwood Bible* (1998)—a novel deeply critical of the resurgence and deeply informed by American multiculturalism. Indeed, *The Poisonwood Bible* is a significant exception to serious literary culture's general inattention to the astonishing, unpredicted Christian resurgence of the last forty years. Kingsolver comprehensively critiques American fundamentalism, attacking a certain version of Christianity on its own grounds of Pauline universalism. Yet the novel's universalism is doubled and ultimately undone by a critical relativism—a dual approach perhaps inspired, I hypothesize, by Walker's experience in writing about African cultural traditions. Its strategic ambivalence in its moments of universalism and relativism makes it symptomatic of a kind of impasse that multiculturalism has faced since the 1970s in its response to the powerful conservative Christian resurgence. As we shall see, Kingsolver's critique of such universalist Christian claims proceeds by generating universalist counterclaims, but also (and more important) by unmasking Christian universalism as merely Western ethnocentrism.

Uprooting Paul

> To be here without doing everything wrong requires a new agriculture, a new sort of planning, a new religion.
>
> *The Poisonwood Bible*

Published to excellent reviews,[1] *The Poisonwood Bible*, perhaps Kingsolver's best-known book, was adopted as an Oprah's Book Club selection in June 2000, one of the volumes that "shifted dramatically toward the so-called literary" the balance of Oprah Winfrey's choices (Lofton 162).[2] The novel tells the story of a fundamentalist Baptist family from Georgia who become missionaries to the Belgian and then independent Congo between 1959 and 1961. The father, Nathan Price, is a patriarch who drags his wife and daughters to a technologically simple and pagan Kikongo-speaking village, where he alienates the population as well as his own family. Disaster strikes the family and the survivors flee, except for Nathan, who stays and goes mad. His wife, Orleanna, and their four daughters alternately narrate the dissolution of both the family and their missionary project, and the novel is narrated in their different voices: from the Valley-girl-before-her-time Rachel, marked by materialism and malapropisms; through the voiceless genius Adah and her wordplay, and the pious Leah, whose faith crumbles and who learns to embrace the culture she has arrived in; to the five-year-old naïve child Ruth-May, who dies of a snakebite.

The novel finds many things disturbing about late-1950s Christian fundamentalism, and, I argue, the conservative Christian politics firmly established in the 1990s while Kingsolver was writing. First, *The Poisonwood Bible* critiques the patriarchal and misogynist content of the father's fundamentalism as he inflicts it on both his family and the Kilanga villagers. This Christianity is an exercise in male power and familial hierarchy, which Kingsolver portrays as the danger of male tyranny inherent in the biblical admonition that wives obey their husbands (Eph 5:22). Kingsolver's second and related critique is that this conservative theology of hierarchy and submission—rather than an alternative progressive one of liberation—is toxic in a colonial and neocolonial setting, when invoked, as Belgium and then the United States do, to justify paternalism and domination. The book's critique is not confined to the arrogance of missionary work, and its prizing of the Word over bread (70), and the fact that, like charity, missions preserve the imbalance of wealth instead of radically redistributing wealth and power (232). Taking a cue from Chinua Achebe's *Things Fall Apart* (1958, credited in the Author's Note), Kingsolver is especially disturbed by Christianity's justification of colonial violence and oppression (120). A third element is Kingsolver's attention to abstract, theological problems, such as suffering and the problem of evil. The narrators wonder aloud about God's responsibility for the destructive floods causing dysentery among village children (217), an ant plague that devastates the countryside (307), the malaria and other diseases that kill many, and slavery (522). *The Poisonwood Bible* questions God's alibi for not intervening in these bad things—some of which are done in his name.

These critiques take form primarily through the characterization of Nathan, who subjugates the women and girls around him and who has no discernible virtue, a portrait of a fundamentalist preacher as ideologue and social totalitarian. Nathan is a patriarch whose values require the domination of the "mess of female minds" (36) in his family, as he puts it, in a way that parallels colonial paternalism. Kingsolver makes the point that patriarchy is to blame for male rule in the household and masculinist European colonial and American neocolonial rule in the Congo. Critics and reviewers have recognized that *The Poisonwood Bible*'s crucial attack on colonialism and neocolonialism is achieved partly through this character, although for some, he is so one-dimensional that the novel's power suffers.[3] Nonetheless, Kingsolver's critique of conservative Christianity dovetails with the novel's important critique of the colonial and neocolonial situation, as becomes painfully clear when Nathan is contrasted with his foil, the village's previous missionary, who has "gone native" but who returns to the village for a visit.

This former missionary's name is Brother Fowles, and he has largely given up the mission of evangelizing. Fowles has married a Congolese woman—a fact that shocks the Georgian Baptists in 1959—and they and their mixed-race children travel the main river on a riverboat. As Fowles puts his new vocation, it's "a little collecting, a little nature study, a little ministry, a little public health and dispensing of the quinine" (248). The novel sets up a simple binary opposition between the good Christian and the bad Christian, and through it establishes a good religion–bad religion dichotomy. Fowles dialogues while Nathan preaches and never listens. Fowles respects cultural differences, while Nathan condemns the partial nakedness of the villagers (27). Fowles is concerned with health, while Nathan cares only whether souls are saved. Fowles, an amateur ornithologist, respects creation; Nathan ignorantly brings over American plants to try to grow on African soil. Fowles questions the composition of the Bible as writing that transcends culture; Nathan knows the Truth and tells everyone else. In short, Fowles is interested in dialogue, not doctrine, while Nathan is obviously the reverse.

Strangely, for a novel so critical of fundamentalist Christianity's ideological certainties, there is almost no moral ambivalence in these two characters. There's a bad Christian, and a good, watered-down Christian. Critics and reviewers have been very sure which side Kingsolver is on, disagreeing only on the Christian contours of the opposition. Cecelia Lynch, for example, argues that *The Poisonwood Bible* contrasts Fowles's "pluralist identity" and syncretizing religious practice with Nathan's "uncompromising Christian dogma" and "neocolonialist" imposition of religious identity (748, 747). William Purcell, on the other hand, convincingly demonstrates that while Fowles's portrayal is intended to suggest St. Francis, the former missionary departs from "orthodox Christianity" not in his views of the Bible, but in his views of nature and immanence (106): nature "confirms" scripture for St. Francis but seems to "supersede" it for Fowles (107–8). As some critics have noted, Nathan may be a caricature that unfairly represents the many twentieth-century missionaries who also evinced Fowles's theological flexibility and commitment to social gospel concerns.[4] Nevertheless, what is not in doubt is the novel's opposition between the two men, and where the author's sympathies lie.

One of the key metaphors through which Kingsolver contrasts these characters is that of plants and gardens. Nathan plants a "demonstration garden" (35) of beans, squash, and tomatoes; as Leah narrates, "It was to be our first African miracle: an infinite chain of benevolence rising from these small, crackling seed packets, stretching out from our garden into a circle of other gardens, flowing outward across the Congo" (36). Nathan begins by planting on flat ground, ignoring the advice of one villager; in the first disaster to strike the project, a torrential rainfall washes the Americans' garden away. In the second attempt, Nathan adapts to local practice by replanting in small mounds and at first seems rewarded by thriving plants—but plants that do not bear fruit. Nathan finally realizes that there are no pollinating insects for these plants, explaining to Leah they need "African bugs. . . . Creatures fashioned by God for the purpose of serving African plants" (80). In case we miss the point, Nathan has earlier cited Jesus's parable of the mustard seed (39), thereby drawing on established Christian imagery of planting, sowing, and bearing fruit.[5] Nathan, in other words, is far too certain that his vegetables, like his faith, can be transplanted. Both fail to thrive because of his willful ignorance of cultural difference. The implication is that, just as Georgia vegetables are inappropriate for Congo ecology, so too is Baptist fundamentalism inappropriate for the Kilanga people: "Christianity is an alien growth that will no more bear fruit in the Congo than Nathan's bean plants" (York 142).

In contrast to Nathan's arrogant obstinacy is Fowles's engagement with Kilanga culture, a point Kingsolver makes with a plant metaphor that addresses the failed garden characterizing Nathan's missionary project. During their dueling scriptures debate, Fowles quotes and then reinterprets Romans 11:16–18, where Paul suggests that the gentiles have, through Christ, been "grafted" onto the Jewish tree, sustained by Jewish roots. As Fowles asks Nathan rhetorically, "Don't you sometimes think about this, as you share the food of your Congolese brethren and gladden your heart with their songs? Do you get the notion we are the branch that's grafted on here, sharing in the richness of these African roots?" (252). Fowles is happy to graft what he thinks are a few Christian ideas—such as monogamy and a prohibition against wife-beating—onto the already established tree of African culture, a grafting of which, by contrast with the garden that will not bear fruit, Kingsolver approves.

Kingsolver's anticolonial critique of Christian fundamentalist missionary work becomes especially clear when examining Fowles's revision of Paul's image of the grafted tree. The most important articulator of proto-orthodox Christianity, Paul is also sometimes considered to be an origin for Western universalism. As my epigraph to this chapter suggests, Paul argued that it is through Christ that the ethnic differences between Jew and Greek (i.e., Jew and gentile) are transcended into a universal religion. I want to read that move in consultation with Daniel Boyarin, a contemporary Jewish rabbinic scholar and cultural critic whose 1994 *A Radical Jew: Paul and the Politics of Identity* was one of the important texts, contemporaneous with *The Poisonwood Bible* (1998), to see Paul's dialectic between the universal and the ethnically particular of critical value for our times. (Another was Alain Badiou's 1997 *Saint Paul: The Foundation of Universalism*.) Like Kingsolver, Boyarin is anxious about the disrespect for difference that seems to attend Christianity's universal claims.

In *The Poisonwood Bible* Fowles quotes part of Paul's metaphor from Romans, which reads in full:

> If some of the branches were broken off, and you, a wild olive shoot, were grafted in their place to share the rich root of the olive tree, do not boast over the branches. If you do boast, remember that it is not you that support the root, but the root that supports you. You will say, "Branches were broken off so that I might be grafted in." That is true. They were broken off because of their unbelief, but you stand only through faith. So do not become proud, but stand in awe. For if God did not spare the natural branches, perhaps he will not spare you. Note then the kindness and the severity of God: severity toward those who have fallen, but God's kindness toward you, provided you continue in his kindness; otherwise you also will be cut off. And even those of Israel, if they do not persist in unbelief, will be grafted in, for God has the power to graft them in again. For if you have been cut from what is by nature a wild olive tree and grafted, contrary to nature, into a cultivated olive tree, how much more will these natural branches be grafted back into their own olive tree. (Rom 11:17–24)

As Paul explains to the predominantly gentile church in Rome (a congregation he did not found, but wanted to visit), the ethnic, descent-based covenant that God had with the Jews becomes extended to gentiles through Jesus Christ. Through this supersession an ethnically specific historical relation to God becomes universal, applicable to all nations. In Paul's image, Jews who do not accept Jesus as the Messiah are pruned from the olive tree that God had carefully cultivated, and in their place are grafted gentile branches. As Boyarin summarizes,

> the metaphor is based on the practice of the grafting of fruit trees. Branches of different sub-species and indeed even of different species can be attached to root-stock such that they form effectively one plant. To perform this operation, however, existing branches often have to be pruned in order to make room for the new ones and also to give them a fair chance at the vitality and nutrients of the root. This is Paul's metaphor, then, for his new formation. The root remains Israel, and just as in the case of a graft, the root-stock defines what the plant, in some sense, is and gives it nutriment, so also the new plant of Christians remain defined as Israel. (203)

As Paul argues, the Jewish branches that have been lopped off are not to be derided, because they can be regrafted to the tree from which they came—but only if they accept the new practices and beliefs. This universalism entails human equality but also the demand for conformity: Christian ideas and Christian practices are true, Paul thinks, and they make their claims on everyone, whether or not certain individuals or cultures accept them.

This universalism is the crux of both Paul's appeal and his problematic effects, according to Boyarin, who suggests that Paul, like other Hellenized Jews in the ancient world, faced a conundrum about how Jewish particularity fit in with other peoples and religions. This tension was the context for "Saul's trouble" on the road to Damascus:

> The Torah, in which he so firmly believes, claims to be the text of the One True God of all the world, who created heaven and earth and all humanity, and yet its primary content is the history of one particular People—almost one family—and the practices that it prescribes are many of them practices which mark off the particularity of that tribe, his tribe. In his very commitment to the truth of the gospel of that Torah and its claim to universal validity lies the source of Saul's trouble. (39)

As Boyarin explains, "Paul was impelled by a vision of human unity that was born of two parents: Hebrew monotheism and Greek longing for universals" (228). It is not that ancient Judaism became universal only through the influence of Hellenistic thought, however, as the previous quotation suggests. Although rabbinic Judaism[6] held that God's covenant was with a particular nation, its theology suggested that "in order to achieve salvation, Jews are required to perform (or better, to attempt to perform) the entire 613 commandments, while non-Jews are required only to perform seven commandments given to Noah that form a sort of natural, moral Law" (233). These so-called Noahide laws included prohibitions against murder, idolatry, theft, and so on, and their existence attests to the way that ancient Judaism already had a universal dimension in that it thought that non-Jews who practiced idolatry were not just practicing differently, but wrongly: it made claims on an outside group. Of course, as Boyarin reminds us, Jews never tried to stop gentiles from eating pork, and thus, as he nicely puts it, "The genius of Christianity is its concern for all of the peoples of the world; the genius of rabbinic Judaism is its ability to leave other people alone" (331n10, 232–33).

But according to Boyarin, the question of universality became urgent as Judaism came into contact with other cultures in "the Hellenistic and Roman periods," compelling Jews like Paul to try to figure out "how the biblical religion fit in a world in which Jews live among other peoples" (25). Responding to these intellectual contexts, a "Hellenistic Judaism" developed, one that Boyarin contrasts with "rabbinic Judaism" during the period. Preconversion Saul was a synecdoche for this Hellenized Judaism, which contained "two nearly contradictory cultural tendencies, one toward a universalism which emphasized the capacity for all human beings to be saved and the other a reaction against this universalism which re-emphasized the particular privileges of the Jewish People" (59). Paul achieved a synthesis through his Christology, Boyarin suggests in his compelling reading of Paul's theology, in which Christ was both flesh and spirit, and in a hermeneutic that held that flesh to be an outward sign of the spirit, just as Israel became an allegory for (and superseded by) those people joined in the universal Christian church. Unlike some other early followers of Jesus, Paul taught that gentile converts to Christianity should not perform Jewish covenantal practices such as circumcision, because this was merely the outmoded sign of a relationship which was now properly the realm of the spirit. As Paul says in the epigraph quoted above, in Christ there is "no longer Jew or Greek": these earlier ethnic religious distinctions are entirely superseded by the universal person in Christ.

While this universalism is marked by a desire for oneness, a respect for human equality, and a concern for those outside one's ethnic group, it comes at a cost, says Boyarin. Though Boyarin defends Paul, whom he sees as the "fountainhead . . . of western universalism" (229), against charges of anti-Semitism (156), he finds that because for Paul "the only possibility of human equality involved human sameness" that Pauline universalism is "inimical to Jewish difference, indeed to all difference as such" (156). Indeed, Boyarin suggests that it is not accidental that this Christian universalism was prone to coercion and imperialism (8), issues entirely germane to *The Poisonwood Bible*'s interest in the historical connection between Christian missionary work and both European imperialism and American neocolonialism. (This universalism—which is how I use the term throughout this book—contrasts with its near-opposite meaning in the liberal Protestant tradition of Universalism that teaches universal salvation regardless of one's religious commitments, or lack thereof.) Boyarin suggests, fruitfully, that Pauline universalism and rabbinic "particularism" both present "enormous ethical and political problems as well as enormous promise," and should be considered a "dialectic" rather than a binary (201).

Boyarin's explication of Paul's universal turn and his grafting metaphor allows us to see just how striking is Kingsolver's revision. If Paul sought to solve the problem of ethnic religious differences by dissolving them into a universal religion, Kingsolver's Fowles entirely reverses this procedure, turning Pauline universalist Christianity into one of many ethnically particular branches that might be (re)grafted onto what are, we infer, a number of ethnically distinct roots. Fowles's reversal of Paul's image—that now gentiles are not being grafted onto the Jewish root, but rather Christians onto an African root—is a possibility contained in Paul's original metaphor, based as it was on many "wild" olive trees and the single "cultivated" one. But if Paul's image of the Christian grafting onto the Jewish root was his way of universalizing a new covenant through belief in Christ, Kingsolver's Fowles's revision of the metaphor de-universalizes the Judeo-Christian cultivated tree, making it no more attractive, important, or true than any other tree: all are de-universalized, opening up the possibility of multiple graftings onto multiple trees.

Kingsolver's central revision, then, reculturalizes Christianity, eliminating its universality, which is associated with the intolerance, arrogance, and imperialism of the Baptist fundamentalist evangelist who has the old-fashioned Pauline understanding of the universal church. Having grafted himself onto the African root, Fowles's new vocation of "a little collecting, a little nature study, a little ministry, [and] a little public health and the dispensing of quinine" no longer makes universal claims. As he says, "I observe a great deal, and probably offer very little salvation in the long run" (250). If the problem diagnosed with Kingsolver's garden metaphor was the act of transplantation, her revision of the grafting metaphor suggests that the one tree of universal Christianity is no longer understood as privileged among other trees.

Culture and Cultivation: Multiculturalism's Impasse

Through these extended plant and gardening metaphors, we begin to see the novel's critical ambivalence and—to return to my opening question about the intersection between the conservative Christian resurgence and multiculturalism—its vacillation between universal and relative claims in confronting Christianity. On the one hand, of course, the relativist logic of these metaphors suggests that what's wrong with Christian theory and practice is simply that they are not African. Once Kingsolver has identified the objection as the act of transplanting the plant, then the problem, in this reading, is not really with the plant itself. If Christianity is inappropriate for the Congolese because they are African, or more particularly Kilanga—if, in other words, it is wrong for Africans because it is not their cultural identity—then how can Christianity be inappropriate for Americans, or wrong for American identity? Objecting to Christianity's participation in the colonizing project of cultural imposition and power, the novel unmasks Nathan's universalist Christianity as a set of (relative) cultural practices and beliefs, and conversely implies via the plant metaphor that Christianity is ecologically appropriate for the United States. In metaphorically treating religion as either an indigenous or alien plant, Kingsolver's novel represents a multiculturalism that comprehends religion as ethnic identification and appropriate culture, agreeing with many of the authors reviewed in this book's first chapter. This is the point, after all, of the novel's garden metaphor, by which Kingsolver shows that Nathan's "message is as irrelevant as his Kentucky seeds to the Congo environment" (Ognibene 26).

Intriguingly, Kingsolver suggests that Nathan's "Kentucky Wonder beans, crookneck and patty-pan squash, Big Boy tomatoes" (35) and pumpkins (41) fail because there are no African pollinators for them (80). But most plants pollinated by animals do not rely on specific insect species for pollination (Johnson 46; Johnson and Steiner 140; Waser et al. 1043). Kentucky Wonder beans are a variety of *Phaseolus vulgaris*, an ancient Mediterranean crop domesticated in the New World; the original bean has been grown in Africa for centuries and is an important protein source in East Africa. It is predominantly self-fertilizing, but can be pollinated by local insect populations and grown in diverse conditions (Graham and Ranalli 131). In fact, historical records attest to the African cultivation of Nathan's four vegetable crops for one to four centuries prior to his attempted garden (Alpern 27–28). The 2004 African Pollinator Initiative report identified Kingsolver's four species—squash, tomatoes, French beans (another variety of *Phaseolous vulgaris*), and pumpkins—as "important commercial commodities within Africa known to benefit from animal vectors for pollination" (5). African insects do, in fact, pollinate Nathan's vegetable species.

Kingsolver is a novelist, of course, and is not required to represent ecological facts accurately. I suggest that Kingsolver, who has bachelor's and master's degrees in biology, ecology, and evolutionary biology, knew that she was altering the facts of botany and horticulture, and that her motivation was the appeal of the cross-cultural garden metaphor so crucial to the novel's themes. Here too, however, *The Poisonwood Bible* has its history suggestively wrong. According to the Pew Forum on Religion and Public Life, Christianity grew from about seven million followers in 1900 in sub-Saharan African to 470 million in 2010—a seventyfold increase, after which Christians made up fifty-seven percent of the region's population.[7] While the faith of many of these African Christians seems nearer to Fowles's grafted syncretism, incorporating traditional African religious practices and beliefs such as sacrificing to ancestors or spirits and the protective power of sacred objects,[8] in several

other ways they are closer to Nathan's American conservative fundamentalist Christianity, opposing with clear majorities abortion, homosexuality, and
prostitution and supporting Bible-based legal practices and political leaders with strong, public religious beliefs.[9] That some conservative Episcopalian congregations (such as the Anglican Church in North America) have
recently sought communion with more traditional African churches as a
critical rejection of liberal Anglican trends of blessing same-sex unions and
appointing gay bishops alerts us to both the continuing appeal of universalist
belief and the relative health of conservative Christianity in Africa. While
Nathan's plants and faith cannot flourish in *The Poisonwood Bible*, they have
actually flourished in Africa.

What might it mean that one of the most compelling fictional treatments
of religion in contemporary American fiction gets its facts so spectacularly
and—in terms of the science, at least—surely purposefully wrong? The
answer to this question, I think, lies in the novel's provocative, metaphorical
undoing of Pauline universalism, and more generally in multiculturalism's
troubled relation to universalism as it seeks to contest truth claims made by
conservative religious traditions. This connection manifests in *The Poisonwood Bible*, which clearly has not abandoned universalism as a ground for
critiquing Christianity in general and the 1950s Baptist fundamentalism of
Nathan specifically—the tradition that would shortly become part of the
groundswell of the 1970s conservative Christian resurgence in the United
States. Universalism, in other words, is a property of Pauline Christianity,
but is not found only there: when Boyarin calls Paul the "fountainhead of
western universalism," he means that universalism's willingness to say what
is right or true beyond one's own ethnic group is in general a kind of claim
that can be made within Western philosophy, law, and metaphysics, thanks
in part to Paul. Thus, *The Poisonwood Bible*'s critique of Nathan's universalist
Christianity is at times generated through universalist counterclaims, as when
Kingsolver pays attention to what seems incoherent or wrong in traditional
Christian theory or practice by raising a number of problematic—indeed,
potentially devastating—ideas. In terms of Christian theory, these include
questions emerging since the nineteenth century out of historical criticism
of the authorship, translation, and editing of the Bible, along with its original
culturally embedded composition. The problem of God's role in relation to
evil and suffering is raised a number of times. As if to register these com-
plaints, Kingsolver has Adah become an epidemiologist especially interested
in that miracle of creation, intestinal parasites. As Adah puts it, "Back then
I was still a bit appalled that God would set down his barefoot boy and girl
dollies into an Eden where, presumably, He had just turned loose elephantiasis

and microbes that eat the human cornea. Now I understand, God is not just rooting for the dollies [i.e., children]" (529). Adah's ironic evocation of Eden underscores how God's creation has always been the site of a fierce struggle for limited resources, one in which children's eyeballs are merely resources driving the natural selection of those microbes. Creation did not start out pristine and good only to be transformed through human agency (as Genesis suggests) but has from the start been the site of violence, disease, starvation, and predation. Environmental violence and suffering are the conditions for, not consequences of, human agency.

More particularly, Kingsolver allusively critiques the problematic contemporaneous Baptist theory and practice in the United States. The novel's temporal and geographical complexity becomes clear as the story of Baptist missionaries in Africa in 1959 evokes the prehistory of the conservative Christian resurgence then taking place across the Atlantic—the resurgence which, in full swing, was the context for the novel's composition in the 1990s. The time of the novel's setting saw an intense resistance to desegregation and civil rights, one shaped by conservative Christianity. As Susan Harding demonstrates, even as Martin Luther King Jr. was putting Christianity to good use during this time, Jerry Falwell was preaching prosegregationist sermons (98), which he later attempted to conceal by removing from circulation published ones (26, 112, 286n24). More broadly, if we look at Southern Christianity in the 1950s—and more specifically the Southern Baptists to which the Price family belongs—we find lots of problems. Although the Southern Baptist Convention passed a resolution supporting *Brown v. Board of Education* soon after it was announced in 1954, rank-and-file church members were not behind it, thus splitting the Convention for a long time. John Lee Eighmy suggests that there was a profound moral failure during this time period: not just the one to intervene into what Eighmy thinks of as secular culture's program of segregation—the Convention could pass a resolution against it but not goad its members to integrate—but the failure to come to terms with its own historical role in justifying segregation.

Violence was endemic to segregation, just as it was to imperialism, and Christianity played some role in justifying that violence. Kingsolver carefully names this moral failure by having Ruth-May recall that a preacher had ascribed to Noah's curse of Ham and to "Jimmy Crow" the need for African American children to be schooled separately from the white Price girls (20). Indeed, the five-year-old reads race in Africa through this Christian segregationist lens, repeatedly referring to the local villagers as the "Tribes of Ham" (20, 50, 123, 215, 238) and confusing the anti-Belgian rebels as being the "Jimmy Crow" (20, 117–18, 120, 123). When Orleanna returns to the United States in the 1960s, leaving her fundamentalist husband behind, Kingsolver pointedly has her become part of the civil rights movement (442). And in a near-anagram, Falwell, who was among those citing Noah's curse on Ham as justification for segregation (Harding 286n24), is replaced by Fowles, the good miscegenating Christian c. 1960. Christian segregationism was the political and cultural ancestor of the conservative Christian resurgence, manifested in the Christianization of the Republican Party and its so-called Southern strategy beginning in the 1970s and very much established by the 1990s when Kingsolver was composing her novel. Kingsolver may "root Nathan's religion in American Puritanism," as Susan Strehle suggests (417), but her more immediate context is the Southern Baptist tradition that was shortly to become a source of energy for the resurgence. With these subtle cues to the genealogy of conservative Christianity, the novel invites us to read its tale about African missions during the Cold War as a commentary on the indigenous conservative Christian resurgence in the United States, which was already producing a backlash in the "second aftershock" of the 1990s. This enables her readers to perceive that the resurgence and multiculturalism were mutually entangled responses to the civil rights movement.

This double register of the novel's conservative racial and sexual moral-ity politics—Kingsolver's eye simultaneously on fundamentalist missionary activity in Africa c. 1959 and on the conservative Christian resurgence of the 1990s as she composed it—suggests its historical complexity. As Hard-ing shows, Christian segregationists like Falwell who preached against the mixing of religion and politics in the 1950s (as a way of opposing the civil rights movement) changed their tune in the 1970s once they saw its suc-cess (9, 23–24). It is not an exaggeration to say that part of the impetus behind the conservative Christian resurgence was, simultaneously, a grudging admiration for what African American churches and their allies had accom-plished by mixing religion and politics, and a desire to push back against those accomplishments. Many conservative Southern churches opened pri-vate schools as desegregation and busing continued apace (27), as a muted but ongoing resistance to the civil rights movement, and the status of whites-only schools became nationally prominent in 1982 when President Ronald Rea-gan "backed the racially discriminatory Bob Jones University . . . in a law-suit against the Internal Revenue Service (IRS), which had denied them tax exemptions under civil rights guidelines" (Wilentz 182). By the late 1970s, conservative Christian racial resentment could not generally be expressed as official policy. As Putnam and Campbell note, white "religious Americans are following the trend [of greater racial equality and tolerance], not setting it" (315). Recalling his own transformation from the practice of Christian segregationism, Falwell reported that "it wasn't the Congress or the courts that changed my heart" but rather "God's still small voice in my heart," as occasioned, he says, by his shoeshine man Lewis, who quietly asked him one day in 1963, "Reverend . . . when am I going to be able to join that church of yours over on Thomas Road?" (quoted in Harding 25–26). While this story is part of the evangelist's efforts "to backdate the end of his active opposition to racial integration" (Harding 26), I am more concerned here with the way in which Falwell, who "often compared the New Christian Right to the Civil Rights movement" (23), can be understood to be generally representative of the way in which the resurgence was a reaction against a crusade that was nonetheless its model. Both, Harding says, were "cultural reform movements mediated by preacherly language" (24).

The Poisonwood Bible's multicultural engagement with the Christian resurgence of the time of its composition proceeds simultaneously along two logics—universalism and cultural relativism—that are frequently complementary but that in a few fascinating moments threaten to undermine each other. This tension is seen particularly in the novel's tentative feminist critique of African cultural practices. We learn, for instance, that the good Christian's grafting includes the mitigation of wife-beating and the unsuccessful attempt to restrict polygamy. But when the village chief seeks to add Rachel to his household as a seventh wife and advises Nathan that she will have to undergo female genital mutilation, Kingsolver hesitates: while Nathan protests that this is "slaughter"—and so this might be a rare instance in which Nathan's cultural superiority might dovetail with Kingsolver's interests in condemning this cultural practice—the author has Orleanna wryly comment, "Since when did he start to care about protecting young ladies" (272). Kingsolver may have declined to critically explore female genital mutilation in Africa after watching the negative reception of another American novelist who had done so in the 1990s—Alice Walker.

While Kingsolver was writing *The Poisonwood Bible* in the 1990s, Walker found herself at the center of critical controversy for criticizing female genital mutilation in parts of Africa in *The Color Purple*, *Possessing the Secret of Joy* (1992), and her documentary film and book *Warrior Marks: Female Genital Mutilation and the Sexual Blinding of Women*, coauthored with Pratibha Parmar (1993).[10] Perhaps most famously, Inderpal Grewal and Caren Kaplan indicted Walker's "Euro-American cultural feminism" (6), arguing that "U.S. multiculturalists cannot address issues of inequalities and differences if they presume the goal of progressive politics is to construct subjects, feminist or womanist, that are just like themselves" (7). The controversy anticipated the conundrum faced by Kingsolver and Boyarin: that a critique based on universalist values ("Torture is not culture," Walker claimed [quoted in Kaplan]) was also a kind of ethical imperialism, one perhaps based on "a secular emanation of Christian culture" (Pecora 42). When asked directly, if rhetorically, about this problem in an interview in *Essence*—"What gives this Westerner [Walker] a right to intervene in our affairs?"—Walker doubled her universalist critique with a relativist claim based on her multicultural subject position: "Slavery intervened. As far as I'm concerned, I am speaking for my great-great-great-great-grandmother who came here with all this pain in her body" (Giddings 87). The white Kingsolver, of course, would not have had this ancestral defense. Perhaps accordingly, she sidesteps this overexposed subject, circumspect on so-called circumcision.[11]

A similar tension is seen when *The Poisonwood Bible*'s core ethos of multi-cultural respect challenges the universalist criteria used to assess national and political practices. The novel's strategy of reculturalizing universalist religion has the occasional consequence of transforming disagreements about ethics into matters of disrespecting or not understanding difference. An excellent example occurs at the end of the novel when the three surviving Price sisters meet briefly as adults. Leah has, like Fowles before her, married a local and tied her destiny to the continent: if not quite a Christian graft, she is at least a white American graft onto an African root. Rachel also lives in Africa, but as a hotel-owning neocolonialist who profits from continued Western political and economic dominance. Adah, meanwhile, has found her voice and become a doctor and epidemiologist. As the sisters discuss the novel's key themes of imperialism and neocolonialism, Leah criticizes American involvement in Africa during the Cold War, including the CIA's aid in assassinating the Congo's first democratically elected leader. Kingsolver has the sympathetic Leah didactically describe such problematic ethics for her reactionary sister Rachel: "Okay, let's take Patrice Lumumba, for example. Former Prime Minister of the Congo, his party elected by popular vote. He was a socialist who believed in democracy. Then he was murdered, and the CIA replaced him with Mobutu, a capitalist who believes in dictatorship. In the Punch and Judy program of American history, that's a happy ending." Leah's political ethics are universalist and not culturally specific to the United States because they can be the grounds for critiquing its practice of sup-porting antidemocratic, murderous, kleptocratic tyrannies in the developing world. The novel clearly approves of Leah's universalist critique in the face of Rachel's indignant (and comic) response to her sister's information, "Leah, for your information I am proud to be an American" (479).

But the novel refuses to perform a similar assessment of African practices and values. In one astonishing episode beginning immediately after Rachel's patriotic deafness to Leah's information, the sisters visit the royal palace at Abomey in modern Benin, built by the Fon kingdom over several centuries and now a UNESCO world heritage site. One of its kings constructed his part of the palace using slaves' blood for the mud walls; he was also buried with forty-one of his wives—that is, he was buried dead but them alive. For Rachel, this is just more indication of African brutality which, she points out to Leah, preexisted European invasion. But Leah and, we are to suppose, Kingsolver, is reluctant to criticize such practices. This reluctance is based on cultural relativism: that "we couldn't possibly understand what their social milieu was, before the Portuguese came" (489). Leah can imagine good explanations, and suggests that "what looks like mass murder to us is probably misinterpreted ritual. They probably had ways of keeping their numbers in balance in time of famine. Maybe they thought the slaves were going to a better place" (489–90). As Leah summarizes the multicultural lesson in the line I paraphrase in the introduction, "You just can't assume that what's right or wrong for us is the same as what was right or wrong for them" (490). This plea, that because of our own cultural subject position we cannot evaluate the practice of building mud walls with slaves' blood or burying one's wives alive when one dies, is a hardline cultural relativism and resistance to universalist ethics of the kind that Rachel has previously exemplified.

What happens in both cases is that criticisms based on universalist criteria are reread as instances of multicultural misunderstanding or disrespect. The novel's Fowlesian strategy of reculturalizing that which was universal means that disagreement about ethics is sometimes transformed into disrespect for difference. This transformation is a consequence, it seems to me, of the logic of Kingsolver's reversal of Paul's grafting metaphor. To return to Boyarin briefly, he suggests that

> Paul holds out to the Jews the possibility of reinclusion in the community of faith by renouncing their "difference" and becoming the same and one with the grafted Israel of gentile and Jewish believers in Christ, but if they do not, they can only be figured as the dead and discarded branches of the original olive tree. There is, on the one hand, what I take to be a genuine, sincere passion for human (re)-unification and certainly a valid critique of "Jewish particularism," but on the other hand, since the unification of humankind is predicated on sameness through faith in Christ, those humans who choose difference end up effectively non-human . . . (204)

Boyarin's framing, however, makes it impossible to disagree about whether Jesus was the Messiah, because alternative beliefs are rendered as disrespect for those who "choose difference." On the one hand, this scheme apprehends the viewpoints of postmetaphysical cultures that have descended from religious traditions with particular metaphysical claims, but whose secularized members no longer make any. That is, Christmas-tree Christians like Norman Mailer's wife, members of a Herbergian culture who do not particularly believe in Jesus's Messiahship (like the British characters talking in the church crypt in Philip Roth's *The Counterlife* [1986] who nonetheless may insist on baptizing grandchildren), cannot disagree with those who deny Jesus's Christhood, since they themselves do not believe it. Roth's secular Christians are indeed, then, as Boyarin suggests, disrespecting difference if they expect everyone to assimilate to their culture. On the other hand, by turning the possibility of disagreement into disrespect for multicultural difference, Boyarin's formulation makes genuine disagreement or argument impossible.

The Poisonwood Bible is one of the relatively few literary novels to engage seriously with the postwar conservative Christian resurgence, and its core ethos of respect animates its critique of both American imperialism and American postwar religion. As Kingsolver has stated on her fan website, Nathan was intended to explore American neocolonialism and Belgian colonialism in the Congo, not represent Christian missionaries.[12] Hers was a book about Western misdeeds in Africa that this self-avowed "pantheist" (Snodgrass 15) had wanted to write for many years, and Nathan became her means. William Purcell suggests that the novel is "a 'political allegory' intended to criticize European and American intervention in Africa. To serve this end, fundamentalist evangelical Christianity is employed as the author's primary metaphor" (109–10). In this respect, Purcell captures one key aspect of the novel's strategic ambivalence. Its occasional aversion to universalist criteria and its metaphorical reversal of Pauline theology suggestively reread Christianity's universalist claims as a set of beliefs and practices of a specific culture.

Universalism's Discontents

But the practice of speaking a rich, tonal language to my neighbors has softened his voice in my ear. I hear the undertones now that shimmer under the surface of the words *right* and *wrong*. We used to be baffled by Kikongo words with so many different meanings: *bängala*, for *most precious* and *most insufferable* and also *poisonwood*. That one word brought down Father's sermons every time, as he ended them all with the shout "Tata Jesus is *bängala!*"

Leah in *The Poisonwood Bible*

As we saw in chapter 1, reconceptualizing religions as cultures has been a core strategy of American literary multiculturalism since the late 1960s. For many of the most important American multicultural writers, religions are not so much celebrated as universal ideas and transcendent truth claims as they are revealed to be specific cultural traditions that undergo historical transformations but are nonetheless sources of contemporary identities. In canonical multicultural texts, universalist critiques of Christian beliefs and practices are supplemented by the idea that specific forms of Christianity are inappropriate for African Americans, Asian Americans, Native Americans, and Mexican Americans. These multicultural writers often insist on recognizing Christianity as part of an American assimilationist national identity, one resisted by their shared multicultural ethos of cultural pluralism and relativism. *The Poisonwood Bible* shares this dual strategy of universalist critique doubled by relativist reculturalization—tilting toward the latter, like multiculturalism generally—and it comes as no surprise by now that some white writers like Kingsolver have learned and pursued the cultural politics of "high cultural pluralism" (McGurl 56).[13]

Kingsolver's novel is thus representative of a multiculturalism that tends to comprehend religion in terms of ethnic identification and appropriate culture, even drawing on a standard multicultural trope of language encoding cultural difference: as the epigraph to this section shows, questions of right and wrong are relativized by linguistic nuances that cultural outsiders cannot hear. But the general secularization thesis in which the pluralist varieties of "American culture-religion" (Herberg 262) were understood also led to our blindness to the return of universalist religious energy that shortly became apparent in the conservative Christian resurgence and its appetite to legislate for those not in its ethnic group. In other words, insofar as the secularization thesis understood religions as cultural communities with little relevant theological content, it ill-prepared us to recognize the universalism of the Christian resurgence—its willingness to say that what is true for us is also true for others—or the issues at stake in the literature that responded, indirectly or directly, to that resurgence. As Michael Kaufmann has recently reminded us, our discipline has been deeply invested in this secularization story (616), even though, says Hungerford, this "interpretation of postwar American religion would turn out to be wrong. Strong, doctrinally specific religious belief was not the shrinking remnant of an earlier form of American religion, but the growing edge of a new form" (7). We have been slow to realize that the secularization we were expecting has been undergoing a decades-long reversal, at least in the United States.[14]

Whereas multiculturalism and the secularization thesis converged on an explanation of religion as a source of social identity, the conservative Christian resurgence pursued its politics through a willingness to say that what is true for us is also true for others as it pursued legislation and judicial action based on universalist ethics. The resurgence faced a political conundrum as it forcefully reentered the public sphere. José Casanova suggests that "fundamentalism cannot survive in a world devoid of shared moral meanings and standards, in a postmodern world in which it would become just another quaint subculture, like that of the native Indians or the Amish, to be added to the 'gorgeous mosaic' of American cultural pluralism" (156). Casanova's argument resonates with Frank Schaeffer's call for conservative Christians to eschew their tendency to speak their own private religious "jive," a description meant to jolt fundamentalists into being less exotic for the purpose of proselytization, but also to encourage political ambition in the form not of pluralist accommodation but universalist transformation of law and society.

Casanova dates fundamentalism's reentrance into the American public sphere to Falwell's political shift from the separatism he had enunciated as late as 1965 and abandoned by 1976 and his formation of the Moral Majority in 1979 (148). That resurgence continued with the later rise of other resurgent groups such as Pat Robertson's and Ralph Reed's Christian Coalition and James Dobson's Focus on the Family. But this broad movement was not simply a dimension of American religious pluralism because "fundamentalism at this point ceases being a privatized, separate religious enclave and reenters American public life as a public religion with claims upon the public sphere of civil society" (156). The conservative Christian resurgence aimed to supersede "a culture of 'pluralism' that most readily embraces diversity in the form of a marketplace of private religious faiths" (Fessenden 192).

The older regime's distinction between private belief and public secularized, civil religion is glossed by Casanova through a quotation from Richard John Neuhaus's *The Naked Public Square*, in which the author describes the newly politicized fundamentalist ambition: "The religious new right . . . *wants to enter the political arena making public claims on the basis of private truths.* . . . Fundamentalist morality, which is derived from beliefs that cannot be submitted to examination by public reason, is essentially a private morality" (quoted in Casanova 165). Thus, concludes Casanova,

> the logic of open public discourse implies that modern societies, while protecting the free exercise of fundamentalism in the private sphere, procedurally cannot tolerate fundamentalism in the public sphere. Fundamentalism has to validate its claims through public argument. This presents fundamentalists with a stark choice. Those who accept the rules of engagement in the public sphere and begin to argue with their neighbors will have to abandon their fundamentalism, at least procedurally. (166)

As we shall see, this transformation, "procedurally," became complicated; as we shall also see, what became more complicated was that sometimes the literature shared the same procedures as the resurgence it sought to register and respond to, including, on some issues, an occasional embracing of its status as a cultural tradition that demanded pluralist accommodation. Many observers, including literary writers, have found it difficult to come to terms with the peculiar double register of conservative Christianity as cultural tradition in need of pluralist accommodation and a universalist set of moral precepts for ethical practice applicable to all.

This entanglement is ultimately the reason that Barbara Kingsolver, and multiculturalism more generally, make a strategic mistake when they abandon the terrain of universalist argument when confronting the conservative Christian resurgence. Near the end of *A Radical Jew*, Boyarin suggests that progressive politics since the 1960s has depended for its advances on questions of identity and respect for group difference (238), but this strategy that has surely run its course. As Rachel's patriotism suggests, identity claims are no longer (if they ever were) the sole purview of progressivism. Boyarin's claim notwithstanding, progressive politics on issues of homosexuality, abortion, and evolution (and indeed civil rights) have been most effective when they adopted the discourse of universal rights, not the discourse of disrespected identity. It makes no sense to propose a strong particularism and respect for difference as antidotes to recent conservative Christian positions outlawing homosexual marriage or same-sex unions, criminalizing abortion in all but an extremely narrow number of circumstances, and introducing creationism in public school classrooms, because these positions take the form of universal truth claims irrespective of cultural difference or individual preference. The willingness to legislate for those who do not agree with its claims is not an accidental byproduct of the resurgence: it is the resurgence.

If it is unsurprising to find conservative Christianity still willing to stake universalist ground—partly the point of Boyarin's notion that Paul is the "fountainhead" of Western universalism—progressive politics, by contrast, has had to face the question of whether Western universalism, now unmasked as a secularized remnant of Pauline theology, might still provide a ground for ethics in a pluralist, global age. In his discussion of secularization and universalism, for instance, Vincent Pecora concedes Talal Asad's charge of ethnocentrism, admitting (with Jürgen Habermas) that Enlightenment universalism is a secularized descendent of Judeo-Christian tradition (48). The question, then, is whether this recognition deactivates universalism in a global context, as the West and its institutions risk the possibility that they will "inevitably promulgate both Enlightenment ideals of knowledge and selfhood and Judeo-Christian ethical-political traditions while weakening indigenous ones" (54). Like Boyarin, Pecora ultimately sees universalism as theoretically (and historically) problematic, but suggests that recognizing its troubled history within the West may sustain its "strategic" usefulness. Thus he asks (with some hope), "Can that vision [of Enlightenment universalism] itself be made sufficiently self-conscious of and hence relatively autonomous from its simultaneously Judeo-Christian and imperialist foundations, and articulated with similar tendencies in other ethical-religious traditions, to be serviceable in a global age?" (66). Pecora's question gets at the crux of the problem: how, in a country whose extraordinary religious pluralism is often experienced through somewhat secularized Herbergian "culture-religions," we might theorize a more historically self-aware and provisional universalism. The question is urgent, given the two most important developments in postwar American religion that are the context for contemporary literary production: the social and political rise of the Religious Right, and the growth and variety of religious identities encouraged by the expansion of non-European immigration since 1965.[15]

Progressive politics has not abandoned universalist terrain, as it often answered the conservative Christian resurgence's interest in legislating what was right and good for all with counterclaims based not on cultural identities but on universalist rights. But literary multiculturalism, as Kingsolver's novel confirms, has a more troubled relation to that resurgence. The establishment of multiculturalism in the United States has brought many benefits, among them acceptance and celebration of cultural difference. However, this social and literary movement has sometimes made it difficult to recognize and conceptually process the other hugely important, if underrecognized, social movement in the contemporary period: the political and social empowerment of conservative Christians. One of the stories of the literary history of the contemporary period is that multicultural commitments complicated American writers' critical responses to the social and political Christian resurgence since the 1970s. It did so because the multicultural critique had successfully taught us that many purported universalist ideas and practices had after all only been culturally specific—that is, Western. How this matters for *The Poisonwood Bible*—and other novels arguably addressing the contemporary Christian resurgence—is that multicultural writers like Kingsolver frequently translated Christian universalism into more familiar terms of culture and identity as a strategy of critique. This brought multiculturalism to a kind of conceptual impasse as it faced the conservative Christian resurgence—an impasse interestingly avoided by recent pragmatic progressive politics. Multiculturalism has been critically attentive to the Christian resurgence, as Walker's "born-again pagan" suggests, and the reverse has been no less true: these movements have been entwined since the 1970s.

If *The Poisonwood Bible* and Walker's born-again paganism are two nodes of intersection indicating the entanglement of multiculturalism and the resurgence, I wish to conclude this chapter by looking briefly at a third: William Paul Young's evangelical Christian bestseller *The Shack: Where Tragedy Confronts Eternity* (2007). Barbara Kingsolver's parents were "medical and public-health workers, whose compassion and curiosity led them to the Congo" ("Author's Note" x), perhaps giving her the desire to return, in her fiction at least, to the geography where she briefly lived as a child. Young, meanwhile, was "raised among a stone-age tribe by his missionary parents in the highlands of what was New Guinea," according to his novel's back cover. Although *The Poisonwood Bible* had a huge readership due to its selection as an Oprah book club choice, its sales and readership are dwarfed by the ten million copies (and, likely, readers) of *The Shack*, which, Kenneth Paradis reports, was number one on *The New York Times* bestseller list for seventy weeks (107). *The Shack* is a conservative Christian literary adaptation of canonical multiculturalism that suggests the appeals and pitfalls of those nodes of intersection between the resurgence and multiculturalism.

In this Christian bestseller, a man travels to a remote cabin seeking answers to the abduction and murder of his daughter years before. The shack is, in fact, the site of the murder, but after receiving a mysterious invitation to it the man finds not the murderer he feared and longed to confront, but three people who help him come to terms with his tremendous loss. There is an African American woman who loves to cook, a fairylike Asian woman who loves to dance and garden, and a Middle-Eastern-looking man who spends time tinkering in the shop. In answer to Mack's terrible pain and rage—and indeed loss of his religious faith in the face of the question of how God could have permitted the abduction and murder of his daughter Missy—this diverse cast helps Mack accept what he cannot understand. His healing is furthered when Mack is introduced to a fourth figure, a Hispanic woman who appears in a cave who helps him understand his own failings, shortcomings, and lack of omniscience.

If this answer sounds familiar, as does, vaguely, the premise of murdered family members, it's because *The Shack* is a reheated and multiculturalized version of the book of Job in the Bible. Like Job, Mack demands an account of God's justice. The book of Job's ultimate answer to the eponymous hero is to change the subject and to respond to the unasked question of God's power rather than the actually asked question of God's justice: Job can't hope to understand the problem of human suffering, God thunders from his whirlwind near the book's end, because he's not God and wasn't around at creation, is not omnipotent, omniscient, and so on. Young's innovation in this story is to update the loss according to the generic expectations of crime procedurals such as *Criminal Minds* and *Law and Order: Special Victims Unit* and our culture's fascination with child abduction and serial murderers. But his really clever innovation is to repackage traditional theodicy by turning God into a multicultural cast. As it turns out, the three people in the shack are actually the Trinity. God the Father is the African American woman—we know because she is described so, but also because she speaks in stereotyped vernacular such as "Sho 'nuff!" and "that's jes' the way I is" (121), and tends to call Mack "honey." The Asian woman, ephemeral, mysterious, and difficult to pin down, is the Holy Spirit. And the Middle-Eastern carpenter is Jesus the Son. Their words are augmented by the Hispanic woman named Sophia, thus rounding out the culturally diverse cast.

Young may hope the reader does not notice that he is putting the old wine of traditional Christian theodicy into the new wineskins of multicultural diversity. Although some Christian readers (on Amazon, for example) criticized the novel's intellectual and theological thinness and charged it with a couple of heresies, *The Shack* offers a more or less standard (if simplified) Christian theology about the problem of suffering. While some readers may share Mack's thinking in the cave that he deserves an answer for why God didn't protect his daughter—the Lord's alibi, in short—Mack is distracted when Sophia shows him instead that he is unable to judge omnisciently or fairly. Our free will demands that God allow suffering in the world, Sophia and the others explain. Why the system has been set up like this is not a question Mack, or Young, asks. (The invocation of Adam and Eve in Eden to explain why there is suffering and pain in our world appears not to be used allegorically, but factually.) The problem of God's goodness and justice, of course, is an old and transcultural one, and even the book of Job itself shows signs, in its complex authorship, of unease over its answers.[16] But Young's ingenuity is to silently rewrite Job into a contemporary setting with multicultural (if stereotyped) mouthpieces; the answers may not make better sense, but the strategy is to doubly displace God's non-answer from the whirlwind in Job with a loving multicultural Trinity, with the least convincing part of the answer provided not by the Godhead itself, but by wisdom.

The Shack is a "homiletic novel" whose "primary job is to inspire in its reader a transformation toward a more Christian way of life" (Paradis 108), a superficial multicultural wrapping for its primary narrative mode of what Paradis terms "typological realism." While Kingsolver and Young can both be understood as adopting lessons from multiculturalism, Kingsolver's response entails a deeper (but, I hope I have shown, problematic) ethical commitment to the principles of cultural pluralism and cultural relativism, as well as a decision not to speak for Africans, while Young's is an expedient if old-fashioned appropriation of voice. In the next chapter, I turn to a far more intellectually and theologically robust Christian response to multiculturalism, Marilynne Robinson's novel *Gilead*.

CHAPTER 3

Christian Multiculturalism and Unlearned History in Marilynne Robinson's *Gilead*

> We can agree, I think, that invisible things are not necessarily "not-there"; that a void may be empty, but is not a vacuum. In addition, certain absences are so stressed, so ornate, so planned, they call attention to themselves; arrest us with intentionality and purpose, like neighborhoods that are defined by the population held away from them.
>
> Toni Morrison, "Unspeakable Things Unspoken"

> If history has any meaning or value, as we must assume it does, given our tendency to reach back into the past (or what we assume to have been the past) to account for present problems, then it matters to get it right, insofar as we can.
>
> Marilynne Robinson, *The Death of Adam*

The Poisonwood Bible's strategy of reculturalizing universalist Christianity is an attempt to grapple with religion's dual register in American society—as a familial or descent-group tradition informing a group's habits and practices, and as a set of ethics and claims that underpin public debates about sexuality, gender, science, race, and national identity. If the return of religion in the contemporary period often takes the form of "weak religion," as John McClure cites Gianni Vattimo as suggesting (*Partial* 12), Kingsolver's tactic could be thought of as a not entirely successful attempt at translating the strong religion of resurgent conservative Christianity into just another culture among many—to shift its register, as it were. Kingsolver and Young incorporate multiculturalism with different levels of success in order to critique or support the energetic doctrine intrinsic to resurgent Christianity. Put another way, Kingsolver and Young live in "a secular age," as Charles Taylor has explained, insofar as the authors and their characters are aware of belief and unbelief as options that exist. They grew up in different "milieux" in which unbelief and belief were "default" options, respectively, as Taylor describes our situation (12), but as adult writers they write within the context of (and indeed with the purpose of addressing) the awareness of other options.

In this chapter I turn to a liberal Christian writer who also writes in this "secular" situation: an author aware of options, including nonbelieving ones, but interested in critiquing the strong religion characteristic of the resurgence. As with *The Poisonwood Bible*, Marilynne Robinson's *Gilead* (one of the texts Hungerford examines) is a novel that must be understood in terms of the coextensive multiculturalism and conservative Christian resurgence characterizing this period. I argue that the downplaying of belief that McClure and Hungerford find in contemporary American literature tends to occur when we (multi)culturalize religion. One of the consequences of this move is a novel like *Gilead*, which tends, like *The Poisonwood Bible*, to treat religion as a form of cultural identity. The liberal Christian Robinson's crafting of her novel as a kind of Christian multiculturalism brings into focus the strategic appeal of suspending doctrinal belief debates, but also the problematic consequences for understanding the religious sensibilities of contemporary American literature.

Gilead is a long letter by the elderly Congregationalist minister John Ames to his young son, in anticipation of Ames's upcoming death and the fact that his son will grow up fatherless. In addition to being a memoir of his growing up in the fictional town of Gilead, Iowa, Ames's letter recollects his memories of his own father and grandfather. The dramatic struggle between them centered on the appropriate form of Christian opposition to slavery: Ames's grandfather, a radical preacher and ally of John Brown, fought with the Kansas Free Soilers and became an abolitionist guerilla along the Missouri border before becoming a soldier and losing an eye in the Civil War. He was opposed by his son (Ames's father), whose opposition to slavery was based on the principles of Christian pacifism. In *Gilead*, the great moral question of whether Christians should oppose slavery violently or peacefully drives a rift between father and grandfather, one that Ames remembers in his 1956 letter to his own son. As with its key intertext, Toni Morrison's *Beloved*, the moral question of slavery attains national significance as examined through the prism of family memory.

Gilead's second and more immediate moral question centers on Ames's feelings toward his best friend's prodigal son, an unhappy rake who had earlier fathered a child with (and then abandoned) a local girl, left his Iowa home, lost his family's Presbyterian faith, and led an unknown life elsewhere. Jack Boughton has returned to Gilead, and Ames, facing his mortality, struggles with jealousy as he fears Jack's attention to his young wife. The novel's questions of grace and forgiveness turn on whether this prodigal son is repentant and changed. As it turns out, his secret is that he has an African American partner and a mixed-race child. Tennessee antimiscegenation law prevents them from legalizing this relationship, as does her preacher father, who is scandalized by Jack's agnosticism.

Gilead thus organizes its two moral questions around what we might call an Africanist presence, following Toni Morrison's contention in her book-length essay *Playing in the Dark* that American literature incorporates Africanist presences that polymorphously figure terror, morality, sexuality, unfreedom, and so on. Morrison's reading of *Huckleberry Finn* along such lines applies in some ways to Robinson's *Gilead*. Jim the escaped slave in Twain's novel is a serviceable presence for thinking through questions of freedom, civilization, restraint, and familial love, and a different kind of Africanist presence allows Robinson to advance her themes of moral clarity, filial loyalty, and the role memory plays in identity construction. But these Africanist presences in *Gilead* are treated seriously and with respect—unlike, ultimately, Jim in *Huckleberry Finn*.[1] Though *Gilead* is not about African Americans as agents and thinkers, they are a crucial presence this novel cannot do without. Through them is constructed the historical setting of this Christian novel by a Christian author with a Christian narrator and characters, as well as its key moral question of the proper shape of Christian opposition to the evil of slavery. This is its ethical topography: in the face of one of the great national sins, what form should Christian resistance take?

But *Gilead*'s moral frame begs the question: should a Christian oppose slavery or support it? "What's so bad about slavery?" we might ask, just as actual Christians did during the period. Because the great divide within American Christendom in the nineteenth century was not between Christian violent resistance to slavery and Christian pacifist resistance to slavery. The divide was actually between Christian abolitionism and what Frederick Douglass called "Christian Slavery."[2]

In fact, in Douglass's *Narrative of the Life of Frederick Douglass, an American Slave*, Christian slavery became so vivid and potentially controversial that he had to write an appendix to the 1845 text designed to correct the impression that he might be "an opponent of all religion" (*Autobiographies* 97). Having escaped bondage, Douglass clarified that his critique of Christianity should be understood "to apply to the *slaveholding religion* of this land, and with no possible reference to Christianity proper; for, between the Christianity of this land, and the Christianity of Christ, I recognize the widest possible difference" (97). While there has been some debate about Douglass's actual theological beliefs and religious faith,[3] there is no question that what makes his *Narrative* so rhetorically powerful is its portrayal of Christian slavery as a matter of old-fashioned hypocrisy. Douglass transforms his abolitionist protest into a debate about the meaning of Christianity itself: the *Narrative* challenges Northern Christians to engage in defining American Christianity precisely through opposing slavery.

We can see the distance between Douglass and Robinson in their portrayals of evangelical religious experience. In one scene in *Gilead*, the prodigal Jack is drawn to a tent revival meeting "down by the river." One man standing beside him is struck by grace and weeps with sincere "repentance and relief" (226); Jack witnesses this jealously because he also longs for redemption—he too knows it would be a relief if he could achieve sincere faith. In contrast, one of Douglass's masters, Captain Auld, attended a Methodist tent revival meeting in 1833[4]—during the Second Great Awakening—where he "experienced religion." But Auld did not become more "kind and humane" after being born again; on the contrary, describes Douglass, "Prior to his conversion, he relied upon his own depravity to shield and sustain him in his savage barbarity; but after his conversion, he found religious sanction and support for his slaveholding cruelty" (52).[5] Douglass continues:

> His house was the house of prayer. He prayed morning, noon, and night. He very soon distinguished himself among his brethren, and was soon made a class-leader and exhorter. His activity in revivals was great, and he proved himself an instrument in the hands of the church in converting many souls. His house was the preachers' home. They used to take great pleasure in coming there to put up; for while he starved us, he stuffed them. (52)

Douglass cites another instance in which Christianity provided a useful justification, as Auld whipped a slave while citing Jesus's line, "He that knoweth his master's will, and doeth it not, shall be beaten with many stripes" (53; see Luke 12:47).

Harriet Jacobs makes similar observations in *Incidents in the Life of a Slave Girl*.[6] Like Douglass, she argues that there is a "great difference between Christianity and religion at the south" (115). After her master and would-be suitor Dr. Flint joined the Episcopal church, Jacobs recalls that "I supposed that religion had a purifying effect on the character of men; but the worst persecutions I endured from him were after he was a communicant" (115). Though it is not as central to the abolitionism of her text, Jacobs engages in the same strategy as Douglass, transforming the question of slavery into that of the meaning of Christianity itself.

It was biblical lines such as the one quoted by Captain Auld, from the New and Old Testaments, to which religious defenders of slavery pointed.

One such apologist for Christian slavery, the president of the South Carolina Baptist Convention, Richard Furman, argued that the New Testament did not dissolve the master-slave bond. Jesus's words, coupled with other references such as St. Paul's admonition that slaves should "obey your earthly masters with fear and trembling" (Eph 6:5; see Jacobs 106) and his instruction to the slave Onesimus to return to his master Philemon (Philem 1:8–16), were used by defenders of slavery to establish its Christian justification. As Furman and other Christians pointed out, neither Jesus nor the Apostles took the opportunity to condemn the institution.[7] And as folk frequently crucified or fed to lions for challenging the moral order of the ancient world, they could hardly be said to have capitulated to local social custom at the expense of what they really thought was a universal transcendent moral truth.[8]

Of course, Christian ideas provided ammunition for both the proslavery and abolitionist sides in the early nineteenth century. Where they differed was that, given passages literally sanctioning slavery in the ancient world, proslavery Christians could be quite specific, whereas abolitionist Christians had to rely more on abstract principles such as the Golden Rule—that it is impossible to own slaves while loving one's neighbor as oneself and doing unto him as you would have him do unto you (e.g., Jacobs 16, 298). Defenders like Furman were aware of such arguments, however, and pointed out that Jesus's admonition did not trump property rights.[9] We might wish that our neighbor give us his riches, but almost no Christians then or now understand doing unto our neighbors—even poor ones—as we would have them do unto us to include the giving up of large portions of one's property.

Thus, slavery's ideological support among Methodist, Baptist, and Presbyterian congregations, all of which split into Northern and Southern conventions over this question, was absolutely central to its history in the United States. Christian support for slavery—as found, for instance, in Furman's famous 1823 apology—was far more widespread and popular across the nation (not just in the South) than were the views of the famous but marginal few who proposed violent Christian opposition to the practice. More common, in other words, were ideas like schoolteacher's thoughts in Morrison's *Beloved* as he goes to reclaim Sethe and her children, that they were "creatures God had given you the responsibility of" (176). Indeed, one historian of proslavery ideology argues that between 1830 and 1860,

> there emerged what could be considered a proslavery mainstream. The Bible served as the core of this defense. In the face of abolitionist claims that slavery violated the principles of Christianity, southerners demonstrated with ever more elaborate detail that both Old and

New Testaments sanctioned human bondage. God's Chosen People had been slaveholders; Christ had made no attack on the institution; his disciple Paul had demonstrated a commitment to maintaining it. (Faust 10–11)

The emerging racial science of the decades before the Civil War was a supplement to this core religious sanction (Faust 11), a fact that places *Beloved*'s schoolteacher's head measuring and division of Sethe's characteristics into "animal" and "human" in 1855 on the cutting edge of this racist discourse (228).

There is not a glimpse of this historical Christian support for slavery in Robinson's *Gilead*. Why is Christian slavery missing? Although almost no Christians today express theological support for the slavery practiced in the United States before the Civil War,[10] why does Robinson not recognize it as a historical perspective? In *Gilead*, narrator John Ames suggests that in writing his sermons he is "trying to say what was true" (19). In this spot at least I think we could say that the narrator and author both conceive of writing—sermons or novels—as forms of truth-telling, or at least trying to get at the true, even given the mystery of existence. But what does it mean that, on this point at least, the novel will not try to say what was true?

Robinson, as the above chapter epigraph demonstrates, has repeatedly insisted on the importance of trying to get "the past" right, "because it matters, and because it has so often been dealt with badly. . . . surely its complexities should be scrupulously preserved" (*Death* 4). As she writes in her introduction to *The Death of Adam: Essays on Modern Thought*, this especially involves reading "major writers, and establish[ing] within rough limits what they did and did not say" (11). Robinson complains particularly about the omission of John Calvin, who has "somehow vanished" from our sense of the past "either as presumed record or as collective act of mind" (13; see also Shy). The act of misrepresentation and misconstrual of Calvin and his thought has large historical reverberations, Robinson maintains, as does the historical blindness at work when we assume "that Thomas Jefferson wrote the Declaration of Independence unconscious of the irony of the existence of slavery in his land of equality" (25). In a later essay, "McGuffey and the Abolitionists," Robinson criticizes "our historiography" for being "too ridden with expectation, which in its workings is like bias or partisanism, incurious and self-protective," with the result that much of the history of Midwest nineteenth-century Christian reformism is misrepresented or omitted (147).[11] As William Deresiewicz points out in his perceptive overview of Robinson's oeuvre and career, the Calvinism and abolitionism of the Midwest must be recovered because "the abolitionists stand for Robinson at the apex of a larger history, a history of the rise and fall of the ideals of democratic government and humane culture" (26). And while there are surely generic differences among history, sermons, and historical novels, I submit that it is fair to ask of this author's work how the "certain [absence]" of Christian slavery "call[s] attention to [itself]," to use the words of the chapter's other epigraph, and what the purpose or usefulness of that absence might be.[12]

Gilead was almost universally acclaimed when it was published in 2004, winning both the Pulitzer Prize and the National Book Critics Circle Award for fiction. It is beautifully written, poignant, and sad without being maudlin, because it is restrained; it is characterized by the "only wisdom we can hope to acquire / [which] is the wisdom of humility," as T. S. Eliot put it ("East Coker" 97–98). It muses on the mystery of time and aging; it brings us to the proper wonder and joy at existence, which continues to "astonish" (Gilead 57); it allows us to see old simple things like water anew, for the first time, always alert to the metaphysical possibilities in metaphor.[13] Robinson's Christianity is short on doctrine and long on wonder, mystery, and wisdom. Gilead is a crossover book, straddling two cultures: it is a Christian novel by a Christian author embraced by the predominantly secular literary world, typically staffed by the coastal liberal elites of the publishing, reviewing, and academic industries. Like her novel, Robinson is widely recognized in this largely secular and liberal world. Her first novel, the brilliant and moving Housekeeping, won the Hemingway Foundation/PEN Award for best first novel and was nominated for the Pulitzer; her third novel, Home, was a finalist for the National Book Award, and her fourth, Lila, won the 2014 National Book Critics Circle Award. She has contributed stories, articles, and book reviews to Harper's Magazine, The New York Times Book Review, American Scholar, and Salmagundi and has taught at the Iowa Writers' Workshop—arguably the most important writing school in the nation—since 1989. While not above inserting herself into the culture wars in the United States, as we shall see, she is (like millions of Americans) a liberal Christian, one who in the fall of 2008 sported a Barack Obama sign in her window in Iowa City (Thompson). What does it mean, then, for this moving and wise Christian novel with a historical setting to evade this complex historical truth about Christian practices of and beliefs about slavery in the nineteenth century?

I think the answer involves reading Gilead on three temporal registers: first, the frame of its narration in 1956, John Ames's letter to his son; second, the frame of many of its recollections about his grandfather and father during the antebellum and Civil War periods; and third, the frame of its composition over what might be as much as twenty years, between the publication of *Housekeeping* in 1980 and *Gilead* in 2004. That final frame witnessed the social and political empowerment of conservative evangelical and fundamentalist Christianity in the United States. Unlike the conservative Christianity that has come to political power in recent decades, Robinson's Christianity is relatively unconcerned with doctrine, is uninterested in sexual morality, and seems to have no patriotic dimension. That the liberal Christian Robinson opposes this recent emergence may be signaled by Ames's rumination on nascent radio and television evangelical broadcasting. As he writes,

> I blame the radio for sowing a good deal of confusion where theology is concerned. And television is worse. You can spend forty years teaching people to be awake to the fact of mystery and then some fellow with no more theological sense than a jackrabbit gets himself a radio ministry and all your work is forgotten. I do wonder where it will end. (208)

Where it ended, of course, was in the emergence of evangelical and fundamentalist Christians—after they had receded from public intellectual and political life for several decades following the *Scopes* trial—in a political coalition with conservative Protestants and Catholics and other social, political, and small-government conservatives in the 1970s and 1980s.

Another person who wondered where it would end was Margaret Atwood in *The Handmaid's Tale*. And in fact, the vision of conservative Christian political empowerment imagined in this 1985 novel appears to be the intertext to which *Gilead*'s title refers: that is, Atwood's totalitarian Christian nation of Gilead lends its name to Robinson's fictional town of Gilead, Iowa, where its political and cultural vision is reworked. Thus while Robinson writes her novel after the empowerment and entrenchment of politically conservative evangelical and fundamentalist Christianity (which Atwood likewise opposes), her political opposition to it takes the form of imagining a more idyllic time before that empowerment—in 1956, just as it was on the horizon—and harkening back to a nineteenth-century moment of imagined moral clarity with a Christian debate about whether slavery should be opposed with arms in addition to the pulpit.

The problem here is that Robinson's opposition to the conservative cultural politics of the postwar Christian resurgence crucially entails a will not to learn its genealogy in the actual Christian support for slavery in America. Even as this postwar Christian writer is critical of the politics of the conservative Christian resurgence, that critique is marked by an evasion of the historical lesson that Christianity provided a vocabulary, not just for abolitionists like Douglass and John Brown, but also for slavery's supporters, like Furman. That crucial ambivalence—that willingness to go both ways—was only marginally less true for the historical 1956 setting of Robinson's novel, a moment when Christianity helped articulate both pro–civil rights positions (as with Martin Luther King Jr.) and anti–civil rights positions (as with Jerry Falwell). H. Shelton Smith makes clear that Southern churches did not give up their theological defense of slavery after the Civil War; rather, this defense translated directly into a theological justification of racial difference and hierarchy in Reconstruction and post-Reconstruction segregation (209–16). In fact, he says, Southern churches became some of the first institutions to practice and advocate formal racial segregation during this period (232). Susan Harding speaks of

> the speed with which interpretations, including official ones, can be revised—or even forgotten altogether. In the 1950s and 1960s, Genesis 9:22 and 24–25 were often cited as biblically mandating segregation, as they had been during the nineteenth-century abolition movement in defense of slavery. Noah cursed his son Ham and his descendants after Ham saw "the nakedness of his father and told his two brothers without." Noah said, "Cursed be Canaan"—Ham's descendants, which, according to popular theology in the South at the time, included Africans and African Americans—"a servant of servants shall he be unto his brethren." As support for segregation gradually eroded during the late 1960s and 1970s, there was no debate about the truth of these Bible verses. They simply stopped being cited. (180–81)

As with the Christian slavery debates, Christians interested in contesting the Christian practices of segregation had to engage with actual Christian doctrine and theological beliefs. Thus Douglass's 1845 *Narrative* opened with a case against the logic of Ham's supposed curse. This biblical story was later cited by Christian segregationists such as Falwell and G. T. Gillespie, and Christian desegregationist Everett Tilson found himself having to address it in a critical counterexegesis more than a century after Douglass in 1958 in *Segregation and the Bible* (16–17, 23–27).[14] And even though, as David L. Chappell suggests, by the 1950s and 1960s many white southern clergy were unwilling to pursue biblical prosegregation theology, they tended to remain silent in the face of civil rights protests (as Martin Luther King Jr. bemoaned), even as others such as Bob Jones or Falwell, who were prosegregation and had considerable influence, openly pursued it (244, 251).

The Christian theorization of King's civil rights politics is widely recognized, although Falwell's resistance to desegregation is not. Falwell founded the Thomas Road Baptist Church in 1956, the year of Ames's narration (and two years after the *Brown* desegregation decision), and his ministry developed the *Old-Time Gospel Hour* for television and radio. Thus Falwell is certainly generally, and perhaps quite specifically, the reference Ames has in mind when he mourns the "jackrabbit" theology of contemporaneous radio ministry (Harding 13).[15] Falwell's ministry began a Christian day school in 1967, the year public schools were required to follow integration plans (27). Unlike *The Poisonwood Bible*, *Gilead*'s evocation of conservative "jackrabbit" theology is silent on that theology's role in justifying segregation's rules of "racial etiquette" (Omi and Winant 62).

I want to suggest that the reason for *Gilead*'s evasion of history—its will to not learn historical lessons—is that Robinson conceives of history as the source of what we have come to call "identity" in contemporary American multiculturalism. If her political intertext is Atwood's *The Handmaid's Tale*, its formal intertext is another 1980s novel, Morrison's *Beloved*—both of which are deeply attentive to historical slave narratives like Douglass's and Jacobs's. In what has become an absolutely canonical text of contemporary American multiculturalism, Morrison tropes and transforms racialized history into a kind of racial memory. In *Beloved*, the lessons of slavery and the Middle Passage become things that cannot quite be learned but rather must be re-experienced—even by contemporary readers—by a kind of memory transference. This becomes apparent in two instances. The first is Sethe's warning to her daughter Denver about her "rememory" of Sweet Home that takes physical form: "Because even though it's all over—over and done with—it's going to always be there waiting for you" (44).

The second is Beloved's memories of the slave ship on the Middle Passage. In this underrecognized scene during her internal monologue at the end of the novel, she remembers someone else's experience of the crossing (248–52). At stake in this model of reincarnation is a notion of racial continuity. Pointedly, Beloved's memory of the slave ship is not that of a European or American slaver: she remembers instead the racially appropriate experience of being in the slave hold as the men and women around her suffer, starve, struggle, and endure. Thus historical American slavery forms contemporary African American identity as traumatic memories that must be recalled or repressed. As Morrison suggested about her novel in a 1989 interview, "I thought this has got to be the least read of all the books I'd written because it is about something that the characters don't want to remember, I don't want to remember, black people don't want to remember, white people don't want to remember. I mean, it's national amnesia" ("Pain" 120). The transformation of the learning of history and culture into a kind of memory to be recalled or repressed is a central trope in contemporary American literary multiculturalism—one might think here of Momaday's "blood memory," or Reed's "racial soul," or Anzaldúa's "genes" and "chromosomes" encoding predisposition to ancient Aztec gods as other examples.[16]

To think of history as forming contemporary identities in this way is not the same as thinking of it as forming specific cultural practices or material conditions. We could say, for instance, that many of today's African American churches have historical roots in slavery, such that specific cultural practices and values might be traceable to slave conditions. This was the lesson that the Reverend Jeremiah Wright tried not very successfully to offer the public in his April 2008 National Press Club appearance after his sermons became a source of controversy during that year's presidential campaign. Or we might examine the possibility that African American religious and cultural traditions suggest continuities with pre–Middle Passage cultures—a theory substantiated by the anthropologists Zora Neale Hurston and Melville Herskovits. Similarly, Henry Louis Gates Jr.'s recent poll of successful and wealthy African Americans led him to argue that they tended to have in common ancestors who became property holders during or shortly after Reconstruction—thus suggesting that contemporary distributions of wealth among African Americans have been substantially influenced by the material conditions passed down through specific families. (Conversely, as Morrison says in her interview, "There are fortunes in this country that were made that way"—that is, by using slave labor ["Pain" 120].) Thus both contemporary cultures and material conditions can be understood as being historically formed: African Americans today might be culturally and financially constrained and empowered by historical occurrences during and after slavery. This is a conception of African American experience that is historical, cultural, and materialist without being a kind of inherited identity.

Morrison would certainly affirm such effects of history, but *Beloved* goes one step beyond them by conceptualizing history through tropes of memory and forgetting. According to Walter Benn Michaels, "whether or not this characterization is accurate, it succeeds in establishing remembering or forgetting as the relevant alternatives. It establishes, in other words, that although no white people or black people now living ever experienced it, slavery can be and must be either remembered or forgotten" (*Shape* 135). *Beloved*'s ghost is thus

> a figure instead for a process, for history itself; *Beloved* is, in this respect, not only a historical but a historicist novel. It is historical in that it's about the historical past; it's historicist in that—setting out to remember

"the disremembered"—it redescribes something we have never known as something we have forgotten and thus makes the historical past a part of our own experience. (137)

For Michaels, the governing trope of *Beloved*—that of memory and trauma—is what transforms historical influence into inherited identity.[17]

Like *Beloved*, *Gilead* imagines memory as the mode by which we know about the history of American slavery. Robinson's novel thus takes up in formal terms—the father writing to his son his memories of his father and grandfather, and their memories of opposing slavery—one of multiculturalism's central tropes, that of treating history as a form of memory. The advantage of treating the history of American slavery as though it were a form of memory to be recollected returns us to the politics of this Christian novel. In the recollections of all her characters—their "rememories," as Morrison might call them—there never was Christian support for slavery. Robinson's formal adoption of multiculturalism allows her to determinedly not learn certain historical lessons about Christianity. Or to put it in the terms of the adopted trope, the advantage of treating history as a kind of memory is the formation of a liberal white Christian identity that "forgets" about the complexity of actual Christian history. Like Morrison, Robinson conceives of the history of American slavery as crucially formative for contemporary identities in a way that exceeds material conditions and cultural continuities. It is because contemporary Christian experience and politics are understood as a kind of multicultural identity (and in this case perhaps a white one) that Robinson cannot acknowledge Christian ideas in favor of slavery—perhaps by having Ames's grandfather preach, as Frederick Douglass argued, that it was a form of hypocrisy and false religion.[18]

If Morrison is right that black and white people do not want to remember slavery, and if Michaels is right that this trope succeeds in establishing the "remembering" and "forgetting" of slavery as the only relevant alternatives, Morrison's novel's project is one of remembering slavery. And in this respect *Gilead* is a kind of companion volume to *Beloved*, in the sense that it is committed to forgetting about Christian slavery. It is almost as though Robinson has taken up Morrison's invitation to recall the experiences of one's ancestors, which in both cases is a racially appropriate process. On the other hand, *Gilead* is concerned not so much with white identity as with Christian identity, or, to put it more finely, a white Christian identity whose whiteness comes in for a critical accounting but whose account of historical Christianity is nostalgic, simplified, and purified.

If I am right that *Gilead* and *The Handmaid's Tale* are both critical responses to the conservative cultural politics of the postwar Christian resurgence, Atwood's novel is more attentive to the historical lessons of Christianity's role in slavery than Robinson's, and Atwood's Gilead comprehends the genealogical links between the contemporary Christian Right and the pro-slavery Christian nineteenth century in a way that is evaded by Robinson's *Gilead*. Atwood displays her literary debt to the autobiographies of Douglass and Jacobs in several different ways: the representation of Christianity as the state ideological apparatus justifying enslavement and subordination of women and African Americans to white patriarchal authority; the notion that this ideology works best when the subordinated themselves share the belief system; the citation of the Bible even as the text itself is deemed too dangerous for the subordinated subjects to read—thus the general prohibition against reading, and consequently the thematic importance of being able to read in Douglass and Atwood; the metaphoric "editing" of the Bible, with some pieces removed, some added; the illicit sexual availability of slave women in a Christian society, attested to in Douglass and Jacobs, as the Commander meets the handmaid outside the state-sanctioned conception ceremonies; the framing of the narrative through an authorizing foreword or afterword; the opposition to the system by some Christian sects, such as the Quakers, who risk participation in underground railroads (of the kind present in Gilead in Ames's grandfather's time), which become in Atwood the "Underground Femaleroad" (246); and the escapee's withholding of the logistical details of the underground route "because some of the stations may still be operating" (246).[19]

Gilead's critical account of whiteness emerges chiefly through the figure of the apostate Jack in his discussions with Ames. In their discussions, the two moral strands of the novel—the grandfather and father's Christian opposition to slavery and the friend's prodigal son's mixed-race family—come together over the latter's concern that there is no longer a Negro church in Gilead, the result of an act of arson years earlier. This is part of Jack's concern about whether the town—and his father—would accept his partner and child if they came to live in Gilead. Jack suggests that the narrator has "influence" in Gilead as the local Congregationalist minister (231)—influence that he has apparently not used previously to urge racial justice or reconciliation. But this is also why Robinson's reference to Atwood is so deeply problematic. Jack is upset that there are no longer any Negroes in Gilead—but of course, there were no longer any Negroes in Atwood's Gilead either. In Atwood's dystopic Christian state, we recall, the "Children of Ham" were being relocated to "National Homeland One"—formerly known as North Dakota (83–84)—in an explicit reference to the South African model of apartheid but also, less explicitly, to the use of the story of Ham in Christian prosegregation thought. In contrast, there has been no official policy expelling African Americans from Robinson's Gilead, but there is likewise no concerted effort on the part of its white spiritual leaders to join with the threatened African Americans when their church is set on fire. "It was only a small fire," Ames protests weakly when Jack brings it up; then later, "a little nuisance fire, and it happened many years ago" (171, 231). This fact is one possibility for Ames's ambiguous musing a few pages later that "this town might as well be standing on the absolute floor of hell for all the truth there is in it" (233), as Gilead seems to have abandoned its original purpose to provide "a place John Brown and Jim Lane could fall back on when they needed to heal and rest" (234)—in other words, as a civilian Christian site supporting Christian abolitionist guerrilla activity in Kansas and Missouri, "set up in the heat of an old urgency that is all forgotten now" (234). The novel ends with Jack leaving the town: he will be able to live with his family in neither Tennessee nor Iowa.

The final scene in which Jack departs, Deresiewicz suggests, is "Robinson's most damning indictment of Gilead's—and, by implication, America's—moral decline" (28). But if *Gilead*'s 1956 setting momentarily registers this question of segregation and antimiscegenation laws, there is no corresponding recognition that support for segregation was often articulated through Christian thought, as was its opposition. Nor is there recognition that this segregationist era is the genealogical link between the proslavery Christian conservatism whose historical presence the novel erases and the racially tinged political empowerment of conservative Christianity at the time of the novel's composition, to whose political values its author is opposed. Thus while Ames's refusal to respond properly to the church burning seems to be Robinson's momentary criticism of modern (1950s) Christianity, that criticism works by contrasting its moral tepidity to the fiery abolitionism of the grandfather, thus representing Christian moral practice as a victim of decline, as though it were not already contaminated by Christian slavery. This contrast is part of the novel's strategy of lionizing a heroic Christian past against which modern times are found wanting, a strategy that ultimately depends, Deresiewicz argues, on a "distortion of American history" that omits secular progressivism (26) but that also, I am arguing, omits Christian support for deeply regressive racial politics. In *Gilead*'s Christian multiculturalism, whiteness is critiqued and repudiated so that Christian identity may be defended and reclaimed.

Christian Ideas, Christian Practice

> In the early years of his ministry, Billy Graham went through a time when he struggled with doubts about the accuracy and authority of the Bible. One moonlit night he dropped to his knees in tears and told God that, in spite of confusing passages he didn't understand, from that point on he would completely trust the Bible as the sole authority for his life and ministry. From that day forward, Billy's life was blessed with unusual power and effectiveness.
>
> Rick Warren, *The Purpose Driven Life*

Part of what accompanies *Gilead*'s remembered account of a sanitized history of Christian practice is a disinclination to investigate Christian ideas. By contrast, the most famous Christian abolitionist novel ever written—Harriet Beecher Stowe's *Uncle Tom's Cabin*—is saturated with Christian debates about slavery, which demanded the author's attention to theology. As was true for Douglass (and others like Angelina Grimké), Stowe understood that this intrareligious debate had to face and defeat actual propositions about slavery. For her, this meant quoting and engaging the very scriptural precedents that sanctioned slavery and the doctrine that had accumulated around them. Like Douglass and Jacobs, Stowe rhetorically transformed the debate about slavery into a debate about the meaning of Christianity itself: thus she enjoined Northern and Southern Christians to redefine slavery itself as un-Christian, and Christianity itself as necessarily always abolitionist. She did the homework of reading Christian defenses of slavery and directly refuted their ideas. Possibly unlike Douglass, whose piety may have been a pose, Stowe was obviously a believer who had moral rage at slavery—even though her novel is unable to envision a place for freed African Americans in America. The abolitionist literature of the period was deeply and necessarily interested in the Christian doctrines for slavery and how to refute them.

By contrast, Robinson's *Gilead* is reluctant to take up questions of doctrine and beliefs. It is not that John Ames (and Robinson, I presume) do not believe in such Christian ideas as the divinity of Christ, the afterlife, and God's essential omnipotence, omniscience, and benevolence. It is rather that, in this novel that reformulates Christianity as a kind of multicultural identity, the reader—like John Ames's son—is gently dissuaded from thinking too closely about Christian ideas or theology. This aversion is part of Robinson's liberal Christian opposition to the doctrinal certainty characterizing much of the conservative Christian resurgence, and it is articulated primarily in terms of Ames's discussions with the apostate Jack. Jack is sincere and penitent, and wants to find a way into, or back to, Christian experience, but at first he seems to have doctrinal problems with Christian orthodoxy. He thus asks the older man, "Does it seem right to you . . . that there should be no common language between us? . . . How can capital-T Truth not be communicable? That makes no sense to me" (170). Ames prefers the term of "grace" (170), that is, Christian experience, to Jack's seeming quest to "be persuaded of the truth of the Christian religion" (171). Importantly, after asking about the disappeared Negro church of Gilead, Jack seems to grow angry and wonders why "American Christianity" waits for the "real thinking to be done elsewhere" (172). Ames likewise becomes upset and, beginning to weep, responds, "I am well aware that people find fault, but it seems to me to be presumptuous to judge the authenticity of anyone's religion, except one's own. And that is also presumptuous" (173). Thus at first Jack's concerns seem to be concentrated around questions of "truth," while Ames insists rather on the "authenticity" of Christian experience: religion is not so much a matter of claims about the true as it is authentic and incommunicable experience.

"I have had a certain amount of experience," Ames muses later, "with skepticism and the conversation it generates, and there is an inevitable futility in it. It is even destructive" (177). He has had young parishioners troubled by confronting Jean-Paul Sartre, André Gide, and unbelief: "And they want me to defend religion, and they want me to give them 'proofs.' I just won't do it. It only confirms them in their skepticism. Because nothing true can be said about God from a posture of defense" (177). Ames will not partake of the tradition of Christian apologetics, justifying God's ways to men. In his disquisition on faith, religion is removed from the realm of possible argument and disagreement—returning us to the initial sense of frustrated incommunicability experienced by Jack. Modern skepticism is "as old as Lucretius," Ames writes to his son (177), suggesting, "In the matter of belief, I have always found that defenses have the same irrelevance about them as the criticisms they are meant to answer" (178). Ames recommends against looking for "proofs" because "They are never sufficient to the question" and are "a little impertinent" (179). Ames, like intellectual Christian discourse, is "not saying never doubt or question" (179), but it is obvious that such doubts and questions must eventually be suspended, not answered. "Be sure that the doubts and questions are your own, not, so to speak, the mustache and walking stick that happen to be the fashion of any particular moment" (179), he writes, in an allusion to his German-educated brother Edward, who returns with his doctorate in philosophy but is unwilling to say grace at dinner.

Ames correctly captures the reality of religious experience: that we do not so much become convinced of the doctrinal truth claims of a religion and then convert as adopt some of them during our childhood or after we have had a religious conversion experience. As social scientists Andrew Greeley and Michael Hout put it in *The Truth about Conservative Christians*, "most people are socialized to a broad spectrum of beliefs in the context of their religious heritage—in short, denomination constrains belief" (24). In this sense, the question of doctrinal proofs probably is moot: if you are already on the road to what *Gilead* portrays as fashionable skepticism, it will likely end with fashionable apostasy, a process the best apologetics-trained preacher will be unable to arrest. But my argument here is that the novel's representation of besieged, minoritarian Christianity in a secular America removes religion from being a set of ideas about eternal and universal truths and relegates it to the domain of what we have come to call cultural identity. Cultures do not do well under questions of proofs: if you are already set on questioning certain practices and values from the point of view of the dominant culture, you may also be set on abandoning those ways no matter what kind of defense is offered—that way assimilation lies.

This is why Ames emphasizes religious experience rather than religious doctrine, even as he continues to call that experience "belief" (144). It is thus true, as Hungerford points out, that in *Gilead* "discourses of belief become religious practices" themselves (121). Jack's problem, suggests Hungerford, is that he takes the discourse of belief to be about the true, rather than about relationships in the believing community to which he wishes to return:

> Belief matters, then, because it is the foundation of relationship between believers and the raw material of their discursive activity. Jack, a professed unbeliever, wants to be convinced through the conceptual content of religious discourse; his difference from his father and from Ames is only underscored by his lack of what Ames calls "sympathy" with theology—his mistaking it for a discourse of answers rather than a discourse of relationship. He mistakes it, that is, for a discourse that could *produce* individual belief rather than a discourse that *enacts* shared belief. (118)

For Ames, religious experience is known to be authentic because of its openness to wonder at the natural world and the mysteries of existence and Being. As with cultural identity, these are not things that are easily represented to outsiders, who may misunderstand what they do not share. Only the self—or other cultural insiders—can judge the authenticity of one's lived religion.

The central subplot of Jack's apostasy is thus actually a drama of assimilation. His mistake is to imagine Christian ideas as though they (only) made universal claims. His loss of faith is the decidedly nonpluralist process of the loss of his childhood Presbyterian culture. As quoted above, this is imagined to be the changing of a "language," with Jack lamenting that there is not a "common language" between him and his father's trusted friend. Because language features prominently in dramas of assimilation, Jack is here figured almost as though he were a second-generation American who has given up his father's tongue and culture in order to adapt to secular American ways. But the trope's power is its transformation of the possibility of disagreement between Jack and Ames about Christian theology into a problem of communication, in which disagreement is rendered impossible because each speaks a different language. Just as no language or culture can be truer than another, no religious tradition can be truer in this model, only different. In moving away from his childhood religion, Jack's apostasy is refigured as a kind of second-generation assimilation—a generation gap—rendering religion as a kind of cultural identity to be lost or, as this novel and its successor *Home* hold out, possibly rediscovered and regained.[20]

Viewing Jack's apostasy as a case of mourned assimilation places *Gilead* concretely within multicultural literature's reconfiguration of familial religion as a resource for contemporary identity formations whose pluralism must be embraced as part of a rejection of assimilation into the broader mainstream. It thus appears that Christian faith as envisioned in *Gilead* owes much to the contemporary conceptualization of cultural identity within multiculturalism, the genealogy of which has crucially entailed a social science stance that suspends religious truth claims. Robinson's work evidently arrived at similar sentiments about the importance of her characters' lived religion, a matter that is still characterized by discourses of faith and belief, though religious authenticity is beyond belief itself. *Gilead*'s faith, with its emphasis on authentic religious experience incommunicable to cultural outsiders, as well as its shyness in discussing Christian doctrine, suggests a provocative reimagining of Christianity as a form of minority culture within the world of contemporary American multiculturalism.

But of course, as Greeley and Hout make clear, religion *is* primarily a matter of familial culture, a fact that makes it entirely apt for *Gilead* and *Home* to imagine Jack's apostasy as a form of cultural assimilation. In their account of recent changes in religious demographics, the social scientists make the case (drawing a different conclusion than Putnam and Campbell in *American Grace* than "shock" and "aftershock"—see, for example, 110–11) that the conservative Christian resurgence was not primarily the result of mainline Protestant or Catholic (let alone atheist or agnostic) conversions to conservative Protestant affiliations (such as Baptist or Pentecostal churches), as was occasionally claimed by conservatives. Though there were conversions from mainline Protestant denominations (such as Episcopalians, Presbyterians like

Jack's family, or Congregationalists like Ames's family) to conservative ones and vice versa, mainline conversions to conservative denominations has "held steady for at least seventy-five years" at about "13 percent" (Greeley and Hout 104). Greeley and Hout see two factors accounting for conservatives' growing share of Protestant numbers in the United States: first, conservative Protestant women have significantly more children, and second, the trend wherein "upwardly mobile Baptists, Evangelicals, and Pentecostals announced their arrival in the middle class by joining the local Episcopal, Congregational, or Presbyterian church" had "dissipated in the 1970s and 1980s" (105–8). In other words, conservative Christian families were raising more conservative Christians and losing them a lot less to mainline Protestant denominations. This demographic partial explanation for the conservative Christian resurgence in the last four decades underscores, of course, that people's religious commitments are usually the result of familial and communal cultures.

Thus Robinson's 2004 liberal Christian protest against the political empowerment of conservative Christianity is achieved by recommending a nondoctrinal Christian cultural identity in place of the doctrine-heavy Christianity that has characterized the emergence of this subculture since the novel's 1956 setting. *Gilead* nostalgically mourns the road not taken: there might have been a wiser, less arrogant and contentious, more spiritually humble and compelling national religious experience instead of the flavor that ultimately became prominent.

All this is fine in one way, except that Christianity has historically been crucially concerned with right belief. Thus when Talal Asad warns us in his critique of Clifford Geertz that the focus on belief as "a distinctive mental state" is not characteristic of all religion, he reminds us that "It is preeminently the Christian church that has occupied itself with identifying, cultivating, and testing belief as a verbalizable inner condition of true religion" (48). Furthermore, and as we have seen, the resurgence has been marked precisely by the introduction of Christian doctrines into the public sphere, sometimes as the basis for public policy. The problem is that the kind of conservative, doctrinal, and fundamentalist politically empowered Christianity that Robinson opposes—the kind of religious force that forms the premise of the Christian dystopia in Atwood's novel—has its very roots in the Christian slavery that Robinson's novel is determined not to acknowledge.

To return to the three temporal frames of Robinson's *Gilead*, Christian slavery transformed quite directly into Christian support for Jim Crow and segregation in ways that extended directly into John Ames's 1956 time frame. But that force in turn underwent similar transformation into the time frame

of the composition of the novel, when conservative politics were characterized by the deep evangelical and fundamentalist influence on the Republican
Party at the very moment that it established most strongly its racial "Southern strategy" across the area known as the Bible Belt—with Ronald Reagan
kicking off his nomination with his approval for "states' rights" in Neshoba
County, Mississippi, where civil rights workers had been murdered, and
George W. Bush's 2000 speech at the fundamentalist Bob Jones University,
which at that time had a white supremacist policy of prohibiting interracial
dating.[21] The question of Christian ideas and practices during the historical
register of *Gilead*'s composition resonates with the repressed Christian ideas
and practices in the historical registers of the novel's 1956 setting and its
remembered past of antebellum America.

Reading Robinson's work within this double contextual frame of multiculturalism and the conservative Christian resurgence of the last forty years
illuminates a few crucial aspects of contemporary American literary history
and Robinson's place in it. The first is the striking fact that the success of
multiculturalism in the literary and academic fields—and in sites where they
overlap, such as universities—has had a deep influence on white writers, as of
course we should have expected it would. If multiculturalism's influence on
Kingsolver is evident in her wholehearted embrace of cultural pluralism and
cultural relativism, Robinson's narrative strategy of examining the American
history of race relations through the mechanics of characters' memories precisely because certain aspects of that history are to be brought into productive identificatory relation to people in the present is another such effect, as
is the converse: that certain other histories are not to be remembered as a
source of contemporary identities. As Morrison has put this twin urgency
in a suitable double entendre, certain histories and stories are "not a story
to pass on" (*Beloved* 324). It is not unexpected that Robinson at the Iowa
Writers Workshop, despite her homes of Idaho and Iowa being "two of
the least diverse states in the Union" (Deresiewicz 26), nonetheless felt the
institutional influence of "high cultural pluralism," especially insofar as such
pluralisms can be imagined, Mark McGurl suggests, in "regional" terms at
centers such as the Iowa Writers Workshop (56, 61).

The second aspect of this simultaneity and confluence of multiculturalism
and the resurgence is the culturalization of religious faith: as with those writers
of the multicultural turn, even writers of faith today are sometimes drawn to
the conceptualization of religion as a form of culture. As McClure shows with
several of his authors, and as I have argued in chapter 1, the multicultural project
of returning to the religious tradition of one's ancestors does not primarily entail
the need to engage with theology or argumentation about the universally true

or good. It is not that Robinson—or these other multicultural writers—lacks religiously based ideas about what is true and good. Rather, multicultural religion is figured as the imperative to be true to one's familial, ancestral, and sometimes even racial religious culture. Robinson's Christian multiculturalism takes its place alongside other religiously inflected cultural pluralisms as a way of resisting assimilation into an imagined secular, dominant society.

The third aspect illuminated by this frame is that it is especially in the sense of this pluralist, Christian multicultural resistance to the secular nation that Robinson takes her place as an author at least partly *within* this Christian resurgence of the last forty years, not as an outside critic. She was raised in "Presbyterianism" (*Death* 237), and her childhood seems to have been marked by a familial religious tradition that was not evangelical ("born again") and especially not fundamentalist; as with many Christians, her childhood religion has been doubled by adult commitment. As her essay collections make clear, she is a critic of modern thought, rejecting in particular its modes of exposure, cynicism, and disenchantment. She repudiates the alliance between neoliberal capitalism and the Christian Right (99, 102). As noted above, the questions of sexual morality crucial to the cultural politics of the resurgence are entirely absent from her fiction and nonfiction. I nevertheless place her partly within the cultural politics of the resurgence because her fiction and nonfiction take on the project of contesting a secularizing history that omits or misrepresents Christian contributions to American history—which places her in an unlikely alliance with conservatives in the Christian resurgence such as Jerry Falwell, Francis Schaeffer, and Tim LaHaye, who seek to establish the Christian identity and history of the nation, as I show in chapter 4. Her historiography, as Deresiewicz suggests and as I have tried to show in detail, is as partial and narrow as that to which it is opposed.

In another vein, her critical stance on evolution in the culture wars likewise places her within the resurgence, particularly in her essay "Darwinism" and her review of Richard Dawkins's *The God Delusion* ("Hysterical"). Although a full review of her ideas on evolution is beyond the scope of this book, suffice it to say that she either does not understand evolution or willfully misrepresents it when she defines it as "the change that occurs in organisms over time" (*Death* 30)—an idea she accepts—and tries to separate that change from natural selection, which is championed by "Darwinists" who have failed "to prove the existence of the process of natural selection, which they freely concede they have not done" (39). This is a definition of evolution and a summary of the science on natural selection that no contemporary biologist would accept; it echoes instead "creation science" claims that culminate in the Intelligent Design movement.

Navigating the terrain of what historical practices and beliefs mean for the present is crucial for a literary history of how American literature has responded to the contemporary Christian resurgence. We need to address not only Christian practice historically and in the present but also theology and the social actuality of Christian belief. The liberal Christian Robinson opposes some of the cultural politics of the conservative resurgence on the level of ideas and values, so she understandably prefers religious experience, dishonestly cleansing "true" Christianity of its history by "forgetting" unsavory aspects. But the Christians she opposes—then and now—thought of themselves as authentic, with right values and practices, ones based in scripture. *Gilead* treats religion as a kind of cultural identity, in addition to downplaying belief and doctrine in the postmodern, postsecular ways that Hungerford and McClure identify. But literary history, with its different mandate, cannot ignore belief or follow Robinson in dividing a true faith from conservative Christianity. That is a good rhetorical strategy for believers and participants like Robinson, Douglass, Jacobs, Stowe, and William Lloyd Garrison. But it is not a good strategy for a literary history of the present, which has to take Christianity as it was actually lived, believed, and empowered in the conservative Christian resurgence following World War Two.

Beyond Belief: Studying Religion in the Twenty-First Century

> One of the main methodological problems in writing about religion scientifically is to put aside at once the tone of the village atheist and that of the village preacher, as well as their more sophisticated equivalents, so that the social and psychological implications of particular religious beliefs can emerge in a clear and neutral light.
>
> Clifford Geertz, "Religion as a Cultural System"

Robinson's preference for religious experience over doctrinal debates was widely noted by critics and reviewers. For instance, in his recent essay wondering about the lack of contemporary "fiction about the quandaries of Christian belief," Paul Elie noted Robinson's exceptional presence in the literary field. *Gilead*'s protagonist, Elie suggested, was the "most emphatically Christian character in contemporary American fiction," and the novel "presented liberal Protestantism as America's classical heritage; it set Ames's wise, tender reverence against the bellicose cymbal-clanging of George W. Bush's White House." That contrast suggests part of the answer to Elie's question: the literary novel of belief receded as Christian belief became more socially visible and politically controversial since the 1970s, and Robinson's 2004 novel should be understood as a liberal Christian repudiation of the conservative Christian resurgence to which it is indirectly addressed and which had reached an apex in the reelection of President Bush that year. As Hungerford notes in *Postmodern Belief*, Robinson is not the only contemporary writer whose religious imagination moves beyond belief, choosing to focus, with many religious studies scholars, on the experience of lived religion and everyday practice instead (see introduction and 109–12). In this reading, Jack's mistake is to put doctrinal theology first, thinking that he has to sort out the truth claims of his childhood religion before he can return to the community of Christian grace and experience.

As a way of concluding this chapter, I want to look at the larger reorientation toward religious practice with which, we can now clearly see, Robinson is aligned. Describing that shift, David Hall suggests that "lived religion" scholarship begins with the observation that historians know a lot about the history of theology, but not so much about "religion as practiced" and the "everyday thinking and doing of lay men and women" (vii).[22] Lived religion scholars consider practice in its widest sense. Two recent essay volumes suggest the range of this "wider reorientation rooted in a rethinking of what constitutes religion" (viii). Hall's collection *Lived Religion in America: Toward a History of Practice* (1997), for example, formulates religious practice to include shrine landscaping in the Bronx, charismatic Catholic scripture reading, infant baptism in early New England, Romantic gift culture, cremation, the rhetorical construction of devotional books, Ojibwa hymn-singing, late twentieth-century wifely submission, the lay liberal beliefs of "Golden Rule" Christians, and the gardening practices of some who wish to be food self-sufficient. A kind of sequel to this volume is Laurie Maffly-Kipp, Leigh E. Schmidt, and Mark Valeri's collection *Practicing Protestants: Histories of Christian Life in America, 1630–1965* (2006), the essays of which encompass diary writing, forgiveness, missionary activity and attitudes to living with indigenous peoples, honoring eldership, education, landscaping, architecture, faith healing, bodily sanctification processes of diet and dress, daily prayer, sympathy, liturgical dance, and aesthetic taste in visual arts. Taking its cue from Geertzian anthropology—that is, as the above epigraph suggests, suspending metaphysical judgments in order to describe religion in terms of cultural dynamics—theories of everyday practice by Pierre Bourdieu and others, and the sociology of community, among other influences (Hall ix), lived religion is a "materialist phenomenology" of religion with "an empiricist orientation" (Orsi, "Everyday" 8). It does not prize the popular over the elite, but does away with this distinction by focusing on the constantly creative use of religious idioms even as it keeps in sight the "complexities of lived religious practices" (10). As Robert Orsi (an originator and still chief theorizer of this scholarly movement) contextualizes this turn,

the word *belief* bears heavy weight in public talk about religion in contemporary America: to "believe in" a religion means that one has delib-
erated over and then assented to its propositional truths, has chosen this
religion over other available options, a personal choice unfettered by
authority, tradition, or society. What matters about religion from this
perspective are its ideas and not its things, practices, or presences. This
is not necessarily how Americans actually are religious, of course, but
this account of religion carries real normative force. . . .

But belief has always struck me as the wrong question, especially
when it is offered as a diagnostic for determining the realness of the
gods. The saints, gods, demons, ancestors, and so on are real in experience and practice, in relationships between heaven and earth, in the
circumstances of people's lives and histories, and in the stories people
tell about them. Realness imagined this way may seem too little for
some and too much for others. But it has always seemed real enough
to me. (*Between* 18)

This shifted perspective, writes Hall, allows the historian of religion to consider practices and beliefs beyond those sanctioned by official institutions,
and to "establish the importance of texts and activities that all too readily are
ignored or trivialized" (ix).[23]

The payoff from this scholarship is high, allowing us to see, to use an
immediate example, that the form of *Gilead* is a devotional practice performed by Ames. As an essay in *Practicing Protestants* suggests, diary writing
has been a religious practice of self-introspection and self-regulation since
John Winthrop—a tradition with which Robinson is likely familiar—and
it included the awareness of the "possibility of self-deception" (Brekus 23).
And though the form of *Gilead* carries what one might call a biblical burden
of leaving a message behind in anticipation of the author's absence,[24] this too
is a useful reminder of how religious experience, for Ames and for Robinson,
entails much more than an abstract and predetermined set of mental propositions. What Orsi and religious practice / lived religion scholarship contest,
in alignment with Robinson, is the idea that doctrine is the necessary core
of religious life.

While this reorientation has been immensely useful for religious studies, it is not without problems or consequences. Most obviously, moving
beyond belief to peoples' lived religions does not mean abandoning the way
beliefs inform practices, and vice versa. Almost all the essays in *Lived Religion
in America* and *Practicing Protestants*, to use them as representative samples,
suggest the intricate and sometimes contradictory ways in which practices

and beliefs inform one another: for example, debates about how to dispose of corpses or ensure the spiritual security of infants frequently turned on (or, indeed, helped produce) beliefs about bodily resurrection and intergenerational covenants. Furthermore, the editors of *Practicing Protestants* note in their introduction that "practice in American Protestant theology has received much of its inspiration from Alasdair MacIntyre's retrieval of Aristotle's virtue ethics." MacIntyre suggests not abandoning belief, but cultivating practice as a way into belief: he notes that "churches can cultivate habits of Christian practice, foster corporate identity, and eventually reinstall belief in the tradition itself. In short, people can be habituated into belief in the truths of Christianity through the practices of the Christian life" (4).

Thus a focus on practice rather than belief leads us not to abandon the latter; on the contrary, as one essayist on honoring eldership among the Ojibwa observes, contemporary practice theologians such as MacIntyre and Dorothy Bass see that "formal practices and cultivated mental disciplines can generate, shape, and sustain the moral, experiential, and meaning-seeking inner life of religion" (McNally 78). Or, as another essayist puts it,

> in the midst of cultural change, practice can have a conserving influence on belief. Modern commentators such as Dorothy Bass remind us that, as the Church Fathers put it, *lex orandi, lex credendi*—prayer shapes faith. Bass and others have called for renewed attention to Christian practice for this very reason. They believe that reviving Christian practice can be a way to strengthen Christian faith at a time when traditional beliefs seem to be waning. As Bass asserts, "we can believe more fully as we act more boldly." (Ostrander 178)

Although we might question Ostrander's assertion that traditional Christian belief was waning in 2006—echoes of Robinson's nostalgic take that the most vital Christianity is in decline—he makes clear the inseparability of belief and practice and that, sometimes, talking about practice is an indirect way of addressing the importance of belief.

Thus while it is useful for religious studies to distinguish between a religious practice and a religious idea, the one frequently entails the other. Nowhere is this clearer than in *Gilead*'s imagined moral topography, where the conflict between violent Christian guerrilla abolitionism and pacifist Christian abolitionist resistance are at once everyday practical ethics with life-and-death consequences and powerful theological propositions. On this terrain Christian belief and Christian practice are not separable: what the grandfather believes about the evil of slavery entails warfare and preaching when bloodied at the pulpit, an ethical choice very much opposed by Ames's father who cannot countenance the violence. The grandfather and father share a common cosmology and Christian theology but other interrelated beliefs and practices pit them against one another. If I have argued in this chapter that Robinson's remembered past sidesteps and thereby "forgets" the much more important Christian conflict between Christian abolitionism and Christian slavery, the inseparability of Christian ideas from Christian practice is even more vivid for that struggle.

Indeed, Christian slavery is precisely one kind of field that ought to be—but is not yet—part of the "more comprehensive map of practices" that Hall calls for in *Lived Religion* (xi). What would it look like, for instance, to consider how Christian prayer and singing were inflected by the quotidian intra-Christian struggles described by Douglass about his new servitude to Edward Covey, "a professor of religion—a pious soul—a member and a class-leader in the Methodist church" who also had "a very high reputation for breaking young slaves" (54):

He would make a short prayer in the morning, and a long prayer at night; and, strange as it may seem, few men would at times appear more devotional than he. The exercises of his family devotions were always commenced with singing; and, as he was a very poor singer himself, the duty of raising the hymn generally came upon me. He would read his hymn, and nod at me to commence. I would at times do so; at others, I would not. My non-compliance would almost always produce much confusion. To show himself independent of me, he would start and stagger through with his hymn in the most discordant manner. In this state of mind, he prayed with more than ordinary spirit. (57)

Douglass's passage is laced with skepticism and irony, producing a critique of Christian hypocrisy as he sees it; a more neutral analysis of religious practice would look at the ways Christian slaveholding households were sites of prayer, worship, meditation, and teaching, but also sites of contestation among those with relations of unequal power. As Hall suggests in a slightly different context, practice "always bears the marks of both regulation and what, for want of a better word, we may term resistance" (xi). Here, Christian practice encompasses patriarchal household authority in which the white slave owner, as Furman counseled, had spiritual responsibility for those beneath him—shades of schoolteacher's sense of the "creatures God had given you the responsibility of." But Christian practice also encompasses micro-level resistance by Douglass, who disrupted the household's morning ritual with his occasional refusal to sing, a refusal he interprets as causing displeasure to Covey, not God.

The wide scope of this scholarship's attention to religious practice should also entail recognizing those practices occurring in Douglass's later observation, made immediately after the above quotation:

> Poor man! such was his disposition, and success at deceiving, I do verily believe that he sometimes deceived himself into the solemn belief, that he was a sincere worshipper of the most high God; and this, too, at a time when he may be said to have been guilty of compelling his woman slave to commit the sin of adultery. The facts in the case are these: Mr. Covey was a poor man; he was just commencing in life; he was only able to buy one slave; and, shocking as is the fact, he bought her, as he said, for *a breeder*. This woman was named Caroline. Mr. Covey bought her from Mr. Thomas Lowe, about six miles from St. Michael's. She was a large, able-bodied woman, about twenty years old. She had already given birth to one child, which proved her to be just what he wanted. After buying her, he hired a married man of Mr. Samuel Harrison, to live with him one year; and him he used to fasten up with her every night! The result was, that, at the end of the year, the miserable woman gave birth to twins. At this result Mr. Covey seemed to be highly pleased, both with the man and the wretched woman. Such was his joy, and that of his wife, that nothing they could do for Caroline during her confinement was too good, or too hard, to be done. The children were regarded as being quite an addition to his wealth. (57–58)

The more comprehensive map of Christian practice would want to include such unhappy scenes of everyday lived experience that intersect with questions of sexuality, marriage and adultery, and capitalism and property. The religious studies scholar and historian would need to disentangle Douglass's moral judgment of "sin" on this loathsome practice, and seek instead to map the codes of marriage, adultery, and procreation that were at once Christian practices and Christian ideas. We could share Douglass's condemnation of Covey's acts, but we will not want to judge them, as he does, to be not Christian at all. They were—descriptively, neutrally—Christian. To decide ahead of time that Covey's adulterous arrangements, or morning hymns, or Auld's scripture-sanctioned whipping of his slave, are not Christian practices is not to create a more comprehensive and accurate historical map of Christian practices, but rather to participate as partisans in the struggle over Christian definition in which Douglass and Furman were engaged. As Hall warns us, scholars must resist the temptation to "abridge, even to censure, the messiness that leaks into everyday life" (x). Christian slavery, like Christian abolitionism, entailed intertwined practices and beliefs, both of which must be included in our struggle to get the past right, insofar as we can, as Robinson has urged us.[25] The same dynamic is true of Christian segregation. Christianity was an innovator and theorizer of segregation during Reconstruction: it provided the ongoing justification for African American inferiority; it confirmed a divine authority for ingrained racial difference; it confirmed fears of social equality and how that might, in churches or schools, lead to racial amalgamation. Although some voices stridently called out for integration during Reconstruction, Baptists, Methodists and Presbyterians quickly developed segregated churches (H. S. Smith 226–44). Indeed, "organized religion in the white South was dominated by spokesmen who held firmly to the dogma of Negro inferiority, and who thus maintained that the system of black-white separatism represented the normal development of a divinely implanted instinct" (304).

Clearly it is not uplifting to dwell on such histories, and this might account for why religious studies scholars and historians of religion sometimes silently edit out of the range of Christian practice, belief, and history those things they do not find in agreement with their version of religion—as Robinson has also done. As historian Drew Faust noted thirty years ago about scholarship on the mid-nineteenth century slavery debates, "a disproportionate amount of this scholarly attention has been devoted to antislavery movements and ideologies. . . . Many scholars have felt uncomfortable contending with zealous defenses of a social system that the twentieth century judges abhorrent" (1). While a few essays in *Practicing Protestants* contain implicit critiques of Christian missionary cooperation with American imperialism, the collection otherwise exemplifies the tendency to assume a normative Christian tradition that is "unified, essentially good, and therefore authoritative" and not "contradictory and oppressive," as the editors cite one critic of this assumption (296n8; see R. S. Smith). Indeed, says Orsi in his introduction to Hall's volume, the scholarship seems to share our culture's normative understanding of religion:

> In a nation in which religion has been so wildly creative and innovative, where there seems to be no end to the fecundity of religious imaginings or to their violent and disruptive consequences, the public discourse of "the religious" instead presents faith and practice in ameliorative and consensual terms. Nothing happens in the space of the sacred, nothing moves, nothing changes, nothing ever spins out of control, no one is ever destroyed there. (11–12)

While "some notion of resistance to power is central to the theory and phenomenology of lived religion"—a description as true of *Practicing Protestants* as of the volume Orsi is describing, Hall's *Lived Religion*—these scholars risk missing "religion's complicity in sustaining structures and patterns of alienation and domination" and the complex ways religion provides "idioms of discipline" (15). "The shared methodology of this collection" and of lived religion may be "radically or phenomenologically empiricist," but, I submit, it is not yet empiricist enough (7).

I hypothesize that lived religion scholarship itself, which emerged shortly after the beginning of the conservative Christian resurgence, is another motivated, largely Christian attempt to imagine an alternative to the doctrine-heavy resurgence that was taking place. Many of the key texts and scholars associated with the recent research on religion and practice—on lived religion in America—have benefitted from research funding awarded by the Lilly Endowment. Hall's *Lived Religion in America* began with a 1994 Harvard Divinity School conference that was partly funded by the endowment's Religion Division (vii). *Practicing Protestants* emerged from the American Christian Practice Project (2002–04), also funded by Lilly (vii, ix), and the three contemporary practice theologians mentioned in the book's introduction and throughout its essays as key influences—Dorothy Bass, Craig Dykstra, and Stephanie Paulsell (2)—likewise have ties to the Lilly Endowment, with Dykstra operating as vice president of its Religion Division. Orsi's *Between Heaven and Earth* acknowledges the Endowment and Dykstra's support for his project (ix). R. Marie Griffith (whose work appears in *Lived Religion*) acknowledges the support of the Lilly-funded Institute for the Study of American Evangelicals for *God's Daughters* (x). I am not making any claims as to the specific practices and beliefs of the scholars whose work appears in these four books (which were all published by excellent American university presses). I am merely observing that the Lilly Endowment's stated interest in Christian practice may have been a motivated liberal Christian response to the Christian Right's emphasis on the importance of conservative doctrine: the construction of an alternative contemporary American Christianity.[26] As Michael Hamilton and Johanna Yngvason observed in *Christianity Today*, Dykstra and Lilly director Robert Lynn "developed a strategy of underwriting scholarship, mainly in theology and in the sociology and history of American religion" (44).[27] Lilly may have had concerns similar to those of its sister Christian philanthropic organization, the Pew Charitable Trusts, some of whose directors grew "troubled by the conservative politics and demagogic character of popular evangelical leaders. But they knew that evangelicalism was a movement of many moods. They saw its scholars as more moderate, better behaved, and less threatening to the status quo than the movement's populist leaders. So for some at Pew, strengthening evangelical scholarship was a way to housetrain an unruly arrival in the public square by encouraging its better instincts" (45). If my hypothesis is correct—that lived religion scholarship emerged partly as a motivated liberal Christian attempt to moderate the growing influence of conservative Christian doctrine in the public sphere—then this fact may help explain why the scholarship tends to avert its eyes from the destructive dimensions of American Christianity.

Our tendency to put beliefs—and the processes of making believe, the practices of faith itself—off-limits to public scrutiny, discussion, and evaluation of specific ideas may be advantageous (even necessary) in a pluralist society. But in his recent *Reason, Faith, and Revolution: Reflections on the God Debate*, Terry Eagleton questions the multiculturalism in which beliefs are treated as socially inert. "Multiculturalism at its least impressive," he says, "blandly embraces difference as such, without looking too closely into what one is differing over." He continues:

> Such facile pluralism therefore tends to numb the habit of vigorously contesting other people's beliefs—of calling them arrant nonsense or unmitigated garbage, for example, as one must of course preserve the right to do. This is not the best training ground for taking on people whose beliefs can cave in skulls. . . . Beliefs are not to be respected just because they are beliefs. (147–48)

For Eagleton, fundamentalism tries to evade political questions by, paradoxically, treating its own beliefs as though they were cultural phenomena that had to be respected in the public sphere: this "antipolitical" fundamentalism is "a form of culturalism, seeking to replace politics with religion" (43).

Against this form of conservative Christianity, Eagleton, like Robinson, seeks in the Christian tradition a source for proper politics and values: the aiding of the poor, the feeding of the hungry, the lifting up of the oppressed. Eagleton's Jesus is a radical redistributionist, utopian, and this-world apocalypticist who provides the model of proper Christian political beliefs and values. While the Christian tradition is a source of proper politics for both Eagleton and Robinson, both theorist and writer downplay Christian ideas and doctrine in favor of a revitalized Christian experience. "Faith, Ditchkins seems not to register," Eagleton says of his conflation of New Atheists Christopher Hitchens and Richard Dawkins,

> is not in the first place a question of signing up to a description of reality, though it certainly involves that as well. Christian faith, as I understand it, is not primarily a matter of signing on for the proposition that there exists a Supreme Being, but the kind of commitment made

manifest by a human being at the end of his tether, foundering in darkness, pain, and bewilderment, who nevertheless remains faithful to the promise of transformative love. (37)

Echoing Hungerford's and McClure's conclusions about the status of belief in contemporary American fiction and contemporary religious studies' preference for lived religion instead of histories of theological change, Eagleton suggests that faith "is for the most part performative rather than propositional" (111). Where New Atheists like Dawkins and Hitchens err, Eagleton contends, is in seeing religion as a mistaken description of the real.

Eagleton and Robinson correctly suggest that Christian experience goes far beyond a list of propositional beliefs; that it is a kind of allegiance to a tradition entailing political and social values. At the same time, however, many Christians will be surprised to hear that several of their tradition's central ideas are a "caricature" crafted by the secular left, according to Eagleton:

> These [New Atheist] intellectuals claim as Christian doctrine the idea that God is some sort of superentity outside the universe; that he created the world rather as a carpenter might fashion a stool; that faith in God means above all subscribing to the proposition that he exists; that there is a real me inside me called the soul, which a wrathful God may consign to hell if I am not egregiously well-behaved; that our utter dependency on this deity is what stops us thinking and acting for ourselves; that this God cares deeply about whether we are sinful or not, because if we are then he demands to be placated, and other such secular fantasies. (50)

Though these are traditional (if simply rendered) Christian beliefs, Eagleton's rarefied Christianity sees them as a straw Christianity held true by "atheistic fundamentalists" (like "Ditchkins") who are the "inverted mirror image of Christian ones," such as Pat Robertson (53).[28]

Rightly anticipating the objection that "the account of Christian faith I have sketched here is the product of an intellectual elite loftily remote from actually existing religion," Eagleton defends "the distinction between what seems to me a scriptural and an ideological kind of Christian faith" (58, 57). For him, Christianity has a true revolutionary origin which has been betrayed by its practitioners over the centuries. Thus, although Eagleton somewhat ambivalently brings questions of belief (and hence politics) back into debates about religion, he purifies an elite "scriptural" Christianity against an "actually existing" social one that is often, as he puts it, "ideological" (58). The purified one is scriptural (his sense of the scriptures, not the sense of conservative Christians) and is posited as having a true origin (55–56); it has become debased and ideological, serving the needs of the rich and powerful. One may prefer Eagleton's version of Christianity to the alternative, but his avoidance of conservative Christianity and his construction of a purified, sometimes nonorthodox, but purportedly scriptural Christianity in its place cannot help scholars come to terms with the conservative Christian resurgence and its cultural politics or genealogy. Eagleton's Christianity is not historical, attentive to how other theologies developed through reference to scripture, or how Christian theology itself was formed through arguments about right-thinking.[29] And while Eagleton suggests that Ditchkins and the like are "fundamentalist" atheists akin to the fundamentalists they (and he) oppose, he is like the fundamentalists in appealing to "scripture" (sometimes as an idea instead of specific passages) and not accommodating different theological interpretations; in his view, he and those who agree with his readings of the Bible do theology, and other people do ideology. Though Eagleton does not shy away from doctrinal debates (in the way that Robinson's Ames does), he, like Robinson except more overtly, addresses problematic Christian theology in history or today by treating it as though it were not Christian, effectively excising it from the history of authentic faith.

Thus, while Eagleton notes the evangelical articulation of nineteenth-century abolitionism (76), he would not recognize Christian slavery as Christian—it would merely be ideology. Like Douglass, Jacobs, Stowe, and Garrison (and, were she to recognize it, Robinson), he would separate the religion of the South from true Christianity.[30] Eagleton, like Robinson and the lived religion scholars generally, can thus be thought of as part of what Putnam and Campbell describe as the "second aftershock" in American postwar religious life: the social, literary, and scholarly reaction to the empowerment of conservative Christian ideas and politics since the 1970s. Their aversion to strong doctrinal articulations of belief and to recognizing the Christian genealogies that lay behind that resurgence is understandable. That aversion is part of the story of how literary writers and critics responded to the resurgence in the last four decades.

Gilead's preference for Christian experience over Christian doctrine suggests a conceptual separation that is undercut both by its own primary moral terrain of Christian abolitionism (and the missing Christian slavery) and the contemporaneous scholarship on religion and practice. Belief and practice can be conceptually distinguished, but for most Christians historically and in the present—and in a way perhaps not true of all other religions, as Asad warns—belief and practice are often mutually dependent, if sometimes tension-filled. This is especially true of the conservative religious and political genealogy that *Gilead* responds to through suppression: practice and belief are always intertwined, as was true for Christian slavers, Christian abolitionists, Christian segregationists, Christian desegregationists, the Christian Right, and liberal Christians such as Robinson or Eagleton—and, perhaps, some of the lived religion scholars. While many of the beliefs common to the resurgence cannot be conceivably disentangled from practice—like the questions of abortion or homosexuality, central fronts in the culture wars—other beliefs (evolution, age of the earth, biblical inerrancy) remain controversial even though they are not obviously implicated in everyday practice. And while questions of biblical inerrancy or miracles are not really the theological terrain on which Robinson's apostate Presbyterian Jack stumbles, making *belief* continues to be a crucial conservative religious *practice*. As Harding puts it, "Fundamental Baptist interpretation rests on a poetics of faith—absolute faith—not a hermeneutics of suspicion," a poetics in which "interpretive practices" such as harmonization and the closing of gaps help produce belief not only in the Bible, but sometimes in Christian leaders as well (88). *Gilead* is an attempt to challenge the dominance of the conservative resurgent Christianity, and to imagine a liberal alternative emphasizing Christian experience and grace rather than doctrine. Its re-relegation of belief to the private sphere of familial culture amid the threat of secular assimilation is one of the ways American literature provocatively reimagines contemporary religion in multicultural terms of cultural pluralism.

CHAPTER 4

Recapitulation and Religious Indifference in *The Plot Against America*

> In a sense, part of what drove the Moral Majority
> and motivates the Christian Right in the U.S.A. is an
> aspiration to re-establish something of the fractured
> neo-Durkheimian understanding that used to define
> the nation, where being American would once more
> have a connection with theism, with being "one
> nation under God"...
>
> Charles Taylor, *A Secular Age*

Not very many novels' publications are preceded by an open letter from the author directing audiences how to read—and not to read—the upcoming work. It is far easier to think of examples of authors responding to and correcting their critics—recall Maxine Hong Kingston to her many ethnographic readers[1]—than of writers preempting certain interpretations. But when Philip Roth wrote in advance of *The Plot Against America* that "Some readers are going to want to take this book as a roman à clef to the present moment in America. That would be a mistake," the warning was prescient ("Story"). The 2004 novel was almost universally received as being about "the present moment in America," even if book reviewers and critics recognized—often quoting Roth's own disavowal—that no simple parallels could be drawn between events in the novel's setting of 1940–1942 and the time of its composition. Indeed, it was impossible to think about a novel published in 2004, composed between December 2000 and December 2003, and titled *The Plot Against America*, as not being about American emergency post-9/11, war hysteria, national propaganda, religious fanaticism, and American exceptionalism.

I argue in this chapter that *The Plot Against America* was in fact a critical response (as several reviewers suggested) to the hugely important conservative Christian resurgence of the last four decades. Like another fictional thought experiment, Margaret Atwood's *The Handmaid's Tale*, it was based on things that had "already happened," as we shall see. The politics of Atwood's novel are clear: as a critique of the Christian resurgence's conservative discourse about women's bodies and sexuality, it worked by comparing those currents to their genealogical ancestors in the theology and practice of Christian slavery. And indeed, women and African Americans were not the only groups with something to fear in Atwood's Christian nation, for its totalitarianism incidentally entailed the forced conversion or exile of the Jews. But the government's aim in Roth's novel, on the other hand, is not conversion but assimilation: not to make Jews into Christians but, as the novel has it, into better Americans. What makes *The Plot Against America* Roth's most multicultural novel is not only his recapitulation of twentieth-century American racial histories, as we shall see, but also his problematic rereading of religious difference as cultural. That revision is a kind of blindness, I argue, and it indicates how disarmed the literary response to the Christian resurgence has been by our paradigm of "multiculturalism." Thus, I disentangle the distinct cultural, religious, and racial models for understanding Jewish identity in *The Plot Against America*. Insofar as Roth revisits the racialism of his understanding of the Nazis to repudiate it, he recapitulates the history of the multicultural turn. But it is this very method that blinds him to the reenergized religious dimensions of the contemporary scene.

Though critics generally agreed that *The Plot Against America* is about the present, figuring out what Roth's fictional alternate history meant for the first decade of the twenty-first century is more difficult. In one of the most important critical debates about the novel to date, for example, Walter Benn Michaels argued that the act of writing an antiracist book in 2004 was part of the neoliberal project of "redescrib[ing] the injustice of class difference as a kind of discrimination" ("Plots" 299). In response, Michael Rothberg suggested that "the novel's evocation of anti-Semitism gone wild might be read less as a literal commentary on the social position of Jews—either now or in the past—than as an indirect indictment of the contemporary Christianization of American public life" (306). Initial book reviewers agreed that the novel was about "the present moment in America." Frank Rich perceived, "Surely 'perpetual fear'"—quoting the novel's opening lines—"defines our post-9/11 world—and the ruthless election-year politics of autumn 2004." Citing the author's disavowal, J. M. Coetzee reflected that "a novelist as seasoned as Roth knows that the stories we write sometimes begin to write themselves, after which their truth or falsehood is out of our hands and declarations of authorial intent carry no weight"; thus "*The Plot Against America* is 'about' the presidency of George W. Bush in only the most peripheral way"—unless one lived in paranoid times, which, it so happens, is what the novel is "precisely" about. In a largely negative review, Ross Douthat in *Policy Review* termed it "the great literary debate of 2004: Does Roth intend to draw parallels between his novel's era and our own—between the creeping fascism of [Charles] Lindbergh and the Bush administration? The answer is almost certainly yes, for all that Roth himself has called it a 'mistake'"—a disavowal that bespoke "a certain disingenuousness" (77), Douthat contended. The critical consensus—though not unanimity—was indeed that *Plot* was to an important degree about "the present moment in America." That consensus linked the Bush and Lindbergh administrations, and several critics further interpreted the novel in terms of the political rise of the Christian Right, the apex of which was—so far—the Bush presidency.[2]

Roth's own generic categories seem intended to forestall links between the novel's setting and its composition. "I had no literary models for re-imagining the historical past," he writes: "I was familiar with books that imagined a historical future, notably '1984,' but much as I admire '1984,' I didn't bother to reread it" ("Story"). There were precedents for Orwell's dystopia in the recent and contemporaneous histories of "Hitler's Germany and Stalin's Russia," Roth noted, but "his book wasn't a prophecy. It was a futuristic horror story containing, of course, a political warning." Like a more recent example—Atwood's *The Handmaid's Tale*—dystopias serve as political warnings for their present because they have an eye on both their contemporary moment of composition and the historical past from which they sometimes draw their models. But while "Orwell imagined a huge change in the future with horrendous consequences for everyone; I tried to imagine a small change in the past with horrendous consequences for a relative few," Roth concludes: "He imagined a dystopia, I imagined a uchronia." Unlike dystopias, according to this scheme, uchronias—alternate histories—have their resonance safely sealed in the past; Roth's, then, is simply "a thought experiment" intended to (in a nice turn of phrase) "defatalize the past."

If Roth's counterfactual novel was supposed to take its references from history, Atwood's 1985 novel imagined a dystopian future in the aftermath of a Christian totalitarian revolution in the United States. Although clearly written with attention to the conservative Christian resurgence of the time—and with particular attention to the debate over abortion inaugurated by *Roe v. Wade* and the specter of state control over women's bodies—Atwood's novel nonetheless took its references from American history. This is what she meant when she said in an interview that "there isn't anything in the book not based on something that has already happened in history or in another country" (Interview 317). Thus the theological underpinning of the totalitarian Gilead and its oppressive control over the lives and bodies of subordinated peoples had "already happened" with Christian slavery. That African Americans were being relocated to a "Homeland" (83) in North Dakota in Atwood's novel has an echo in contemporaneous South African policy, but it also has a historical echo in the forced removal of the Cherokee nation in the early nineteenth century.

At first, the politics of Roth's historical allusions are not quite as clear as Atwood's. As a speculative history—what if the fascist Charles Lindbergh had run against and beaten President Roosevelt in the 1940 election?—it foregrounds questions of national identity and, indeed, identity as such. For the novel has everything to do not just with the riddle of American exceptionalism and difference ("it can't happen here!" becomes "could it have happened here?" or, indeed, "is it happening here?"[3]), but with the question of Jewish difference itself. In fact, the novel theorizes Jewishness by recapitulating the history of other racialized minorities in the United States. What puts the factual in this counterfactual history is not so much the historical backdrop of the Holocaust in Europe, but Roth's attention to the specific histories of American minorities in the 1940s and 1950s. Using the language of segregation, relocation, and concentration camps, Roth's alternate history alludes to the specific midcentury histories of African Americans, Native Americans, and Japanese Americans during and following the war.

Roth's Multicultural Plots

The novel's plot thus turns on the question of what Jewish difference is and how one might eliminate it. Our readerly suspense comes from the possibility that the fascist Lindbergh might follow the historical precedent of the fascist Hitler in pursuing "the total disappearance of the Jewish population" from the nation (324). And of course, it's not at all difficult to imagine how this kind of Jewish difference might have been construed as a plot for the novel, since this is the historical context evoked in its introduction. "Israel didn't yet exist, six million European Jews hadn't yet ceased to exist, and the local relevance of distant Palestine . . . was a mystery to me," Philip frames the novel in its opening pages (4). Nazi Germany's answer for eliminating Jewish difference was animated, the conventional view has it, by a racial ideology based on inherited biological supremacy and immutable, essential difference. Once difference is so constructed, supremacy may be attained by formal and informal rules of subordination (as in the United States during this period with segregation, but also with other practices of racial formation) and, if the elimination of such difference is the goal, by strategies of eugenics or genocide. The anti-Semitic ideology of the

Third Reich frequently articulated itself through religion, but its core concept has been understood as an essentially racial struggle between Aryan and Jew, as Jackson Spielvogel suggests (265–67). This ideology was able to draw on a Christian anti-Semitism inherited from "medieval Christian opinion" (267) and was shaped by nineteenth- and twentieth-century ideas emerging from social Darwinism, eugenics, and racial anthropology. It conceived of difference as group-based, inherited, immutable, hierarchical, and natural. What began as a religious distinction constructed by early proto-orthodox followers of Jesus[4] became, with various historical twists and turns, a racial distinctiveness crucial to modern thinking.[5] A plot based on this racial understanding of Jewish difference is the premise for Philip K. Dick's 1962 uchronia *The Man in the High Castle,* in which Germany and Japan win the Second World War and Germany globalizes the Final Solution in part by constructing a death camp in New York within the territory of its puppet-controlled eastern United States. Although Roth is probably not familiar with Dick's uchronia, its story of the remaining American Jews trying to escape detection is one thought experiment of how it could have happened in the United States, a story in keeping with Roth's understanding of the Nazis' model of Jewish racial difference.

But Hitler's fascist and racial solution to Jewish difference is not Lindbergh's fascist solution in *The Plot Against America* because Lindbergh conceives of Jewish difference as cultural instead of racial. Lindbergh's kinder, gentler fascism thus proposes a program of accelerated and state-enforced assimilation as the proper "resolution of America's Jewish Question" (281). His administration forms an Office of American Absorption (OAA) with the announced purpose of "encouraging America's religious and national minorities to become further incorporated into the larger society," though, notes narrator Philip, the only minority group so targeted seems to be Jews (85). One OAA program, called Just Folks, is formed to "remove hundreds of Jewish boys between the ages of twelve and eighteen from the cities where they lived and attended school and put them to work for eight weeks as field hands and day laborers with farm families hundreds of miles from their homes" (85). One of Just Folks's most enthusiastic participants is Philip's idolized older brother Sandy, who spends a summer on a Kentucky tobacco farm. The OAA is headed by the quisling Rabbi Bengelsdorf, who happens to be married to Philip's mother's sister, who in turn explains that "Sandy and the other Jewish boys like him in the Just Folks program should serve as models not only for every Jewish child growing up in this country but for every Jewish adult" (107). The unstated intention of Just Folks is to introduce a generation gap between Jewish adults and their children, a gap to be properly bridged when adults become more like their assimilated children, not when children return to their parents' ways. Sandy's sojourn is so successful that Philip fears he will change his last name to Mawhinney, move back to Kentucky, and "hand himself over to the Christians so as never again to have anything to do with Jews. Nobody needed kidnap him because Lindbergh had kidnapped him already" (196).

The next year, the OAA introduces a new assimilation program called Homestead 42, billed as a "relocation opportunity" (204) for "emerging American families" who are to move from established urban centers to more rural townships "where parents and children can enrich their Americanness over the generations" (204–05). The implicit goal is to destroy the communities and neighborhoods that nurture Jewish cultural difference. The Roths are to move to Kentucky, while other families have been invited to Montana, Kansas, or Oklahoma, where there are "very few" Jews (206). The Roths are to homestead very near Sandy's Just Folks farm, as it turns out, and they will be the only Jews in Danville, Kentucky. And while the radio commentator Walter Winchell fears the Homestead 42 program will end in "concentration camps à la Hitler's Buchenwald" (228), others, like Aunt Evelyn, who helps run Homestead 42, see it as an opportunity for Philip to become "something more than another Jewish child whose parents have made him too frightened ever to leave the ghetto" (216). A later passage in which Philip channels his uncle-by-marriage's language explains the thinking of Bengelsdorf and the OAA. For these "highly assimilated" (269) upper class German Jews, who had "been born to wealth and were among the first Jewish generation to attend elite secondary schools and Ivy League colleges," it was the clannishness of "poorer" working-class Jews in the northeast that provokes anti-Semitism in the gentile population. The way to solve the perception of Jewish difference, then, is to enable Jewish children especially to escape their "segregated existence" (269–70) and to "enter the American mainstream" (270). One other way Homestead 42 breaks down barriers of segregation is the Good Neighbor Project, wherein gentile families are introduced into the apartments and houses vacated by homesteading Jewish families who have left the city, thus integrating the Jewish character of the neighborhood (280).

Segregation, relocation, concentration camps: as must be clear by now, Roth's alternate history of the nation owes much to the actual American history of race relations. Indeed, these allusions evoke the specific histories of African Americans, Native Americans, and Japanese Americans during and following the war. More particularly, they evoke a social science model of ethnic assimilation that was systematically extended to racialized minorities between 1940 and 1965, in a move that shifted American literary, judicial, and official consciousness from thinking of these groups as being marked by racial differences to thinking about them as being marked by cultural differences. In *A Genealogy of Literary Multiculturalism*, I show that the sociology of the University of Chicago, led by Robert Park, had a series of wide-ranging intellectual, policy, and literary influences in these years.[6] The most immediate was the treatment of interned Japanese Americans during the war. Although the fear that animated the internment itself was a racial one—the idea that Americans of Japanese descent, even those born on American soil, retained a kind of biological loyalty to the Emperor of Japan—it was sociology's instrumental replacement of race by culture that allowed the theoretical innovation for how one might wrap it up with the government-approved goal of the disappearance of Japanese American difference, now conceived as cultural. Beginning with college students, many *Nisei*—second-generation Japanese Americans—were permitted to leave the internment camps of the West during the war to finish their degrees at colleges and universities in the Midwest and East. It was a sociology doctoral candidate—a student of a student of Robert Park—who inspired this program based on the explicit sociological argument that migration disrupted cultural continuity and that Japanese American youth were far more American culturally than their Japanese-born immigrant parents. This program became the basis for the policy of dispersal near the war's end: Japanese American families were encouraged—coerced—to settle away from the West Coast and from other Japanese American neighborhoods. As with Roth's Homestead 42, the problem of difference is cultural, and is generated by the "clannishness" of ethnic communities, families gathered together on the East or West Coasts, and the solution is the dispersal of those communities into the hinterland and more rural townships, where "Americanness" can be enhanced through the generations. Thus in John Okada's *No-No Boy*, a Japanese American novel about the internment deeply influenced by this sociology, one character recommends to another that he should "Go someplace where there isn't another Jap within a thousand miles. Marry a white girl or a Negro or an Italian or even a Chinese. Anything but a Japanese. After a few generations of that, you've got the thing beat" (164).

Dillon Myer, the head of the War Relocation Authority, oversaw the policy of resettlement and dispersal near the war's end. It was his partial success in running this coercive policy of assimilation that led President Truman to appoint him to head the Bureau of Indian Affairs in 1952, where he administered the policy of Native American Relocation. As with the resolution of the internment camps, Relocation was premised on the sociological truths of how cultural continuities among socially insular groups—whether Japanese

Americans on the West Coast or Native Americans on reservations—could be severed through generation gaps and migration. Whereas Japanese American resettlement moved families from urban centers to rural areas, Native American "Relocation"—a word echoed in *The Plot Against America*—moved young Native men from their reservations into urban centers, mostly on the West Coast. (Relocation is the policy under which Abel is moved to Los Angeles after being released from prison in N. Scott Momaday's *House Made of Dawn*.) As with Roth's Just Folks program, assimilation by generation gap and migration is officially hastened by removing children from their more parochial families. While in Roth's novel this functions more as an extended summer camp, because the children return to their homes, in Sandy's case it has the same desired effect of driving a wedge between the child and parental culture.

As historian Richard Drinnon has argued, with these two programs Myer was an agent of a coercive liberal consensus about Americanization and race. In this respect, these programs and historical precedents entirely fit with what we might call the liberal fascism of Roth's President Lindbergh. For many African Americans, in contrast, this liberal sociology was a theoretical apparatus to be embraced, beginning with Richard Wright's *Native Son* (1940), through Park's training of various African American sociologists and his influence on Gunnar Myrdal's *An American Dilemma* in 1944, to Myrdal's, and sociology's more broadly, theoretical underpinning of the NAACP's desegregation cases culminating in *Brown v. Board of Education* in 1954 and, indeed, the civil rights movements that were enabled by *Brown*. Liberal sociology cut both ways, and it did so because it replaced racial difference with cultural difference. In *The Plot Against America*, then, Jewish Americans join Japanese Americans, African Americans, and Native Americans as being redefined as culturally distinct and racially equal.

So, when Philip, in his disquisition on Jewish difference, argues, "What they were was what they couldn't get rid of—what they couldn't even begin to want to get rid of. Their being Jews issued from their being themselves, as did their being American. It was as it was, in the nature of things, as fundamental as having arteries and veins, and they never manifested the slightest desire to change it or deny it, regardless of the consequences" (220), he seems at first to be returning to the language of biology—"nature" and organic difference as fundamental as the "arteries and veins" of one's body—and hence to veer dangerously close to the illiberally fascist racial ideas of Hitler rather than the liberally fascist cultural ideas of Lindbergh. But Roth is only repeating a standard trope in American multicultural literature of describing learned cultural differences as though they were unlearned natural differences based in bodies and blood. Roth is trying to say, like Toni Morrison, Ishmael Reed, Amy Tan, N. Scott Momaday, Gloria Anzaldúa, Frank Chin, and other multi-culturalists, that difference runs deep—or more particularly, that resistance to assimilation does.[7]

These historical allusions reinforce—indeed, turn the screws of—the critique offered by Stanley Crouch and Walter Benn Michaels. The novel, Crouch says, "moves along as though that bestial level of social bigotry was not a highly visible *fact* of American life at the time that 'The Plot Against America' is imagined to have taken place, between 1940 and 1942." "Roth's great sin," writes Crouch, was that his thought experiment depended on introducing an imagined virulent anti-Semitism into a nation where it displaced (by ignoring) the actual history of violence and racism against African Americans. Thus, Michaels maintains, Roth's idea that "it very easily could have happened here" is superseded by the fact that "of course, it did happen here, only not to the Jews" ("Plots" 288); that is, with respect to lynching or being denied rooms in hotels, we are looking at the history of African American experience. I am adding, then, that "it did happen here," not only to African Americans, but to Japanese Americans and Native Americans as well. This series of historical allusions to the actual experiences of other racialized minorities in the twentieth century makes the novel into one of many multicultural novels that register the transformation of racial difference into cultural difference. What the novel recapitulates, therefore, is not only the history of other racialized minorities in America, but the history of multi-culturalism's constitutive turn against the liberal assimilationist consensus in the middle decades of the century described in chapter 1; it recapitulates reactions like those of Toni Morrison, who was anxious about the cultural politics implied in *Brown v. Board of Education* (which pathologized African American culture) and who would criticize the assimilationist social science undergirding the Supreme Court decision in her first novel, *The Bluest Eye*, and N. Scott Momaday, who rejected the assimilationism of Relocation in his most famous novel, *House Made of Dawn*.[8] This recapitulation makes *The Plot Against America* into Roth's most multicultural novel, not just in terms of its ethos of cultural pluralism and cultural relativism, but likewise—and in ways that parallel other important multicultural works by writers such as Reed and Anzaldúa—in terms of its transformation of religion into a form of culture. In my disentangling of racial, cultural, and religious notions of Jewish difference, then, the histories of other US racial minorities are evoked in *The Plot Against America* in order to establish the more correct notion of their cultural difference, American longevity, and dynamic health—a strategic move characteristic of post-1970s American multiculturalism. I turn now to a discarded third model of difference—religious distinctiveness—in order to assess Roth's literary intervention in the contemporary period.

Roth's (Con)Version of the Jews

In the middle of the book, a lyrical passage takes up the question of what we have come to call Jewish American identity, and here it appears that, whatever difference Jews have, it cannot really be considered a matter of religious difference. A meeting of the Jewish employees of Metropolitan Life and their families who are imminently to be "relocated" (218) across the country is the occasion for Philip's meditation on this Newark community, who are "very similar people at the core" (219). And though one of the things they share is their local rabbi, Philip explains, "Their being Jews didn't issue from the rabbinate or the synagogue or from their few formal religious practices, though over the years, largely for the sake of living parents who came once a week to visit and eat, several of the households, ours among them, were kosher" (220). Indeed, his description of the families' practices and beliefs tends to remove them from the domain of the religious:

> To be sure, each Friday at sundown, when my mother ritually (and touchingly, with the devotional delicacy she'd absorbed as a child from watching her own mother) lit the Sabbath candles, she invoked the Almighty by his Hebrew title but otherwise no one ever made mention of "Adonoy." These were Jews who needed no large terms of reference, no profession of faith or doctrinal creed, in order to be Jews, and they certainly needed no other language—they had one, their native tongue, whose vernacular expressiveness they wielded effortlessly and, whether at the card table or while making a sales pitch, with the easygoing command of the indigenous population. (220)

Thus while their local rabbi presides over "Rosh Hashanah and Yom Kippur" celebrations, he is not otherwise deeply involved in these families' lives, not only because he is "really not very brilliant," as Philip's father says (219), but also because he is identified with a kind of religiosity that is not the source of their Jewish difference.

In this respect, the fascist President Lindbergh seems to agree with Philip the narrator (and, I am suggesting, Roth the author) that Jewish difference is not really a religious difference. A more apt precedent for a plot in *The Plot Against America*, if that difference were understood to be religious, would be something like the Spanish policies for eliminating religious differences during and after the *Reconquista* of the Iberian Peninsula by the

Spanish monarchs of Aragon and Castile. Just as the *Reconquista* ended, "a few months after the surrender of Granada, on 30 March 1492, an edict was issued ordering the Jews to accept baptism as Christians within four months or to leave the kingdom" (O'Callaghan 671). Both Muslims and Jews were forcibly converted or deported in the decades that followed, with some 300,000 Jews converting soon after 1492 (Smedley 65). For Spain, the transformation of the religiously different into the religiously same meant precisely a change in the "rituals," "devotions," "professions of faith," and "doctrinal creeds" of the subjects, to draw on language used by Philip above. The *conversos*, as the converted Jews were known, became Christians through baptism, and were expected to acknowledge the Christian creeds, with the Inquisition introduced (supposedly) to guard against backsliding and heresy. Although conversions frequently took place "as a consequence of an immediate and real fear of death" following pogroms (O'Callaghan 606–607), other reasons included the chances for social, political, and commercial advancement, and occasionally open disputes about whether Jesus was the Messiah or not.[9] One historian suggests that many of the *conversos* "tried to merge inconspicuously into the general population," while others "secretly returned to Judaism" (Gerber 121). "With utmost secrecy" and in fear of the Inquisition, such *anusim* ("forced ones") "avoided forbidden foods, fasted meticulously, prepared their homes for the Sabbath, and kindled the Sabbath candles" (121).[10]

The story of the Iberian *conversos* became entangled with another model of Jewish difference as time went on, however. According to historical anthropologist Audrey Smedley, the experience of the *conversos*—or, rather, the Christian experience of suspecting that *conversos* were backsliding or secretly practicing their Jewish religion—helped formulate a Western ideology of inherited social identity that planted some seeds for the idea of biological racial difference. The Inquisition "was designed to weed out recalcitrant converts, or 'secret' Jews, by investigating personal behavior and genealogies for evidence of Jewishness. Some of the seminal ideas that later became basic ingredients of a racial worldview were set into motion during this period of rising Christian intolerance and rampant persecution of Jews and Moors." Since "social stigma" attached to anyone whose family had been investigated by the Inquisition, it offered (for a fee) "'certificates of Limpieza de Sangre' (literally, 'purity of blood')" which assured the bearer a pure genealogy (Smedley 66). Although not quite a full-fledged ideology of race, this imagining of Jewish difference in terms of blood and ancestry rather than practices and doctrine began to shift the conceptual grounds of group-based difference in the West—an evolving notion of difference that the Spanish shortly brought with them to the New World. It's one thing to suspect the new Christians of backsliding or secretly returning to Jewish ritual and doctrine. It's another to begin to imagine them as incapable of fully or authentically adopting a different set of religious practices and values because of their ancestral heritage, now imagined as a property transmitted in the blood. As Smedley shows, Jews were at the center of modern conceptions of racial difference well into the twentieth century.[11]

This history of forced conversion is, of course, one of the things that had already happened that Atwood draws on for *The Handmaid's Tale*. As the narrator muses when trying to guess the identity of a hooded, hanged body, "You don't get hanged only for being a Jew though. You get hanged for being a noisy Jew who won't make the choice. Or for pretending to convert. That's been on the TV too" (201). In Gilead, the "Sons of Jacob" must choose between forced conversion or emigration to Israel, with a set of spies set up to seek out secret Jews. With her eye on the conservative Christian resurgence, Atwood imagines that the "Jewish problem" from its perspective is a matter of faith, not biology (as it still evidently is for the "sons of Ham" who are sent to national homelands in continental North America). Atwood's *conversos* and *marranos* echo the Spanish experience of the *anusim* following the Reconquista, and it's not at all difficult to imagine such doctrinal coercion and ritual resistance as a possible plot for Roth's novel. The characters are already in place, in fact: Philip's father is precisely "a noisy Jew," but what he's noisy about is his claim to America and his defense of American freedom and democracy.[12] There is a kind of religious, metaphysical experience in *The Plot Against America*, but it takes the form of the nation itself, not Jewish religious traditions. Thus when the Roth's family's thoughts turn to pilgrimage in the chapter titled "Loudmouth Jew," they head to Washington, DC and the national monuments in a wholly non-ironic claiming of America. Because Jewish difference is not understood as religious, encouraging or coercing conversion to Christianity is neither the program for Lindbergh nor the danger Roth imagines in this counterfactual history.

While it is not in the cards in *The Plot Against America*, it's not as if the conversion of the Jews was not in the air during this time period, especially among the Christian Right: witness the hugely successful *Left Behind* series of Christian fundamentalist apocalyptic bestsellers, in which the end times is heralded by the conversion of the Jews—or at least 144,000 of them, with the rest dying along with other unsaved people in the final tribulations.[13] Sixty-five million copies of this twelve-part series have sold since they began publication in 1995, and as Jonathan Freedman points out in

Klezmer America, the books combine anti-Semitism with what he calls a kind of "philosemitism," one very active among the conservative Christian resurgence:

> The novels are intensely interested (as is the religious right at large) in Jews generally and in the State of Israel specifically as intimate, if not essential, parts of the story of Christianity itself. They are, to a certain extent, signs of the increasingly palpable philosemitism on the Christian right, although, given their emphasis on the conversion of the Jews as a necessary precondition of the Apocalypse, this is a philosemitism of which Jews might wish to be wary. (142–43)

One of the series' authors, Tim LaHaye, became a significant leader in the Christian resurgence of the last thirty years or so, helping to organize Jerry Falwell's early ministry and later fundraising for the Institute for Creation Research, which promoted the introduction of young-earth geology and biology into high school classrooms.

In a great plot device that says everything about dehistoricized and decontextualized fundamentalist hermeneutics, one Jewish leader in this series converts after the Israeli government commissions him to "conduct an exhaustive study of the messianic passages [in the Hebrew Bible] so the Jews would recognize Messiah when he comes" (LaHaye and Jenkins, *Tribulation* 319)—an examination no one had apparently ever undertaken before. The study confirms fundamentalist beliefs about the end times and that Jesus must have been the Christ. In fact, this rabbi and scholar Tsion Ben-Judah's study is figured as a way of solving the lack of Jewish religiosity: as he puts it, "much of Judaism, even in the Holy Land, has become secular and less biblically oriented. My research project was assigned almost as an inevitability. People have lost sight of exactly what or whom they are looking for, and many have given up" (327). Ben-Judah's journey to faith is helped, of course, by the fact that he's able to interview the resurrected Moses and Elijah, who appear at the Wailing Wall in Jerusalem witnessing about Jesus. But it is only by reading scriptures as fundamentalist Christians do that he comes to full belief, and reveals his research findings to the world on CNN (389–97).

Ben-Judah is joined by the Israeli Chaim Rosenzweig, who begins his journey to belief after witnessing the miracle of divine intervention saving Israel from an unprovoked Russian air attack in the first novel (*Tribulation* 107). Unlike Ben-Judah, Rosenzweig begins the series as a secular Jew, and though he becomes gradually convinced about the truth of Christianity throughout the series—and is actually kind of helpful to God's plan, given that he personally assassinates the Antichrist in book six—he does not fully convert until the seventh novel, *The Indwelling*, when he is faced with his mortality during a possible plane crash. Sincere belief and sincere repentance on his knees in the plane aisle save the man's soul, giving him a literal mark of the elect on his forehead. Thus, as Freedman suggests, "the secularity of the secular Jew remains fundamentally problematic for LaHaye and Jenkins" (148).[14] When these two Jews convert, they change their religious practices and beliefs, like the other 143,998 Jews they represent. And while these authors' premillennial dispensationalism is a twentieth-century theological innovation, their interest in Jewish conversion is in continuity with the longstanding Christian preoccupation with Jewish religious difference, as the Spanish experience suggests. While the *Left Behind* series is an extreme (but not marginal) expression of the conservative Christian resurgence, and imagining Jews in general as religiously different might be a kind of Christian fantasy, it is the operative Christian fantasy of the resurgence as it has developed over the last forty or so years.

Roth's attention to the history of Christian anti-Semitism by including references to two figures in particular—Gerald L. K. Smith, a minister and the publisher of *The Cross and the Flag*, and Father Charles Coughlin, the Catholic priest famous for reactionary anti-Semitic radio broadcasts during the 1930s and early 1940s—appears at first to suggest just such religious dynamics. Smith, Roth reports in his historical Postscript, was an ally of Coughlin and Henry Ford, and "his anti-Semitic magazine, *The Cross and the Flag*, blamed the Jews for causing the Depression and World War Two." He also "maintained that Roosevelt was a Jew, that *The Protocols of the Learned Elders of Zion* was an authentic document, and, after the war, that the Holocaust had never taken place" (384). When radio broadcaster Walter Winchell ends one broadcast with the question, "How long will Americans remain asleep while their cherished Constitution is torn to shreds by the fascist fifth column of the Republican right marching under the sign of the cross and the flag?" (230), Roth's reference to Smith's publication invokes the history of American Christian anti-Semitism of the 1930s and the 1940s. Smith, indeed, argued that America's status as a Christian nation was under threat; he was pro-segregation and anti-communist.

Coughlin, meanwhile, introduced early in the novel as "the Detroit-area priest who edited a right-wing weekly called *Social Justice* and whose anti-Semitic virulence aroused the passions of a sizable audience during the country's hard times" (7), is a better known figure of American Christian anti-Semitism from the 1930s and 1940s, whose radio broadcasts reached tens of millions. Coughlin's politics were anti-communist, anti–New Deal, anti-Semitic, and sympathetic to European fascists such as Hitler and Mussolini; his weekly magazine serialized *The Protocols* in 1938. Although as a Catholic he had a more vexed relationship to the idea of a Christian America in the 1930s,[15] Coughlin sometimes framed anti-Semitic violence as a Christian backlash against supposed Jewish provocation (as with the murder of Christians in the USSR under Communist direction—see D. Warren 155–56). Roth invokes Coughlin's logic when narrating America's version of *Kristallnacht*: when anti-Semitic rioters rise up in Detroit, they firebomb two of "Coughlin's 'Communist' targets" (266) that are actually Jewish cultural and worker organizations. "By nightfall," the novel reports, "several hundred of the city's thirty thousand Jews had fled and taken refuge across the Detroit River in Windsor, Ontario, and American history had recorded its first large-scale pogrom, one clearly modelled on the 'spontaneous demonstrations' against Germany's Jews known as *Kristallnacht*, 'the Night of Broken Glass,' whose atrocities had been planned and perpetrated by the Nazis four years earlier and which Father Coughlin in his weekly tabloid, *Social Justice*, had defended at the time as a reaction by the Germans against 'Jewish-inspired Communism'" (266).

Thus, with Smith and Coughlin, Roth invokes an American Christian history of paranoia and demagoguery; there is a way in which these figures anticipate contemporaneous American Christian media demagogues such as Glenn Beck, Ann Coulter, and Sean Hannity. But, obviously, there is a key difference, a difference that goes to the heart of my argument about *The Plot Against America*: the anti-Semitism of yesterday's Christian Right has been transformed into the philosemitism (to again use Freedman's useful term) of today's Christian Right, with a particular emphasis on support for Israel. Smith's anti-Semitic and anti-miscegenation views were very much bound up in the racial worldview in which he imagines exclusion and resistance, not conversion, as the solution for Jewish difference. While Coughlin's vocabulary about Jews was both racial and religious (see, e.g., D. Warren 137, 155, 164), his sympathy for the Nazis similarly suggests an essentialist conceptualization of difference with no genuine possibilities for religious transformation. Their presence in the novel underscores the way in which Roth frames historical anti-Semitism as emanating from the racial worldview, against which he poses cultural difference and pluralism. But Coughlin and Smith's real anti-Semitic successors today are with the fringe Christian Identity movement, as Freedman notes, not the mainstream Christian Right, for which such ideas are an "embarrassment to the movement" (162). Today's philosemites among the Christian Right imagine the imminent conversion of the Jews religiously and doctrinally, a mass conversion expressly articulated in the *Left Behind* series but more often diplomatically unspoken by other political and media figures within the resurgence.

Roth's Religious Indifference

The Plot Against America continues to use the language of Christian and Jew, but Christian, like the latter, is generally drained of religious significance that in any case is more or less located safely in the past. Thus, Philip and his friend Earl take to following "Christians" on the bus, even to their homes where, in one instance, they glimpse a Christmas tree complete with an angel on its top—an angel who is probably Jesus, thinks Earl, since Jesus is the "chief of the angels" (120). This is, Philip knows, "the culmination of our quest" undertaken to follow Christians because "Jesus Christ," Philip muses, "by their reasoning was everything and who by my reasoning had fucked everything up: because if it weren't for Christ there wouldn't be Christians, and if it weren't for Christians there wouldn't be anti-Semitism, and if it weren't for anti-Semitism there wouldn't be Hitler, and if it weren't for Hitler Lindbergh would never be president." In the scheme developed by this child narrator, the meaning of Christianity is not so much distinct religious practices or doctrinal beliefs—these are incidental rather to Christianity's core of anti-Semitism. And while we might be warned away from such a serious conclusion because this idea comes from a child and is attached to the amusing idea of Jesus as an angel,[16] on the other hand the notion that Christianity's absolute core is anti-Semitism is more or less the point revealed in the final chapter of Roth's earlier (1986) novel *The Counterlife*. As Zuckerman discovers when he journeys to the heart of Christendom by marrying an English wife, what holds Christianity together is not so much a distinct set of religious practices or values, but a communal identity bound around a center of anti-Semitism. While at first this discovery is prompted by his sister-in-law's dark warning that his mother-in-law will demand a baptism of their child, there is no sense in which baptism is attached to any metaphysical or spiritual dimension. It is rather a sign of belonging, a serious demand by one community for recognition and ownership. And so the culmination of Zuckerman's journey, even while it extends to exploring churches whose stones were first laid by Normans, speaking in church crypts after Christmas service, and encountering Anglo-Saxon people in the heart of ancient Christian Britain, reveals the core of this Christian identity to be an age-old anti-Semitism with no discernable religious dimension. Or rather, we could say that just as whatever religious energy Philip's father has is refocused around the idea of America, whatever religious energy remains in Christianity has been more or less boiled down to a residue of us-and-them affect.

Thus while *Plot*'s language is that of Jew and Christian, we should understand the difference between the two as not so much animated by religious distinction as by cultural belonging. The language refers less to universal and metaphysical claims about Jesus and more to ethnic differences that need to be maintained. It is Bengelsdorf who captures this dimension, praising Lindbergh's attempt to "raze those barriers of ignorance that continue to separate Christian from Jew and Jew from Christian" (110). While this sounds like an earnest plank within the program of multiculturalism, Bengelsdorf, as we have seen, is the traitor who helps to run Lindbergh's program of making Jews into better Americans. This language drains Jewish difference of any religious dimension, and in so thoroughly culturalizing the Jews, it ends up culturalizing the Christians as well. Not only is there nothing really religious about the Jews, but there is nothing religious about Christians either.

Most Jews, of course, will not be surprised to hear that one can be a Jew without religion—without, that is, performing certain practices or ascribing to specific beliefs, notwithstanding Michaels's claim that "There are lots of things that, as a Christian or Muslim or Jew, you are required to believe, and if you don't believe them you can't count as a Christian, Muslim or Jew" (*Trouble* 177). (Indeed, Michaels himself concedes this point.[17]) Nor will contemporary scholars of religion, who have turned away from belief in recent decades, as we have seen in chapter 3, be surprised by Roth's exploration of a Jewish American identity that requires no distinct mental states. The emphasis on belief as a distinct mental state, after all, was a Christian innovation that colored Western conceptions of religion for a long while, as Talal Asad has warned us. Thus it is, the *Encyclopedia Judaica* reminds us, that in the Hebrew scriptures

> there are no articles of faith or dogmas in the Christian or Islamic sense of the terms. . . . The reason for the absence of a catechism in both the Bible and the rabbinic tradition is probably twofold: in Judaism the primary emphasis is not on profession of faith but on conduct (Avot 1:17); and speculative and systematic thinking is not characteristic of the biblical or the rabbinic genius. Dogmatics entered Judaism as a result of external pressure; contact with alien religious systems, which had formulated theological doctrines, compelled Jewish thinkers to state the basic creeds of their own faith. In a sense, Jewish dogmatics forms part of the larger category of Jewish apologetics. (Abrahams et al. 290)

Other Jews, and certainly other scholars of religion, however, may be surprised to find that the Judaism in *Plot* has not only gone beyond belief, but beyond practice as well. Though there are remnants of religious practice in

Philip's household, as we have seen, and in the Jewish community in New-ark, it is repudiated by Philip as the basis for their Jewishness. Attention to practice rather than belief in our definition of what counts as religious (as the recent lived religion scholarship has developed, for instance) does not render *Plot*'s Jewish community as really religious rather than a vibrant, indigenous, but non-transcendent and non-metaphysical culture.

Nor will this point come as a surprise to those who have been reading Roth for decades. Indeed, it might be safe to say that almost everything Roth has ever written, as well as almost everything his critics have written about his work, has had to do with Jewish and Jewish American identity, at least in passing, and often centrally. But no one reads Roth as a particularly religious writer, nor does he think of himself as one. His oeuvre has never treated Jewish American and Jewish identities with sustained interest in whatever religious dimension that identity once held. Specific religious practices and beliefs have often been the sites of interethnic comedy for Roth, whether in terms of the suicidal blackmail on the question of the virgin birth in "The Conversion of the Jews," using rit-ual devotion as seeming pretext for special treatment in "Defender of the Faith," *Portnoy's Complaint*'s mockery of silly Christian ideas, or horse-trading religious rituals and holidays for the mixed child in *American Pastoral*. As *Portnoy's* nar-rator's father rages, referring to the idea that Jesus the Jew was the Messiah, "I assure you, Alex, you are never going to hear such a *mishegoss* of mixed-up crap and disgusting nonsense as the Christian religion in your entire life" (40). Portnoy likewise vehemently disagrees with Christian belief:

> The Jews I despise for their narrow-mindedness, their self-righteousness, the incredibly bizarre sense that these cave men who are my parents and relatives have somehow gotten of their superiority—but when it comes to tawdriness and cheapness, to beliefs that would shame even a gorilla, you simply cannot top the *goyim*. What kind of base and brain-less schmucks are these people to worship somebody who, number one, never existed, and number two, if he did, looking as he does in that picture, was without a doubt The Pansy of Palestine. In a page-boy haircut, with a Palmolive complexion—and wearing a gown that I realize today must have come from Fredericks of Hollywood! (168)

(Roth's Pansy of Palestine anticipates the flower-garlanded, fair-skinned Jesus who looks down with disappointment on Morrison's Pecola.) In *American Pastoral*, meanwhile, we know that Jewish difference is not imagined primar-ily religiously by the comic transcription of the Swede's father's negotia-tion (an "inquisition") of the Swede's engagement with his Irish American Catholic fiancée. Here, religion is reconceptualized as a series of holidays that can be negotiated in a mixed family (391). Roth, in my reading, is merely elaborating on Will Herberg's observation that the metaphysics of the three religious traditions and their doctrinal specificities were on the wane.

If Roth imagines Christians, like Jews, to be essentially cultural groups, Michaels on the other hand suggests (rhetorically at least) that it is impossible to be a Christian or a Jew in any meaningful nonreligious, purely cultural way: "Fundamentalist Christians are not an ethnic group or a culture. They are people who believe in things like the inerrancy of scripture, the sinfulness of homosexuality, the divinity of Jesus," suggests Michaels (178). In fact, however, the conservative Christians who became powerful social and political actors since the 1970s were a set of cultural groups—but one that (unlike contemporary American Jews) made distinct universal claims on those outside its group. As we saw in chapter 3, recent social science research on the Christian Right has confirmed that, as is true of other religious groups, "denomination constrains belief" (Greeley and Hout 24). The United States may be a gorgeous mosaic of religious pluralism, but most Americans remain within the religious traditions in which they are raised. Greeley and Hout's work suggests a partial demographic reason for the conservative Christian resurgence, one based around these denominational contingencies: conservative Protestant women tend to have more children than those in liberal denominations, and—in a change from previous decades before the 1970s—"upwardly mobile" members of conservative denominations feel less need to join mainline or liberal Protestant denominations upon entering the middle class (105–08).

Thus, to use Michaels's examples, the conservative Christians who believe in the inerrancy of scripture, the sinfulness of homosexuality, and the divinity of Jesus are likely to have been raised in familial and church cultures that believe precisely these things. Likewise, the pressure to assimilate to mainline or liberal Protestant denominations that have more nuanced views in these areas seems to have lessened in the last three or four decades. So, while it is clear that fundamentalist and conservative evangelical Christians are largely a conglomeration of descent-based cultural groups, the resurgence generally and importantly speaks the language of universality, personal commitment, and conversion. It is this peculiar double register of the Christian resurgence—the way it functions both in terms of a religion extending its universal and metaphysical claims to everyone and a kind of descent-based cultural identity within the broader frame of American multicultural reality—that has made it difficult to apprehend, especially since many commentators (and literary writers) remained committed to viewing religion in terms of secularized social communities.

My argument is not that Roth should have plotted his *Plot* so as to entail the conversion of the Jews, à la *The Handmaid's Tale* or the *Left Behind* series, or that he should treat religion seriously and without comedy. Rather, I am arguing that in a novel in an important sense about "the present moment in America"—and, more to the point, a novel with an eye on the contemporary Christianization of America—religion is not graspable as a phenomenon. It is reread as a kind of cultural difference. If this is a metaphor—in which cultural difference is the vehicle for the tenor of religious faith, assimilation the vehicle for conversion—it is a metaphor that does a certain kind of work, a metaphor with consequences: it generates insight only at the cost of a sort of blindness to an immensely important social and political shift in the last four decades. *The Plot Against America* embraces a model of Jewish and Christian ethnic identities from which religious tonalities have been evacuated. It is deaf to religion, and so, if the many commentators are correct who have seen the novel as being about the Bush presidency, even in an indirect way, and American emergency after September 11, 2001, it is an extremely odd misrecognition of the present moment.

How strange it is to write in 2004 a book about American emergency and difference that utterly drains religious signification from the national picture. Indeed, the novel's treatment of assimilation as a kind of conceit for conversion fundamentally misapprehends the vectors of one of the most crucially formative social and political movements of the contemporary period. For Roth, the question of conversion has perhaps always been a strange and alien one. When telling the story of the debate held at the start of his career at Yeshiva University in 1962—where he was famously asked, as he sat on the panel beside Ralph Ellison, "Mr. Roth, would you write the same stories you've written if you were living in Nazi Germany?" (*The Facts* 127)—Roth remarks on his wife Josie's "pointless conversion" to Reconstructionist Judaism (126). It is pointless partly because Roth is a secular Jew, but also because, according to Roth,

> being a Jew had to do with a real historical predicament into which you were born and not with some identity you chose to don after reading a dozen books. I could as easily have turned into a subject of the Crown by presenting my master's degree in English literature to Winston Churchill as my new wife could become a Jew by studying with Jack Cohen, sensible and dedicated as he was, for the rest of her life. (126)

Josie became after her conversion "some sort of simulated Jew" (126). There aren't any conditions, in other words, in which a gentile could become a Jew, or a Jew a gentile. This is merely the conundrum of "the issue of Jewish self-definition and Jewish allegiance" (129) that was Roth's "luckiest break" (130) to have been struck with so forcefully so early in his career at the Yeshiva seminar, giving him material for his next half-century of literary work. Fair enough. But in terms of equipping him for the religious energy that would overtake the nation during that career, it is difficult to imagine poorer preparation.

The paradigm of multiculturalism in general—and probably the experience and upbringing of Roth specifically—disarms the ability to apprehend what that other seismic shift has been about, and how it operates. Roth's career, and certainly *The Plot Against America*, are increasingly comprehensible within literary multiculturalism. There are great benefits to this model, both for literature and for citizens. But this paradigm has made it difficult to apprehend the conservative Christian resurgence, partly because that resurgence has operated partially within, and alongside, our multiculturalism of the last four decades. If *Plot* is a novel that aims to critique contemporary Christianization or the politics of the resurgence, it fails in this regard precisely because it cannot seem to imagine Jewish difference as religious. Imagining Jews as religiously different might be a kind of Christian fantasy, after all, but it is the dominant conservative Christian fantasy of the contemporary period. *The Plot Against America* indicts instead the pre-multicultural "liberal consensus"—or liberal fascism if you will—of forced assimilation that was operative more than a half century ago. But the kind of claims made by the resurgence, we have seen, happen on the level of universal religion, not relative culture. The resurgence occasionally frames itself through multiculturalism, pleading for tolerance for creationism in science classrooms or terming fact-reporting news as a kind of liberal subject position or suggesting that textbooks and academics have suppressed the true Christian history of America. But Roth's multicultural tactic of criticizing assimilation cannot equip him to interrogate the politics of the conservative Christian resurgence, and in that sense, *The Plot Against America* fundamentally misapprehends the religious energy that characterizes our contemporary moment.

Christian America

> By 1976, [Falwell] was preaching that *This idea of "religion and politics don't mix" was invented by the devil to keep Christians from running their own country.*
>
> Susan F. Harding, *The Book of Jerry Falwell*

By the time Philip Roth published his uchronic vision of a Christian America in 2004, the nation had seen decades of post–civil religion debate about the ways in which the United States should be considered a Christian country. As a way of concluding this chapter, I want to turn, in contrast to Roth, to the Christian Right's vision of what Christian America looked like in the resurgence's first decades. As with Roth's uchronia, their vision was a reimagining of American history that reworked the past so as to make identity claims for the political present. If Roth did not quite understand that the conservative Christian resurgence's terms were willing conversion rather than coerced assimilation, he did see that their vision of the Christian history of the nation, as resurgent writings show, entailed that all Americans, including non-Christians, embrace the moral order and ethical positions of the resurgence.

One such vision was offered by Francis Schaeffer IV in his influential 1976 *How Should We Then Live?* This conservative evangelical middlebrow interpretation of the history of Western art, philosophy, and religion offered an overview of the "rise and decline of Western thought and culture," as the subtitle had it, and, as a film documentary, helped politically activate the conservative Christian resurgence. Schaeffer was, like C. S. Lewis, the kind of conservative Christian author one turned to if one wanted a more intellectually complex account of theology, apologetics, and modernity than those offered by most fundamentalist writers (see, e.g., Frank Schaeffer, *Crazy* 280). In Francis Schaeffer's decidedly Protestant account of Christian civilization, the humanism of the Renaissance and Enlightenment culminated in the modern world's abandonment of absolutes. It was up to present-day Christians to try to reclaim the biblical worldview that modern society had abandoned, for only that retrieval could save civilization from the specter of authoritarian government.

In one chapter describing how some Reformation ideas became secularized, Schaeffer explains his sense of America's Christian roots:

Not all the individual men who laid down the foundation for the United States Constitution were Christians; many, in fact, were deists. But we should realize that the word *Christian* can legitimately be used in two ways. The primary meaning is: an individual who has come to God through the work of Christ. The second meaning must be kept distinct but also has validity. It is possible for an individual to live within the circle of that which a Christian consensus brings forth, even though he himself is not a Christian in the first sense. . . . Many of the men who laid the foundation of the United States Constitution were not Christians in the first sense, and yet they built upon the basis of the Reformation either directly through the *Lex Rex* tradition or indirectly through Locke. (110)

Schaeffer's historical sketch suggests the way one could be culturally Christian even if one was not a born-again, Bible-believing Protestant. Intriguingly, and as I argue in chapter 1, it is in this very capacity that many inaugural multicultural authors suggested—around the same time as Schaeffer—that America and its founders were Christian. But this larger agreement about the importance of locating America within a Christian cultural tradition led evangelicals and multiculturalists to different conclusions: recommitment to or repudiation of the Christian past, respectively.

Calling on Christians to engage the world, Schaeffer urged his conservative readers to help return America—and, indeed, the Protestant West—to its original Christian worldview. Only the Protestant tradition was capable of this job, for only it had held on to the otherworldly absolutes grounded in the Bible, a transcendent source of meaning and values by which one could align right action and right belief. Schaeffer thus often finds himself in agreement with the diagnoses of the modern condition made by modern painting or modern literature. Sympathetic to the youth culture of the "long Sixties," he argues that it arrived at a social and moral impasse because its modern humanism offered no ground for ultimate meaning. Science views "man" as a mechanical machine; government, academic and "technocratic" elites seek to govern through the assurance of well-being and material accumulation (225); and while many have turned to drugs or rock music to assuage the emptiness, they will not ultimately suffice.

Schaeffer's tone is explanatory rather than preachy. He ran an international mission in L'Abri, Switzerland at which many North American youth touring Europe and seeking answers dropped by to talk about art, politics, religion, and philosophy. *How Should We Then Live?* represents Schaeffer's synthesis, tying the story of the art those youths had seen in European museums to the modern crises of spiritual malaise and the loss of absolutes. It is an evangelical work aimed at those young seekers, but it is also a diagnosis and a program for Bible-believing Christians, whom it warns, "As the memory of the Christian consensus which gave us freedom within the biblical form increasingly is forgotten, a manipulating authoritarianism will tend to fill the vacuum" (245). Schaeffer calls on Christians to engage the world in order to influence it, suggesting that "*Such Christians do not need to be a majority in order for this influence on society to occur*" (252; emphasis original). Schaeffer saw the nation's heritage as considerably more biblically-derived than did Bellah (who leaned on Rousseau to outline its basic beliefs, such as they were), and his call for Christians to influence the nation collapsed the public/private split upon which Bellah delineated civil religion in the domain of the former.

In some important respects, the European-based Schaeffer represented an important thread in the conservative Christian resurgence considerably distinct from the Southern fundamentalism still reeling from Supreme Court decisions on integration, school prayer, and evolution. It was through an alliance between such strains that the Religious Right was born, Harding reports: "During the 1970s, Falwell had helped to close the ranks among a broad spectrum of fundamentalisms. During the 1980s, he divided them down the middle, hiving off those who would forsake much of their biblical separation from the world, and allying them with conservative evangelicals who were already more at ease in the world but had lately become alarmed about its moral state and the prospect of accommodating to it" (129). This alliance eventually included "two key figures, the fundamentalist (proto-evangelical) Jerry Falwell, and the (ex-fundamentalist) evangelical Francis Schaeffer IV" (130), explains Harding, who suggests that Schaeffer had a "reputation that was novel, even radical, at the time, namely, that of an intellectually respectable evangelical who was also a biblical inerrantist" (130). While I think Schaeffer is more fundamentalist that Harding allows,[18] the significant difference between the two conservative Christian leaders becomes apparent in Schaeffer's discussion of race, where he condemns contemporaneous and historical racism. As he puts it, "Today's Christians, by identification with their forebears, must acknowledge these inconsistencies in regard to a twisted view of race. We can use no lesser word than *sin* to describe those instances where the practice was (or is) so far from what the Bible directs" (114). Schaeffer suggests that the moral problems of "accumulated wealth" and "slavery based on race" were wrong, "and often both were present when Christians had a stronger influence on the consensus than they now have—and yet the church, as the church, did not speak out sufficiently against them" (113). The weasely language Schaeffer uses here—"slavery based on race"—allows him to silently disregard the Bible's approval (for him, the sole source for moral absolutes) of ancient world slavery based on reproduction, capture during warfare, and debt.[19] Nonetheless, Schaeffer's repeated denunciations of racial slavery and racism give his conservatism a different shape than the Southern fundamentalism that had previously justified Christian slavery and then Christian segregation, and which continued in the 1970s to appeal to white racial resentment.

Similarly, Schaeffer's condemnation of "the lack of compassionate use of accumulated wealth" (114) that he sees emerging from the Industrial Revolution and continuing into the present suggests a concern for social justice issues that was different from what would come to be the movement conservative values that would shortly remake the Republican Party. To be sure, Schaeffer sees the political impulse toward "radical redistribution of the wealth in the world" to be one of the dangers facing modern society (dangerous because that redistribution would alter international power relations and make everyone a little poorer overall, he believes), and throughout the book he is intent on countering the continued appeal of Marxism (248). But in recalling the "tragic" "acceptance" of those opposed to helping the Irish during the potato famine "on the grounds that they should help themselves and that to do otherwise would encourage them to be lazy" (116), Schaeffer's *How Should We Then Live?* seems unable to imagine the eventual alliance developed in movement conservatism between the Christian Right and the small-government, big-business-friendly, supply-side economics segment of conservatism recently represented by Republican vice-presidential candidate Paul Ryan's articulation of what we might call the "hammock theory" of welfare effects.[20] As with any alliance, it had its rough edges.[21]

Schaeffer's appeal to Christians to influence their country did not include a continued sense of racial resentment or racism that, for him, was negated rather than supported by biblical absolutes: in this sense he was appealing to Christians who shared the antiracism of the civil rights movement rather than those who felt their way of life had been assaulted by it. Schaeffer focuses instead on the pressing ethical problem of abortion, which for him is a culmination of the humanist worldview that sees humans as machines. The Supreme Court's recent decision in *Roe*, Schaeffer asserts, resulted from its departure from the Christian consensus about life and its turn instead to an "arbitrary absolute" in deciding when life began (220). While noting that the Kinsey sex studies also seemed to suggest that there was no right and wrong in sexuality (224), Schaeffer is notably non-preachy on questions of sexuality and premarital sex—except for the lengthy analysis of abortion, which might lead, he suggests, to the use of euthanasia, genetic engineering, and population control technologies by the elite.

It was Schaeffer's stance on abortion that would later become a lynchpin in the developing conservative Christian resurgence. Two years after *How Should We Then Live?*—the book and then the documentary—he authored the five-part film *Whatever Happened to the Human Race?* with C. Everett Koop, who would later become President Reagan's surgeon general. The film, "widely credited with turning the tide of popular evangelical opinion against abortion" (Harding 191), suggested that killing a fetus is killing the image of God and that abortion would lead to "state-mandated, mandatory infanticide and euthanasia of unwanted individuals and groups" (192). (Thus, in *Left Behind*, women's unborn babies are raptured, while the Antichrist, soon to be anointed Secretary General of the United Nations, calls those raptured unborn babies "fetal material" [259].) What it also did, argues Harding, was to make the Christian position on abortion prolife by default (193). Schaeffer's film version of *How Should We Then Live?* in 1977 likewise cemented the developing Religious Right alliance by emphasizing abortion and helping to turn conservative evangelicals away from the relatively prochoice evangelical president Carter toward the steadfastly pro-life Ronald Reagan. Falwell and "Schaeffer were allied in the same basic project: dismantling the complex of psychological, social, and intellectual constraints and taboos that discouraged fundamental Christians from entering upper-middle-class professions" (Harding 147) and using their new social and political clout to bring America back to its Christian heritage.

The film also marked an important milestone for conservative Protestants in overcoming their hostility to Catholicism and becoming willing to ally with it partly through this issue of abortion. According to Schaeffer's son Frank (who suggested the book and documentary *How Should We Then Live?*, which he directed), Schaeffer at first did not want to include a lengthy discussion of abortion, seeing it as a Catholic issue.[22] But the way conservative Protestants grew to adopt the Catholic position on this ethical question—and eventually sidelined as non-Christian any prochoice values, Harding suggests—helped forge the alliance of the conservative Christian resurgence which, though mostly run and theorized by conservative Protestants, proclaimed a large tent theoretically open to Catholics, Mormons, and Jews (Harding 145). Conservative Protestant respect for the longstanding prolife Catholic position helped bury a previous generation's political anti-Catholicism, thus clearing the way for the larger alliance of the Religious Right to come.

Indeed, one has the sense from Frank Schaeffer's fiction that this shift in fundamentalist attitudes toward Catholics occurred within his own family. The Schaeffers took their summer vacations in the small Italian fishing village of Portofino, he reports in *Crazy for God* and *Why I Am an Atheist Who Believes in God*. In his autobiographically inspired novel *Portofino* (1992), written after he had broken with Christian fundamentalism, the child narrator's missionary family dwells in a foreign country trying to convert the local pagans. Unlike Kingsolver's Baptist family among the Africans, however, the narrator's Presbyterian family are proselytizing to Swiss Catholics; even on vacation in Italy, he remains "a fundamentalist Protestant child of the light in a dark, corrupted ocean of Roman Catholic paganism and alcohol-consuming superstition" (44). Clearly modelled after his own childhood at his parents' mission in Switzerland, the novel reflects through its narrator on "the youth of Europe" who "were either backslidden Protestants, who had forgotten their great Reformation heritage . . . or worse, Roman Catholics who were in bondage to the Pope and Satan and were in the dark because they had never heard the real gospel or had been born again to a new life in Jesus as their personal Savior" (47). *Portofino* satirizes this 1960s fundamentalist sense of Catholic superstition and idolatry. It also portrays the child narrator's growing awareness that other families "knew we were strange people" (234) who used public prayers of thanksgiving as opportunities for preaching the Word—as well as Tolstoy's truth that unhappy families are unhappy in their own unique ways.

Situated as he was in the Swiss mountain village of L'Abri, there is a certain cosmopolitanism to Francis Schaeffer's intellectual and spiritual diagnosis and subsequent political project that was missing from the Christian conservatives whose home remained the United States. Schaeffer shared with them the vision of a more specifically Christian American past and the fear of liberal technocratic elites who would gradually come to run the government and take away the freedom originally granted by the biblically based worldview, but his vision refused the racial animus that ran deep in Southern fundamentalism. One could imagine that, in his more thoroughly Christian America, there would be no deportations of African Americans to Homeland One or forced conversion of Jews, à la Atwood's Christian nation in *The Handmaid's Tale*. Indeed, for Schaeffer, and even for his less intellectually sophisticated colleague Tim LaHaye in his fictional apocalyptic world of the end times, forced conversions would make no sense because they would betray the way God personally calls some people (including Jews) to proper belief, and not others. The *Left Behind* series imagines the conversion of some of the Jews, something that could never be accomplished by widespread coercion because conservative Christianity understood faith as a private matter between one's conscience and one's God.[23]

Schaeffer's *How Should We Then Live?* was the starting point for a similar resurgent book, Tim LaHaye's *The Faith of Our Founding Fathers* (1987). Lacking Schaeffer's intellectual breadth, it is a narrower, more overtly political tract focusing on "the evangelical Protestants who founded this nation" (1)—the true history of which must be recovered because "history was deliberately raped by left-wing scholars for hire" (6) and "history revisionists" (5). For LaHaye, the ills of 1980s America—pornography, abortion, sexual immorality, drug use, and a secular humanist Supreme Court bent on removing all traces of religion from the public sphere—could only be solved by a determined return to the biblical principles that characterized the Christian consensus of the Founders. Many of the key themes of the conservative Christian resurgence are present in LaHaye's influential book. When he ends with the suggestion that "if a majority of our citizens, most of whom have deep religious and moral yearnings, can be enlisted" (199) in a broader movement at the ballot box—thus using the very words in Falwell's "Moral Majority," founded eight years before with LaHaye's help—then conservative Christians would be able to rescue the country before "an elitist minority of secularists continue to lead this nation into impotence, stagnation, and slavery" (200).

Much of LaHaye's book consists of biographical sketches of the fifty-five delegates to the Constitutional Convention, to demonstrate their commitment to what the author calls (borrowing Schaeffer's phrase) the "Christian consensus" of the time. Some sketches are longer than others; some delegates signed and others didn't; some were more demonstrably religious than others. But while LaHaye not infrequently asserts that "many of the delegates" would be "comfortable" in "our Bible-believing churches of today" (144), the problem he runs into is the wide gap between the public religious pronouncements of the Founders (as he quotes them) and the specific ethical claims about abortion, pornography, sexual immorality, and prayer and Bible-reading in schools that animated the politics of the conservative Christian resurgence. Indeed, the evidence LaHaye is able to provide suggests that, in public at least, the Founders were much more likely to speak in eighteenth-century language of (as is demonstrated in a long section on Washington) Supreme Being and Author, without reference to Jesus or the Bible. The public language of the Founders that LaHaye quotes is the antecedent deist language to Bellah's civil religion, not the evangelical language of born-again conversion or the inspired Word of God in the Bible. The lone exception seems to be Washington's "personal prayer book" (110) with its prayerful reference to Jesus Christ, which leads LaHaye to conclude, "An objective reading of these beautiful prayers verifies that were George Washington living today, he would freely identify with the Bible-believing branch of evangelical Christianity that is having such a positive influence on our nation" (113). But while this work is frequently cited by conservative Christians, "the University of Virginia, which houses the Papers of George Washington, and the Smithsonian Institution have concluded, based on the handwriting, that it was not written by Washington."[24]

The implication of LaHaye's argument is that the unspoken, unwritten biblical principles of our Founding Fathers would have entailed opposing abortion, homosexuality, evolution, sex education, sex outside of marriage, and pornography, and supporting school prayer, Bible reading in schools, abstinence-only sex education and other "traditional family values" (197). LaHaye expresses the fury of many conservative Christians about the Supreme Court, which had "resolutely misinterpreted the Constitution so as to increase the scope and power of the federal government and to separate it almost entirely from God and Biblical principles," noting, "it has become both secular and hostile to religion" (190). In LaHaye's reading, recent Supreme Court decisions on school prayer, Bible readings, evolution, and abortion reversed the Founders' intention regarding the first amendment clause that religion be protected from government intrusion (61).

LaHaye clarifies that "I do not claim that this country was founded as a Christian nation, even though many of the original states were established as Christian colonies"; rather, "it was a nation so predominantly Christian that the culture evidenced what the late Dr. Francis Schaeffer called 'a Christian consensus'" (33). He means by this distinction that the Founders did not write the Constitution to found a theocracy (it couldn't be, given the narrative of America as a site of religious freedom), but that America makes no sense and can't work without recognizing the Christian beliefs and biblical principles of the Founders. That Christian basis is the organizing principle that makes sense of the Founding documents and of the nation's divine mission, which are currently being undercut by secular humanists. Non-Christian Americans, though citizens, need to recognize the Christian consensus of the moral majority, and submit to the biblically based legislation and moral codes that they may not personally share. The Christian history of the nation thus entails universalist claims on the present, as we have seen.

This vision of a Christian America has been powerfully compelling, even as other thinkers and writers in the resurgence have, over the years, not necessarily made LaHaye's distinction between a theocratic nation and one founded on the Christian consensus. Indeed, near the end of Francis Schaeffer's life, according to his son, he came to regret the alliance of the Religious Right he had been instrumental in developing, "saying privately that the evangelical world was more or less being led by lunatics, psychopaths, and extremists, and agreeing with me that if 'our side' ever won, America would be in deep trouble" (*Crazy* 335). Schaeffer's concession that in order to imagine national history as Christian one had to understand that term in two senses—personally born-again, and culturally—was not always shared by other Christian conservatives who came to dominate the brain trust of the resurgence. Jerry Falwell, for instance, claimed, "Any diligent student of American history finds that our great nation was founded by godly men upon godly principles to be a Christian nation" (quoted in Lepore 120). If "the Puritans bequeathed to subsequent generations a desire to record America's origins not as religiously and racially plural but instead as white and Protestant, and to read the nation's subsequent history through the lens of the Puritans' providential design" (Fessenden, *Culture* 32), as is surely true of the conservative Christian resurgence, that design entailed rewriting the Founders' Deism as a more biblically based Christian Theism.[25]

The resurgence's development of a parallel academic, publishing, and media ecosystem meant that the notion of a Christian nation has continued to be made by leaders with powerful voices, but also at a grassroots level in school boards across the land. Glenn Beck, Sarah Palin, and Bill O'Reilly made public proclamations about America's Christian origins, reports Jill Lepore in her 2010 study of the Tea Party (156–57), even as, to use her example, a Texas school board member trained at Pat Robertson's Regent University School of Law and a "visiting professor of law at [Falwell's] Liberty University," could assert that the United States was "a Christian land, governed by Christian principles" (158). As with the creation-evolution controversy to which I turn in chapter 6, school board–level pressure had large consequences for textbook publishing because of Texas's large market (12).[26] Authors and publishers are under pressure to provide more amenable accounts of the Christian history of the nation than they might otherwise see as correct. This battle over American history, reports Lepore, had been brewing since the 1970s, particularly over the Bicentennial celebrations in 1976 (68, 73), but it reached a milestone with the Tea Party in the early twentieth-first century:

> Whatever else had drawn people into the movement—the bailout, health care, taxes, Fox News, and, above all, the economy—some of it, for some people, was probably discomfort with the United States' first black president, because he was black. But it wasn't the whiteness of the Tea Party that I found most striking. It was the whiteness of their Revolution. The Founding Fathers were the whites of their eyes, a fantasy of an America before race, *without* race. There were very few black people in the Tea Party, but there were no black people at all in the Tea Party's eighteenth century. Nor, for that matter, were there any women, aside from Abigail Adams, and no slavery, poverty, ignorance, insanity, sickness, or misery. Nor was there any art, literature, sex, pleasure, or humor. There were only the Founding Fathers with their white wigs, wearing their three-cornered hats, in their Christian nation, revolting against taxes, and defending their right to bear arms. (95)

As reviewed in the introduction, Tea Party members are demographically whiter than Republican Party members in general, but they also desire more religion in government even more than they desire smaller government and less taxation.

It is this vein, perhaps, that Leslie Silko has one of her many characters in

Almanac of the Dead, a corrupt right-wing judge, articulate his conservative values through his sense of a betrayal of the "Christian nation": "The judge, like all dedicated conservatives, understood the greatest dangers to a nation lay within, among its own people who had become degenerate and had betrayed their Christian nation" (648). Although the judge's Christianity is not expressed in the born-again language used by Acosta, Walker, or Mailer, Silko names the trope of the Christian nation fallen away from its true roots that powerfully emerged during the conservative Christian resurgence in the period between when she wrote *Ceremony* (published in 1977) and *Almanac* (published in 1992). The liberal Silko portrays the judge not as a duped conservative mind; the irony arises from the fact that while the author politically opposes her character, she actually agrees with his characterization of America as a Christian nation—as we have seen was true of many other multicultural writers during this period. The apocalypse about to erupt at the end of *Almanac* will result in the destruction of the Christian nation: this is not a reformist political proposal, but one that imagines, à la the Paiute prophet Wovoka's vision, the imminent disappearance of all things white and European, including the religion whose God did not arrive with the Europeans, in contrast to kidnapped Africans. In this sense, the judge's idea that "the greatest dangers" to his Christian nation "lay within, among its own people," is entirely apt. It is when its indigenous inhabitants—not just Native Americans, but also Mexican Americans now realizing they are Indians, and African Americans to whom indigeneity has been extended—return to their ancestral gods that the Christian nation in *Almanac* will begin its collapse. In another entangled moment, the multicultural Silko shares with some conservative Christians not only the naming of the nation's Christian identity, but a hunger for apocalypse, a hunger growing in the 1980s that was to come to literary fruition in LaHaye and Jenkins's *Left Behind* series, and one that has her, like them, reading the signs of imminent apocalypse.

For many conservative Christians such as LaHaye, imagining the true Christian history of the nation entailed making the Founders into Protestant evangelicals, and the Constitution into a document intended to promote the religious basis of the country. It also entailed a purification of origins, with Michelle Bachmann, for instance, contending "that the Founders worked tirelessly to end slavery" (Lizza), and a turn to what became known, especially in the post-*Brown* and post-*Roe* years, as Constitutional Originalism (as with LaHaye's call for only "strict constructionist" judges to be appointed to the Supreme Court [200]) in which we discover the Founding Fathers' true Christian intentions. But originalism, writes Lepore, is "lousy history":

And it has long since reached well beyond the courts. Set loose in the culture, and tangled together with fanaticism, originalism looks like history, but it's not; it's historical fundamentalism, which is to history what astrology is to astronomy, what alchemy is to chemistry, what creationism is to evolution. (123–24)

I conclude this chapter with the suggestion that the conservative Christian resurgence's construction of the Christian history and identity of the nation should be understood in both multicultural and postmodern terms. It was multicultural insofar as it agreed with multiculturalists on the historical Christian religious identity of the nation, but also in the way in which recognizing the religious identity of our ancestors was the important first step in developing our own choices for religious identities today. "My faith is the faith of my fathers," Mitt Romney proclaimed in 2007 (quoted in Lepore 122), a comment that could be heard as a slightly defensive version of being true to one's ancestral faith (like Walker or Anzaldúa) in the face of continued ambivalence about Mormonism. (Evangelical pastor-turned-candidate for the Republican presidential nomination Mike Huckabee had somewhat awkwardly raised questions about Mormon doctrine in late 2007 [Chafets]). But it could also be considered a public affirmation of the universal validity of the founding of the Christian nation. If the resurgence's interpretation of the Christian intentions of the Founders and the Constitution was symptomatic of the postmodern condition wherein we find ourselves trying "to think the present historically in an age that has forgotten how to think historically in the first place" (as Fredric Jameson famously put it [*Postmodernism* ix]), its prescription used the multicultural logic of following in the paths of our ancestors' religion. But there was another way the resurgence's history could be understood as postmodern: as LaHaye's condemnation of "history revisionists" suppressing the true Christian history of the nation suggests, history as a field of inquiry was not to be left to academic experts who, in the name of purported objectivity and neutrality, had managed to improperly secularize American history and identity. The denial of elite expertise—the insistence that so-called experts in a range of fields were speaking from liberal, secular humanist subject positions and not from neutral conclusions after having objectively gathered and weighed the evidence—became one of the crucial postmodern facets of the conservative Christian resurgence, as we shall see in the second half of this book.

Part Two

Postmodern Entanglements

CHAPTER 5

Thomas Pynchon's Prophecy

> It's a Puritan reflex of seeking other orders behind
> the visible, also known as paranoia, filtering in.
>
> Thomas Pynchon, *Gravity's Rainbow*

The literary history I have begun to map in
the previous four chapters tries to account for the way in which the rise of
the Christian Right coincided with the emergence of multiculturalism, and
indeed the unusual and significant entanglement of the two movements. We
begin to apprehend their shared vocabularies and ways of thinking about
religious communities when we recognize their common delineation of the
Christian history and identity of the nation as a starting point for (re)discov-
ering the powerful affective appeal of the faith of one's ancestors. This recognition and affirmation was premised on a stronger version of the Christian
nation than the civil religion consensus had articulated in mid-century. We
have since travelled some distance from Schaeffer's careful 1977 distinction
between personal Christian commitment and a larger Christian civilization
and LaHaye's 1987 qualification that while the Founders may have shared
an evangelical Protestant faith, they didn't quite intend to found a Christian
nation as such. Today's Tea Party, as Lepore reports, has abandoned these fine
distinctions, honing the message of the Christian nation.

This story becomes yet more complex when we take into account the
question of the postmodern—its stances and methods, its uncertainties and
indeterminacies—which is the subject of these next four chapters. We glimpse
the three-threaded complexity of this literary history of the present as we
attend to multiculturalism, postmodernism, and the conservative Christian

resurgence, in noting how, at times, the Jamesonian postmodern problematic of trying to do history in an age that has forgotten how is answered with multicultural solutions. LaHaye's critique of mainstream history is that liberal humanists have improperly secularized the story of America, and that what purports to be a neutral, fact-derived account of the role religion played in the founding of the nation and the lives of the Founders is a partial, ideologically freighted reading by those with an axe to grind. To right that wrong means, for LaHaye, both correcting the portrayal of the faith of the Founding Fathers and exhorting the nation to return to its Christian origins. LaHaye, in my view, is symptomatic of the postmodern condition as Jameson outlines it: his is another partial, partisan history, but one that is decidedly not better than the account he critiques.

A subtler example of a multicultural solution to the postmodern problem of doing history, I have argued, is found in Marilynne Robinson's work. While she offers a more intellectually complex and compelling American history than LaHaye, it is motivated in part by a similar sense that academic history has improperly erased Midwest Christian abolitionism and its key contribution to national history. But Robinson's historical sense of mid nineteenth-century Christianity is as prone to historical omission as the history she questions. *Gilead* is a good example of the entangled triple questions of multiculturalism, postmodernism, and the conservative Christian resurgence animating this study: in the face of the difficulty and partiality of writing histories, it adopts the key multicultural trope of treating history through the prism of familial memory and as the source of contemporaneous (Christian) identities and affect. Its Christian multiculturalism uses history to perform the same kind of identity work as often occurs in contemporary literary multiculturalism.

In these next four chapters I develop this question of the postmodern, focusing specifically on what is already evident in these examples: the epistemological and, indeed, political problems of expert authority. Although the challenge to expert academic history was explicit in the resurgence's insistence on the forgotten or secularly edited true Christian history of the nation, it was to two other areas of academic expertise that the movement took most notable exception. These areas had been constitutive of fundamentalism since their serious challenges to Christianity in the nineteenth century: the science of evolution and the historical-critical methods developed in Bible scholarship to analyze the authorship, editing, and transmission of scripture. Both fields of expert authority turned on the proper way to interpret design—textual or natural—and American writers responding to the conservative Christian resurgence often took up questions of reading and interpretation, featuring, in fact, characters who—and plots which—rely on the acquisition of proper

interpretive expertise. In featuring and calling into question the expert authority needed to adequately read what these fictions sometimes disclose as the
sacred writing still visible in our world, the novels address the question of the
postmodern, but also the intriguing occasional convergence between the postmodern and the resurgence. As with multiculturalism, the easy assumption
that postmodernism must be naturally opposed to the certainties of conservative (often fundamentalist) Christianity in the United States misses their larger
confluence and alignment, a fact that sometimes made it difficult for literary
writers to apprehend what the Christian Right was, and how it operated.

Recognizing the postmodern crisis in expert authority allows a different mapping of the postmodern and religion than those offered by John
McClure and Amy Hungerford. As we have seen, for McClure, the return of
the religious in contemporary fiction takes the form of "weak religion" characterized by alternative, non-systematic, non-institutional, non-doctrinally
focused religiosities. While these "postsecular" spiritualties characterize
a number of authors or characters examined in *If God Meant to Interfere*
(Anzaldúa, Reed, and Kingsolver's Brother Fowles, for example), this formulation of the intersection of religion and postmodernism cannot account for
the return of strong religion in the form of the conservative Christian resurgence. This religion, we have seen, is doctrinally emphatic, universalist rather
than relativist, politically engaged, and embedded in a traditional (and growing) network of church, school, and media institutions. For the same reason,
I offer a different map of religion and postmodernism than Hungerford's
characterization of postmodern religion as belief without content, belief as
rhetorical and stylistic practice. That scheme makes good sense of some of
the texts examined in this book (Robinson's *Gilead*, in particular), but is not
sufficient, I think, for approaching the question of the content-rich, doctrinally active Christian resurgence.

Paying attention to these three terms of the resurgent, the postmodern, and the multicultural allows us, I contend, to better map the interfaces
between the secular and the religious. In his critique of the "master narrative
of secularization," Charles Taylor suggests that in fact the religious and the
secular have a long history of interfacing in complex, dynamic, and uneven
ways. His analysis suggests that the unevenness of American secularization in
the twentieth century is part of a larger Western history of new possibilities
rather than declining faith. As he poses his question,

> Put this way, and very schematically, we can ask: what stopped people
> (that is, almost everybody) from being able to adopt stances of unbelief
> in 1500? One answer is: the enchanted world; in a cosmos of spirits

and forces, some of them evil and destructive, one had to hold on to whatever was conceived to be the mainstay of good power, our bulwark against evil. Another answer was: that belief was so interwoven with social life that one was hardly conceivable without the other. And these two answers were originally connected: some of the interweaving involved collective uses of good, Godly power against the dangers of the spirit world; ceremonies like "beating the bounds" of the parish illustrate this.

Negatively, and leaving aside all the construction that went into this, the intervening centuries have seen the dissipation of the enchanted cosmos (some elements of belief in enchantment remain, but they don't form a system, and are held by individuals here and there, rather than being socially shared). Then there came the introduction, within the context of the modern moral order, of a viable alternative to belief, of forms of exclusive humanism, in turn followed by a multiplication of both believing and unbelieving positions, which I have called the "nova". . . . We no longer live in societies in which the widespread sense can be maintained that faith in God is central to the ordered life we (partially) enjoy. . . .

If we want to carry this account on as a "subtraction story", we might say that secularization, defined as the loss of social matrices of belief, hence decline and fragilization, has at last brought about a "level playing field", because these matrices previously conferred a preferential advantage on belief. But this very idea is absurd, since what we really have is not a playing field at all, but a very accidental terrain; there are lots of tilts, but they don't all slide in the same direction. The tilt of the Bible Belt is not that of the urban university. (530–31)

Recognizing this multiply tilted "accidental terrain" on which the secular interacts with the religious in twentieth- and twenty-first-century American society allows us to see the danger in the simplest understanding of using the word "postsecular" to characterize the contemporary moment—that is, as a time of reenchantment and belief that came after a thoroughly secular age. (This is an error, I should be clear, that I do not think McClure makes.) It is obvious that, as Taylor here says, the "nova" continued to multiply in the twentieth century—he calls the proliferation of options after World War Two a "super-nova" (377)—as many possibilities were encouraged by immigration reform that ceased the de facto preference for immigration from nations with Christian heritages, or were rediscovered (as with writers like Reed, Anzaldúa, and others discussed in chapter 1), outright invented (consider the science-fiction-influenced invention of Scientology by L. Ron Hubbard), and so on. The list of possible positions of belief and unbelief—our super-nova—is very long.

But my focus is on one such set of religious traditions that had, indeed, never gone away, but whose return nonetheless caught many observers off guard. Attending to its history shows us how complex the secular-religion interface is, and has been. Even in the era of supposed secularization—its high tide in the United States, which we could maybe locate in the half-century between *Scopes* and the founding of the Moral Majority, or the election of Jimmy Carter—should not be understood as a time of the retreat back into private life of public religion. In fact, this "secular" midcentury consensus had a place for (Christian) religion in public life: in school prayer and Bible reading, in community standards that entailed silence on evolution and sex education in public school classrooms, and outside school, in the continued appeals to religion as sites of nation-building and -articulation (Bellah's civil religion, the Cold War struggle against atheistic Communism, how "the phrase 'one nation under God' quickly claimed a central position in American political culture" in the 1950s [Kruse 111]) or community belonging (as with Herberg's "culture-religion" in an era of increased church and synagogue membership and construction). Even in this most secular period of American public life, the everyday was still shot through with religious language, ideas, belonging, and affect. The question of the "postsecular" misleads when it is understood as what happens after secularization.[1]

The quiescence of mid-century Christianity must be understood as only a *relative* quiescence: it was an era of vibrant, often public, religiosity (as Putnam and Campbell note), a status quo that was about to be broken open by the civil rights movement, by the sexual revolution, but also by what appeared, to traditional Christians, to be fresh secular demands (about evolution, school prayer, Bible reading, contraception, and abortion) on them and their children, events that violated what we might think of as the truce terms of the midcentury "secular" compromise. Books like *How Should We Then Live?*, *Faith of Our Founding Fathers*, and the *Left Behind* series articulate this conservative Christian sense of embattled faith suffering from aggressive public secularization, and the central motivation to push back against the forces of godlessness leading the country to ruin. But they also speak to conservative Christians' growing feelings of alienation from their own country, especially following the social changes of the "long Sixties." The spiritual alienation felt by this group in the 1960s would come to fruition in the "aftershock" religious formations that became publicly articulated and mobilized in the 1970s and 1980s.

One similar, spiritually alienated American who was not yet activated by resurgent politics was the protagonist of *The Crying of Lot 49*, Oedipa Maas. In this chapter I want to make a series of related claims for reading Thomas Pynchon's 1966 novel as a prolepsis of the conservative Christian resurgence and the national spiritual quandary in which that resurgence took place. My first claim is that the novel names the spiritual emptiness of the protagonist and her society, a kind of a waste land four decades after T. S. Eliot's diagnosis. The moment here, of course, was the civil religion consensus outlined by Bellah and Herberg; as we saw in chapter 1, it was this civil religion against which both multiculturalism and the resurgence reacted, in part by (re)turning to more energetic religious traditions. I want to argue that Oedipa's spiritual emptiness c. 1966 is similarly redolent of this civil religion—its official national status, its relative blankness, its inability to jolt her out of her spiritual ennui. *The Crying of Lot 49* is a classic articulation of modernist spiritual emptiness within modernity, a comic sequel to *The Waste Land*, the W.A.S.T.E. land 44 years later.

My second claim is that insofar as the novel investigates the "exitlessness" of everyday life, in its search for an alternative spiritual resource it is also about Oedipa's way of reading the world, and as such, it serves as a kind of allegory about faith, a lesson in motivated reading. Oedipa's desire to read the world's design—or at least discern the outline of a shadowy conspiracy operating in history, very reminiscent of *Mumbo Jumbo*'s ancient religious plots—exemplifies what we can begin to outline as a postmodern desire for design in our world. Oedipa's investigation is as much about bringing herself to her world as it is about uncovering a design already there, however, and we follow her footsteps in this metaphysical detective novel we are watching the process of how to make belief, how to make believe. If her desire to read reenchantment into her world is a sign of postmodern desire for design amidst disenchantment, her methods for doing so—extended research and consultation with experts—are, I argue, neither postmodern nor anticipatory of the resurgence itself, which tended, as I show in chapters 6 through 8, to treat expert knowledge in the field-leveling terms outlined by Jean-François Lyotard in *The Postmodern Condition*.

My third claim is that, just as it is useful to consider *The Crying of Lot 49* in terms of the insufficiency of an officially sanctioned American civil religion, it is likewise useful to consider its portrayal of paranoia in terms of another mid-1960s sociological treatise, Richard Hofstadter's 1964 *Harper's* essay "The Paranoid Style in American Politics." Pynchon's novel is all about paranoia, as critics have widely recognized, but I argue that we should read its development in Oedipa not as an age-old universal human phenomenon, but as a quite specific cultural-historical formation that reached one high point, Hofstadter suggests, in Barry Goldwater's 1964 campaign. Historians have recognized that the Goldwater campaign was an important milestone in the long, five-decade arc of the Christianization of the Republican Party, and I suggest here that in articulating Oedipa's state of paranoid disinheritance and alienation, Pynchon is proleptically capturing something of the energy that Hofstadter names and that Bellah believed was a disappearing residue. In its spiritual diagnosis, its analysis of motivated reading, and its surprisingly specific sociological portrait, *The Crying of Lot 49* begins to capture—and in some fascinating ways, fails to capture—the nation on the cusp of the conservative Christian resurgence. Pynchon's novel was a kind of prophecy, which I mean in the ordinary, idiomatic sense of "imagining a future outcome," but, more important, of diagnosing the spiritual ills of the community, a vocation to which prophets (both Hebrew and classical, such as those in Eliot's *Waste Land*, for instance) are called.

Other Orders behind the Visible

> At this point, one is tempted to make some conjectures about those formal pleasures, which involve the consolations of what is nowadays so often loosely called "paranoia." Far from being some ultimate nightmare state beyond simple forms of anxiety and delirium, "paranoia" in that sense strikes me as a preeminently reassuring thing, almost as good as a belief in God or providence.
>
> Fredric Jameson, "Reviews"

The spiritual emptiness that attends Oedipa's everyday life makes her into a kind of American everywoman. Led by clues emerging from her deceased ex-husband Pierce Inverarity's estate, Oedipa discovers the seeming existence of the Tristero, a five-hundred-year-old alternative mail-delivery network of outsiders and rejects. Tristero's appeal, Oedipa realizes late in the novel, is that it appears to be "a network by which X number of Americans are truly communicating whilst reserving their lies, recitations of routine, arid betrayals of spiritual poverty, for the official government delivery system"; indeed, it might represent "a real alternative to the exitlessness, to the absence of surprise to life, that harrows the head of everybody American you know, and you too, sweetie" (141). As her conclusion suggests, Oedipa's daily routine—a Tupperware party, shopping for groceries for dinner, tending her herb garden, drinking until her husband returns from work—is merely a manifestation of the larger "spiritual poverty" within which "everybody American" lives. Oedipa has no spiritual resources: this Southern California housewife is without family, besides her husband, without church, and without neighborhood. While the Tupperware party implies a network of social acquaintances, the novel emphasizes Oedipa's social and psychological isolation from other people. Its occasion is thus a change in this previous existence of "a fat deckful of days which seemed (wouldn't she be the first to admit it?) more or less identical" (2), a life characterized by "the sense of buffering, insulation . . . absence of an intensity, as if watching a movie, just perceptibly out of focus, that the projectionist refused to fix" (10).

Her representative status is suggested by her second husband Mucho's dream of the used-car lot where he used to work, in which "a salad of despair . . . the unvarying gray sickness" covered the used cars, and where a buyer would "exchange a dented, malfunctioning version of himself for another, just as futureless, automotive projection of somebody else's life" (5). What used to wake Mucho screaming from his dreams about the lot—before he begins using LSD—was the sign hanging above it: "the National Automobile Dealer's Association. N.A.D.A. Just this creaking metal sign that said nada, nada, against the blue sky" (118). As in Ernest Hemingway's "A Clean, Well-Lighted Place," to which this episode alludes, we drink or take drugs against the nothingness that harrows our heads. The sense of belonging offered by Herberg's religious communities or national mission by Bellah's civil religion is not enough for Oedipa and Mucho, or for us. Theirs are not, as the resurgent evangelical bestseller would pithily put it decades later, "purpose driven lives" (R. Warren).

Pynchon's diagnosis of American "spiritual poverty" is frequently articulated through images suggesting a prior loss of traditional religious meaning, and in this sense it's a classic diagnosis of spiritual poverty in the wake of apparent secularization. Thus, as Oedipa begins to uncover clues to Tristero's existence—the secret historical conspiracy that might represent a "real alternative" to American spiritual poverty—she wonders if the clues "were only some kind of compensation. To make up for her having lost the direct, epileptic Word, the cry that might abolish the night" (95). As this reference to the hymn to Logos that opens the Gospel of John suggests—the reference, we have seen, that forms the core of Momaday's sermon by Tosamah—the novel establishes Oedipa's problem in fundamentally religious terms: what can take the place of the Word in seemingly post-Christian, secular America? For all its humor and pop-culture irreverence, then, *The Crying of Lot 49* is a serious diagnosis of its protagonist's religious condition in modernity. Intriguingly, Pynchon uses the same metaphor of "buffering" that Charles Taylor does in *A Secular Age* to describe our existences disengaged from a larger enchanted cosmos. If "the boundary between agents and forces is fuzzy in the enchanted world; and the boundary between mind and world is porous"

(39), this porosity has been closed for the "buffered self" (38), who "no longer fears demons, spirits, magic forces" (135). The buffered self experiences no mystery, is cut off from the transcendent, and yet, as Taylor says, may feel a lack in her "lived experience"

> where we experience above all a distance, an absence, an exile, a seemingly irremediable incapacity ever to reach this place; an absence of power; a confusion, or worse, the condition often described in the tradition as melancholy, ennui (the "spleen" of Baudelaire). What is terrible in this latter condition is that we lose a sense of where the place of fullness is, even of what fullness could consist in; we feel we've forgotten what it would look like, or cannot believe in it any more. But the misery of absence, of loss, is still there, indeed, it is in some ways even more acute. (5–6)

The Crying of Lot 49 is the story of one such buffered self.

One early scene's accumulation of religious imagery gives us a particularly sharp sense of Oedipa's post-Christian loss. She drives to San Narciso, a fictional suburb of LA where her ex-husband based his business empire, and looking down on it is reminded of the "printed circuit" she had seen as a child in a transistor radio. The comparison prompts a reverie worth quoting in full:

> The ordered swirl of houses and streets, from this high angle, sprang at her now with the same unexpected, astonishing clarity as the circuit card had. Though she knew even less about radios than about Southern Californians, there were to both outward patterns a hieroglyphic sense of concealed meaning, of an intent to communicate. There'd seemed no limit to what the printed circuit could have told her (if she had tried to find out); so in her first minute of San Narciso, a revelation also trembled just past the threshold of her understanding. Smog hung all round the horizon, the sun on the bright beige countryside was painful; she and the Chevy seemed parked at the centre of an odd, religious instant. As if, on some other frequency, or out of the eye of some whirlwind rotating too slow for her heated skin even to feel the centrifugal coolness of, words were being spoken. She suspected that much. She thought of Mucho, her husband, trying to believe in his job. Was it something like this he felt, looking through the soundproof glass at one of his colleagues with a headset clamped on and cueing the next record with movements stylized as the handling of chrism, censer, chalice might be for a holy man, yet really tuned in to the voice, voices, the

music, its message, surrounded by it, digging it, as were all the faithful it went out to; did Mucho stand outside Studio A looking in, knowing that even if he could hear it he couldn't believe in it? (14)

This striking passage is remarkable not only in terms of the religious language by which it marks Oedipa's "odd, religious instant," but also in the way in which it registers those signs as failed communications, as a kind of experience no longer within Oedipa's reach. The transistor card and suburban street ways are a kind of "hieroglyphic" writing Oedipa cannot read; the Greek root of "hier," *hierós*, meaning sacred and holy, suggests what is illegible to Oedipa. While the reading of holy writing might pertain to many religious traditions, the passage progressively narrows to a Judeo-Christian set of references. Thus out of the eye of the whirlwind "words were being spoken"—a reference to God finally speaking to Job at the end of that eponymous book—but they are words she cannot understand, "on some other frequency." The "revelation" is likewise forestalled, unlike the apocalypse given by the angel to St. John of Patmos at the beginning of the book of Revelation; it is taking place, somewhere, but is out of her reach, not understood. The narrator compares Oedipa's awareness of religious meaning from which she has been excluded to her husband Mucho's difficult participation in his own job. Mucho is akin to an unbelieving priest watching with envy his "holy man" colleague who still believes, and whose ritual objects recall the "chrism" carrying holy oil for anointing, the censer for holy incense, and the chalice for the sacramental wine of the Eucharist to serve "the faithful."

We get a sense in this passage and in others—such as the registering of the loss of the "Word" Oedipa suffers from—that this character's religious condition is at stake and that, more particularly, what the novel is diagnosing (again like *The Waste Land*) is not just a generalized sense of spiritual emptiness but rather a more particular description of a specifically Christian religious tradition no longer accessible to her.[2] While what solved the "loss of the Word" for Eliot was actually the rediscovery of the Word—as well as an accompanying political project, as Michael Lackey has argued[3]—for Oedipa it is only the possibility of the disinherited Tristero. Edward Mendelson early and firmly established this "religious" reading of *The Crying of Lot 49*, arguing that

> Pynchon uses religious terms and hieratic language not simply as a set of metaphors from which to hang his narrative, not merely as a scaffolding (as Joyce, for example, uses Christian symbols in *Ulysses*). The religious meaning of the book does not reduce to metaphor or myth, *because religious meaning is itself the central issue of the plot.* (119–20)

Tristero's presence, Mendelson shows, suggests the existence of a sacred world whose presence Oedipa interprets as the novel progresses. Thus "The manifestations of the Trystero [as it is sometimes spelled] . . . are always associated in the book with the language of the sacred and with patterns of religious experience; the foils to the Trystero are always associated with sacrality gone wrong" (117). In Mendelson's reading, the generic traits of the detective story are undercut insofar as the final mystery is not fully solved by its end.[4] Instead, confounding the detective's empiricism, the novel is a kind of allegory for the problem of belief: that the signs and clues of the sacred exist, but must finally be believed in as a faith decision. But if, "as in all religious choices, no proof is possible" (Mendelson 119), Oedipa further realizes that the desire to believe may have produced the supposed clues themselves.

Pynchon develops this central question of belief through two metaphors that recur throughout the novel: that of the maiden in the tower weaving the world, and the planetarium projector illuminating worlds and constellations. Both metaphors for Oedipa's quest reveal that her investigation of ontological mystery—the Tristero as a parallel, sacred presence, impinging onto this world in discernible clues—is likewise an epistemological conundrum insofar as the signs she thinks she is reading in the external world may be "woven" or "projected" by her own spiritual need. As the narrator describes in the first chapter, Oedipa is to have "all manner of revelations" about "what had remained yet had somehow, before this, stayed away" (10). She interprets her buffered sense of apartness and insulation in terms of a Remedios Varo painting she had seen years before. The central panel of a triptych titled *Bordando el Manto Terrestre* (embroidering the earth's mantle) depicts

> a number of frail girls with heart-shaped faces, huge eyes, spun-gold hair, prisoners in the top room of a circular tower, embroidering a kind of tapestry which spilled out the slit windows and into a void, seeking hopelessly to fill the void: for all the other buildings and creatures, all the waves, ships and forests of the earth were contained in this tapestry, and the tapestry was the world. (11)

The self-recognition occasioned by the painting makes her weep. As the existentialist-modernist language of the passage suggests—"seeking helplessly to fill the void"—the things of the earth that make meaning and which fill the void are crafted by ourselves. No outside, transcendent meaning rescues Oedipa (or us) from the solipsism implied in the meaning we make to fill the void because "the tapestry was the world."

This metaphor poses Pynchon's construction of the central problem of religious faith: do we believe in the transcendent because we intuit its real existence, or do we believe in something unseen simply because we need transcendent meaning, even if we must imagine it into being? Indeed, Oedipa comes to sense that if there is "magic, anonymous and malignant, visited on her from outside" (12)—perhaps thinking of the hooded figure, not described in the novel but existent in the painting, who stands above the embroidering girls in the tower, stirring a pot—it is keeping her where she is, overseeing her embroidery. The reader is left with the possibility that the signs of Tristero uncovered during the rest of the novel may actually be Oedipa's inventive embroidery as she seeks a religious escape to the "exitlessness" of everyday life—the possibility that "her discovery of what she was to label the Tristero System or often only The Tristero" might possibly "bring to an end her encapsulation in her tower" (31).

The planetarium projector is the other extended metaphor Pynchon uses to describe the ambiguity of whether Oedipa is discovering Tristero's ontologically independent existence or whether she is, through her paranoia, inventively connecting unrelated historical traces into an alternative to her existential exitlessness. The metaphor is first suggested by the director of the faux Jacobean tragedy she sees with her co-executor Metzger. After the play, Oedipa questions the director about the looks of "ritual reluctance" (55) characters give one another as they ponder the coming of the Tristero, a knowing silence finally broken when one character speaks the name "Trystero" (58). While Oedipa seeks an origin for the strange silence in the words of playwright Wharfinger's script—as a stage direction perhaps—the director suggests she should not be "so hung up with words." The play exists, he argues, not in the words but in his head:

> That's what I'm for. To give the spirit flesh. The words, who cares? They're rote noises to hold line bashes with, to get past the bone barriers around an actor's memory, right? But the reality is in *this* head. Mine. I'm the projector at the planetarium, all the closed little universe visible in the circle of that stage is coming out of my mouth, eyes, sometimes other orifices also. (62)

The allusion to Christ's incarnation—"To give the spirit flesh"—alerts us to the religious implications of the director's point.

The possibility that "reality" exists not in external texts and words but as mental projection is developed by Oedipa shortly after when she wonders if her relation to Pierce's will might be analogous to the director's relation to the text of *The Courier's Tragedy*—in which case, her job as "executrix" (1) means that

> it was part of her duty, wasn't it, to bestow life on what had persisted, to try to be what Driblette was, the dark machine in the center of the planetarium, to bring the estate into pulsing stelliferous Meaning, all in a soaring dome around her? (64)

Oedipa writes the words "*Shall I project a world?*" in her notebook—beneath the Tristero sign of the muted post horn copied from a bathroom stall wall—musing, "If not project then at least flash some arrow on the dome to skitter among constellations and trace out your Dragon, Whale, Southern Cross. Anything might help" (64–65). As with the embroidery in the tower, the metaphor of the planetarium projector suggests that whatever signs of the historical Tristero Oedipa might find would be lifeless until she brought them together, making "Meaning" out of them. The reference to constellations gives us a clue to how this process works: the actual stars are real, but the constellations that "connect the dots" are shapes imagined by humans, with geographically and culturally distinct communities imagining different shapes, names, and stories. Our invitation to imagine religious meaning-making as a kind of mythic projection is sealed by the final naming of one such constellation, the Southern Cross. The possibility that the "revelations" in the rest of the novel are largely Oedipa's inventive constellation-tracing is reiterated when her search for clues is glossed as "this, what you might have to call, growing obsession, with 'bringing something of herself'—even if that something was just her presence—to the scatter of business interests that had survived Inverarity. She would give them order, she would create constellations" (72). The distinct possibility rendered here is that whatever meaning she discovers in the Tristero may be "just her presence" after all, a constellation ordered and brought to life by her mind alone.

Having established this ambiguity early, the novel sustains it throughout, pointedly refusing to show us the final revelation wherein a Tristero representative might finally reveal himself in the flesh to bid for Pierce's stamp collection in the "crying" (that is, auctioneering) of Lot 49. Oedipa confronts the paradox of faith near the end of the novel, when one character suggests she may be being played in a "hoax," a possibility that "had occurred to her" although she had "been steadfastly refusing to look at that possibility directly" (138). This prompts a final reverie in which she recognizes the "symmetrical four" possibilities that would explain the Tristero clues, because, she now must acknowledge, "Every access route to the Tristero could be traced also back to the Inverarity estate" (141, 140). The options are the following:

1. The historical Tristero is real and she has discovered in it "a secret richness . . . a network by which X number of Americans are truly communicating whilst reserving their lies, recitations of routine, arid betrayals of spiritual poverty, for the official government delivery system . . . a real alternative to the exitlessness, to the absence of surprise to life, that harrows the head of everybody American you know, and you too, sweetie."
2. She is "hallucinating" Tristero and the clues, projecting, as it were, the continuing existence of Tristero as a spiritual alternative.

3. Tristero isn't real and she is not hallucinating the clues, but rather "a plot has been mounted" against her directed gothically from beyond the grave by Pierce through his will.

4. She is "fantasying some such plot" constructed by Pierce, her paranoid construction of a constellation. (140–41)

As she examines the "symmetrical four," she realizes that "this, oh God, was the void" (141). The symmetricalness hinges on two axes: true external existence (Tristero or Pierce's plot) vs. paranoid projection (hallucinating Tristero, fantasizing the plot), but also on whether this is really about Tristero (Tristero or hallucinating it) or whether this is all about Pierce (Pierce's plot or fantasizing it).

As I show in the next three chapters, the problem of trying to read the world's or history's design tends to recur in contemporary American fiction interested in religion, and it is by virtue of the difficulty of reading sacred writing—the ambiguity of the clues, the only partially legible script, the mystery of the symbol—that a faith decision is permitted, or indeed necessitated. But I would like to suggest that Pynchon's critics, who tend to emphasize the indeterminacy and ambiguity of the novel (see, e.g., Eddins 89–91 for his brief review of this trend), have missed the fact that these "symmetrical four" possibilities are not actually equally probable, Oedipa's fears notwithstanding. In fact, the faith decision Oedipa must make is only based on the first possibility, and not between a real Tristero on the one hand and a plot, hallucination, or fantasy on the other. Rather, the faith option Oedipa faces is whether to believe that the historical traces of the Tristero, which are more or less reasonably verified by the novel, remain sealed in the past as incidents without intention toward her, or whether they bespeak an active alternative to the exitlessness of her life, a conspiracy of underground communication in the historical present to which she might one day belong.

The Quest for the Historical Tristero

> If there is something comforting—religious, if you want—about paranoia, there is still also anti-paranoia, where nothing is connected to anything, a condition not many of us can bear for long.
>
> Thomas Pynchon, *Gravity's Rainbow*

Intriguingly—and importantly, I shall shortly argue—confirmation of Tristero's historical existence comes via the two experts who remain available to Oedipa at the end of the novel, even after her realization that "they are stripping away, one by one, my men" (126), including her husband, her psychiatrist, her lover, and the director of the play. Emory Bortz, the Renaissance drama expert who edited an edition of *The Courier's Tragedy*, and Genghis Cohen, the philatelist employed to assess the value of Pierce's stamp collection, are still offering expert advice on the historical traces of the Tristero to Oedipa by the novel's end. These two confirm the external presence of Tristero within history, thus obviating the possibilities that Oedipa is hallucinating it or fantasizing Pierce's plot (options 2 and 4). Bortz confirms that the line containing the word "Tristero" during the performance of *The Courier's Tragedy* that Oedipa sees exists only in a "pornographic" and parodic edition of the play housed in (intriguingly, for my argument) "the Vatican library" (125, 124). Through textual references in various historical documents, Oedipa and Bortz are able to piece together a history of the Tristero, seemingly begun by Hernando Joaquín de Tristero y Calavera in 1577, who claimed to be a "rightful heir" to the "Thurn and Taxis monopoly" (131–32) of postal service in Europe. (The latter was an actual postal service co-opted by emerging nation-states in Europe.) Tristero and the movement he began think of themselves as "The Disinherited," and take "disinheritance" to be their "constant theme" (132). Similarly, Cohen confirms that some unusual stamps—"forgeries" containing hidden signs suggesting Tristero's struggle with official postal systems (145)—predate Pierce's collection, as does other manuscript evidence suggesting an awareness of Tristero's struggles (142–44).

Option 3—that Pierce has set up a plot against Oedipa to make her believe in a fake Tristero—is thus the only plausible alternative, but the plot would have to be too far-reaching to be really probable. It would require, for instance, the participation of both Bortz and Cohen, actively deceiving Oedipa according to Pierce's will. Pynchon carefully plants the suggestion that this is possible for Bortz, because he now teaches at San Narciso College, which, Oedipa realizes, was partly funded by donations from her late husband (140). But while it is hypothetically possible that Bortz has somehow been "bought" by Pierce as part of an elaborate plot, it is difficult to see how that deception could include the retroactive fabrication of the historical clues about Tristero, which would have to include manuscript forgeries that somehow made their way into the Vatican library, microfilm of which Oedipa sees and which are the basis of an alternative non-Bortz edition of Wharfinger's play published in New York, outside of Pierce's geographical sphere of influence (124, 127). The probability of the plot option becomes worse when we come to Cohen, "the most eminent philatelist in the L.A. area" but who, Pynchon also carefully suggests, can be linked back to Pierce because he is retained "on instructions in the will" (75). Cohen independently confirms the historical existence of the Tristero, as well as the "forged" stamps they have created (142–45). (That is, the forgeries were not created by Pierce in order to fool Oedipa, but by the historical Tristero itself in order to resist official postal services.)

The plot possibility is rendered even less plausible by the novel's extensive discussion of the physical evidence attesting to a historical Tristero predating Pierce—the preexisting 1893, 1934, 1947, 1954, 1958 (144), and 1940 (77) stamps, an "outdated" stamp catalogue, and a 1865 article discussing internal Tristero divisions (142), but also the seventeenth-century Wharfinger parody housed in the Vatican library (124), Wharfinger's own historical notes that source his mention of Tristero in a prior account by Diocletian Blobb, whose manuscript is in Bortz's collection and which Oedipa also reads (129–130), and other clues: "obscure philatelic journals furnished her by Genghis Cohen, an ambiguous footnote in Motley's *Rise of the Dutch Republic*, an 80-year-old pamphlet on the roots of modern anarchism, a book of sermons by Blobb's brother Augustine" (130–31). Might these physical texts, many of which Oedipa sees and which purport to be prior to Pierce, nonetheless be part of Pierce's hoax as well? It is hypothetically possible. But this reading of the novel is unsatisfying, because *The Crying of Lot 49* does not invite us to doubt the physical evidence that (in its fictional universe) is said to actually exist. For a plot in which everything is a hoax on the protagonist to work, there has to be a big final reveal, à la *The Truman Show*, or at least significant hints that the archival evidence presented along the way is a modern (as opposed to old) forgery—without such a reveal or hints, the (unrecognized) hoax is on the reader as well. The simpler, more probable explanation is that these are actual historical traces of a historical Tristero (within the novel's fictional universe, of course) rather than the more convoluted idea that Pierce's hoax includes forging Early Modern publications *and* play editions, stamp pamphlets *and* stamps dating back to 1893, and locating actual experts—experts in both their respective areas of Renaissance drama / philately *and* deception—who can act to play along. My reading acknowledges and preserves the hypothetical possibility of a hoax, hallucination, or fantasizing, but it sees one interpretation as being considerably more likely to be the case. Beyond the initial hints that Bortz and Cohen may be tied to Pierce's estate, the novel gives no support to the idea that the physical, historical evidence of Tristero is part of such a grand deception.

If it is improbable that a plot has been constructed against Oedipa by Pierce's estate, then while the four possibilities might be "symmetrical" schematically (in terms of internal/external and historical/contemporary), they are asymmetrically probable. In fact, only one possibility is probable: the actual historical existence of Tristero. Its existence seems confirmed by Oedipa herself one night as she wanders the streets of San Francisco, geographically outside the range of Pierce's estate. She confirms the historical trace through multiple sightings of the muted horn but also seeing W.A.S.T.E. (We Await Silent Tristero's Empire) in action (88–101) and discovering that people have continuing relation to that trace; they derive (some kind of) meaning and community out of it. That this evidence itself could be hallucination or fantasizing is undercut by the fact that Bortz and Cohen attest to Tristero's historical existence. (In other words, these two options are not compatible with Bortz's and Cohen's external evidence, even if they are part of a plot, while the plot option is not compatible with Oedipa's San Francisco sightings, even if she is hallucinating or fantasizing.) Tristero's historically verified existence is thus the real object for Oedipa's faith decision: can she, and should she, believe that its historical design continues into the present, perhaps signaled by the various underground groups who are communicating via the W.A.S.T.E. system named after Tristero? The novel's question is not whether Tristero really exists, but whether the spirit of the Tristero conspiracy—the living intentionality of the disinherited—is a current existential possibility for Oedipa. What would be "compensation for loss of the Word" is this continued existence into the present of an entity that might "bend to her alone . . . and begin to speak words she never wanted to hear" (40), and which she might join as another alienated American seeking an alternative to the exitlessness of her life. Oedipa is frightened by Tristero's existence, but more important, she desires it.

Oedipa independently confirms through her walk the continued existence of W.A.S.T.E., even if it is used by people who don't know its origin or full history, or who Tristero really was. Unlike Oedipa, most W.A.S.T.E. users are not consulting specialists and looking at old manuscripts in order to get to the origin of the mystery that is at the center of their daily lives. And this is finally what confirms Tristero as an analog for religion, but also for Christianity more narrowly in *The Crying of Lot 49*. To be sure, as Dwight Eddins notes, even the false versions of Tristero would end up having religious implications: "A hoax set up to resemble an elaborate conspiracy is in itself an elaborate conspiracy; and insofar as it aims to control the whole sense of reality of its victims, it is gnostic in design" (93)—thus, a hoax about Tristero would have "religious significance not dependent upon . . . Tristero's autonomous existence" (93). But I am arguing that once we see how *The Crying of Lot 49* prefers one of the symmetrical options it hypothesizes, the religious references of the novel begin to refer more specifically to the question of how reasonably verifiable historical events or personages can be brought into living relation for contemporary lives through faith.

Pointedly, Oedipa is first led to one of her experts—Emory Bortz, on Jacobean drama—through her interest in the manuscript variations in Wharfinger's *The Courier's Tragedy*. The line she hears during the performance mentioning "Trystero" has been changed in Bortz's edition (81). When she finally meets Bortz, her question to him to learn "something about the historical Wharfinger" is met with derision by one of his graduate students, who compares her quest to the search for "The historical Shakespeare . . . . The historical Marx. The historical Jesus" (124). That Oedipa's quest to discover the origin of Tristero (her reason for asking about the playwright) is compared to the search for the "historical Jesus" supports this religious reading of Pynchon's novel, but also places Oedipa in a fascinating distinction from the conservative Christian faith practices that, I am arguing in this book, would shortly remake the nation in a social and political movement that Pynchon is partly intuiting in his 1966 novel.

Christianity has struggled for almost two centuries with two emergent bodies of knowledge that have challenged some core assumptions. The first is the science of evolution, which I discuss in chapters 6 and 7. The second is the historical critical method developed largely in the nineteenth century to examine the historical authorship, editing, and transmission of the Bible. These are two modern modes of expert authority that have challenged, on the one hand, the idea of the young earth and God's direct creation of human and other species, and on the other, the idea that the Bible is a divinely inspired or dictated document with a coherent theology that is relatively unmediated by culture, history, or a tradition of editing. Fundamentalist Christianity—as opposed to other Christian traditions of belief and practice—is marked by its rejection of these two projects of scientific and historical expertise within modernity. Fundamentalist resistance to these modes of modern expertise sometimes take the form of what we might call mere "premodern" refusal of facts and evidence. But, more interestingly for this literary history of how American fiction has responded to the conservative Christian resurgence in the contemporary period, fundamentalist resistance to these modes of modern expertise also takes postmodern forms, as I discuss in the forthcoming chapters, thus allying the conservative religious resurgence with the very tendencies sometimes displayed in contemporary "secular" American literature. For now, it is enough to note that Pynchon evokes one of these modes of modern expertise, the search for the historical Jesus, to which the reader of *The Crying of Lot 49* is invited to compare Oedipa's search for the historical Tristero.

It is useful to briefly review this tradition of scholarship because it sheds light on the ways that Oedipa's religious quest is very like, and at other times very dissimilar to, the conservative Christian resurgence that I am arguing Pynchon partially anticipates in this mid-1960s novel. Albert Schweitzer's 1906 *The Quest for the Historical Jesus* was an important early culmination of the historical-critical method of New Testament studies and the quest for the historical Jesus. As we saw in chapter 4, Francis Schaeffer identified this book for its pernicious effects. The quest itself was very much active in the 1960s as Pynchon was writing his novel, having been invigorated by the 1945 discovery of the Nag Hammadi library of Gnostic texts, including noncanonical gospels, and the 1956 excavation of the Dead Sea Scrolls, texts of an ancient Jewish community contemporaneous with Jesus. The "quest for the historical Jesus" uses the historical-critical method of New Testament scholarship to try to determine what the historical Jesus more probably said and did, as opposed to later theological traditions about who he was and what we should believe about him. The historical method views the Gospels as valid but complicated sources of historical information, even though they are not eyewitness accounts (they are written documents based on earlier oral traditions) and even though they were written by early followers with specific theological views. The basis for historical Jesus scholarship is an understanding of manuscript evidence—traditions, transmissions, editings, variations, and so on—that rely on expert judgments about which manuscripts are more likely to preserve an author's original words. This scholarship of ancient manuscript evidence (not dissimilar to Bortz's) is laid out in Bruce Metzger's *The Text of the New Testament: Its Transmission, Corruption, and Restoration*, the first of several editions of this famous undergraduate textbook published by Oxford in 1964, just as Pynchon was writing his novel. As Metzger summarizes the principles by which scholars adjudicate manuscript variations (of the kind Oedipa is investigating), manuscript traditions can be considered better (that is, closer to what the original author more probably wrote) when: they are earlier; they are independent of one another; they preserve "the more difficult reading" (that is, for the scribe, "who would be tempted to make an emendation" of theologically awkward material); they are shorter (because a scribe would generally be more likely to add rather than delete); they display "verbal dissidence" insofar as they appear unharmonized (when making Old Testament quotations, for instance); and they appear in a "less refined grammatical form or less elegant lexical expression" (because a scribe editing for style would attempt to "make a smooth text" when copying) (209–11). The textual scholar should apply these principles with a sense of context and the author's style, not mechanically, Metzger counsels (210). The hint that such questions of biblical textual authority and historical investigation are on Pynchon's mind shows up in his naming

Oedipa's co-executor after the brilliant young New Testament scholar at the beginning of a long and productive career: Metzger.

We can give an example of the second principle (of the independence of sources) through reference to *The Crying of Lot 49*, where it is intriguingly used not to locate the "historical Jesus" but instead the historical Tristero. Oedipa's information, we have seen, comes from two primary sources: Wharfinger's play (or rather the parodic Schurvamite edition of it [127–28]), which attests to the early historical existence of Tristero, and the Tristero-horn stamps from Pierce's collection. They are in turn interpreted for her by two experts: Bortz and Cohen, the former drawing on older manuscripts and the latter, other experts. These scholars are independent of one another—neither has influenced the other—and Oedipa herself verifies the muted post-horn and the existence of W.A.S.T.E. on her nighttime walk through San Francisco. These may not be three independent attestations of Tristero, however, because Oedipa may be hallucinating Tristero's existence or fantasizing Pierce's plot (options 2 and 4). Bortz and Cohen may not be independent because both might be tied back to Pierce's estate (option 3). Thus, as sources of knowledge about the historical Tristero, each is possibly compromised but not useless when combined with the other two historical sources: together, they make it more probable that the historical Tristero did exist, and that option 1 is actually true.

Thus when it is suggested to Oedipa that she "Write down what you can't deny. Your hard intelligence. But then write down what you've only speculated, assumed. See what you've got" (138), the method of disentangling assumptions and theological speculation from "hard intelligence" is reminiscent of the historical-critical method used by New Testament scholars. As examined in chapter 1, Oscar Zeta Acosta's confrontation with his own Baptist faith is broken when he undertakes a "comparative study of the Synoptic Gospels" in which he looks for, among other things, the "inconsistent" (*Autobiography* 133). Inconsistency doesn't necessarily mean something didn't happen, however. While multiple independent attestation increases the historical probability of a saying or event, so too can inconsistency if that textual variant would have caused theological difficulty for an early proto-Christian community passing that tradition down.

Thus, in the principle of multiple attestation, scholars look for multiple independent sources for Jesus's words and actions. Acosta's "Synoptic Gospels" are called such because Mark, Luke, and Matthew share many stories and traditions, often word for word; by contrast, the Gospel of John is understood to be a later independent tradition. Where the three synoptic gospels share stories, Mark is understood to be the probable origin—in other words, the writers of Luke and Matthew had access to Mark, probably a written version. Conversely, Luke has stories that appear nowhere else, and as these are not eyewitness accounts, scholars have named "L" as the oral tradition source of this material; "M" is the oral tradition source for some of Matthew's unique stories. One of the early discoveries of the historical method was that occasionally Matthew and Luke shared stories that are not found in Mark; contemporary scholarship posits the existence of a hypothetical source, probably written, called "Q," which we don't have a copy of, consisting mostly of saying of Jesus, that must have been used as a source for Matthew and Luke, but not Mark or John. The earliest Christian writer was Paul in his letters, who does not seem to have had access to any of these written gospels (since he never quotes from them or refers much to the words and deeds of Jesus). Other early traditions are of value to Bible scholars, such as some of the Nag Hammadi material—particularly the noncanonical Gospel of Thomas—which may include other historical and relatively early texts, and non-Christian sources, such as writings by the first century CE Jewish historian Josephus, who attests to some events like Jesus's crucifixion. Thus, the more Mark, M, L, Q, Paul, and John suggest the same story, the more likely it is to have actually happened, as opposed to its being in Mark and Luke alone (because the latter used Mark as a source text). Using criteria of multiple independent attestation as well as others, New Testament scholars today say that it is extremely probable that the basic events of Jesus's life—his baptism by John the Baptist and his execution by crucifixion by Pontius Pilate—actually happened. This basic outline is very well historically attested—notwithstanding New Atheist claims about "the highly questionable existence of Jesus" (Hitchens 114)[5]—making it vastly improbable (even though remotely hypothetically possible) that he was the creation of a later hoax. By contrast, the story of the woman caught in adultery being brought to Jesus for judgment, while edifying in many ways, is considered less likely to have really happened because it is contained only in the Gospel of John (7:53–8:11), and is not in that book's earliest manuscripts.[6]

I have used an analogous method to this historical criticism to suggest that the multiple attestations and early historical records suggest that the historical Tristero, like the "historical Jesus" mentioned in the novel, almost certainly did exist. Cohen's and Bortz's attestation obviates half of the symmetrical four possibilities, eliminating the "interior" axis in which Oedipa is either hallucinating Tristero or fantasizing Pierce's plot. Both confirm the externality of Tristero, as either historical or Pierce's plot: because both see the signs, they can't just be Oedipa's projections. When we combine Cohen's and Bortz's affirmation of the external with the fact that the (we then know) non-hallucinating, non-fantasizing Oedipa sees the various Tristero post signs in San Francisco and the W.A.S.T.E. system in action in areas that are not linked back to Pierce, these pieces of evidence together strongly suggest that the only option left is for the historical Tristero. Although critics have interpreted Oedipa's scheme of the symmetrical four as being equally possible, Pynchon gives enough evidence in the novel to reasonably conclude that one of the four options is considerably more likely. The consequence of this probability is that the faith decision that Oedipa faces in *The Crying of Lot 49* is not *whether* Tristero was, or *what* it was, but whether it continues to exist in the W.A.S.T.E. system of which she could possibly become a part. Oedipa's scholarly search for the historical Tristero—like the search for the historical Jesus to which the novel compares her quest—confirms its presence, but only in an inactivated way.[7] What Oedipa the fledgling scholar intuits rather than comprehends—but what the users of W.A.S.T.E. do seem to understand, even if they don't know about its origin—is that the network of the disinherited has to be brought into relation to the self in terms of everyday life. In this realm of religious experience Oedipa's research can only get her so far. What she is really seeking in her search against the exitlessness of everyday life is to bring the disinherited network into relation to her buffered self, to have faith in its continued intention toward her.

Oedipa Maas, Young Republican

> One side of American evangelicalism was becoming a movement of the disinherited.
>
> George M. Marsden, *Fundamentalism and American Culture*

My argument, then, is that *The Crying of Lot 49* names the religious situation in the United States c. 1966. In Oedipa's spiritual condition, understood to be shared by "many Americans," we see the insufficiency of the liberal civil religion consensus outlined by Bellah and Herberg in the 1950s and 1960s—the watered-down official national theology linked to civil rights. Pynchon locates in Oedipa the desire for a more direct and personally intentioned design in the world at the heart of our need for religious belief. For all its prescience about the religious energy and desires of his society, however, Pynchon's portrayal of the fledgling scholar studying old manuscript variations, while fitting for a metaphysical detective story, does not quite capture the shape of the religious resurgence that would overtake the nation in the next decades. In this last section of this chapter, I wish to argue for the sociological accuracy of Pynchon's portrayal of another part of this religious energy—that he grasped not only the disinherited and untapped religious energy of the nation, but also the way in which that energy was becoming attached to the conservative political reaction to the civil religion / civil rights consensus, a reaction that was termed at the time of Pynchon's writing to be the "paranoid tendency in American politics."

The phrase, of course, is Richard Hofstadter's famous shorthand diagnosis of the reactionary political formation that had crystallized in the Barry Goldwater campaign of 1964 against President Lyndon Johnson. I think it is useful to understand *The Crying of Lot 49* in the context of two important contemporaneous essays that in some sense portrayed an emerging political-religious tension in the nation: Bellah's famous 1967 essay on "Civil Religion" that I examine in chapter 1, and Hofstadter's "The Paranoid Tendency in American Politics," published in *Harper's Magazine* in November 1964 during the election. In the section that follows, I read Oedipa's disinherited search for religious meaning in terms of the "paranoid tendency" that she shares with Goldwater's followers, and the way in which the religious energy was already bending toward conservative social and political norms: when Oedipa declares "I'm a Young Republican" (59), we see the seeds of the religious-political alliance that would profoundly affect American society in the next decades.

The Goldwater movement exemplified a "style of mind" that Hofstadter called "the paranoid style simply because no other word adequately evokes the qualities of heated exaggeration, suspiciousness, and conspiratorial fantasy" (3). While its immediate predecessor was McCarthyism's anticommunism, Hofstadter recognizes a long American tradition of suspecting national subversion by Masons, Catholics, and others. Whatever the enemy, Hofstadter suggests that the paranoid style was a way of reading history in which the enemy was not caught in history, but was its agent (32): it found "a 'vast' or 'gigantic' conspiracy as *the motive force* in historical events. History *is* a conspiracy, set in motion by demonic forces of almost transcendent power, and what is felt to be needed to defeat it is not the usual methods of political give-and-take, but an all-out crusade" (29). Whereas prior eruptions of the paranoid style envisioned an outside enemy, its manifestation in postwar anticommunism of the McCarthy and Goldwater eras held that the enemy was already in control of parts of the government. Hence, Hofstadter suggests by citing Daniel Bell, the modern Right "feels dispossessed: America has been largely taken away from them and their kind, though they are determined to try to repossess it and to prevent the final destructive act of subversion" (23). This communist plot is, as Masonry was believed to be in the previous century, "a standing conspiracy against republican government. . . . constituting a separate system of loyalty, a separate imperium within the framework of American and state governments, inconsistent with loyalty to them" (16).

Interestingly, the paranoid style produces a mode of reading in which there are no accidents or errors by American leaders. Rather, errors in geopolitical calculation or a lack of military strength is seen as intentional subversion under orders from the Kremlin (27). The "higher paranoid scholarship" is "nothing if not coherent—in fact, the paranoid mentality is far more coherent than the real world, since it leaves no room for mistakes, failures, or ambiguities. It is, if not wholly rational, at least intensely rationalistic" (36). And while this movement may occasionally manufacture "facts," Hofstadter suggests, "What distinguishes the paranoid style is not . . . the absence of verifiable facts . . . but rather the curious leap in imagination that is always made at some critical point in the recital of events" (37).

Paranoia, the suspicion of conspiracy, the motivated reading of historical facts, the "leap in imagination," the hidden agent of history, the subversive and alternate system of loyalty, the scholarship of coherence, the feeling of dispossession—all of these elements of the paranoid style are richly echoed in Oedipa's gradual revealing of the Tristero. The key difference, of course, is that the paranoia of Goldwater's followers was the suspicion by previous insiders that their country has been taken away in a process of subversion and dispossession, and their politics was aimed at reestablishing their proper inheritance. *The Crying of Lot 49* remaps this experience of dispossession and paranoia, such that it is Tristero, the conspiratorial outsider group, that is the true inheritor of the nation that has been taken away from them; for this reason, the back mythology of the Tristero as the "disinherited" uncovered by Bortz is crucial. That is why it is important to recognize Oedipa's attraction to the group that she gradually uncovers: I agree with Mendelson's assertion of her desire for Tristero to exist, rather than Eddins, who sees Tristero in terms of a demonic "cabalistic gnosticism" (12) that seeks oppressive control over history and nature. Indeed, near the end of the novel Oedipa muses that "Perhaps she'd be hounded someday as far as joining Tristero itself, if it existed, in its twilight, its aloofness, its waiting" (150).

Being "hounded" by that which one ultimately religiously desires might seem like an odd metaphor, but it echoes the central image in Francis Thompson's 1893 poem "The Hound of Heaven." A more contemporary literary parallel to the simultaneity of religious desire as subject and object—that is, running from the promise of fulfillment that one desires—and one more obviously patterned on evangelical culture, comes in Dorothy Allison's account of being saved in *Bastard Out of Carolina* (1993). Bone, the child narrator in Greenville, South Carolina, begins to get religion—"I gave myself over to the mystery of Jesus' blood, reading the Bible at the kitchen table after dinner and going to the Wednesday-night services for young people" (146)—and tries to proselytize to her uncle Earle. As Bone ultimately learns, Earle understands religious desire is best felt as an outsider: as he puts it, recalling the Sunday School pictures of his youth, "Jesus got the lost one in his arms. Jesus wants you, each and every one of you. He'll climb mountains, walk the hot sands, brave the night winds, search among the many for the one not found. And you are never so valuable as when you stand outside the fold, the one God wants" (147–48). He continues, "I like it that they want me, Catholics and Baptists and Church of Gods and Methodists and Seventh-Day Adventists, all of them hungry for my dirty white hide, my pitiful human soul. Hell! None of them would give two drops of piss for me if I was already part of their saggy-assed congregations" (148). Bone shares the evangelical affect his language suggests: "What I really like was how he talked about Jesus. . . . He talked about Jesus like a man dying for need of him, but too stubborn to sit down to the meal spread within reach. . . . The hunger, the lust, and the yearning were palpable. I understood that hunger as I understood nothing else, though I could not tell if what I truly hungered for was God or love or absolution" (148). Bone imagines her uncle, like Thompson's speaker, "as if every muscle in his body was fighting off God" (149), and she arrives at her own method of staying in the liminal space, the lost lamb who doesn't want to be found quite yet: "I came close to being saved about fourteen times—fourteen Sundays in fourteen different Baptist churches" (151). She is transfixed by "that moment of sitting on the line between salvation and damnation with the preacher and the old women pulling bodily at my poor darkened soul. I wanted that moment to go on forever" (151). The adolescent narrator's love of gospel music is betrayed, however, when she realizes how it is embedded in the Southern practices of Christian segregation (170). She eventually turns her back on religion, declining its enduring appeal like another biographically inflected fictional Southerner, Cormac McCarthy's Suttree, who, witnessing a baptism scene at a river, is also invited to be baptized and to join the service at a "Gospel tent" meeting in the evening: "But Suttree knew the river well already and he turned his back to these malingerers and went on" (125). My point in invoking *Bastard Out of Carolina* and *Suttree* is that being outside the religious community can be, nonetheless, a site of strong religious desire, even when, as with Oedipa, that desire is leavened with fear.

Thus, unlike the Goldwater "New Right" that, in a paranoid style, sought to find and eliminate a subversive enemy, Oedipa's paranoid style is aimed at finding (and maybe joining) this pre-political conspiratorial group of the dispossessed. Whereas for Hofstadter the Goldwater movement aimed to identify and eliminate the conspiracy, for Pynchon the Goldwater movement *is* the conspiracy. Intriguingly, it is Genghis Cohen, the stamp authority, who wears a Goldwater sweatshirt (76), and he also shows up to the auction at the end of the novel. The Goldwater-supporting Cohen is a seeker, like Oedipa the "Young Republican."

One of the best accounts of *The Crying of Lot 49*'s political and sociological portrait is Casey Shoop's "Thomas Pynchon, Postmodernism, and the Rise of the New Right in California." Shoop reads the novel in terms of its portrait of the "southern Californians" Oedipa realizes she knows little about and of how the 1966 election of Ronald Reagan as California governor heralded the rise of the New Right. The 1964 Goldwater presidential campaign was a "dress rehearsal" for the rise of the New Right and its challenge to the Northeastern, liberal Rockefeller Republican establishment, Shoop says (59). Pynchon has his eye on this transformation, as his political allusions suggest: "Pynchon's choice of a moderate Young Republican from a prior generation is thus highly motivated, for it emphasizes the degree of disorientation and uncertainty experienced in this transition from the fifties to the sixties" (68). This disorientation is highlighted by Oedipa's encounter with Berkeley leftist radicalism (66), but also by the political geography of discovering the southern California conservativism that was the emergent political power base of the Goldwater New Right. Thus, says Shoop, the "set piece for postmodern criticism" (69) wherein Oedipa looks down on the San Narciso suburb (cited above), often read in terms of the paranoid projection of meaning onto randomness, can better be understood via the novel's remark that Oedipa "knew even less about radios than about Southern Californians" (14). It is a description of actual emergent political geography: that Southern California, and the Southwest more generally, would become an incubator for the political New Right's challenge to northeastern Republicanism in the 1960s (Shoop 69–70).

Shoop mentions Goldwater, but focuses on the rise of Governor and then President Reagan, and the political realignment occasioned by the rise of the New Right. What he does not mention is the co-emergence within the New Right of the fundamentalist and conservative evangelical Christian resurgence that likewise energized this political alliance, beginning in the 1960s but especially coming to power in the 1970s and later. My contribution to Pynchon scholarship, then, is to synthesize Shoop's excellent sociopolitical analysis of the novel with the longstanding attention to the religious sensibilities of *The Crying of Lot 49* by suggesting that it is precisely this conservative religious energy and its political shape that is being prophesized in the novel. Indeed, by 1965 Hofstadter had already realized that he had underestimated the importance of Christian fundamentalism in his previous analyses of the "pseudo-conservatism" of the McCarthy and Goldwater eras.[8] It was "an element whose importance has become increasingly evident in the past decade" (67); indeed, the "re-emergence of fundamentalism in politics . . . is a notable development of the past fifteen years" (72). The conservative Christian alliance of the contemporary period was partly enabled by the Cold War: whereas Baptists were generally hostile to Father Coughlin in the 1930s, they generally supported the lay Catholic McCarthy, suggesting that anticommunism helped fundamentalists abandon their traditional anti-Catholicism "in order to take part in right-wing ecumenical anti-Communism" (70). Hofstadter further noted, "Fundamentalist leaders play a part in right-wing organizations far out of proportion to the strength of fundamentalism in the population at large" (74), and, intriguingly for Shoop's thesis, remarks that "southern California" has a larger portion of fundamentalists than many other areas (76). What Hofstadter in 1965 was in the process of recognizing was the brewing religious energy on the cusp of a large resurgence that was difficult for secular observers to see: "Fundamentalist-evangelical America was, in fact, so long divided or quiescent as a political force that many intellectuals have forgotten that it still exists" (79). In Goldwater's time, that energy's animus was Cold War anticommunism as well as hostility to the civil rights movement and federal intervention into Southern segregation—Goldwater had a "Southern strategy," noted Hofstadter (99), one later advanced by Nixon and then perfected with Reagan's electoral run in 1980. (What would be added to the mix in the 1970s was the potent force of gender and sexual politics with *Roe v. Wade* and the Equal Rights Amendment.)

Pynchon's evocation of the Goldwater candidacy and his portrayal of Oedipa as a confused "Young Republican" looking for spiritual answers in southern California is a fascinating snapshot of a nation in religious transition. As Daniel K. Williams suggests in *God's Own Party: The Making of the Christian Right*, the Christian resurgence's beginning was not exclusively and necessarily Republican—especially given the fact that the traditional Bible Belt was mostly composed of white Southern Democrats. The rise of the Religious Right was intertwined with the realignment of Southern politics in the context of the civil rights movement, and Goldwater's candidacy was a watershed in this transition, as Williams explains,

> fundamentalists who thought that Washington had abandoned American values considered Barry Goldwater a godsend. In a Republican Party that was still heavily influenced by northeastern business interests

and moderate liberals, Goldwater's straight-shooting conservative rhetoric, southwestern heritage, virulent anticommunism, and hostility to
almost all federal social spending put him on the far right of the nation's
political spectrum. For many young Republicans, including the campus
activists in the staunchly conservative Young Americans for Freedom,
that was exactly what they wanted. Goldwater was especially popular
among conservative activists in southern California, a center for the
Sunbelt conservatism that later became the dominant political ideology
in the Republican Party. (72)

As the geography here suggests, realignment in the South took place by way
of a struggle between the Northeast and Oedipa's and Goldwater's territory
of the Southwest. The "Young Americans for Freedom" Williams mentions
is the "YAF" at Berkeley mentioned in the novel (83), part of young conservatives' reaction to the counterculture movement of the 1960s. Another
Southern California Goldwater supporter was Tim LaHaye, who moved to
San Diego in 1956 after his training at Bob Jones University (Williams 73);
in those early days before *Faith of Our Founding Fathers* and the *Left Behind*
series, LaHaye gave talks in favor of Goldwater (Williams 73) at local John
Birch Society chapters, a right-wing political cause on Pynchon's radar (36)
that widely supported the candidate (Hofstadter 111). The Southern Californian LaHaye financially and theologically supported the nascent Institute
for Creation Research when Henry Morris opened it near San Diego in
1972. Morris later "set up the first museum of creation and earth history"
in 1977 (Harding 218, 215). LaHaye and Morris were Southern by training,
both associates of Falwell, but Southern California was the location of their
ministries.

While neither Goldwater nor Reagan were born-again Christians, they
spoke the language and articulated the values of the conservative Christian
resurgence in ways that marked the growing integration of the Christian
Right and the Republican Party. *The Crying of Lot 49* begins to name this
network of religious faith and conservative politics that came to fruition in
the decades following the novel's 1966 publication, as well as its particular geography in the Southwest. In Oedipa's search for Tristero, Pynchon
prophesizes the religious restlessness and desire of the mid-1960s for this
disinherited, alienated Young Republican, placing our human will to believe
into a specific historical locale that was about to erupt in a historically particular way with lasting effects.

If Pynchon diagnoses this not yet sufficiently answered midcentury conservative religious desire, my argument has been that Oedipa's method as a

religious seeker—tracking down ancient manuscript variations, consulting the relevant experts—was not proleptic of the interpretive habits of most resurgent Christians. And yet, Pynchon's invocation of the role of expert authority in answering religious questions was directly relevant to the shape and methods of the resurgence that would soon come into formation—and, indeed, to the shape and methods of the postmodern that Pynchon's work is sometimes said to herald. As Eddins (2–4) and McClure (*Partial* 27–28) note, Brian McHale's scheme for differentiating postmodernist from modernist fiction places *The Crying of Lot 49* as a liminal text marking Pynchon's transition from one "dominant" to another. McHale argues that in the course of their careers, an influential, transitional set of writers showed the move from the modernist dominant to the postmodernist dominant, including Samuel Beckett, Alain Robbe-Grillet, Carlos Fuentes, Vladimir Nabokov, Robert Coover, and Pynchon. As he describes, epistemological questions of narratorial reliability, tale transmission, multiple perspectives, withheld evidence, and limitation tend to characterize modernist fiction (9–10), while ontological questions of the existence of the world, or other worlds, of the self and of other selves tend to characterize the postmodernist dominant (10)—keeping in mind the fact that both sets of questions are present in both dominants. As he explains,

> intractable epistemological uncertainty becomes at a certain point ontological plurality or instability: push epistemological questions far enough and they "tip over" into ontological questions. By the same token, push ontological questions far enough and they tip over into epistemological questions—the sequence is not linear and unidirectional, but bidirectional and reversible. (11)

McHale places *Crying* well on the way from the epistemological to the ontological, but not quite there. He compares Pynchon's novel to Henry James's *The Turn of the Screw*, writing of the two heroines' epistemological quandaries that

> the difference between *The Turn of the Screw* and *Lot 49*—and it is a crucial difference—is, of course, that James's governess is herself unaware of the alternatives, believing in the "ghostly" explanation from the outset; the teetering between alternatives goes on "above her head," a problem for students of literature but not for her. Whereas Oedipa is only too aware of her alternatives. Once a student of literature herself, she understands the ambiguity of her situation as clearly as her readers do. In this respect, as in others, she is an exemplary late-modernist heroine. (24)

But McHale bases this reading on the idea that, as with James's novel, "there is finally no way to decide between the alternatives" because the "evidence is so finely balanced that one hesitates between the epistemological and the ontological lines of explanation, without finally resolving the hesitation" (24). That is, McHale sees, of the four "symmetrical options" Oedipa analyzes, that the first three are epistemological in nature and that the last one—that Tristero really exists—is the single ontological one, but that the text refuses to privilege one of these options. Thus, for McHale, the novel pauses at the edge of the postmodern without tipping over into it.

I think McHale is mistaken in taking the novel's own description of the hypothetical, symmetrical four at face value because, as I have argued, the novel clearly tilts in favor of the fourth, ontological possibility: that, Oedipa's apparent equivalence of the four options notwithstanding, Tristero—the fantastic, otherworldly presence that even in "secular" form (136) promises to answer Oedipa's religious desire—has most probably historically existed and that the primary question the novel poses is not whether Tristero existed, but what that historical existence means for religious desires and communities in the present. Nonetheless, McHale's delineation of the way in which epistemological indeterminacies can be milestones on the path to an ontological pluralism in postmodernism is suggestive of the intersection between postmodernism and the conservative Christian resurgence.[9]

I would like to argue that the resurgence manifested as a kind of epistemological and ontological pluralism: a Christian postmodernism in which other ways of knowing circulated in a complex network that could legitimately be considered an ontologically different sphere—other than our official secular one—that was in communication with the sacred. This may be the meaning, finally, of the revelation that Oedipa is about to witness at the end of the novel as she waits with Cohen for "the crying of Lot 49"—that is, the auctioning of Pierce's stamp collection, including its Tristero forgeries, which seems to have attracted a mysterious bidder. When the auctioneer is described as "spread[ing] his arms in a gesture that seemed to belong to the priesthood of some remote culture; perhaps to a descending angel" (152), Pynchon's biblical allusion is complete: the crying of Lot 49 by a descending angel looks much like the descent of the Holy Spirit to the waiting apostles 49 days after Easter during the Pentecost. As Mendelson notes, "the novel ends with Oedipa waiting, with the 'true' nature of the Trystero never established: a manifestation of the sacred can only be believed in; it can never be proved beyond doubt" (135), a lingering ambiguity Mendelson links to Oedipa's doubt that she may be hallucinating or fantasizing. But if I am correct in my reading that the novel has reasonably demonstrated that Oedipa is doing neither of these things, the question becomes, rather, whether she might be about to witness a new indwelling of the Holy Spirit, as Pynchon's allusion invites us to think. Could Oedipa, "hounded," be about to have a kind of religious experience during which, infused with a new spirit, she enters into the religious community and mysteries of the elect—an elect that, until now, has seen itself as disinherited from the nation it should rightfully possess?

We might imagine an ending to *The Crying of Lot 49* in which Oedipa discovers and joins Tristero; a Tristero that has decided, in fact, to forego its operational secrecy and separation and to assert its rightful claims as the true inheritor of the nation not through sabotage or subterfuge, but by encouraging its members to take what is rightfully theirs by joining the political process and wielding influence over the Republican Party, which already seems to have members (in Oedipa and Cohen) who are looking for a way out of the exitlessness and lack of transcendent meaning in everyday American life. Their search is for an exit to her sense of what both Pynchon and Taylor call "buffering," an exit that might lead to an awareness of the other, sacred world that lies alongside our own, the possible existence of which had been broached earlier with Oedipa's rumination, "Behind the hieroglyphic streets there would either be a transcendent meaning, or only the earth" (150). The desire for transcendent meaning, perhaps inscribed in the sacred writing of the streets themselves, makes obvious that Oedipa seeks a way out of her secular predicament.

My argument is not that Pynchon's Tristero is a metaphor for the conservative Christian resurgence that had not yet happened, with Pynchon a supernatural seer able to foretell the future. Rather, it is that *The Crying of Lot 49* locates a nascent intersection of religious desire and political geography that would, in the next decade, begin to coalesce through specific networks and articulate specific policy demands. It is at that intersection, finally, that I think it most useful to consider the particular epistemological uncertainty and ontological pluralism known as the postmodern emerging. As we shall see in the next three chapters, what I would like to call the Christian postmodern has emerged on the terrain of epistemological uncertainty but also as a kind of ontological pluralism in which the conservative Christian resurgence would consider itself to be, in effect, to use the novel's definition of a miracle, "another's world's intrusion into this one" (97). The resurgence understood itself to be organizing its politics as a reflection of sacred demands: that is, to reorder American society to reflect transcendent truths that had been revealed through the Bible. It was a demand for the secular to be beaten back in favor of the sacred, which had been improperly displaced from American public society and politics. The sacred sphere had existed alongside the secular to which it now turned its attention through a series of church, academic, media, and publishing networks that cultivated a different sphere of Christian postmodernist scholarship in historiography, creationism, and the Bible. It was a parallel world, epistemologically and ontologically distinct from the mainstream America it claimed as its rightful inheritance.

CHAPTER 6

Science and Religion in Carl Sagan's *Contact*

> An atheist is someone who is certain that God does not exist, someone who has compelling evidence against the existence of God. I know of no such compelling evidence.
>
> Carl Sagan, interview with *U.S. Catholic*

One of the most important arenas of resurgent conservative Christian political engagement has been evolution, its most visible conflict with scientific authority. When President George W. Bush in 2005 suggested about evolution and its new rival Intelligent Design that "both sides ought to be properly taught . . . so people can understand what the debate is about" (quoted in Humes 245), he was reprising presidential candidate Ronald Reagan's preference, explained to a gathering of "some ten thousand" fundamentalist Christians in Dallas in 1980, that because evolution was "a scientific theory only," if it was going to be taught then "the biblical theory of creation" should be taught beside it (quoted in Webb 217). By the time President Bush recommended this seemingly even-handed approach to education, it had become part of the "God debates" of the opening years of the new millennium. Books by "New Atheists" like Richard Dawkins, Christopher Hitchens, Daniel Dennett, Sam Harris, and others charged religion with fomenting ignorance (especially on evolution, but with science in general) and violence, among other sins. Coming as they did after the 9/11 terrorist attacks, these writings' hostility to religion often looked like, or took the form of, a hostility to Islam more particularly. But in an American context, books with titles such as *The God Delusion* and *God Is Not Great: How Religion Poisons Everything* signaled a wider assault on cultural matters by newly militant atheists.

The mutual animosity and incomprehension was palpable. A telling example could be found in Richard Dawkins's documentary *The Root of All Evil?*, in which he interviews Ted Haggard, evangelical pastor of New Life Church in Colorado Springs and president of the National Association of Evangelicals, in 2006 just before he resigned after being outed by a gay prostitute who confessed to their crystal methamphetamine–fueled sex sessions. To Dawkins's incredulity, Haggard asserts that "some evolutionists" have contended that the human eye could not possibly have formed itself "by accident," thus resuscitating (as we shall see) William Paley's chief example of the argument for design in his 1802 *Natural Theology*. The documentary shows Dawkins's anger and Haggard's sad condescension as he describes the "intellectual arrogance" of which he says Dawkins's atheistic evolution is representative.[1]

Even to other, less theologically and politically conservative observers, Dawkins represented a new, overreaching atheistic attack on faith. Perhaps the response best known in literary critical circles was Terry Eagleton's conflation of Dawkins and Hitchens into "Ditchkins" (as we saw in chapter 3). Kenneth Miller, a Christian cell biologist who was an expert for evolution during the Dover Intelligent Design trial of 2005, contended, "The backlash to evolution is a natural reaction to the ways in which evolution's most eloquent advocates have handled Darwin's great idea, distilling from the raw materials of biology an acid of hostility to anything and everything spiritual" (189). Writers like Dawkins, Daniel Dennett, and E. O. Wilson "have gone well beyond any reasonable *scientific* conclusions that might emerge from evolutionary biology," and their "triumphant excess" (185) provoked a backlash by those who consider this strident atheistic materialism to be incompatible with their beliefs: "The triumphalists of materialism now act as though this last achievement is enough to exclude the spiritual. The reactionists of creationism respond in kind, tilting comically at evolution's windmill with every trick at their disposal" (190). In their proselytizing zeal, the New Atheists, Frank Schaeffer notes, "remind me of my missionary parents" (*Why* 72).

Given the heated rhetoric of the New Atheists and their fundamentalist opponents, it is difficult to recall an earlier yearning for a mutually respectful coexistence between science and religion. Intriguingly, the Dawkins at the center of the God debates in the 2000s and 2010s began his writerly career as a science popularizer, with his *The Selfish Gene* (1976) and *The Blind Watchmaker* (1987) explaining aspects of evolution to lay audiences. I want to turn in this chapter to another science popularizer, Carl Sagan, who, unlike the New Atheists of recent years, sought middle ground in the struggle between science and religion. An astronomer by training and probably best remembered for his 1980 PBS documentary *Cosmos*, Sagan wrote several popular science books and a 1985 novel called *Contact*. Sagan recognized evolution as the most visible site of conflict between science and resurgent Christianity, and he gives it a prominent place in his novel. I turn to this underappreciated popular science fiction novel to examine how Sagan situated the science vs. religion debate in 1980s America. First crafted as an unrealized screenplay with his wife, Ann Druyan, the novel—and later the slightly different 1997 movie on which it was based—could be thought of as a scientist's novelistic discussion of the authority of science and religion during the period. *Contact* merits our attention because it is a novel by America's premier science communicator, famous by 1985 for *Cosmos*, aiming for a fictional détente between science and religion—one in which both sides would recognize the validity of the other, the battle defused through the genre's power of imagining interior worlds and dialogically situating competing discourses.

In the year the film came out, another famous American science communicator, Stephen Jay Gould, proposed that science and religion were "non-overlapping magesteria": that is, domains of separate inquiries, with science confined to questions of material facts and religion addressing questions of ultimate meaning and morality. Gould tried to separate the combatants by suggesting that there really was nothing to fight about—though he conceded that there were some gray areas where the non-overlapping magesteria rubbed against one another, creating friction. But Sagan's novel suggests that some areas in fact overlapped significantly. His rumination on the relative authorities of science and religion was attentive to the religious beliefs and experiences marking the period, a popular science writer's perspective on the resurgence and its cultural and scientific "politics," but it also attempted to arrive at a common ground between them in a way that produced some unexpected results. The two decades between Sagan the conciliator and Dawkins the New Atheist combatant suggest a hardening of positions, but also how the struggle between science and religion has turned into a surprisingly postmodern phenomenon—a kind of postmodernism I assess in the second half of this chapter.

The Voice from the Sky

Now this Scripture-derived framework also sustained a certain kind of understanding of the world, interwoven with those underlying the cosmos ideas. The understandings of things as signs, and as signs addressed to us by God, entrenches the fixity of the cosmos in its short time-scale. The world around us is God's speech act, and in the context of the Bible story this seemed to leave no room for any other story but the standard one, that the world as we see it issued in the beginning from the hand of God.

Charles Taylor, *A Secular Age*

"Where is everybody?" wondered Italian physicist Enrico Fermi in 1950 as he pondered the simultaneous vastness and emptiness of space. Fermi was lunching with colleagues at the Los Alamos National Laboratory, and the question had sharpened because of recent advances in physics, radio astronomy, and rocketry—as well as, jokingly, a rash of purported sightings of flying saucers. What became known as the Fermi Paradox was the contrast between high estimates of the number of extraterrestrial civilizations and the total lack of evidence for any alien life.[2] Later expressed in the Drake Equation, which was "a way to quantify our ignorance" (Davies 77) by attempting to codify the many variables involved in estimating extraterrestrial intelligence—based on billions of stars, the age of the universe, the presumed millions of planets, the assumption of widespread life and estimates of evolved intelligence, of which a number would arrive at radio astronomy—the Fermi Paradox wondered whether the universe's silence was a case of misapprehended or hidden clues to presence, or our accurate apprehension of absence.[3]

It was a religious question as much as it was a scientific one.[4] Some of the possible answers to the Fermi Paradox echoed longstanding philosophical and religious assumptions: that, for example, our planet's ability to support life was totally unique or at least extremely rare, contrary to optimistic calculations of thousands of life-bearing solar systems in our galaxy. With a data set of only one—our own planet—all estimates about the existence of intelligent life elsewhere were based on huge assumptions about the variables in the Drake Equation, even if some of them have grown somewhat smaller due to scientific advances allowing for the detection of extrasolar planets in the last decade or so.[5]

When astronomer and science communicator Carl Sagan wrote his novel *Contact* in 1985, the religious reverberations of the Fermi Paradox were very much on his mind. The novel tells the story of the brilliant radio astronomer Ellie Arroway, who devotes her professional life to the Search for Extra-Terrestrial Intelligence (SETI). One day her research program picks up a strong, coded transmission from the Vega star system twenty-five light-years away; the palimpsest structure of what they call "the Message" contains a blueprint for what becomes known as "the Machine." Earth's international, cooperative decision to build the Machine is the occasion for the novel's political, religious, and philosophical discussions, with Ellie as the central focalizer as she becomes embroiled in the debates and the action leading to its construction. As it turns out, the Machine is a station on a kind of multigalactic metro operated by a consortium of extraterrestrial species. The Machine takes Ellie and four other human representatives to the center of the galaxy, where each meets an alien who appears (in order to not distract or frighten them) as a deceased or living loved one. After their return through the wormhole, however, the five's claims are met with skepticism: no time elapsed on Earth while they were gone, and they have no photographic or material evidence of their journey, prompting some to suspect a hoax. The novel ends somewhat inconclusively for the travelers: their stories are not publically released, but the aliens' final instruction to Ellie to seek deep within pi another coded message appears to bear fruit as she discovers a pattern, mathematically visible at last.

Sagan understands that the Fermi Paradox and the novel's premise of humans contacted purposefully by extraterrestrials entail religious implications that are as deep as the scientific ones they raise. The Message, after all, comes from the heavens, a kind of revelation from beings far more powerful and wise than ourselves. In answering the question of whether humans are alone, the novelistic premise likewise investigates the questions of who we are—true anthropology can begin at last—and ultimate meaning. Sagan investigates especially the international response to the Message in the late Cold War context of 1985, as the shared global experience of detecting an extraterrestrial presence eases both East-West and North-South tensions, bringing the planet together through the project of recording and decoding the Message and then building the Machine. But he is likewise as interested in the religious responses to the unexpected voice from the sky, as human religions begin to grapple with what this new revelation means for their doctrinal, social, and moral systems. While the Message hastens millennialist expectations for many sects (the Machine is not finished until December of 1999), Sagan is most interested in the consequences of the new revelation for Christianity.

The tension between science and religion, reason and faith, is the novel's core dialectic; it is prepared early, sustained throughout by the plot and the substantial dialogue between Ellie and various religious characters, and is the focus of the novel's hopeful conclusion. *Contact's* twenty-four chapters always begin with an epigraph or two, often religious in nature—quoting, for instance, William James on God and universal laws (277), the Dead Sea Scrolls (325), St. Augustine on demons (109), Euripides on the existence of the gods (157), and the Bible (401), to give a random sample. Urged by her mother, the adolescent Ellie joins a local Bible study run by "one of the respectable Protestant denominations, untainted by disorderly evangelism" (20), but the leader's inability to answer questions raised by basic contradictions—why are there two accounts of creation in Genesis, and different genealogies of Jesus in the Gospels of Matthew and Luke?—seems to confirm the adolescent's natural skepticism (and precocity). Her sense of what the novel calls the "numinous" instead grows when Ellie becomes enamored of astronomy and science, as Sagan develops the portrait of the scientist who has a keen and proper sense of wonder at the natural world.

Sagan portrays religion as not just an aspect of Ellie's individual awareness, but a social phenomenon unsettled by the reception of the Message. *Contact* suggests that there would be a range of creative responses to evidence of intelligent extraterrestrial life. Some religious sects are certain the Message is from God; others believe the Devil is the source (119). Even before it is decoded, it exercises a "steadying influence" on Cold War geopolitics (119), where nuclear disarmament between the US and USSR is already in its early stages, and a tentative global hopefulness takes hold. This hopefulness and shared sense of unity and purpose is not greeted warmly by all, however. Millennialist groups looking forward to apocalyptic end times—Sagan calls them "chiliasts," from the ancient Greek word for thousand, given to those who believe that Christ will return to rule for one thousand years before the final judgment day—cannot decide whether the Message is presaging the end or delaying it. Sagan writes,

> Some chiliasts held that the imminent arrival of the Third Millennium would be accompanied by the return of Jesus or Buddha or Krishna or The Prophet, who would establish on Earth a benevolent theocracy, severe in its judgment of mortals. Perhaps this would presage the mass celestial Ascent of the Elect. But there were other chiliasts, and there were far more of these, who held that the physical destruction of the world was the indispensable prerequisite for the Advent, as had been unerringly foretold in various otherwise mutually contradictory ancient prophetic works. The Doomsday Chiliasts were uneasy with the whiff of world community in the air and troubled by the steady annual decline in the global stockpiles of strategic weapons. The most readily available means for fulfilling the central tenet of their faith was being disassembled day by day. (120)

This is a fairly accurate reading of Christian fundamentalist apocalypticism in the 1980s, which would soon turn its imagination away from the Cold War and toward what President George H. W. Bush called the "new world order" in 1990, an imagination made anxious by the "the whiff of world community" whose most spectacular literary manifestation was the *Left Behind* series.

Contact develops the novel's religious themes through two Christian "fundamentalist" characters. Just as Kingsolver, in an attempt to be even-handed in her critique of resurgent conservative Christianity, presents a "good" watered-down Christian and a "bad" fundamentalist one, so too does Sagan present his readers with a sympathetic, reasonable Christian and a more narrow-minded, somewhat duplicitous Christian ideologue. Through their portraits, and as the above quotation on millenarianism suggests, what becomes clear is that Sagan is talking not just about a general, dehistoricized Christianity as he develops his novel's religious themes, but quite specifically the conservative Christian resurgence as it was already impacting politics, science, and society in the 1980s as he wrote it.

Palmer Joss is the sympathetic Christian who eventually befriends Ellie and, the novel's conclusion hints, may become her romantic interest as well. Once a carnival performer with the earth tattooed on his torso and an aptitude for quoting Ovid, Palmer was hit by lightning one day and had a near-death experience in which he saw a "Godlike" figure at the end of a tunnel (133). "He had been truly and literally reborn" (134) Sagan writes of Palmer's experience (without, perhaps, a precise sense of what "literally" means), and Palmer apprenticed to Billy Jo Rankin Sr., the fundamentalist preacher who happened to be present when Palmer woke from the lightning strike. ("Am I gonna live or die?" Palmer whispers to Rankin Sr. as he wakes; Rankin responds, "My boy, you're gonna do both" [133].) Thus Sagan portrays Palmer as a kind of middle-way reasonable fundamentalist:

> Soon Joss found a preaching style that was his own, not so much exhortatory as explanatory. In simple language and homely metaphors, he would explain baptism and the afterlife, the connection of Christian Revelation with the myths of classical Greece and Rome, the idea of God's plan for the world, and the conformity of science and religion when both were properly understood. This was not the conventional preaching, and it was too ecumenical for many tastes. But it proved unaccountably popular. (134)

Contrasted to Palmer is Rankin Sr.'s son, Billy Jo Rankin Jr., whom the novel portrays as a theologically inflexible fundamentalist who is somewhat of a huckster. Indeed, Rankin Jr. claims to have "the actual amniotic fluid that surrounded and protected our Lord" (135), a saintly relic improbably attributed to a late twentieth-century Protestant fundamentalist. Palmer is "appalled" by this claim, "not so much that Rankin would attempt so transparent a scam but that any of the parishioners were so credulous as to accept it" (135). What marks Palmer's reasonableness, then, is his public denunciation of his mentor's son, and that "he railed against other deviant forms of Christian fundamentalism" such as the snake-handling Pentecostal sects still active today (135): "Joss argued that in every religion there was a doctrinal line beyond which it insulted the intelligence of its practitioners" (135). Eventually, Ellie meets Palmer and Rankin together for a kind of informal debate between science and religion. It is primarily between Ellie and Rankin, with Palmer functioning as listener and moderator.

While this nutshell description of the two fundamentalist characters may make it seem as though their presence is awkward and tangential to a novel about humanity's first contact with extraterrestrial intelligence, this is not the case. Sagan perceives that conservative Christianity has a kind of political muscle that would make it relevant to the reception and action following contact. Here again the differences between them matter: Palmer "made it a rule not to meddle in politics" (137), Sagan says, but according to one character is also "very influential. He's been close to three presidents, including the present incumbent," who "is inclined to make some concession to Joss" (138). Palmer Joss, then, is figured as a kind of young Billy Graham figure—patriotic but with a nonpartisan reputation (undeserved, Kruse has recently shown), known as a pastor to Presidents of both parties, widely respected, and not really a crusader for creationism in public schools, "in erudition and moral authority, the preeminent Christian fundamentalist preacher of his day" (137)—though with more of an interest in finding a "middle course" on issues of science than Graham was known for. Though not as highly respected, Rankin is no less influential: he is able to pick up the phone and call the President, urging her to "send an honest-to-God Christian" on the Machine, which he believes is going to fly "straight to God or the Devil" (245).[6] Partly because of his political influence, the President decides not to send the agnostic Ellie, choosing rather another scientist whose mild religiosity is salted with a better sense (than Ellie) of when to keep his mouth shut about potential conflicts between science and religion.

It is the political muscle of resurgent conservative Christianity that leads the President's science adviser to suggest a meeting with Palmer Joss. To Ellie's surprise, Rankin Jr. also attends, he and Palmer having reconciled despite their differences. Ellie's discussion with the two fundamentalist Christians suggests Sagan's sense of the shape of the science vs. religion debate in the 1980s, but also begins to outline the problematic resolution that the novel ultimately puts forward. The timeliness of the novel is reflected in the fact that Sagan sets their discussion at a so-called creation science museum.

Although the novel does not have much to do topically with evolution—apart from its presumption (shared with the Fermi Paradox) that if life began elsewhere, it would have to develop through evolution, which might result in intelligent life and advanced civilizations[7]—its crucial set piece dialogue between Ellie the scientist and the two fundamentalists occurs in the location it does for the good reason that evolution was the loudest confrontation between the two magesteria when Sagan was writing his novel. The "Bible Science Research Institute and Museum in Modesto, California" (158) does not really exist, but Sagan's geographical choice for his fictional creationist museum was apt: as we saw in chapter 5, southern California was an important site of fundamentalist Christian political organization, including the early ministry of Tim LaHaye, and San Diego was the home of the Institute for Creation Research (ICR). Sagan's novel was prescient, foreseeing the widespread appeal of using a museum—an intrinsically modern institution devoted to the public display and communication of curated expert knowledge—to further the aims of conservative religious orthodoxy. The ICR opened the first "museum of creation and earth history" in 1977, and it was "composed of a one-room collection of exhibits supporting creationism and the biblical record" (Harding 215). This one-room "museum," I hypothesize, must have been Sagan's model for his fictional creationist museum, but in the decades that followed, more elaborate and well-financed examples have been developed, including one at Jerry Falwell's Liberty Baptist College in the mid-1980s (Numbers 319; Harding 219), a much-expanded Creation & Earth History Museum opened by the ICR in 1992, and, perhaps the most spectacular example, the Creation Museum, opened in Petersburg, Kentucky (outside Cincinnati) in 2007. In Sagan's museum, Ellie sees a prominent display of "a plaster impression from a Red River sandstone of dinosaur footprints interspersed with those of a pedestrian in sandals, proving, so the caption said, that Man and Dinosaur were contemporaries. . . . The conclusion drawn in the caption was that evolution was a fraud" (158); another display is titled "The Fallacy of the Expanding Universe" (173). Intriguingly, a photo in creationist Henry Morris's *History of Modern Creationism* of an early ICR Museum of Creation and Earth History diorama shows a furskin-clad human next to a brontosaurus and their mingled footprints, suggesting Sagan's probable familiarity with this model for his fictional museum (figure 1). The simultaneity of humans and dinosaurs is one of the signal tropes of creation science—one possibly prepared for the American public by the *Flintstones* cartoon.[8]

The theological discussion at Sagan's fictionalized creation museum centers on the respective authorities and methods of religion and science. Science, Ellie explains, prizes skepticism because it realizes that scientists make mistakes: thus the need to "test the ideas. You check them out by rigorous standards of evidence" (161). Rankin defends fundamentalist reading practices by arguing that predictions made in the Old Testament about Jesus prove that biblical revelation is true, but Ellie questions that reading practice, suggesting that biblical contradictions and apparently unfulfilled predictions—like Jesus returning in the lifetime of his hearers—betray the way fundamentalists

FIGURE 1. Institute for Creation Research Museum of Creation and Earth History diorama. A fur-clad human regards a grazing dinosaur in an early diorama at the Institute for Creation Research's Museum of Creation and Earth History, founded in 1977. The simultaneous existence of humans and dinosaurs—which actually lived about sixty-five million years apart—is a recurrent theme in creation science and a staple for its museums' displays. This exhibit may have been the inspiration for *Contact*'s depiction of a creationist diorama showing "dinosaur footprints interspersed with those of a pedestrian in sandals, proving, so the caption said, that Man and Dinosaur were contemporaries." Photo from Henry M. Morris, *A History of Modern Creationism* (San Diego: Master Book Publishers, 1984), 271.

"only quote the passages that seem to you fulfilled, and ignore the rest" (163). Ellie thinks there would have been better ways for a being who was really "omnipotent, omniscient [and] compassionate" to leave "a record for future generations, to make his existence unmistakable" (163). Such an unmistakable message would have contained information unavailable to the historical human writers of scripture—perhaps some scientific observations—and, furthermore, God could continue to show his presence in contemporary generations, as he seems to regularly do in the Hebrew Bible (164). Ellie doesn't accept Rankin's counterargument that God is present in spirit and through the Bible, available to millions of Christians.

They likewise differ on the question of the Message and its origin. What becomes clear in their discussion is that the Message is compared to the model of revelation: it might be from God or from Satan, the fundamentalists think, but the larger question is that humanity appears to have, in the Message, a real revelation from a superhuman intelligence in the heavens—"a voice from the sky," as Palmer puts it (165)—that transcends culture and language. The problem with revelation as Ellie sees it (and probably Sagan too, we may infer) is that "If your God wanted to talk to us through the unlikely means of word-of-mouth transmission and ancient writings over thousands of years, he could have done it so there was no room left for debate about his existence" (170). The Message, by contrast, is "clearly authentic":

> Radio telescopes are humming away in countries with different histories, different languages, different politics, different religions. Everybody's getting the same kind of data from the same place in the sky, at the same frequencies with the same polarization modulation. The Muslims, the Hindus, the Christians, and the atheists are all getting the same message. Any skeptic can hook up a radio telescope—it doesn't have to be very big—and get the identical data. (169–70)

Sagan thus sets out the culturally and historically embedded composition of the Bible, whose original "data" are no longer examinable except through this conflicted and corrupted account thousands of years later, as the relevant context for understanding the universality, immediacy, and verifiability of this other Message from the skies.

But when Rankin, like other resurgent Christian conservatives of his time, declares, "This is a Christian country," Ellie somewhat surprisingly claims that "I'm a Christian and you don't speak for me" (166). What she means by this, it turns out, is that she thinks Jesus is "an admirable historical figure," and his Sermon on the Mount is "one of the greatest ethical statements" (167), but that he "was only a man" (168), a definition of "Christian" that would satisfy few resurgent Christians. Ellie has been brought up in a Christian civilization, to use Schaeffer's distinction, but is not born again, especially since she is an agnostic. Their discussion ultimately ends with a strange, but, we shall see, telling complaint from Ellie to the fundamentalists that "I resent the idea that we're in some kind of faith contest, and you're the hands-down winner" (172). She asks, "Are you willing to put your life on the line for your faith?," and declares "I'm willing to do it for mine" (172). What Ellie refers to as her "faith" is science, and the form of the test would be to hold her face just outside the reach of the museum's heavy Foucault's pendulum, which swings in an arc delimited by the law of gravity.

The theological debate between religion and science takes up the whole sixteen-page chapter, and with it, we can begin to perceive Sagan's yearning for a reconciliation between the two magesteria, both of which are "bound up," Ellie says, with "a thirst for wonder." As Palmer concludes, "Perhaps we are all wayfarers on the road to truth" (173). Thirty years later, in the age of the combative "New Atheists," it is perhaps not as easy to imagine such a rec-onciliation as it was when Sagan wrote his novel. Fascinatingly, he imagines the shape of that reconciliation to be equivalency—a possibility suggested by Ellie's use of the word "faith" to refer to her personal convictions about natural scientific laws and the fundamentalist Christians' personal convic-tions about God's existence and active presence in the world. In the next section I analyze that equivalence, as seen in the aftermath of the Machine's journey to the center of the galaxy, before turning, in the final section of the chapter, to the questions of postmodern expertise and authority that Sagan's novel raises during the conservative Christian resurgence.

The Father's Code

> It has often been maintained that God has given us two revelations, one in nature and one in the Bible and that they cannot contradict each other. This is cer-tainly correct; but when one subconsciously identifies with natural revelation his own interpretations of nature and then denounces theologians who are unwilling to mold Biblical revelation into conformity with his interpretation of nature, he is guilty of serious error. After all, special revelation supersedes natural revelation, for it is only by means of special revelation that we can interpret aright the world about us.
>
> John C. Whitcomb and Henry M. Morris,
> *The Genesis Flood*

Contact's reconciliation works by establishing careful parallels between reli-gious faith and the scientific enterprise as seen in Ellie's journey in the

Machine and what the world in turn learns (and does not learn) about it through her testimony. In what must be recognizable by now as a trope in contemporary religious-themed literature like Anzaldúa's *Borderlands*, Reed's *Mumbo Jumbo*, Pynchon's *The Crying of Lot 49*, and, we shall see, Brown's *The Da Vinci Code*, protagonists must learn to look below surface patterns to see the truth below, with decoding becoming a kind of religious activity. The Message itself is a four-layered palimpsest. The first level is the broadcasting of prime numbers (impossible for natural phenomena to produce) to get attention. Behind them lies the first Earthly television broadcast powerful enough to be heard by the aliens' listening outpost at Vega—Hitler's opening of the 1936 Olympic Games in Berlin, the replaying of which causes much initial consternation on Earth. Within that rebroadcast lies the third layer, the actual blueprint for the Machine; and the fourth, nestled among its pages, is the math- and science-based "primer" enabling humans to read it, a Rosetta stone of truly universal language. Though the first US Machine is destroyed through an act of sabotage claimed by many groups, including Doomsday Chiliasts, a second built of test parts has been secretly put together in Japan. Because the Christian chosen to go on the Machine is killed during the sabotage attack, Ellie becomes the American representative, taking the journey alongside a Soviet physicist, a Chinese engineer, an Indian biologist, and a Nigerian physicist.

The Machine takes the five to the center of the galaxy, and each separately meets the image of a loved one constituted from the dreams of the voyagers. For Ellie, it is her father, who had died when she was a child. From him, Ellie learns that many alien civilizations cooperatively operate the "subway" of wormholes through which the Machine travelled to the "Grand Central Station" at the center of the Milky Way (366, 363). "We could tell you were in deep trouble" by the Berlin broadcast, the alien-as-father explains, and "thought you could use a little help. Really, we can offer only a little," help that takes the form of the Contact itself, the invitation to Earth to join cooperatively in the Machine project (359). The alien explains to Ellie that she should think of the universe not as "a wilderness" but as "cultivated": alien civilizations from many galaxies have embarked on "engineering" projects, one of which seems to be the creation of the massive radio galaxy known as Cygnus A, six hundred million light years away. "The problem," he explains, "is that the universe is expanding, and there's not enough matter in it to stop the expansion" (364). (Just such an eventual heat death of the universe terrifies the protagonist in Thomas Pynchon's famous short story "Entropy": "Callisto had learned a mnemonic device for remembering the Laws of Thermodynamics: you can't win, things are going to get worse before they

get better, who says they're going to get better" [2671].) The alien cooperative is trying to make things better by engineering a portion of the universe
with sufficient matter to thwart its heat death.

Ellie's alien mentor leaves her with a couple of mysteries before sending
her home. The first is that the subway system across the galaxies preexisted
any of the current alien civilizations: the "subway builders" made all the
transit stations and then, abandoning them, "Billions of years ago, they all
went somewhere. We haven't the slightest idea where" (366). The current
intergalactic engineers are just the "caretakers" because "maybe someday
they'll come back" (366). As if this bombshell were not enough, Sagan drops
a second: Ellie is instructed that deep within a "transcendental number"
(370) like pi lies another message coded in prime numbers—a pattern, Ellie
correctly interprets, "built into the fabric of the universe" (368). Before she
can get an answer to her key question—"Well, for heaven's sake, what does
the [new] Message say?"—it is time for the Five to return to Earth via the
Machine (368). Without explaining why, Ellie's alien-father tells her that the
"tunnel" will be closed "for a while at least" (371).

While the humans' meeting with the aliens is the climax of the novel,
the culmination of its thematic focus on science and religion occurs when
they return to Earth, and it is here that Sagan intriguingly suggests their
equivalence. That he fully intends this saga to be understood for its religious
ramifications is clear when Ellie muses, as she climbs aboard the Machine for
the return home,

> how . . . theological . . . the circumstances had become. Here were
> beings who live in the sky, beings enormously knowledgeable and pow-
> erful, beings concerned for our survival, beings with a set of expectations
> about how we should behave. They disclaim such a role, but they could
> clearly visit reward and punishment, life and death, on the puny inhabit-
> ants of Earth. Now how is this different, she asked herself, from the old
> time religion? The answer occurred to her instantly: It was a matter of
> evidence. In her videotapes, in the data the others had acquired, there
> would be hard evidence of the existence of the Station, of what went
> on here, of the black hole transit system. There would be five indepen-
> dent, mutually corroborative stories supported by compelling physical
> evidence. This one was fact, not hearsay and hocus-pocus. (371–72)

But Sagan purposefully dashes Ellie's "hard evidence." From the perspective of Earth, no time elapsed during the daylong journey. Furthermore, the
many hours of video evidence recorded is simply gone, with the cassettes merely
"blank" (376). The Five brought back nothing physical, and left nothing

behind. There is no "evidence" of the journey other than the oral testimony of the Five.

In fact, Sagan closely models the "good news" that Ellie and the other four bring home, I would like to argue, on the gospels about Jesus Christ that circulated among his early followers ("gospel" etymologically derives from the Old English phrase for "good news"). The US military official who debriefs Ellie accuses the Five of perpetrating a hoax with the help of a powerful industrialist. He suggests the ploy is "straight religion" (379) in its content: "Meeting your father in Heaven and all that, Dr. Arroway, is telling, because you've been raised in the Judeo-Christian culture. You're essentially the only one of the Five from that culture, and you're the only one who meets your father" (379). He calls their claims of interstellar faster-than-light travel "black hole mumbo-jumbo" (386), thus confirming, with Ishmael Reed, Frank Chin, and John Okada, that this is the phrase we use to describe the crazy religious beliefs of other people. The official blackmails Ellie by saying that the United States will release false files saying she's crazy if she goes public with her story. Like early followers of Jesus attesting to his resurrection and his messiahship and speaking in tongues, Ellie and the rest of the Five will be deemed mad if they tell their tale. The official story becomes that the Message was real but that the Machine did not work (410).

The truth of the matter thus comes down to a faith decision initiated by an oral tradition that spreads the good news—recapitulating, not repudiating, the development of early Christianity. Ellie has had a profound religious experience that she can't prove, and one of the first people to accept her story is Palmer Joss. Using religiously infused language, he suggests that people will "believe" Ellie's story when it is told; she is, he says, a new "witness" for modern times (421). Ellie's tale of the Machine ascending to the stars, after all, had already been "foretold" in the story of Jacob's ladder: "a ladder set up on the earth, and the top of it reached to heaven: and behold the angels of God ascending and descending on it," Palmer quotes to Ellie, who seems to silently accept it (421; see Gen 28:12). What's important to realize here is the way in which Sagan's narrative framing of Ellie's experience emerges to confound her earlier objections to religion: that it is based on subjective experience rather than objective proof; that (she earlier complains to Rankin and Palmer) rather than supposedly speaking privately to what Rankin earlier calls "millions of people in this country [who] have been born again" (164), God should "make his presence completely unambiguous" (165) by publically appearing; and that supposed prophecies that fundamentalists constantly find in the Bible occur because they "only quote the passages that seem to you fulfilled, and ignore the rest," as she earlier protested (163). Now, Ellie has only a subjective experience of aliens who pointedly refrain from public appearance, and whose existence and technology appears to have been prophesied millennia ago in the Hebrew Bible.

The novel presses the parallel by having Ellie compose a "samizdat" (415) record of the events, a clandestine written testimony, and then give the first copy to Palmer, to accompany the oral tradition about the Machine's journey presumably being propagated by the Five. Although the gospels were not eyewitness accounts of Jesus's life, the parallel between Ellie's gospel and those of the New Testament is upheld: the truth, held by the world to be madness, must be taken on faith and without proof, circulated first by oral tradition and then in a few written texts. (As the risen Jesus says to Thomas in John 20:29, "Have you believed because you have seen me? Blessed are those who have not seen and yet have come to believe.") Eventually, the world will know the truth as it waits for beings from the stars to open the tunnel again, this time with a probable visit: although the aliens haven't promised, "I am coming soon," as the resurrected Jesus did at the end of the first century (Rev 22:12), the sense of expectant return will build as the new "good news" is shared by the Five.

Having established this set of parallels between science and religion, and between the Five's good news and early Christianity's gospel, we can see *what* Sagan is doing, but to what end is a little more obscure. The ambiguity and possible irony of the situation is captured by the epigraph to his penultimate chapter, which quotes 2 Peter 1:16—"We have not followed cunningly devised fables . . . but were eyewitnesses" (401). Although 2 Peter's author claims to be Jesus's disciple Peter, and was understood traditionally to be so, critical-historical Bible scholars view the work as pseudepigraphical—that is, authored by someone who falsely claims to be someone else—and of origin in the early second century. Thus, 2 Peter's claim to being an "eyewitness" of "the power and coming of our Lord Jesus Christ" (2 Peter 1:16) is not true. Sagan uses this line as an epigraph to the chapter in which Ellie provides her eyewitness account to Palmer, and in which she writes her own samizdat edition of her experience. Is Sagan, not realizing the dubious status of its authorship and firsthand claims, sincerely invoking the idea of writing and speaking a true eyewitness account, thus placing Ellie's scientific experience in the tradition of religious revelation? Or does he know full well the dubious claim of 2 Peter and is slyly juxtaposing the two "eyewitness" accounts, thereby suggesting that Ellie's (and the other Fives') truer, scientific account should properly replace the earlier credulity we had toward religious revelation?

To rephrase this question in its largest terms, has Sagan staged the 1980s conflict between science and religion in such a way as to reveal their essential equivalency, or in such a way that suggests that true science is now properly ready to replace false religion as the revelatory mode wherein we might truly apprehend the numinous? The novel's ambiguity on that central question is heightened in the last chapter, titled "The Artist's Signature." Two events occur here. First, the supercomputers that Ellie has directed to delve deep into pi—following the alien's hint—discover a nonrandom pattern of ones and zeroes in the white noise of random numbers:

> *Hiding in the alternating patterns of digits, deep inside the transcendental number, was a perfect circle, its form traced out by unities in a field of noughts.*
> *The universe was made on purpose, the circle said. In whatever galaxy you happen to find yourself, you take the circumference of a circle, divide it by its diameter, measure closely enough, and uncover a miracle—another circle, drawn kilometers downstream of the decimal point. There would be richer messages farther in.* (430–31)

The "artist's signature" bespeaks "an intelligence that antedates the universe," and Sagan emphasizes that its universal language of math is truly transcultural: "It doesn't matter what you look like, or what you're made of, or where you come from. As long as you live in this universe, and have a modest talent for mathematics, sooner or later you'll find it" (431). While I leave a larger analysis of this religious structure of revelation—that God communicates to us indirectly by leaving messages behind—for chapter 8, suffice it to say here that Ellie's "new project" of "experimental theology" (426) resulting in the discovery of God's message in pi is Sagan's affirmation of the religious structure of revelation, an affirmation begun with the novel's parallel between early Christianity and the testimonies of the Five. As one book reviewer put this finale, "Sagan produces a scientific rabbit out of his hat" that "makes retrospective sense" of earlier religious discussions (Nicholls 6).

The other revelation, as it were, in the last chapter is that Ellie's stepfather—who married her mother after her father died and for whom Ellie has an intense lifelong antipathy—is actually her biological father, while her supposed father was actually her real stepfather. Ellie was the outcome of an adulterous affair with the very person Ellie later erroneously thought of as her stepfather in her mother's second marriage, she learns from an old letter from her mother after the latter's death at the very end of the novel. So what?, we might ask of this convoluted stepchild plot. It seems the father is the symbol of authority: "The imposter had turned out to be the real thing. For most of her life, she had rejected her own father, without the vaguest notion of what she was doing" (429). Sagan's language paralleling her scientific search alerts us to this plot's metaphorical meaning: "They had been right to keep the truth from her. She was not sufficiently advanced to receive that signal, much less decrypt it" (430). It is difficult to avoid the impression that the switched-fathers plot is a metaphor for the switched-authority plot: that Ellie, by the novel's end, has come to accept the authority of religious faith, the real father whose authority she previously and erroneously contested.

This respect for the authority of faith is suggested in Sagan's sympathy for the self-educated and scientifically literate Palmer and the hard-nosed scientist Ellie: both share a sense of wonder at the universe, and seem to be good examples of Palmer's earlier musing, "Perhaps we are all wayfarers on the road to truth" (173). *Contact* ultimately reconciles science and religion by constructing Ellie's voyage as a kind of religious experience that is subjective, without proof, intensely spiritual and meaningful, and communicated orally to others who then must make a faith decision. Palmer's journey at first seems parallel. He too has had a subjective experience strengthened by faith, but one that he tries to integrate with modern human knowledge. But although we know less about him, his portrait is somewhat strangely drawn. The novel calls both Palmer and Rankin "fundamentalist" Christians. But when, at the Creation Science museum, Ellie teases them by suggesting that they think the Earth was created by God in 4004 BC—a reference to James Ussher's conclusion, calculated through biblical genealogies and still widely accepted today by fundamentalist Christians—Palmer replies, "No, we don't believe that, do we, Brother Rankin? We just don't think the age of the Earth is known with the same precision that you scientists do. On the question of the age of the Earth, we're what you might call agnostics" (171). Rankin's silence suggests his acquiescence.

This is a strange concession for a "fundamentalist" to make, and it calls into question Sagan's comprehension of this type of Christianity. Crucial dioramas at creation science museums—including the one described in Sagan's fictionalized one—have humans and dinosaurs sharing the same chronological and geographical place: in fundamentalist belief, they simultaneously existed before Noah's flood, which wiped out the dinosaurs on a recently created Earth no older than 10,000 years. Indeed, when William Jennings Bryan seemed to concede an older earth during the *Scopes* trial, some fundamentalists thought he had given away too much to modern science. The fundamentalist belief that forms much of the backbone of the post-1970s conservative Christian resurgence has indeed generally repudiated this earlier concession, as Harding suggests:

During the 1920s, the "day-age" position, which held that a day of creation may have lasted thousands of years, was common sense among Bible-believers. The other belief common among conservative Protestants until the 1960s was known as the "old earth" position or the "gap theory," which supposed that millions of years may have passed between "In the beginning" and the six days of Edenic creation. Both positions allowed that many thousands, if not millions, of years may have passed since the events recorded in Genesis and thus permitted conservative Protestants to accommodate much mainstream geology and even some evolutionary views in the form of theistic evolution. But Bible-believing common sense changed after the 1960s, when a veritable creationist revival displaced these positions with a new, "strict creationist" position. According to strict creationism, "God created man pretty much in his present form at one time within the last 10,000 years." The strict position, also called "young earth" and "day-day" (a Genesis day is a twenty-four-hour day), "virtually co-opted the creationist label from the old orthodoxy." (213)

While it is possible that both Palmer and Rankin hold to the older "day-age" creationist position, their desire to meet in the creation science museum would imply an affirmation of its young-earth theology. Sagan's portrait of fundamentalist belief is often keen and insightful—as when he locates in Rankin the apocalyptic appetite that characterizes much of fundamentalist millennialism. In other aspects, however, he misses his target—as when he has Rankin purport to have in his possession the amniotic fluid of Jesus's mother Mary. Like Kingsolver's Nathan, who improbably wants to incorporate the (Catholic) Apocrypha (that is, the deuterocanonical books) into Baptist teaching, Sagan's ascription of a holy relic to his Protestant fundamentalist character is a plot device that stretches the credibility of the portrait.

Where this matters most is the portrait of Palmer's search for a middle way—the portrait of what seems to be a fundamentalist creationist (of either the old earth or young earth variety—the evidence is ambiguous) who yearns for a reconciliation between science and religion. As Sagan describes Palmer's position, "In debates on the teaching of 'scientific creationism' in the schools, on the ethical status of abortion and frozen embryos, on the admissibility of genetic engineering, he attempted in his way to steer a middle course" (136). There are, of course, many, many Christians who yearn for a reconciliation between science and religion as well. But they are not the fundamentalists who have generally steered the course of the conservative Christian resurgence when it comes to issues such as creation science (or abortion). They are the theistic evolutionists such as Kenneth Miller, cited above: Christians, many of them working scientists, who accept mainstream evolution and geology and who see a role for God as Creator of the universe and then Savior. My argument here is that Sagan mislocates the drive of fundamentalist belief, and in so doing crucially misunderstands "scientific creationism" and the contemporary conservative Christian resurgence at the heart of his novel's portrait of the struggle between science and religion and the eventual reconciliation between the two. There is no Palmer Joss style of fundamentalist. Those seeking a middle ground are the theistic evolutionists, not the fundamentalists who have generally set the tone and platform of resurgent politics.

In the next section of this chapter, I turn to creationist belief in order to shed light on Sagan's misapprehension. *Contact* correctly sees evolution as the most contested territory in the science vs. religion debate of the 1980s. But what has only slowly become apparent in the years since the conservative Christian resurgence began in the 1970s is that resurgent creationism is entangled with postmodernism. As I show in the last section of this chapter, resurgent creation science should not be understood as an antimodern battle or a yearning for premodern conditions. In substantive but unrecognized ways, contemporary creationism is postmodern in its strategy and worldview—a fact, we shall see, that substantially characterizes the conservative Christian resurgence as a whole.

Christian Postmodernism

> Intelligent design is the science that studies how to detect intelligence. Recall astronomer Carl Sagan's novel *Contact* about the search for extraterrestrial intelligence (or SETI). Sagan based the SETI researchers' methods of design detection on scientific practice. Real-life SETI researchers have thus far failed to detect designed signals from distant space. But if they encountered such a signal, as the astronomers in Sagan's novel did, they too would infer design. Intelligent design research currently focuses on developing reliable methods of design detection and then applying these methods, especially to biological systems.
>
> Intelligent Design theorist William Dembski

One sees the new social power and respectability of resurgent conservative Christians in the contemporary period by contrast to an earlier mockery of creationist belief in a key modernist novel, Ernest Hemingway's *The Sun Also Rises*. The middle of this 1926 work contains some strange repartee about the *Scopes* "monkey trial" of the previous year in Tennessee. The dialogue at first appears puzzlingly out of place, as the characters discuss the American legal case while fishing at the remote Irati River, near Burguete in rural Spain. Jake, the narrator, has read about the recent death of William Jennings Bryan, the populist Democratic presidential candidate, fundamentalist Christian, and counsel for the prosecution during the *Scopes* trial, who died on July 26, 1925, just five days after the trial ended. Jake and his friend Bill make fun of Bryan and his beliefs in the scene that follows. On learning the news while eating a picnic lunch of roast chicken and boiled eggs, Bill announces, "I reverse the order. For Bryan's sake. As a tribute to the Great Commoner. First the chicken; then the egg" (126). Playing on the creation vs. evolution debate that lies behind the chicken-and-egg question, Bill recognizes Bryan's creationist views that God created species as they exist today, not that the species of "chicken" first arrived via randomly mutated genes in a new egg, and proceeds to eat the chicken first, and the egg last. Parodying the language of religious celebration, Bill "gestured with the drumstick in one hand and the bottle of wine in the other," saying "Let us rejoice in our blessings. Let us utilize the fowls of the air. Let us utilize the product of the vine. Will you utilize a little, brother?" (126). Bill exhorts his parishioner, or fellow monk, that they should not undertake science's demystification of the origin of species, adopting the caricatured evolutionary understanding that we are descended from the apes: "Let us not doubt, brother. Let us not pry into the holy mysteries of the hencoop with simian fingers. Let us accept on faith" (127). The conversation trails away from there, as they cite H. L. Mencken, the famous journalist whose barbed coverage of the *Scopes* trial set the national tone for mocking backward fundamentalist belief in the tradition of which Bill's parody can best be understood.

The dialogue stands out as an oddly precise historical reference in this novel of postwar ennui, changed sexual attitudes, and the rootless cosmopolitanism of what Gertrude Stein called the "lost generation." Nonetheless, the fishing, like the almost-lost "afficion" of the Pamplona bullfighting, is a site of spiritual authenticity in *The Sun Also Rises*, and both spiritual experiences contrast with the emptiness of institutionalized religion. We should hear, then, this dialogue that follows shortly on Bill's mockery of Bryan—

"Listen, Jake," he said, "are you really a Catholic?"
"Technically."
"What does that mean?"
"I don't know" (128–29)

—as well as Jake's earlier rumination that "I was a little ashamed, and regretted that I was such a rotten Catholic, but realized there was nothing I could do about it, at least for a while, and maybe never, but that anyway it was a grand religion, and I only wished I felt religious and maybe I would the next time" (103) as suggestive of the religious picture of modern Europe in which old institutionalized beliefs and practices no longer provide the spiritual sustenance palpably missing from the characters' lives. The strange creationism-mocking scene thematically makes sense in this modernist novel, but its presence also suggests the way in which modernist literature—like Eliot's *The Waste Land*—helped formulate a kind of secularization thesis for literature and literary critics wherein we imagined that strong Christian belief was properly disappearing and that its residual presence could be safely mocked (or, for Eliot, mourned and eventually reclaimed).

The Sun Also Rises is part of a literary consensus that fundamentalist belief lost the *Scopes* trial. Because of the media trouncing that creationism received during the trial we sometimes forget that, in fact, Tennessee's antievolution statute was legally upheld, surviving into the contemporary period. Indeed, "By 1929, most states of the old Confederacy had imposed restrictions against evolutionary teaching by law, legislative resolution, or administrative ruling" (Larson, *Trial* 83), a situation that held for forty years until the Supreme Court's *Epperson v. Arkansas* decision in 1968, which voided regulations against teaching evolution for violating the Establishment Clause. Creationists responded by beginning a number of initiatives and organizations, including the Institute for Creation Research, opened in 1972, and with new legislation and regulations requiring equal time for both evolution and creation science. This "equal time" approach included a 1973 Tennessee statute and a 1974 Texas Board of Education ruling that stipulated that evolution in classrooms be taught as a "theory" and as "only one of several explanations" (quoted in Larson, *Trial* 139). The ICR was the source of legislation demanding "equal time" for creation science in classrooms in the 1970s, and in 1981 "bills were introduced in about twenty states requiring, in effect, that the Genesis account of creation, *as science*, with all biblical references deleted, be taught alongside evolution" (Harding 216).

Even when such efforts were not upheld in court they had a chilling effect on textbook publishers, as *Time* reported in 1981:

> To preserve sales, textbook publishers are beating a none too stately retreat from evolution after giving it strong emphasis in the post-Sputnik editions of the 1960s, which aimed at more and better science teaching. To enter the lucrative Texas market, many biology textbook publishers now bow to a requirement by the state's school board and include a statement that evolution is clearly presented as theory rather than fact. More significant, according to Gerald Skoog, 45, professor of education at Texas

Tech University, textbooks now say less about evolution. Between 1974 and 1977, the section on Darwin's life in *Biology*, a text published by Silver Burdett, was cut from 1,373 words to 45. Discussion of the origins of life went from 2,023 words to 322. Text devoted to Darwin's view of evolution shrank from 2,750 words to 296. Sections on fossil formation and geologic eras were deleted entirely. (Pierce)

These efforts culminated in the 1981 Louisiana "Balanced Treatment for Creation-Science and Evolution-Science Act," which, as the name suggests, treated the two accounts as equally valid and equally scientific, and which required "creation science" to be taught whenever evolution was. A challenge to the statute percolated its way between federal and state courts between 1982 and 1985 (while Sagan was writing *Contact*), staying in the news as the most visible creationist challenge to the teaching of evolution. Its unconstitutionality was affirmed by the 1987 *Edwards v. Aguillard* Supreme Court decision that confirmed that the statute violated the Establishment Clause; a concurring opinion noted the influence of ICR teachings in the Louisiana act (Larson, *Trial* 186).

The Institute for Creation Research behind this "equal time" legislation was founded in 1972 by Henry Morris, the co-author, with John C. Whitcomb, of *The Genesis Flood: The Biblical Record and Its Scientific Implications* (1961). *The Genesis Flood* was an immensely influential work that revived "flood geology" and made the case for young-earth creationism in what looked like scientific argumentation. It argued that geological formations like the Grand Canyon and worldwide fossil strata were actually the record of Noah's flood, in which God repented of his creation and wiped out all living animals except for Noah's immediate family and a pair of every animal (except dinosaurs, thus explaining their extinction). As Harding describes the work, "Confronting as it did the conservative Protestant establishment in the name of a more biblically literal truth and simultaneously steeped in scientific and scholarly trappings, *The Genesis Flood* was an instant sensation" (214). Indeed, the book is full of illustrations of geological formations, tables of data, diagrams, equations, and footnotes to standard scientific accounts and peer-reviewed scientific articles. With sections on the "Hydrodynamic Selectivity of Moving Water" (Whitcomb and Morris 273), "Antediluvian Radiocarbon Proportions" (374), coral reefs, petroleum deposits, atmospheric carbon dioxide, and more, *The Genesis Flood* looked like it was speaking the language of science: that is, was doing science.

As Harding's description of the book suggests, this new young-earth creationism was not merely a return to old truths, but was rather an innovative synthesis of biblical truths with scientific discourse:

Whitcomb and Morris's insistence on young-earth and strict, day-day positions enabled them to reclaim the authority of scriptural literalism with regard to the Genesis account, authority which had been lost in the Scopes trial finale when Darrow decried the inconsistency of Bryan's day-age position. . . . But Whitcomb and Morris hoped to do more than recoup lost ground by promulgating a strictly literal creationist position. What made their rhetoric of strict creationism culturally productive and innovative rather than merely reactive was its assumption of the very apparatus that had defeated them, the apparatus of science. (214)

Morris's Institute for Creation Research engaged in this same innovative use of the apparatus of science to advance young-earth "scientific" creationism. Its use of the scientific apparatus was central to the development of creation science museums, beginning with the ICR Museum of Creation and Earth History, which opened in 1977, and which, I hypothesize, must have been the model for the one in Sagan's novel (H. Morris 272n1). Its claim to the status of science allowed the ICR to generate legislation to evade the *Epperson* decision outlawing the teaching of creationism in schools by suggesting the new strategy of using creation science to "teach the controversy" (as the call later became) about the supposed scientific problems with evolution.

Having historically contextualized creation science's innovation in terms of the conservative Christian resurgence, I want to turn to its successor. The history and politics of creation science has been well documented and its tactics much discussed.[9] Less well-documented and understood is its successor, the Intelligent Design movement, which, after the 1987 *Edwards* decision decreeing that "creation science" was still religion, gradually came to replace creation science as a plausible conservative Christian legislative answer to evolution; as such, it is the contemporary successor to the creationist debate in which Sagan set his novel.

Focusing on the Intelligent Design movement allows for a productive inquiry into the intersection between postmodernism and contemporary religion. Like McClure and Hungerford, I see the need for an account of contemporary religion and postmodernism that is more complicated than a simple opposition between them. An example of such can be found in Hardt and Negri's *Empire*, where they suggest that

it seems to us that postmodernists and the current wave of fundamentalists have arisen not only at the same time but also in response to the same situation, only at opposite poles of the global hierarchy, according to a striking geographical distribution. Simplifying a great deal, one could argue that postmodernist discourses appeal primarily to the winners in the processes of globalization and fundamentalist discourses to the losers. (150)

This account of fundamentalism is certainly wrong in the US context, where the "winners," I contend, could be both postmodern and politically powerful conservative Christians. We need a finer-grained account of the intersection between postmodernism and religious revivalism than that found in Hardt and Negri—an account that recognizes that postmodernism is not opposed to all the possibilities opened up by Taylor's postwar "super-nova"—and a more specific attention to the Christian resurgence than that offered by McClure or Hungerford. This labor allows us to understand the problems facing Sagan's hopes for reconciliation.

Proponents of Intelligent Design (ID) hold that "certain features of the universe and of living things are best explained by an intelligent cause, not an undirected process such as natural selection" (Discovery). It generally accepts the geological age of the earth and many examples of evolution,[10] but argues that evolution by itself is unable to account for the complexity of all life, the beginning of life, the development of intelligence, and so on. It contends that an ideology known as "Darwinian orthodoxy" based on naturalism and materialism has wrongly excluded the possible supernatural ordering of our universe. ID theorists such as Michael Behe suggest there are numerous examples of "irreducible complexity" in organisms, based on Darwin's own observation, "If it could be demonstrated that any complex organ existed, which could not possibly have been formed by numerous, successive, slight modifications, my theory would absolutely break down" (189). Similarly, William Dembski, citing information theory and complex systems theory, suggests that instances of "specified complexity"—similar to Behe's irreducible complexity—indicate that a design process beyond random mutation and natural selection is at work, possibly implying the existence of an unnamed Designer. Though Intelligent Design authors are officially agnostic as to who or what this Intelligent Designer is, it has become clear, especially in the last decade, that its proponents are exclusively Christians and other theists; there are no atheist ID proponents. Fascinatingly and not coincidentally, ID theorists—such as William Dembski in the epigraph to this section—have repeatedly cited Sagan's *Contact* for its portrayal of the scientific search for intelligent patterns amidst random noise as a model for their idea of looking for design.[11]

Developed primarily at the Discovery Institute, a conservative think-tank in Seattle, the origin of Intelligent Design lay, strangely, in a moment suggestive of postmodern science. According to journalist Edward Humes, the "godfather" (63) of Intelligent Design was Phillip E. Johnson, a University of California, Berkeley lawyer, and the moment of inspiration—echoes of William Paley stumbling on a watch—came when Johnson stumbled upon

Dawkins's *The Blind Watchmaker*. Comparing it to Michael Denton's *Evolution: A Theory in Crisis*, Johnson "saw Dawkins's writing as beautiful, powerful, persuasive rhetoric—but he also recognized in it the same tool great lawyers use to defend bad cases: compelling arguments that, in Johnson's estimation, seemed very slim on supporting evidence" (66–67). With no prior scientific training, Johnson began to draft a "brief" to be used against evolution. That brief became his 1991 book *Darwin on Trial*, which, alongside books by Denton, Behe, Dembski, and the Discovery Institute's textbook *Of Pandas and People* (1989), advanced the claims of Intelligent Design against the modern consensus on biological evolution. When the textbook was adopted by the Dover, Pennsylvania school board in 2004 for inclusion in high school biology classrooms, some parents sued the school board, charging that it was a form of creationism. The very modern (systematic, evidence-weighing, expertise-respecting) 139-page 2005 decision *Kitzmiller v. Dover* reviewed the supposedly scientific claims of ID and agreed that it was a form of creationism.[12]

I would like to suggest that Intelligent Design—and its historical and theological ancestor, creation science—are postmodern forms of science comprehensible in the terms developed by Jean-François Lyotard. Lyotard's well-known tenet defining the postmodern as "incredulity toward metanarratives" (xxiv) at first seems at odds with the theological assumptions and certainty of most of the conservative Christian resurgence. But his deeper argument conceiving of science as a set of "language games" was prescient. Lyotard analyzes science as a series of performative "moves" in a kind of game played with other scientists, rather than as denotative utterances describing the real or the true. As in chess, the game is playable only because the rules are recognized by the community of players. Influenced by J. L. Austin and Ludwig Wittgenstein and emphasizing linguistic pragmatics rather than denotation, Lyotard argues that scientific utterances are those which conform to certain rules and are recognized as such by others within the scientific community. Each "addressee" of a scientific utterance is likewise a potential "sender" of a scientific utterance. A scientific utterance pragmatically succeeds not if it can be proven to be true—not, that is, if it is understood as pure denotation, as accurately representing an empirical real. Rather, it succeeds when its addressee agrees that a "proof" can be had for the utterance. As Lyotard puts this distinction, "Not: I can prove something because reality is the way I say it is. But: as long as I can produce proof, it is permissible to think that reality is the way I say it is" (24). Those proofs, of course, come in the form of other linguistic signs, further shifting science from the positivist realm of accurate description of the real to the performative and pragmatic realm of what Austin calls "felicitous" utterances. Scientific research and its publishing apparatus are the arena for "moves" within the game of science, premised on an "agonistics of language" (10) wherein senders try to trump other senders' utterances.

As Fredric Jameson summarizes this vision,

> the cognitive vocation of science would however seem even more disastrously impaired by the analogous shift from a representational to a nonrepresentational practice. Lyotard here ingeniously "saves" the coherence of scientific research and experiment by recasting its now seemingly non- or postreferential "epistemology" in terms of linguistics, and in particular the theories of the performative (J. L. Austin), for which the justification of scientific work is not to produce an adequate model or replication of some outside reality, but rather simply to produce *more* work, to generate new and fresh scientific *énoncés* or statements, to make you have "new ideas" . . . or, best of all . . . again and again to "make it new" . . . . (Foreword ix)

What interests me in Lyotard's account of the postmodern is not so much his point that science legitimates itself through forms of narrative knowledge that it disavows (emancipation, professional management), as his description of an agonistic pragmatics of scientific utterances that removes science from the realm of describing the real and shifts its questions to those of participants, audiences, and the recognition of expertise.

Lyotard's adoption of pragmatics to describe science was an outsider's view of the rhetorical structure of scientific research. When Austin analyzed pragmatic utterances, his point was that "I now pronounce you man and wife" and "I christen this ship the USS Enterprise" did not use language referentially to describe things that already were, but creatively to enact the things they spoke into being only because their conventions were recognized by the audiences and the speakers were understood as empowered. But science uses language referentially: when geologists claim the Earth is 4.5 billion years old or that all species originate through evolution, they make referential claims about referents that are there whether we speak about them or not. Their language is descriptive, and the referents about which they speak preexist the speech act; thus science proceeds by trying to analyze whether previous referential claims accurately describe their referents. This distinction between reference and pragmatics is probably why science generally ignored Lyotard's use of speech-act theory to describe the scientific enterprise—*The Postmodern Condition* was never reviewed by any scientific journals as far as I can tell, and scientists in Quebec may have wondered, if they knew about it at all, whether this was the best use of the provincial funds used to commission *La Condition postmoderne* in 1979. It was true that, institutionally, speakers have to be recognized and want their utterances deemed acceptable to their audience of fellow scientists; it is also true that, institutionally, the practice of scientific research is often "agonistic" in ways that Thomas Kuhn and others had described; and it is obviously true that science researchers attached to universities are indeed under professional pressure "simply to produce *more* work," as Jameson put it. But scientists do not usually, and do not institutionally over time, ignore the way utterances match emergent and evolving consensuses of the real in the way that Lyotard ignored the descriptive dimension of scientific utterances.

Although science generally has continued to conduct itself as a modern enterprise, ignoring Lyotard's theory entirely, I would like to argue that the "postmodern condition" of science he outlines is a fairly good description of the workings of Intelligent Design. In particular, Lyotard's recognition of the questions of legitimation and audiences in scientific rhetorical practices allows us to see Intelligent Design and its predecessor creation science as postmodern phenomena. My argument is that the conservative Christian resurgence's engagement with evolution takes the form not of a refusal of the modern: it is not (simply) an antimodern rejection of scientific knowledge and authority. Rather, and as Karen Armstrong has counselled us, it is better to read contemporary fundamentalisms as using modern techniques and methods (369). The fundamentalist (and more broadly in this case, conservative evangelical) contest with science appears to use modern rhetorical structures and methods of mainstream science; it is innovative in its contest with modernity in the way outlined by Armstrong (see, e.g., 178–79), an innovation whose particular form is Lyotardian postmodernism.

A good example of the postmodern science of Intelligent Design is its view of the bacterial flagellum, as developed by Michael Behe. The bacterial flagellum is a kind of whiplike motor that powers various tiny creatures through water, and though it is often described in biology textbooks as a kind of machine, the motor actually functions through "a complex series of separate chemical components that must be assembled in total for the system to function" (Humes 138). This became for Behe a primary example of irreducible complexity. After reading Johnson's book, Behe developed this idea of irreducible complexity into his 1996 book *Darwin's Black Box*, using the bacterial flagellum as one chief example. As Behe writes, "here again, the evolutionary literature is totally missing. Even though we are told that all biology must be seen through the lens of evolution, no scientist has *ever* published a model to account for the gradual evolution of this extraordinary molecular machine" (72). Behe and Johnson were among a delegation from the Discovery Institute that briefed Republican leaders, including "more than fifty senators and congressmen" in 2000, about the gaps in evolutionary theory and the need to "teach the controversy," which might include the notion of irreducible complexity and the bacterial flagellum (Humes 140, 166). For Behe, the flagellum was like a mousetrap: neither machine's parts made any sense—had no other uses—outside of the whole it was currently used for.

The bacterial flagellum appeared 353 times at the Dover trial (Humes 256), becoming the object of debate with the mousetrap to which it was analogized. But as biologist Kenneth Miller demonstrated, the pieces of the mousetrap could indeed be used for other things (264). When put on the witness stand at the Dover trial, Behe admitted that his theory of the irreducible complexity of bacterial flagella was testable in a laboratory experiment that might take about two years, or ten thousand bacteria generations, to see if something like a flagellum might begin to evolve in a condition that gave advantages to more mobile organisms. But Behe contended that such an experiment "would not be fruitful" (306), and like other supposed examples of irreducible complexity (e.g., the immune system or the blood–clotting cascade [Behe 74–97]), scientific research refuting them—that is, showing that these examples of irreducible complexity were in fact reducible—have not led him to abandon the propositions. More important, Forrest and Gross note that the scientific literature on how "the contemporary flagellum is descended from earlier, simpler systems" is well-established and widely available, but generally ignored by Behe and other ID authors (77). One need only look at the Discovery Institute's web pages today—as well as its in-house blog *Evolution: News and Views*—to see that none of these discredited ideas and examples has been abandoned. What makes Intelligent Design particularly postmodern, then, is that no bad or discredited idea is discarded.

The key ID notion of irreducible complexity, of course, is a descendent of William Paley's 1802 *Natural Theology* and its primal scene wherein Paley imagines stumbling upon a watch. Unlike a previously stumbled-upon stone, which shows no intentionality, "when we come to inspect the watch, we perceive (what we could not discover in the stone) that its several parts are framed and put together for a purpose" (7). For Paley, the complexity of the watch's interlocking parts is evidence of design: "the inference, we think, is inevitable; that the watch must have had a maker" (8). Paley reasoned that the human eye, as a similarly intricate structure, had to have been designed by a creator with a purposeful goal. It was Paley, of course, to whom Darwin directly responded with a different account of how something might appear designed, an explanation popularized and updated in a book like Dawkins's *The Blind Watchmaker*. Thus, according to the consensus on evolution, that which seems to have been intelligently designed does indeed need an explanation for that design—one that evolution provides.[13]

In the postmodern condition, those expert consensuses about the outmodedness of the analogy (as Dawkins discovered when Haggard mentioned the eye as an example) no longer stand: thus the Intelligent Design textbook at the heart of the *Dover* trial, *Of Pandas and People*, updated Paley's analogy by wondering what would happen if a pickup truck were left near a "native village." "It would come as no surprise," the textbook suggests, "if they wondered *who* was responsible—if they envisioned some kind of intelligence like their own" (Davis and Kenyon 56). "Even a primitive tribe" would reason, based on analogy to its own tools, that while the truck is subject to physical laws, "*the truck does not form spontaneously as a result of these laws*" (56–57). These and other examples are forms of what Dawkins calls "the Argument from Personal Incredulity" (*Blind* 38)—the fallacy that because this idea of complexity happening through natural processes is incredible, it must not have happened naturally at all. That this discredited analogy can reappear without responding to the problems identified with the original analogy of the watch shows both how there can be no resolution (or "progress") or conclusions to any of these ideas in postmodern science, but it also shows how the Intelligent Design movement is ultimately engaged in bad faith arguments. Not only is no erroneous idea ever discarded; the strategy of muddying the water by recycling old canards is revealed.

Perhaps the best example of this process of recycling discredited ideas in order to keep the dialogue going—to prolong the adversarial game, to try to generate controversy that can then be taught—is with the publishing history of the textbook itself. During the *Dover* trial, lawyers for the plaintiffs uncovered *Of Pandas and People*'s old manuscript drafts. As it turned out, in its first incarnation it had been a creation science book called *Creation Biology* until the 1987 *Edwards* decision outlawing the teaching of creation science, at which point "suddenly *Pandas* stopped being about creation science and started being a book about intelligent design." As Humes puts it,

> this in itself might not have been a problem—there is nothing sinister about correcting a book to make it consistent with a Supreme Court ruling. Indeed, that would have been a good thing, [philosophy professor and plaintiff witness Barbara] Forrest said, except the book was not changed in any substantive way. Instead, every reference to creation and creationism in the book was simply changed to "intelligent design,"

and "creator" was changed to "designer" or "intelligent agency." There were more than 250 such substitutions in all—but there were virtually no other changes in the text. (285)

This history of composition seems decidedly dishonest, a Machiavellian exercise in bad faith, but only from the modern perspective that locates science as a discourse of truthful representation, of denotative utterances that can be adjudicated by experts to be more or less referentially accurate. But seen from the point of view of postmodern science, it is merely the efficient use of existing material for further linguistic utterances, and a great example, to use Jameson's allusion to modernism, of "making new" that which is old. Thus, Forrest and Gross note, Behe continues to declare the "irreducible complexity" of biochemical systems within cells *and* the lack of evolutionary explanations for them, despite many articles describing evolutionary processes for these very things. They conclude, "The fact that he *continues to make these accusations*, however, indicates either that (1) Behe has not reviewed the scientific literature seriously, (2) he has done so and does not recognize the significance of it, or (3) he is aware of the literature and ignores it in order to maintain his point in purity for the nonspecialist, biochemically naïve audiences to which it is addressed" (74–75).

The postmodern science of Intelligent Design is one symptom of a crisis in expert authority, what Lyotard calls "delegitimation" due to our incredulity toward science's modern narrative justifications of speculation and emancipation (37). And while there may be some truth to Lyotard's contention that this has occurred partly because of the splintering of "compartmentalized" scientific expertise wherein "no one can master them all," I am less interested in the origin of this crisis than in how delegitimation appears to be working on the ground, entangled with the postwar Christian resurgence. This crisis is not one that exists within the scientific community, where an established consensus exists about evolution as the cornerstone of modern biology (and is the basis for ongoing research into many unanswered questions), and in which Intelligent Design and creation science are seen as simply incorrect in denotative terms. Rather, it is a crisis of authority within the social order, where the American public and media are generally much less prone to defer to expert authority on this matter and others.

Thus while Dembski writes that "Enlightenment rationalism and scientific naturalism" face "impending collapse" not because of questions raised by "postmodernity" but because in this "information age" the "only coherent account of information is design" (*Intelligent* 14–15), I would like to suggest that Dembski, like many conservative Christians interested in Design, is practicing the kind of postmodernism that he purports to disdain. It is not against postmodernism that the Christian resurgence strives, but through postmodernism that it solves the seeming contradictions between traditional theology and the science of evolution.

Importantly, then, there is actually a dual audience for Behe, Dembski, and other Discovery Institute authors: mainstream scientists whom they hope to draw into conversation and the lay public with limited or no expertise in scientific questions whom they hope to confuse. This is the logical end of the pragmatics of language that Lyotard lays out: while still agonistic, the purpose of an Intelligent Design utterance—or the creation science utterance before it—is to provoke addressees in the scientific community to reply with another refutation of Intelligent Design ideas. If they do not, the public is to understand that the scientific community is not making felicitous statements according to the pragmatics of scientific utterances because they are breaking their own rules (of evidence, debate, citation, neutrality, and so forth) when they refuse to engage with "new" claims—thus suggesting the larger cultural argument ID authors make that scientists are dishonest sore losers addicted to their own institutional power and blind to their materialist, naturalist ideology, now renamed "Darwinian orthodoxy." It has long been recognized that scientists are in a catch-22 position with creationist utterances. If they don't address and correct the old discredited ideas, science's public mission of education is undercut. But if they do address them, that process gives credence to the ideas they are discrediting because in Lyotardian terms it appears as though the creationist has been recognized as a legitimate sender by the scientific community.

While Lyotard suggests that "Consensus is a horizon that is never reached" (61), in fact a consensus on evolution does exist, a consensus that is the basis for continuing research into many unanswered questions. It is possible in principle that this paradigm might be eventually challenged and overturned by future research. As Lyotard writes about the weight that a consensus or paradigm can exert, "Countless scientists have seen their 'move' ignored or repressed, sometimes for decades, because it too abruptly destabilized the accepted positions, not only in the university and scientific hierarchy, but also in the problematic" (63). While members of the Intelligent Design community might argue that this characterizes them—harbingers of a yet-unrecognized paradigm shift—my argument is that the pragmatics actually point to an audience of lay people, not of other scientists, given their inability to "present peer-reviewed genuine data from original research" (Forrest and Gross 142). As Forrest and Gross show in gruesome detail, scientists and theologians associated with Intelligent Design (such as Behe,

Dembski, Paul Chien, and Douglas Axe) have produced no peer-reviewed science articles on the topic and appear to have no active scientific research programs (see chapters 3 and 4, and 6 and 7 more generally).[14] And as they describe the unhappy task facing the scientific critic of Intelligent Design, "any attempt on the part of the critic to keep up [with the newest version of recycled material] means climbing onto the ID treadmill: response and counter-response. Many a potential critic of an ID production must decide, after a glance at the large body of serious literature in his own field to be read, that life is too short and the gain for the pain of this ID treadmill is much too small" (116). Thus, for example, Forrest and Gross write of early creationist author Henry Morris's 1974 textbook *Scientific Creationism* and Morris's contention about "the inability of mutation and natural selection . . . to generate information," continuing, "the absence of response until very recently from serious scientists to such arguments is not evidence of their having ignored them. On the contrary, the arguments have been examined and found unworthy of the time and effort needed to reply in kind and at length" (280–81).

Both creationists and the scientific community know that the real audience is not one another but rather the audience witnessing the exchange. (Indeed, Creation Museum leader Ken Ham attributed to the publicity of his debate with Bill Nye "the science guy" at the museum in 2014 the "miracle" of a fundraising surge that will allow the museum to build a 510-foot replica of Noah's Ark [Two-Way].) And while the scientific community's countercreationist utterances are meant to convince the lay public of the truthful accuracy of their denotative utterances, the same is not true for Intelligent Designers, for whom the task is merely to show the public that they can play the game and speak the same language, which is enough to generate the legitimation crisis in scientific expert authority.[15] As Forrest and Gross argue of William Dembski's *Intelligent Design*, most of his readers "are likely happy with what sounds like a good bottom-line result . . . . They are delighted that a fellow true believer can speak for them in those arcane languages" of "statistics, mathematics, thermodynamics, information theory, or biology" (125). For theologically conservative Christians who care about expert authority—and some do not—systems like Intelligent Design or creation science provide intellectual cover for already-established faith positions. They do so not by providing good alternative explanations—they are not good—but by leveling the playing field of scientific discourse.

My argument here is that though many Christians on the one hand and postmodern theorists and practitioners on the other might understand one another oppositionally (an understanding not confined to these players, as

Hardt and Negri's construction shows), there is in fact a meaningful entanglement between postmodernism and the conservative Christian resurgence on this question of evolution—and, we shall see, other questions where expert authority comes into play. Another way to put this would be to say that the postmodern collapse of expert authority has cleared a space for increased participation by conservative Christian truth claims. As self-identified evangelical Christian academic Crystal L. Downing puts it in *How Postmodernism Serves (My) Faith: Questioning Truth in Language, Philosophy and Art*, "Lyotard's suspicion toward metanarratives is a reaction against the arrogant confidence of modernists [that is, those who embrace modern science, empiricism, and reason] who, thinking they have a special handle on truth, disdain narratives based on faith" (75). What is valuable about postmodernism, Downing suggests, is that it levels the playing field between faith and reason: thus, citing Richard Rorty, Downing concludes that postmodernism suggests that "all truths, including those of science, are human: intellectual constructions taken as true by groups of people who share the same interpretation of reality" (75).

In this scheme, science and reason are no better or truer than religion and faith as "interpretations" of reality. Downing cites journalist and science popularizer Robert Wright (erroneously calling him a scientist, though he received undergraduate training in evolutionary psychology) as describing his own "faith" in natural selection—"not *blind* faith, really, since the faith rests on the theory's demonstrated ability to explain so much about life. But faith nonetheless; there is a point after which one no longer entertains the possibility of encountering some fact that would call the whole theory into question" (quoted in Downing 76). While Wright's point could be described as entrenched paradigms, it is glossed by Downing thusly: "He sounds like numerous Christians, including myself, who attest that their faith is reinforced by Christianity's 'demonstrated ability to explain so much about life'" (76). If Wright's word choice seems infelicitous, we should recall that Sagan has Ellie describe her own scientific enterprise and sense of wonder as her "faith."

While Downing's argument might strike some as a caricature of postmodernism, I would like to suggest that it is not. Downing correctly understands the possibilities that some accounts of postmodernism open up for traditional, orthodox Christian theology. Thus she writes:

> This explains why Lyotard and Rorty regard scientific explanations of reality as similar to religious ones: both must be judged by their internal coherence rather than their correspondence to reality. After all, they would ask, how can one judge a system's correspondence to "reality" if reality is precisely what that system defines? . . .

> I want to direct attention to how these postmodern thinkers unwittingly served Christianity. When Lyotard established scientific rationality as a "language game with its own rules . . . on par with" other forms of knowledge, he destabilized the idea that only reason and empiricism can access truth. His word *par* allowed Christians to join the intellectual country club as legitimate players in the game of knowledge, for it signaled that all truth claims are situated on presuppositions—rules shared by the players in the language game—that must be taken on faith.
>
> In other words, postmodernism brings us back to the *credo ut intelligam* (I believe in order to understand) of Augustine and Anselm. Thus, while most modernists considered Christian faith as a superstitious human construction doomed to fall, like James Ussher's biblical timeline, postmodernists asserted that this modernist idea was itself a human construction. (76)

As her reference to Ussher's chronology suggests, there are limits to what kind of Christian utterances can be legitimately made. Indeed, the embrace of creationism is a major part of what evangelical scholar Mark Noll calls "the scandal of the evangelical mind," in his book of the same title (see especially 188–99).

Thus postmodernism for Downing allows for old-earth Intelligent Design, but not young-earth creationism. Though young-earth creationists

> assume that they are standing firm for their faith with a rock-solid foundation, they don't realize that the Christian house built on such a foundation has such huge cracks in it that no one believing even the most conservative scientific estimates for the world's age would dare to move in. Thus, in the minds of many intelligent design scholars, rather than preserving Christianity, "young earth" creationists are making it intellectually unten(ant)able. Like skyscrapers in California, the house of Christian faith as expressed in the Apostles' Creed will stand longer if Christians allow theories about the earth's age to move. (118–19)

A footnote further distinguishes young-earth creationism from old-earth Intelligent Design: "I am not indicting the 'intelligent design' movement, even though 'young earth' creationists usually identify with it. Two of the most intelligent Christian philosophers I have met endorse a form of 'intelligent design.' Both, however, argue that the earth is far older than 'young earth' creationists allow" (118). The footnote ends with an endorsement of Dembski's *Intelligent Design*, published, as is Downing's book, by InterVarsity Press, which we now must recognize as a publishing clearinghouse for Christian resurgent postmodernism.[16]

Though the unmasking of Intelligent Design as reheated old-earth creationism by the 2005 Dover decision had evidently not yet happened by the time Downing's 2006 book went to press, her principle nonetheless stands. To the extent that postmodernism imagines expert, empirical knowledge as sets of language games divorced from their referents, they are human constructions no better or truer than religious faith. To be sure, thinking Christians still have a duty to try to harmonize their faith with emerging knowledge—thus Downing's preference for the old earth rather than the young earth. As with other forms of Christian apologetics, the intellectual task is to bring the new information into alignment with already-existing beliefs. That harmonization is made much easier by the newly levelled playing field of human knowledge, in which scientific mastery becomes merely one language game set amidst other choices, such as traditional religious belief. What Downing has suggested is the use of postmodernism for Christianity, I have demonstrated as the specific procedure of Intelligent Design and creation science before it. While scientists in general have ignored Lyotard's theory of postmodernism, and continue to measure research in terms not of pragmatic linguistics but rather whether their models accurately describe reality, the postmodern collapse of expert authority outlined by Lyotard has been embraced by the conservative Christian resurgence. As theologian Mark C. Taylor remarks about this movement, "While claiming to reject relativism, the New Religious Right's promotion of intelligent design as a plausible alternative for understanding human life leads to a subjectivism that undercuts scientific inquiry. This tactic is part of a larger strategy to discredit science in ways that are epistemologically disingenuous and politically dangerous" (405n27).

Sagan's novel begins with an attempt to reconcile science and religion in the late twentieth century, "struggling toward a common ground with a brand of sophisticated religion," as one reviewer put it (Benford), but strangely ends up levelling the playing field in a similarly postmodern way, arriving unintentionally at an epistemologically postmodern position. The novel is not formally postmodern: in its lack of formal experimentation and its didacticism and reliance on traditional exposition, dialogue and character, it is exemplary of what John Barth had characterized as "The Literature of Exhaustion" years before, the way most postwar fiction was written as though experimental modernism never occurred, preferring instead nineteenth-century realist styles. But *Contact*'s equation of Ellie's research as a kind of "faith" (as she calls it), and its resolution of the Fives' new gospel as a kind of oral tradition that must be believed rather than demonstrated by evidence suggests the novel's larger imaginative project of understanding both science and religion as equally legitimate pathways on the road to truth, to use Palmer's terms. This reading is premised, as we have seen, on Sagan's misunderstanding of what "fundamentalism" entails, but I suggest that the novel also misunderstands the sincerity of at least some Christian resurgent apologetics. As the rhetorical language games of scientific creationism and Intelligent Design sometimes demonstrate, the primary goal is not the search for truth (as Sagan's Palmer imagines), but rather the harmonization of reality with already existing religious truth claims.

This is ultimately why religiously motivated critics of Sagan have substantially misread the novel's lesson. Daniel J. Silver, for instance, in *Commentary*, argues that the possibility in *Cosmos* and the premise for *Contact* is that

> the discovery of such alien intelligence would, Sagan was convinced, offer ultimate vindication of the Darwinian challenge not only to the creationist "myth" but to the entire structure of Jewish and Christian teleology. Once human beings were shown to be neither unique nor all that special, the vanity that propped up religious faith—for Sagan, a kind of covert narcissism by which humans projected their own imagined centrality onto an ersatz "supreme being"—would be discredited once and for all. Man, having been demoted, would be able to see clearly at last. (53)

Silver's certainty about Sagan the secularist colors his interpretation of the film (and novel before it), leading him to see its representation of religion as insincere and "unscrupulous" (54), and to miss its extensive sympathy for religious experience, and its final, almost postmodern resolution of the conflict between science and religion. Other film reviewers argued it was "burdened with the bias and plot of the original novel by militant atheist Sagan" (Wall 3), and that the aliens' lack of ability to provide "the meaning of existence" to Ellie (Newman 34) shows that the film's message is that there is no transcendence or ultimate meaning. But while the film in a few ways sharpens the conflict between science and religion,[17] in others ways it deepens their resolution: there is no Rankin, there is no creationist museum, and by reducing the Five to Ellie's One, Ellie herself does not even have a community of faith. Or rather, the sympathetic Palmer Joss, whom the film makes into her early lover, becomes the willing hearer of her new testament, which he, unlike Thomas, will believe without evidence. Other critics of the film—such as Antonio Sison, comparing it to Ezekiel's mysticism, and Gregory Sadlek, comparing Ellie's journey to Dante's in the *Paradiso*—have more correctly noted the film's essential religious sympathy. Indeed, given the way the film and novel divided critics, Sadlek wonders if "one of the reasons for this disparity may be that some critics confuse religion with orthodox belief. They do not see that scientific longings can be religious at their very core" (28). Given that Sagan had considerable creative influence on the screenplay, we should not be surprised.

Carl Sagan's *Contact*, then, brings us to one intersection between post-modernism and the conservative Christian resurgence. Sagan's sought-for compromise, his middle ground, evoked a Deism of a bygone era, but "What Deism in its various forms wanted to reject," Charles Taylor reminds us, "was seeing God as an agent intervening in history. He could be agent qua original Architect of the universe, but not as the author of myriad particular interventions, 'miraculous' or not, which were the stuff of popular piety and orthodox religion" (275). The Deistic Author who leaves a code in pi is too weak a figure for the tastes of the conservative Christian resurgence, which is why LaHaye tries to attribute belief in a more Theistic, doctrinally-sectarian and personal Jesus to the Founders. Nonetheless, Ellie's personal religious experience and her testimony of that experience suggests a closer align-ment with the conservative Christian resurgence that the novel has its eye on. Both Sagan's Deism and the more personal experience of the numinous that the novel sympathetically portrays might be thought of in terms of the "super-nova" that, Charles Taylor suggests, marks the available religious options of the postwar period. My analysis here of what I am calling "Chris-tian postmodernism"—articulated by Downing and practiced by Intelligent Design theorists and scientific creationists before them—is meant to sug-gest yet another resurgent possibility within that supernova. To be sure, the lines separating these positions are fuzzy: the Deism Sagan's code seems to suggest is the kind of Author that Intelligent Design purports to find (even as most of its supporters and theorists find their practices and beliefs char-acterized in terms of a more personal and traditional God), while the kind of resurgent Christian postmodernism practiced by Intelligent Designers is actively opposed by other scientists who are non-resurgent Christians like Ken Miller. Within this increasing array of possible religious subjectivities in the super-nova, Christian postmodernism is particularly appealing to con-servative Christians because it promises to solve a couple of longstanding theological problems in a way that responds to, by partially adapting, mod-ern ways of knowing. The theological problems of evolution and revelation entailed questions of theodicy that were in fact constitutive of the earlier rise of Christian fundamentalism, and the way contemporary American writers addressed them are the subject of the next two chapters.

CHAPTER 7

Evolution and Theodicy in *Blood Meridian*

> The kid spat dryly and wiped his mouth with the
> back of his hand. A lizard came out from under a
> rock and crouched on its small cocked elbows over
> that piece of froth and drank it dry and returned to
> the rock again leaving only a faint spot in the sand
> which vanished almost instantly.
>
> Cormac McCarthy, *Blood Meridian*

The opening pages of Cormac McCarthy's *Blood Meridian* introduce the character of Judge Holden at an evangelical tent revival meeting held in Nacogdoches, Texas in 1849. The anonymous protagonist of the novel, called only "the kid," has slipped into Reverend Green's "nomadic house of God" (6) to get out of the rain. He hears the preacher describe the constancy of God's love—"Dont you know that he said I will foller ye always even unto the end of the road?" including "these here hell, hell, hellholes right here in Nacogdoches" where the temptations of alcohol and prostitution await (6). This conviction of human sin coupled with God's promise of constancy set the stage for a presumable altar call: Reverend Green will invite his tent revival audience to recognize their own sinfulness and need for redemption and that only faith in Jesus Christ, who died for our sins, offers the salvation they need.[1]

This evangelical invitation to be born again is interrupted by the judge—perhaps the most enigmatic and terrifying character in all American literature—who steps into the tent to address the audience with charges of imposture and iniquity. "Ladies and gentlemen," the judge begins,

> I feel it my duty to inform you that the man holding this revival is an
> imposter. He holds no papers of divinity from any institution recog-
> nized or improvised. He is altogether devoid of the least qualification

to the office he has usurped and has only committed to memory a few passages from the good book for the purpose of lending to his fraudulent sermons some faint flavor of the piety he despises. In truth, the gentleman standing here before you posing as a minister of the Lord is not only totally illiterate but is also wanted by the law in the states of Tennessee, Kentucky, Mississippi, and Arkansas. (7)

The Reverend begins reading from his Bible in defense, but the judge continues to detail the charges, "the most recent of which involved a girl of eleven years—I said eleven—who had come to him in trust and whom he was surprised in the act of violating while actually clothed in the livery of his God" (7). Reverend Green protests with the novel's first hypothesis as to the judge's true identity: "This is him, cried the reverend, sobbing. This is him. The devil. Here he stands" (7). No matter: the judge turns the screw, adding that "Not three weeks before this he was run out of Fort Smith Arkansas for having congress with a goat. Yes lady, that is what I said. Goat" (7). The revival meeting dissolves at this point into a mob as members of the audience begin shooting at Reverend Green. The postscript to the episode is the judge's nonchalant admission, as he afterwards buys the kid and others drinks at a tavern, that "I never laid eyes on the man before today. Never even heard of him" (9).

The readers of McCarthy's 1985 novel had likewise never heard of this fictionalized evangelical preacher, but the outrageous sexual charges the judge brings against him might have sounded familiar.[2] Although pedophilia and bestiality were not among the usual catalogue of sexual sins, the 1980s were known for regular scandals featuring fundamentalist and evangelical preachers, often situated in the South in what had been known as the Bible Belt. This was in particular the era of the televangelist scandals: of Jimmy Swaggart, Jim and Tammy Faye Bakker, Oral Roberts, and others. It is not possible that McCarthy had his eye on these scandals as he was composing *Blood Meridian* in the early 1980s, however, simply because the scandals with Swaggart and the Bakkers occurred in the late 1980s, making them the context for early readers of the novel but not for its composition. There had been other, less-known scandals in Southern congregations, but perhaps it is best to say that, if these were not quite what McCarthy had in mind, then certainly the evangelical revivalist culture of the scene would have been readily recognizable to his audience.[3] McCarthy emerged from an intensely religious culture, and his novels, critics agree, are among the most religiously resonant of the serious literature being produced today. But what would it mean not only to pay attention to the religious imagery and references in this novel largely set in 1849–1850 but to listen to it carefully against its compositional background of the post-1970s conservative Christian resurgence?

Listening for that presence does not assume that McCarthy is encoding messages about the resurgence in his work but rather that it is the specific cultural formation for its religious resonances and that the religious meaning of his novels must be understood in its context. Sometimes this way of listening for the resurgence is simple—as in the instance of the tent revival that begins *Blood Meridian*, or the scenes of evangelical baptisms in this (268–69) and other McCarthy novels—and is merely evidence of the continuing religious energy of American culture, as the several "Great Awakenings" in American history attest. Indeed, the tent revival the kid attends in Nacogdoches in 1849 is at the tail end of the Second Great Awakening, which often featured itinerant preachers holding camp meetings over several days, including notably in frontier societies. The kid would not have been the first impoverished social outcast on the frontier to escape boredom or the weather by listening to a revivalist preacher. Including a reference to the Second Great Awakening during what Mark Taylor has called the Fourth Great Awakening is a way of calling our attention to this continuing religious energy in America.[4]

While this cultural presence of evangelical Christianity clearly connects the time of *Blood Meridian*'s composition to its historical setting, I want to read the novel against a less-obvious theological issue that connects the 1980s to the mid-nineteenth century: that of evolution. As we shall see, *Blood Meridian* is replete with images, scenes, and language that evoke the nineteenth-century sciences of geology and biology. Behind this presence are the deep theological problems that evolution presented Bible-believing Christians—as then, so now. Evolution is a problem not just for literalists who are committed to a young earth and to the direct divine creation of human origins—the group that represents only one part, although at times the most vocal and powerful part, of the contemporary Christian resurgence. Evolution, I argue, has also been deeply problematic for nonliteralist Christian theology. If Carl Sagan's *Contact* situates it as the most heated site of conflict between science and religion, *Blood Meridian*—the other 1985 American novel intensely interested in the interpretation of God's design in the natural world—suggests that the desire to read design in our world runs up against crucial problems of theodicy to which evolution seems to point; against this backdrop it is especially rewarding to read McCarthy's most famous novel.[5]

A Gnostic McCarthy?

> Now that the Nag Hammadi discoveries give us a
> new perspective on this process [of the formation of
> early Christian orthodoxy and the New Testament
> canon], we can understand why certain creative per-
> sons throughout the ages, from Valentinus and Herac-
> leon to Blake, Rembrandt, Dostoevsky, Tolstoy and
> Nietzsche, found themselves at the edges of orthodoxy.
>
> Elaine Pagels, *The Gnostic Gospels*

Critics have long been attentive to the religious language and meanings in McCarthy's work, especially *Blood Meridian*. Amy Hungerford has recently suggested that the style of the novel reminds us of the "sacred aura" of the Bible (79), and that the judge in particular "sounds both like Christ telling parables and like Milton's Satan addressing his fiends" (90). Insofar as the judge and the narrator sound alike, religious authority trumps the religious content of the novel, ultimately conferring "a godlike status on the author" (96). Whereas Hungerford sees the kid carrying around a Bible he cannot read in these terms of authoritative style displacing religious content, Doug-las Canfield suggests that it might be evidence "for a Christian existentialist reading of the end of the novel" (47). But "the question," Canfield asks, "if this novel is a theodicy, is whether there is any other agency that counts, that does not serve the warrior ethic and a brutal imperialist Manifest Destiny" (44). He finds the answer in the figure of the kid, who seems at least at times to "witness" against himself, in the novel's language, even as he partakes in its violence (45), and in the epilogue that in Canfield's estimation represents the coming of civilization to the frontier (48). Interestingly, even a self-avowed atheist like Canfield, trying to find some shreds of "Christian existentialism" (47), is moved to rescue a benevolent God from the evidence of the novel and indeed, as we shall see, from the evidence of history and natural history.

A similar problem exists for another approach to the religious dimension of *Blood Meridian*: that of reading it for its Gnostic suggestions, championed by Leo Daugherty in 1992 and Petra Mundik in 2009. The substantial virtue of this approach is that it makes sense of a number of strange images, allusions, and episodes and is an especially strong account of the figure of the judge who is, one of the characters recognizes, a "mystery himself, the bloody old hoodwinker" (263). As Daugherty and Mundik summarize the scheme, in Gnostic cosmologies there was originally a good, divine realm of the spirit, created by a good supreme being and in communion with it. This original unity and goodness was broken, perhaps by an outside force or by one of the lesser created deities, either of which took upon itself the creation of the material universe, including humankind (Daugherty 122).

In Gnostic theologies, it is Yahweh, the traditional Jewish and Christian God, who creates this lesser material realm, trapping a divine spirit or spark from the original good spiritual realm in human beings. This spirit or "pneuma is actually a fragmented spark of the divine which has fallen into, or in some cases, been maliciously trapped in the evil manifest cosmos" (Mundik 73). In this cosmology, our divine spirit must find knowledge—gnosis— of its true antecedence and through this knowledge eventually escape the evil materiality of world and body, reuniting with the divine sphere. Often a messenger is sent—Gnostic Christians understood this to be Jesus—to convey in secret sayings this true understanding of the alien spirit that longs to escape the material body, a message which is not understood by all. The archons, or lords of the material realm, work to keep the divine sparks trapped in material bodies, and the spirits housed in human shells ignorant of their real nature: to this end, Yahweh introduces Mosaic laws and rules of conduct. As can be seen in this nutshell description, Gnosticism upends traditional orthodox Christian theology by redescribing Yahweh as the evil god of the material realm intent on keeping his human creatures ignorant of the divine nature of their spirits. It is for this reason that the community Bart Ehrman refers to as the "proto-orthodox" followers of Jesus contested Gnostic accounts, along with other belief systems they termed "heresies," in the first few centuries of the Common Era (*Lost Christianities*, 123–24).

Although obscure and—let's face it—more than a little bit goofy, this system of religious belief seems to offer a fairly robust explanation of some of the confusing allusions, episodes, and imagery in *Blood Meridian*. Particularly strong is its account of the judge who, it is suggested several times, seems to have supernatural capabilities. In Daugherty's and Mundik's complementary schemes, the judge is an archon whose command of the material world and its modes of life is consistent with the fact that, as one of the novel's many "as ifs" would have it, "he seemed much satisfied with the world, as if his counsel had been sought at its creation" (146). Some of the judge's most "godly" claims seem to make sense in this scheme (Daugherty 125), as does his role as the spiritual guide of the murderous Glanton gang who keeps them ignorant even as he encourages their warfare both in theory ("War is god" [261]) and in practice (as with the creation of gunpowder out of "our mother the earth [who] was round like an egg and contained all good things within her" [136]). Thus the judge's obscure parable (148–52) sows confusion in the Glanton gang, not the secret understanding that might aid the recognition of their divine spirits. The judge may be Yahweh's "archonic overseer" (Daugherty 127), and the "false graver" he employs in the kid's dream may be his method of employing false exchange systems (128). This Gnostic reading also makes some sense of the novel's incredibly obscure epilogue, as the figure who moves across the plain striking fire out of the rock is in fact a coming Gnostic savior who tries to enkindle the fire—the divine spark—from out of the world's material bodies (130).

As Mundik also notes, this Gnostic cosmology makes sense of the repeated references to fear and evil as the metaphysical foundation of our world (76), and, speaking of the judge, suggests that "The demiurge has no desire to alleviate human suffering, or to intervene in humanity's slow self-destruction, as he is a malevolent, bloodthirsty deity, and the manifest world is his sadistic playground" (78). The judge has no origin (81) and the novel's conclusion suggests he will never die; he, like Yahweh, simply judges things according to whether they are inside or outside his will (82–83). Unlike Daugherty, Mundik sees the judge's coldforger as establishing false religions, not false exchange systems (86), but both agree that the epilogue "is absolutely central to a Gnostic understanding of the novel" (88). Thus, concludes Mundik (citing the judge), "McCarthy's preoccupation with God's refusal to 'interfere in the degeneracy of mankind' is thoroughly Gnostic" (78).

The Gnostic reading is compelling but not perfect, and carries with it the additional commendation that Elaine Pagels's *The Gnostic Gospels*, which provides an accessible scholarly account of the Gnostic texts found at Nag Hammadi in 1945, was published in 1979, just before McCarthy began to write *Blood Meridian* intensively.[6] But the overarching problem with this account is that it requires us to conclude that McCarthy believes in its bizarre cosmology. In the Gnostic reading, the ethics of the novel rest on the notion that the kid carries a spark, as indicated by his supposed misgivings about his violent acts—something Mundik connects to *The Road*, where the "father reminds the son throughout the journey through the apocalyptic wasteland that they are 'the good guys' because they are 'carrying the fire'" (97n71). The only thing that makes the novel not nihilistic, that is, is the kid's spark and the final presence in the epilogue of a Gnostic savior who proceeds across the plain trying to strike the spark out of human materiality. Because the final ethical vision of *Blood Meridian* would depend on these two readings, I submit that the Gnostic interpretation of the novel requires us to take seriously the idea that McCarthy takes Gnostic cosmology seriously.

But why would he? One of the biggest problems with this belief system is the obviousness of its attempt to salvage a good God out of a world of evil and suffering. Gnosticism does this by distancing the original good deity from the facts of human and animal suffering for which he is not responsible. Of course, this was merely a new solution to an old problem. Judaism and Christianity had solved the problem of evil in a number of different ways, the first of which (textually, if not historically) was the story of Adam and Eve in the Garden of Eden: that creation was made good, but suffering and evil were introduced through human agency. The Judeo-Christian tradition likewise developed other explanations in its sacred texts—sometimes contradictory ones, as Bart Ehrman explains (see *God's Problem*). Indeed, the Gnostic tradition was an extreme way of solving the age-old problem of how the world can seem to be going so wrong if it is under control of a God who has our interests at heart. As Ehrman summarizes, one of the earliest explanations for suffering was the Hebrew prophetic tradition, in which "Israel suffers military, political, economic, and social setbacks because the people have sinned against God and he is punishing them for it" (*Lost Christianities* 117). In this explanation, suffering is punishment for sin, and the promise of Exodus, that God "would intervene on their behalf when they were in dire straits" (117), is maintained on both a national and personal level.

The problem with this theology, Ehrman suggests, "is that it does not explain why the wicked prosper and the righteous suffer," especially if the people do return to God (117). Ehrman suggests that this problem led to "variant theologies in ancient Israel," including that of the book of Job (alluded to in *Blood Meridian* [117]), and that of the apocalyptic tradition. Jewish apocalypticism kept God in ultimate control, but temporally distanced him from the world by seeing human suffering as the result of a cosmic struggle in which God would ultimately triumph. Ehrman explains:

> Jewish apocalypticists developed the idea that God had a personal adversary, the Devil, who was responsible for suffering, that there were cosmic forces in the world, evil powers with the Devil at their head, who were afflicting God's people. According to this perspective, God was still the creator of this world and would be its ultimate redeemer. But for the time being, the forces of evil had been unleashed and were wreaking havoc among God's people. (118)

Jewish apocalyptic prophets such as John the Baptist and Jesus asserted that God was going to imminently reassert his control over history and destroy the forces of evil in a day of reckoning and judgment.[7]

But what would happen if God did not reassert that control, and the end did not come soon, as the apocalyptic prophets had promised—including Jesus in his line, "Truly I tell you, there are some standing here who will not taste death before they see the Son of Man coming in his kingdom" (Matt 16:28)? Ehrman argues that for some Jews and early followers of Jesus, this led to "another radical modification" in the theology of suffering: namely, Gnosticism. In this scheme, the earlier assumption that "the world was created by

God, who is the good and all-powerful divine force behind it" is called into question because of human suffering. "Maybe," the new thinking went, "the suffering in this world is not happening as a punishment *from* this good God [the thinking of the prophetic tradition, as well as Job's counselors] or *despite* his goodness [the thinking of the apocalyptic tradition]. Maybe the God of this world is not good" (119). In this developing theology, the God of this world either wants humans to suffer or does not care because he is "evil, or ignorant, or inferior" (119). As I have suggested above, the true God is now reinterpreted as a distant antecedent—further removing him spatially, temporally, and causally from human suffering—who did not create the world, but existed as a divine spirit with ultimate priority. This God is still good, and is trying to reach us with a divine messenger. Thus, Ehrman hypothesizes, Gnosticism "may well have derived, ultimately, from a kind of failed apocalypticism" in a process that reinterpreted Jesus "away from his own apocalyptic roots" (119).[8]

So, in Mundik's Gnostic interpretation of *Blood Meridian*, the excellent question that the judge rhetorically poses to the Glanton gang—"If God meant to interfere in the degeneracy of mankind would he not have done so by now?" (153)—is answered by the idea that the evil or uncaring creator has no desire to alleviate the suffering. But this Gnostic reading defers rather than answers the novel's central question of theodicy, here expressed by the judge's question: that is, why doesn't the real God, the true good spirit, intervene in degeneracy, evil, and suffering? To send a few messengers at distinct historical moments who speak in riddles that only a select few can understand is clearly not a satisfying answer for theodicy, thus calling into question (again) this God's goodness, power, or knowledge. Gnostic theology also belittles suffering by treating it as illusory: thus, in the Gnostic Gospel of Philip, Jesus's final words on the cross—"My God, my God, why have you forsaken me?" (Mark 15:34)—are understood to be spoken by the merely material being of Jesus that housed the divine spirit of Christ (see Ehrman, *Lost Christianities* 224). In fact, another Gnostic text, the Coptic Apocalypse of Peter, pictures the living spiritual Christ floating "above the cross, glad and laughing," while "he into whose hands and feet they are driving the nails is his physical part," the discarded suffering body of Jesus (quoted 186–87). Too bad, in other words, if you actually live in a body. In this theology, pain and suffering are merely illusions one has to see through. Tracing Gnosticism's possible intellectual antecedence through Jewish apocalypticism to the prophetic tradition of the Hebrew Bible, as Ehrman does, makes painfully obvious how it was another attempt to provide an alibi for God—to explain why he is not here now to stop suffering and why he is not responsible for it in the first place. To read *Blood Meridian* as a Gnostic text is ultimately to make McCarthy into a kind of apologist for God, justifying God's ways to men in the tradition of Milton and C. S. Lewis.

An Anti-Theodicy of Evolution

> But mechanistic theory fragilized faith . . .
> because mechanism undermines enchantment, the expression-embodiment of higher reality in the things which surround us, and thus made the presence of God in the cosmos something which was no longer experience-near, or at least not at all in the same way. God's power was no longer something you could feel or see in the old way; it now had to be discerned in the design of things, the way we see the purposes of the maker or user in some artificial contrivance, a machine—an image which recurs again and again the discourse of the time, particularly in the simile likening the universe to a clock.
>
> Charles Taylor, *A Secular Age*

I contend that a better way to understand the religious meaning of *Blood Meridian* is not to make McCarthy into a Gnostic apologist for God but to see the novel as an indictment of God's responsibility for suffering in his material world. Like the creationists of his time, McCarthy discerns in the natural world the character of the creator; but in contrast to their accounts and signaled by the myriad references to evolution in his book, the suffering entailed in evolution implies an antitheodicy in which human and animal suffering make impossible the classical notion of God as all-powerful, all-good, and all-knowing.

Fittingly, it is the judge who ties together many of the strands of evolution in the novel. The judge is a practitioner of the nineteenth-century scientific disciplines involved in evolution: the geologist who affirms an ancient earth against those who quote scripture (122); the botanist pressing leaves (133); the ornithologist preserving birds (206), a probable allusion to Darwin's important 1835 research on the adaptation of finches on the Galapagos Islands; and the paleontologist studying fossils. In one scene, the narrator describes,

> at all desert watering places there are bones but the judge that evening carried to the fire one such as none there had ever seen before, a great femur from some beast long extinct that he'd found weathered out of a bluff and that he now sat measuring with the tailor's tape he carried and sketching into his log. All in that company had heard the judge on paleontology save for the new recruits and they sat watching and putting to him such queries as they could conceive of. He answered them with care, amplifying their own questions for them, as if they might be apprentice scholars. They nodded dully and reached to touch that

pillar of stained and petrified bone, perhaps to sense with their fingers the temporal immensities of which the judge spoke. (262–63)

The judge's discovery of the dinosaur fossil from a bluff recapitulates the fact that many early specimens in the eighteenth and nineteenth centuries were first discovered emerging from cliff faces undergoing natural erosion. His concluding words to his students—"Your heart's desire is to be told some mystery. The mystery is that there is no mystery" (263)—is likewise an allusion to evolution's demystification of the origin of species, now found not in supernatural creation but in the simple natural processes of natural selection working on random mutation. This "singling out the thread of order from the tapestry," as the judge puts it, is the kind of disenchanting scientific mastery that separates him from the "man who believes that the secrets of the world are forever hidden" and thus who "lives in mystery and fear" (207–08).

The narrator likewise alludes to the developing picture of evolution in the mid-nineteenth century when he describes in one chapter heading, "The judge collects specimens—The point of view for his work as a scientist" (194). This narrator compares the Glanton gang to "gorgons shambling the brutal wastes of Gondwanaland" (180)—that is, to dinosaurs wandering Gondwana, one of the two supercontinents making up Pangaea that existed between 510 and 180 million years ago. The novel constantly calls humans "apes" (4, 68, 78, 95, 154, 159, 208, 248, 296), a figure of speech that recalls one of the most contentious popular understandings of Darwin's theory: that we are descended from apes. Likewise, the epigraph about scalping found among three-hundred-thousand-year-old fossils draws the reader's attention to violent practices by Homo sapiens, the evolutionary ancestor of today's anatomically modern humans. The epigraph cites Tim White, who, not incidentally, studies human evolution at Berkeley; his research focus for the last decade or so has been cannibalism (xi). The timeframe of the novel, 1849–1850, is roughly ten years before Darwin's famous synthesis of evolutionary ideas through his introduction of the mechanism of natural selection. These ideas were circulating during this period, and Darwin would shortly provide "the thread of order" by locating natural selection as the design mechanism in *On the Origin of Species*.

My location of the controversies surrounding the sciences associated with evolution during both the setting of *Blood Meridian* and the time of its composition does not mean that all the "scientific" discourses present in the novel are taken seriously by McCarthy. On the contrary, my reading has the advantage of interpreting the judge not as an archon with godlike knowledge but as a sleuth on the cutting edge of scientific mastery circa 1850, whether those ideas ultimately turned out to be right or wrong. Thus the judge's forays into phrenology (249) and racial anthropology (88–89) suggest that for all his supernatural powers, he is actively trying to figure things out during his time period. He is a scientist of his time, which includes getting some things wrong. Likewise, the social Darwinism *avant le mot* that animates Captain White's white-supremacist ideology (35–36) is amusingly if horrifically disproved when his group of filibusters is utterly destroyed by the Comanche, who have comfortably culturally adapted the horse-based warfare introduced by Europeans onto the continent. He imagines that the question of who will govern the Southwest will be answered in terms that anticipate Herbert Spencer's slogan "survival of the fittest" as applied to races and nations. The mistake of Captain White and Captain Glanton is to believe that military supremacy is the sign of a group's biological superiority—the same mistake social Darwinism would later make (but that Darwin himself did not)—rather than a cultural or environmental advantage that was historical and transitory.

Perhaps the most important way *Blood Meridian* invites readers to think about the religious context and religious meaning of evolution is its interest in seeing the system as a product of design. Like other nineteenth-century natural historians, the judge understands that the world might hold signs of the mind of God. Thus, in another scene of scientific instruction in the novel, the geologist judge one evening breaks open rocks,

> in whose organic lobations he purported to read news of the earth's origins, holding an extemporary lecture in geology to a small gathering who nodded and spat. A few would quote him scripture to confound his ordering up of eons out of the ancient chaos and other apostate supposings.
> The judge smiled.
> Books lie, he said.
> God dont lie.
> No, said the judge. He does not. And these are his words.
> He held up a chunk of rock.
> He speaks in stones and trees, the bones of things. (122)

Besides recapitulating the mid-nineteenth century's debate between the Bible's attestation of a young earth and the developing geological evidence advanced by Charles Lyell—whose discovery of vast "eons" was the precondition for Darwin to hypothesize that a natural selection might function analogously to artificial selection (i.e., breeding)—the judge's extemporaneous lecture suggests that the natural world provides a kind of writing ("these are his words") wherein the intention of God might be discerned.

The judge's "lecture in geology" was inspired by a similar scene in Samuel Chamberlain's memoir *My Confession: Recollections of a Rogue*, which was the historical source for many of the Glanton gang's characters and episodes in *Blood Meridian*. Of "Judge Holden of Texas," Chamberlain writes "Who or what he was, no one knew, but a more cool blooded villain never went unhung. He stood six foot six in his moccasins, had a large fleshy frame, a dull-tallow colored face destitute of hair and all expression" (306). That McCarthy had evolution on his mind when composing *Blood Meridian* is suggested by the fictional elaboration he made to the historical Judge Holden. Chamberlain's Holden seems to have had expertise in botany, geology, and archeology: thus the historical Holden gave a "scientific lecture on geology" to the Glanton gang which, according to Chamberlain, "no doubt was very learned, but hardly true, for one statement he made was 'that *millions* of years had witnessed the operation producing the result around us,' which Glanton, with recollections of the Bible teaching his young mind had undergone, said 'was a d——d lie'" (311). As John Sepich notes, the scene "gives the reader an appreciation of the judge's uncommonly advanced education; for example, Sir Charles Lyell's revolutionary *Principles of Geology* was published in England in 1833, but Lyell's work did not become current in North America until his visits there in the 1840s" (17).[9] McCarthy added to the historical Holden's expertise in geology, botany, and archeology the additional sciences of ornithology and paleontology.

These last two were particularly associated with evolution—the first, as noted above, a probable allusion to Darwin's work on finches in the Galapagos—and this elaboration gives us an additional clue that in working up his source material McCarthy purposefully incorporated references to evolution. Chamberlain's Holden in fact gives two lectures on geology in *My Confession*, and intriguingly, when asked regarding one of these, on the erosion of the Grand Canyon (a lecture scene Chamberlain later painted; see figure 2), "'how he knew all this,' this encyclopedian Scalp Hunter replied, 'Nature, these rocks, this little broken piece of clay (holding up a little fragment of painted pottery, such as are found all over the desert) the ruins scattered all over the land, all tell me the story of the past" (318). Chamberlain's Holden, the natural historian who asserts that "these rocks . . . tell me the story of the past," becomes in McCarthy's judge the natural theologian to whom God "speaks in stones and trees, the bones of things."

The genealogy of this critical figure of natural theology—nature read for signs of the divine creator—links Darwin's intellectual precursors to the debates about evolution while McCarthy was composing *Blood Meridian*. The proximate origin of the figure famously lay in William Paley's 1802 *Natural Theology*, which, we saw in chapter 6, had for its primal scene Paley stumbling upon a watch. The watch's complexity showed evidence of

Lecture on Geology, by Judge Holden.

FIGURE 2.   Judge Holden delivers a "scientific lecture on geology" in Samuel Chamberlain's memoir *My Confession: Recollections of a Rogue*, the inspiration for many characters and episodes in *Blood Meridian*, including the judge's "lecture in geology." Chamberlain painted the scene from memory many years later. Chamberlain's Holden, the natural historian who asserts that "these rocks . . . tell me the story of the past," becomes in McCarthy's judge the natural theologian to whom God "speaks in stones and trees, the bones of things." Image courtesy of West Point Museum Collection, United States Military Academy.

intention and design, thought Paley, unlike the previously stumbled-upon stone. Paley reasoned that the human eye had a similarly intricate structure, and thus had to have been designed by a creator with a purposeful goal. For Paley, such intricacies and purposefulness of adaptation in the animal world were not only evidence *that* there was a creator, but also evidence *for* the character of the designer. Thus one could conclude by reading nature that the attributes of the Deity included "Omnipotence, omniscience, omnipresence, eternity, self-existence, necessary existence, spirituality" (231) as well as "Unity" (234). The goodness of the creator could likewise be inferred because the design of contrivance is "in a vast plurality" beneficial (237), and because the Deity added pleasure and joy, which outweigh pain. Paley was notably anxious about predation, writing, "From the confessed and felt imperfection of our knowledge, we ought to presume, that there may be consequences of this economy which are hidden from us: from the benevolence which pervades the general designs of nature, we ought also to presume, that these consequences, if they could enter into our calculation, would turn the balance on the favorable side" (244).

The importance of Paley's design inference cannot be overstated for the history of evolution and the controversy that has attended it ever since. Paley was admired and quoted by Darwin, who appreciated Paley's point about organisms' suitability to their environment. But Darwin conceived of a different mechanism for adaptation, and the idea he arrived at was natural selection operating on forces such as random mutation across eons of time. Thus the adaptability and complexity that life shows does not result from an intentional process; in Richard Dawkins's reworking of Paley's central figure, the watchmaker is blind. Nonetheless, religious opposition to evolution has frequently expressed itself using figures in which nature is read as signs of the creator and his attributes. Taking its cue from William Paley almost two hundred years earlier, the Institute for Creation Research—which, as we saw in chapter 6, was behind efforts to legislate creationism into American classrooms while McCarthy was writing *Blood Meridian*—reads nature not only as evidence for divine creation, but evidence of the character of the creator.[10] The famous astronomer Fred Hoyle's remark that compared natural selection to the chances of "a hurricane blowing through a junk yard and chancing to assemble a Boeing 747," frequently quoted by creationists, likewise argued that improbability implied intention (Dawkins 234).[11] The Intelligent Design movement's textbook *Of Pandas and People* similarly updated this figure in their notion of a truck left close to a "native village," as we have seen.

These two arguments from Paley—that nature shows evidence of design, and that we can read that design for evidence of the character of the creator—were the context of McCarthy's composition of *Blood Meridian* insofar as they were the conclusions of the creation science of the 1970s and 1980s that was being legislated into high school biology classrooms across the South. It is thus not accidental that the allusions to evolution in the novel often take the form of scenes of instruction wherein the scientist judge lectures his scripture-quoting students—such as the "lecture in geology" cited above. In my brief sketch of the legislative and judicial history of creation science and of the controversy raging across the South in chapter 6 I emphasized the states of Tennessee and Texas because McCarthy moved from the former to El Paso in 1977.[12] My argument then is that we need to read *Blood Meridian* against this contemporaneous 1970s and 1980s backdrop of the debate between fundamentalist Christianity and evolution.

McCarthy has had a lifelong interest in science and has been associated with the interdisciplinary science Santa Fe Institute for a quarter-century. Unlike many living writers who have institutional homes in university English or creative writing departments, McCarthy's presence as a fellow (and now trustee) at the Santa Fe Institute puts him in daily contact not with literary critics and theorists but with particle physicists, theoretical biologists, paleobiologists, climate change scientists, complex systems theorists, and so on (Kushner). From his (uncompleted) University of Tennessee studies of engineering and physics to his current role as "interdisciplinary translator among the heavy thinkers" and proofreader for Santa Fe scientists' papers and books, McCarthy has been immersed in scientific conversation and research for decades.[13] "I'm here because I like science, and this is a fun place to spend time," he recently told a reporter: "I'm not here because I'm a novelist. I just managed to sneak in. I haven't read a novel in years" (quoted in Flood). Indeed, while McCarthy began writing *Blood Meridian* as early as 1975, the bulk of its composition came after his move to El Paso and with a Mac-Arthur Foundation "genius grant" in 1981; the Wittliff Collections' "Guide to Cormac McCarthy Papers" suggests 1980–1985 as the chief timeline of the novel's various drafts.[14] While receiving his MacArthur award, McCarthy met and became close friends with the foundation's director, the particle physicist Murray Gell-Mann, who went on to found the Santa Fe Institute in 1984.[15] McCarthy later moved to the Santa Fe area to be closer to the Institute, where he found his intellectual home. Thus his composition of *Blood Meridian* in the early 1980s coincided with the early emergence of his eventual intellectual network of cutting-edge scientific researchers and with widespread media attention to the intense creation science vs. evolution debate in Texas, Tennessee, and other Southern states. It is entirely probable that McCarthy would have been paying attention to the most famous science vs. religion controversy while he was writing his novel (as was Sagan during this same period, we have seen), as well as the Paleyesque arguments that animated creationist ideas.[16]

But my argument is not that the judge represents the forces of modernizing atheistic evolutionary science against the scripture-citing but (à la the master narrative of secularization) religious-belief-imperiled Glanton gang. Rather, it is that the novel itself, like the judge, accepts the two Paleyesque design inferences, that we can discern evidence of a designer in the natural world and that the natural world is a kind of writing wherein we can read the character of the designer. Like the fundamentalists' creation science and the later updated nonfundamentalist creation science of Intelligent Design, McCarthy works within the tradition of Paley's natural theology, discerning in nature evidence of God's character.[17] Unlike them, however, he finds that evidence disturbingly suggestive of a God utterly unrecognizable to traditional Christian theology. McCarthy's dark reinterpretation of Paley's natural theology thus suggests one way that American fiction responded to the growing social and political power of the evangelical and fundamentalist Christian resurgence emerging from the South since the 1970s, a revival that came to dominate the nation in the decades to come. *Blood Meridian* takes the resurgence's theological claims seriously, working those claims through to their logical conclusion.

In my reading, then, the judge is not an archon trying to conceal the truth about the good divine spirit but is rather the interpreter of the dark design, reading the fossil record of extinct species and systemic violence as the words of the God who chose to fashion his living creatures through evolution. The judge takes the position of today's theistic evolutionists who accept the evidence of an old earth and speciation through evolution, teasing out the character of the creator through the signs of his creation. Unlike the Christian evolutionists, however, the judge—and McCarthy—take seriously Paley's design inferences. Or rather, a better way to put it would be to say that in the judge McCarthy creates a character who is an enthusiast for the design found in the natural world. This is no Gnostic scheme wherein God's goodness is preserved through a complicated alibi; rather, the judge as evolutionary scientist and philosopher of war recognizes the divine design in natural history, which is, the novel contends, the material from which human history emerges in continuity.[18] Or to put it in the terms of the judge's question quoted earlier—"If God meant to interfere in the degeneracy of mankind would he not have done so by now?" (153), the source for this book's title—the answer is simply that this violent degeneracy is part of God's own design.

Blood Meridian thus recognizes what Christian theology since Darwin has struggled to resist: that there is no way that a God who is omnipotent, omniscient, and benevolent would choose evolution through which to work. The crucial component of evolution from this perspective is not its seeming randomness but rather the component of natural selection.[19] Darwin referred to natural selection as "the great and complex battle of life" (80; quoted in Barton et al. 458). As the science of evolution has revealed, there are "other evolutionary processes such as mutation, random drift, recombination, and migration" (Barton et al. 458) but natural selection is "the most important evolutionary process" because it "is the only process that leads to adaptation" (457):

Although many processes shape evolution, natural selection is special because it alone creates complex, functioning organisms. All other processes tend to degrade what has been built up by natural selection, simply because these processes act at random with respect to function. Mutation makes random changes in DNA sequence that, if they have any effect at all, tend to disrupt function. Migration introduces genes from elsewhere, which tend not to be adapted to their new environment. Similarly, recombination and random drift will, on average, disrupt genotype frequencies that have been built up by selection so as to increase fitness. (463)

Evolution, the increasing adaptive functionality and complexity of an organism, only works because of selection pressure. If all organisms are permitted to pass on their genes, there will be change but no selection and hence no evolution. The system, therefore, requires selection pressure to work: the less-adapted organisms on average and over vast amounts of time must not be permitted to pass on their less-adaptive genes. Natural selection, then, requires predation and starvation. Predation creates selection pressure because it is a kind of arms-race of predator and prey species: both will evolve. Similarly, Darwin's insight about natural selection was predicated on the work of Malthus: resource shortages would provide selection pressure where predation did not, weeding out the less adaptive genes.[20]

We see these signs of predation and starvation everywhere in *Blood Meridian*. The recognition that he is food for other creatures is perhaps behind the shriek of terror that the already-wounded Sproule utters when he awakes one night to find a "bloodbat" feasting on his neck (69). And while the chief predators of humans in *Blood Meridian* are other humans, there are many instances of humans being food for animals, whether by wolf (63), coyotes (44), buzzards (64), bear (143–44), pigs (189), or vulture (273–74). Similarly, there are many instances of humans preying on animals. The desert setting of the novel models the way the limited food and water resources place selection pressure on the organisms that live there or pass through. Amidst the many bones that the kid and the Glanton gang always come across (e.g., 258), the lizard slurping the kid's spit (66; cited in the epigraph to this chapter) stands out as exquisitely adapted to the desert ecology for which his species evolved. The kid, by contrast, is several times at risk of death by dehydration or starvation. *Blood Meridian* presents us with an ecosystem of finely balanced predation and starvation, wherein humans and nonhuman animals are integrated and mutually implicated. We are watching, as we read the novel, the two crucial forms of natural selection pressure at work.

Creationism's Theodicy

> The judge stood this great pillar of stained and petri-
> fied bone before him and he told of the eons since
> the beast walked the earth. . . .
>
> What was life's plan? said the judge. What was the
> plan for this great fool of a beast?
>
> *Blood Meridian* draft

It was, of course, the problem of predation that made Paley so anxious, reasonably, in his *Natural Theology*; what he did not know was that predation was at the
very root of the mechanism of natural selection whereby the evolution of organisms occurred. The scandal of natural selection for theology may partly account
for the continuing attraction of literalist, Bible-based accounts of creation, which
entirely sidestep the problems of theodicy posed by evolution. Indeed, as William Hoesch, writing for the Institute for Creation Research, reflects,

> what a man does with the fossil record tells a lot about his worldview. Is
> it the result of a world-covering deluge? Or did this sorry chronicle of
> pain, suffering, and death precede humans (and the reign of death) by
> millions of years? A lot hangs on this question. Defending the goodness
> of God in a world full of suffering is a difficult job. The job is made nigh
> unto impossible if we place at God's feet the carnage of the fossil record.
>
> Try to imagine God standing on His newly created Earth and call-
> ing it "very good" when under his feet lay the ruined remains of
> former life forms buried in various positions of agony and stages of
> decay. Yet all Christians who believe in an old Earth must embrace this
> picture. Some defend it by claiming we Americans get too sentimental
> over animals; only human suffering matters. Others say human suffer-
> ing is, in itself, a "good" thing. Most ignore it.[21]

Through Paleyesque design inferences, this young-earth creationism contends that it would be impossible to harmonize the "carnage," "agony,"
and "decay" of evolution with a good, biblical God. If my argument in this
book is correct—that McCarthy had his eye on the most famous religion
and science debate while composing *Blood Meridian*, as challenges to creation
science legislation inspired by the ICR were making their way through the
courts on their way to the *Edwards* decision—then this historical simultaneity contextualizes the Paleyesque theological conclusions circulating in the
novel. Although theology is still charged with the task of providing an alibi
for God, this is much easier to supply when only several thousands, not billions, of years are at issue. Indeed, while the young-earth creationists have

turned their backs on knowledge, the theological account of suffering and death they produce is coherent: in their scheme, death enters the system only with Adam, and the carnage of the supposed fossil strata is actually the record of Noah's flood. In both cases, violence is a just punishment from God, not an intrinsic property of God's original creation.[22] Without the need of natural selection to supply increased adaptability—or the alternative "irreducible complexity" ingeniously supplied by an Intelligent Designer—the problem of God's responsibility for biological suffering is almost entirely evaded.

In contrast to fundamentalist Christianity, the thoughtful, critical theology that apprehends the problem that evolution poses has tended to find itself abandoning some of the qualities of the classical notion of God. A representative example might be John Haught's *God After Darwin: A Theology of Evolution*.[23] Haught is an illuminating representative partly because he illustrates the complex range of Christian positions one might have on evolution; in fact, he testified against Intelligent Design in the famous *Kitzmiller v. Dover* (2004) case that dealt it a crushing defeat. He is a scientifically literate Catholic theologian who accepts the age of the earth, evolution, and natural selection as the mechanism that chiefly drives it and disputes the Intelligent Design notion that there are examples of supposed "irreducible complexity" in evolution that suggest there have to have been divine supplements every once in great while to an otherwise natural process.

In *God After Darwin*, Haught attempts to answer a theological problem similar to that which made Paley anxious: the question of what suffering means for the character of the creator God. Haught recognizes that evolution poses a serious, possibly lethal, problem for theodicy, and attempts to arrive at a strong explanation. As he describes the question,

> How could a powerful and compassionate creator permit all the suffering, aimless wandering, and obscene waste that we behold in surveying the millennia of evolution? How could a lovingly concerned God tolerate the struggle, pain, cruelty, brutality, and death that lie beneath the relatively stable and serene surface of nature's present order? (22)

Indeed, the most important challenge evolution poses to theology is not common descent, but rather that evolution extends the timelines of already existing questions of theodicy: "Darwin has extended the story of life's innocent suffering considerably, leading us down pathways of pain and bloodletting that stretch back through many millions of years. His 'dangerous idea' has uncovered regions of terror and torture that we had never known about before" (24).

Though Haught describes the problem in terms strikingly similar to the ICR writer, he is unable to dismiss the problem as never having happened. The theological solutions he arrives at include the idea of God co-suffering with his creation (50) and perhaps an afterlife for organisms (54), both compatible with the classical notion of God. God's self-sacrificing love means that God has stepped back and allowed his creation to raucously choose new options in the vast temporal space of possible organism designs. The unfolding universe, especially its evolved organisms, "cannot yet be perfect" (59). Thus, concludes Haught, "By holding these and all cosmic occurrences in the heart of divine compassion God redeems them from all loss and gives eternal meaning to everything, though in a hidden way that for us humans only faith can affirm" (60).

Haught's account is both orthodox and surprisingly heterodox, and is revealingly silent on some crucial problems. The orthodoxy comes from the Christian idea of the suffering Jesus. But how Jesus's suffering "redeems" the untold trillions of organisms who have been eaten by faster, stronger prey is difficult to say, unless it merely means that God remembers their being eaten, or that all the animal and human prey get to start over in some sort of envisioned future afterlife—an animal heaven. (But as James Dickey famously reminds us in his poem "The Heaven of Animals," predator heaven needs lots of prey; it's tough to be a fawn in wolf paradise.) Haught's heterodoxy comes with the idea, drawn from Pierre Teilhard de Chardin, that the universe cannot yet be made perfect, but is in the process of becoming so (40–41). In this case, "evil and suffering could be thought of as the dark side of the world's ongoing creation" (41). Teilhard, in turn, saw evil and "physical suffering" as the "*statistically inevitable by-product*" (196) of creation, the inevitability of which suggests a limit—chosen or exterior—on the Creator. In this kind of process theology, suffering and pain are products of a system not caused by human agency à la the Genesis account of original sin; rather, they are the systemic limits within which a no-longer-omnipotent Creator crafts his work. As another process theologian's book title—Charles Hartshorne's *Omnipotence and other Theological Mistakes*—suggests, one of the qualities of the classical God is jettisoned in this account. The critical silence in Haught's work is the question of God's responsibility for choosing to craft his creation through the method of natural selection. The idea that God had no choice but to accept the suffering entailed in the mechanism of natural selection within evolution means God is constrained by a choice he has made. But self-constraint entails responsibility for the consequences of that constraint, which does not get theology around the theodicy question it is trying to answer.

Another method of trying to avoid the problematic theodicy of evolution is by focusing on the evolutionary development of altruism, as Kenneth Miller does in *Finding Darwin's God: A Scientist's Search for Common Ground Between God and Evolution.* Miller in general is not as disturbed as the ICR folk or Haught by the suffering and pain involved in evolution, suggesting that "cruelty is relative" (245) and that "we cannot call evolution cruel if all we are really doing is assigning to evolution the raw savagery of nature itself" (246). The first response is cynical, and the hypothetical distinction of the second between evolution and nature evades the fact of God's responsibility for both. But for Miller, the development of altruism shows that "evolutionary success, it turns out, is rooted a little deeper than shallow self-preservation" (248). Indeed, E.O. Wilson points out that

> it might be supposed that the human condition is so distinctive and came so late in the history of life on Earth as to suggest the hand of a divine creator. Yet in a critical sense the human achievement was not unique at all. Biologists have identified about two dozen evolutionary lines in the modern world fauna that attained advanced social life based on some degree of altruistic division of labor. Most arose in the insects. Several were independent origins, in marine shrimp, and three appeared among the mammals, that is, in two African mole rats, and us.

But these and other[24] recent accounts of the evolution of altruism and kinship cannot rescue evolution from the theological problems it poses because we are still left with the simple fact that God chose the brutality and suffering of natural selection to arrive at the altruistic social behavior of humans that only eventually and partly mitigated these things. *Blood Meridian*, in fact, may be moving in this direction: it is possible, as many critics have done, to read the kid's maturity as "the man" by the end of the novel as evidence that he has withdrawn from, or developed a moral conscience beyond, the violence of his youth with the Glanton gang. We don't have to imagine that he somehow had "clemency for the heathen," as the judge puts it, to see the man's new reluctance to kill, as with the Elrod episode in which he tries to talk his way out of a confrontation but is provoked into killing in self-defense (333–36). And indeed, there are other moments of altruism in the novel. But while this reading seems the most reasonably optimistic interpretation of *Blood Meridian*, the eventual arrival at altruism through evolution does not mitigate the theological problem that God chose the brutal system of natural selection operating over billions of years in order to craft social altruism in humans—as well as ants and mole rats.[25]

"Inevitably," Haught concludes his chapter, perhaps sensing the limits of his solution, "all theodicies fail" (59). Process theology's response to evolution, here represented by Haught and Teilhard, is to sacrifice one of the classical attributes of God, his omnipotence, and maybe his omniscience too. In contrast, *Blood Meridian* is a kind of Paleyesque thought experiment that likewise concludes that the classical notion of God cannot be correct, and proceeds along the different track of giving up God's goodness. Both these theological responses to evolution are intellectually coherent. That these nonclassical Christian theologies prefer to discount God's omnipotence and/or omniscience rather than his benevolence as *Blood Meridian* does is understandable: I would choose that too. But the uncomfortable point is that we must now choose, no longer able to have all three. These are logically satisfying answers, but they are ones that conservative resurgent Christians do not accept as they are outside of traditional Christian theology. What ends up being remarkable, then, is the gap between the generally conservative theology animating the resurgence in the last four decades and the generally liberal, intellectually robust, apologetics-oriented Christian belief system—what Dembski calls "academic theology"—that has adapted to new knowledge by rethinking classical concepts (*End* 8).[26] That gap appears to be unbridgeable.

Reading *Blood Meridian* for its attention to the theological problems that evolution poses allows for a fresh interpretation of its famously puzzling and enigmatic epilogue, in which a "man" progresses across a plain digging with a steel tool that "strikes fire in the hole" and is followed by "wanderers in search of bones and those who do not search" (351). As Mark Busby has reviewed, critics have read the epilogue historically (as the closing of the frontier by fencing or railroad; see Sepich and others), as a mythic Prometheus come to contest the judge's power (Harold Bloom), as a Gnostic savior (Mundik and Daugherty), and in terms of Christian existentialism (Busby). Each interpretation has merits and limitations. In suggesting another possible reading, I think it is important to remember that the epilogue is not the novel's first scene of looking for bones; we have seen these activities in the figure of the judge, who has sought them out and perhaps dug holes to find them. Given that the judge has previously suggested that God speaks "in stones and trees, the bones of things," it is not surprising to find the final figure digging through rocks, followed by those who seek bones. What if this figure, who is usually understood to be a new character because he is unnamed, is actually an old character—the one, we have just heard, who says he will never die (349)? What if the judge's scientific work carries on across the plain as he digs new holes? The "track of holes" across the prairie, the epilogue tells us, seems like "a validation of sequence and causality as if each round and perfect hole owed its existence to the one before it." In this reading, the holes may mythically represent the progress of paleontology as it seeks to establish "sequence and causality" in the fossil record of biological development. Intriguingly, one manuscript draft of the epilogue has "each round and perfect excavation" instead of the eventual "each round and perfect hole"—a word more precisely suggestive of the scientific labor of fossil hunting.[27] The division of the wanderers into those who seek bones and those who do not seek may merely refer to those who accept this fossil evidence and those who reject it, as we have already seen, during the judge's disquisitions on paleontology and geology. These others who do not seek bones may be those who do not want to know about these new words of God, precisely because they are words that convey a different kind of knowledge about his character, as Hoesch so clearly saw. The epilogue's final image thus returns us to the scientific inquiries into evolution frequently alluded to in *Blood Meridian*, as well as to the natural theology controversies occurring in the 1840s and the 1980s as we read rocks and bones as the words of God.

Indeed, the problem of what it means that God set up the universe this way and of the human ability to question that system is raised early in *Blood Meridian* during a discussion between the kid and a hermit he boards with one night in the desert:

> The old man swung his head back and forth. The way of the transgressor is hard. God made this world, but he didnt make it to suit everybody, did he?
> I dont believe he much had me in mind.
> Aye, said the old man. But where does a man come by his notions.
> What world's he seen that he liked better?
> I can think of better places and better ways.
> Can ye make it be?
> No. (20)

We do not actually have to have experienced other, better ways in order to imagine them. We can perceive, with the kid, that God did not craft his world to suit us, in the sense of having particular concern for us as a group or as individuals. The system of suffering that God chose—if indeed he did choose it—bespeaks a creator for whom creaturely pain and death are not important.

We should consider *Blood Meridian* to be a kind of theological intervention into the contemporary moment of the conservative Christian resurgence, one grounded in the specific history of recent American debates about evolution. Agreeing with both conservative and liberal Christian positions that the Paleyesque design inference tells us something important about the character of the creator, the novel suggests that the former is in error in trying to preserve the classical outlines of God, and that the latter has not carefully considered the reasonable alternative that God is unmoved by human and animal suffering—or, worse, has actively willed it through evolution. Implied in McCarthy's vision is not just an anti-theodicy of who God is, but also an anthropology of who we are. In the last paragraph of *Origin of Species*, Darwin writes, "Thus, from the war of nature, from famine and death, the most exalted object which we are capable of conceiving, namely, the production of the higher animals, directly follows" (490). It is perhaps this "war of nature" to which the judge refers in *Blood Meridian* when he declares to the Glanton gang, "War was always here. Before man was, war waited for him. The ultimate trade awaiting its ultimate practitioner" (259). While we are agents of suffering and destruction, that is not because we were their first cause, but rather because we resulted from a process in which those elements are intrinsic and constitutive.

CHAPTER 8

The Postmodern Gospel According to Dan

> Fact: . . .
> All descriptions of artwork, architecture, documents,
> and secret rituals in this novel are accurate.
>
> Dan Brown, *The Da Vinci Code*

If religiously inflected literature in the contemporary period sometimes features a kind of sacred writing in nature that needs interpretation, a scientist figure is required to detect the divine patterns in our world. McCarthy's judge and Sagan's astronomer arrive at hidden revelations promising to reveal the mind of God, working in the natural theology tradition that old-fashioned creationists since Paley and refashioned Intelligent Designers were likewise claiming. But when the hidden signs are historical rather than natural, one needs a differently qualified protagonist. Perhaps someone trained in literary criticism, like Pynchon's Oedipa, who examines Renaissance plays and the world around her for hieroglyphs. Or someone like Pa Pa LaBas, whose knowledge of the Work and the loas has prepared him to discern the epic historical struggle between Jes Grew and the Wallflower Order. But what if the sacred code in history took not a literary form as in Pynchon or music and choreography as in Reed, but was a designed pattern recurring in art and architecture? What if Western art carried, to recall Pynchon's phrases, a coded history, a density of concealed meaning, an intent to communicate? How would one know what the code said, understand the hidden language? For that task, one would need a symbologist.

Just such a "symbologist" is the protagonist of Dan Brown's famous religious-mystery pop thriller *The Da Vinci Code*, published in 2003. Paired with a French "cryptologist," the Harvard symbologist Robert Langdon races through famous architectural sites in France and England on a treasure hunt for the Holy Grail. The clues have been left by a murdered art curator, but they also lie in the art and architecture of Europe, hiding in plain sight. Their search leads them to the shadowy "Priory of Sion," a conspiratorial group dedicated to preserving the secret that Jesus and Mary Magdalene were married and bore children whose descendants survive to this day. This explosive knowledge about Mary Magdalene—who is in fact the "Holy Grail," an embodiment of what the novel refers to as "the sacred feminine"—has been suppressed for centuries by the Catholic Church and its agents who, the novel contends, crafted the Bible by excising references to Jesus's humanness and his true relation to Mary. By the novel's end, the protagonists have made contact with the Priory and uncovered the secret, including the identity of the descendants of Jesus and Mary. While this hidden truth could be the basis of a new revelation to the world, the novel contends that the mystery of the sacred feminine is already the subject of ongoing revelation in Western art, music, and literature.

It was not the first time that the notion of a Jesus and Mary marriage had been the basis of a controversial novel (and then film): years before, *The Last Temptation of Christ* caused an uproar over its representation of Jesus's "last temptation" of starting a family with Mary instead of dying on the cross. Echoing this previous controversy, Christian reviewers of Brown's novel were similarly dismayed by its premise, with many concerned that naïve readers would read the novel for historical information, especially given its initial claims to documentary veracity (cited in the epigraph above). Indeed, critic Victoria Nelson, reviewing the data that thirteen percent of Americans believe Christ's death was faked and he had a family with Mary (106), suggests not unreasonably that Brown's novel was already having such an effect. Seeing it as "a direct attack against the foundation of the Christian faith," many Christian reviewers, pastors, and lay people decided they needed to "speak out" (Erwin Lutzer, quoted in Goodstein). The novel, said these critics, contained "attacks against the Christian faith" that nonetheless "ironically provide Christians with a unique opportunity for effective evangelism" (Maier). The film and novel were "a systematic attack on the divinity of Jesus Christ" filled with "bizarre counterfactual propositions" (Hagen). The movie version was no improvement on the novel, as it "promotes the mischievous fictions that masquerade in the book as the revelation of historical secrets" (Hurtado). Many Christians were moved to wonder about *The Da Vinci Code*'s popularity; it seemed to be an attack on basic Christian ideas, but it also "hit a cultural nerve" (Bock, "Christian"), and was itself, as Eric Plumer put it, "a sign of the American culture wars" (xvii).

Indeed, conservative Catholic *New York Times* columnist Ross Douthat saw the novel as the intellectual culmination of "revisionist" historians who had aided and abetted do-it-yourself spirituality and rejected Christian orthodoxy—a rejection to which he (like others) attributed the declining demographics of mainline Protestantism (*Bad* 149–81).

What struck other reviewers and critics more specifically was the novel's anti-Catholicism, with one publication placing it among "the Five Most Influential Anti-Catholic Books" since the Protestant Reformation (Lockwood). Beginning with the premise that Constantine and the Church fathers edited the Bible to exclude female power represented by Mary in particular and the sacred feminine in general, the novel's plot also entailed members of the shadowy Catholic organization Opus Dei simultaneously pursuing the Grail, and willing to murder for it. Indeed, Langdon and Sophie, the cryptologist, race to find the Grail before it can be found by a murderous Opus Dei monk named Silas, whose albinism signals his embodiment of evil, as with McCarthy's judge, Abel's antagonist in Momaday's novel, and even Melville's white whale.[1] Victoria Nelson argued that the novel could be understood in the tradition of a "fantasy pop culture religion I like to call faux Catholicism" originating in the "Protestant anticlerical Gothic novels of the eighteenth century" (88). The Gothic evinces a sense of Protestant anticlericalism, but, insofar as it was "the first Western literary genre operating implicitly in the vacuum left by the departure of religious belief" (90), is also permeated by a sense of secularization and disenchantment. Faux Catholic novels like *The Da Vinci Code* draw on Catholicism's status as "the only church besides the Orthodox that provides full historical continuity from the beginnings of Christianity" (88), but they also, as with the Gothic in general, resolve initial mysteries with "a rational explanation" (93).

When it is revealed that the monk and an Opus Dei archbishop, whom the reader is led to believe are behind the search to find and destroy the evidence of the Holy Grail, have actually been manipulated by Langdon's friend, the Grail-hunter Leigh Teabing, this final plot-twist initially appears to cancel the novel's anti-Catholic message. But as Nelson suggests, "even though, as Robert Langdon declares at the end of *The Da Vinci Code*, the Vatican and Opus Dei are 'completely innocent,' once again I suspect this last-minute plot reversal may be lost on the vast majority of readers, who take away with them the idea, foregrounded for most of the story, that Opus Dei was really behind it all" (97). Langdon's judgment likewise ignores the novel's initial premise that the truth about Mary and Jesus was the subject of a historical cover-up by the church to deceive the masses. Nelson concludes, "The Catholic Church has reason to be upset about *The Da Vinci Code* because the function it serves in secularizing Jesus is not really to promote a dialogue about Christianity, as both Brown and its apologists have rather ingeniously argued, but rather to help deliver a death blow to the Christian Trinity as it has been understood by all denominations, not just the Catholic Church" (105). Thus, Brown's "depiction of the Roman Church's past constitutes a greatest hits of anti-Catholicism," wrote Douthat of *The Da Vinci Code* and its predecessor *Angels and Demons*, novels that "end with a big anti-Catholic reveal (Jesus had kids with Mary Magdalene! That terrorist plot against the Vatican was actually launched by an archconservative priest!)": "Having dismissed Catholicism's truth claims and demonized its most sincere defenders, Brown pats believers on the head and bids them go on fingering their rosary beads" ("Dan").

I want to argue in this chapter, however, that beneath the anti-Catholic veneer of *The Da Vinci Code* lay a deeper attack on Protestantism. *The Da Vinci Code* is a bad novel, but its outsized influence on contemporary religious beliefs—perhaps finding particular receptivity among the growing number of Americans citing "none" as their religious identification (Putnam and Campbell 566)—and its cultural significance as a wildly popular antiresurrection narrative in the post-9/11 years of the new millennium, suggest it merits critical attention. Brown's novel can best be thought of as a postmodern attack on the Bible, the sacred, inerrant status of which is considerably more important to Protestant theology than to Catholic teaching. The novel's postmodernism lay not in its form—its prose is turgid and plodding, traditional without any of the artistry of tradition—but in its historical claims about Jesus, the early church, and the Bible's authorship and composition. What seems to be the anti-Catholic content of the novel's shadowy European plot and exposition is better understood as an attack on the biblical theology characteristic of the Protestantism at the core of the conservative Christian resurgence. Christian fundamentalism, after all, originally defined itself as a rejection of two nineteenth-century sciences: biological evolution and the historical-critical methods investigating the manuscript history, authors, and editors of the Bible. The importance of the Bible's status as the Word of God was not confined to fundamentalists, however; many born-again, Bible-believing, conservative evangelical Christians might not be biblical literalists, but they still see the text as having divine authority and divine origin. Catholicism in general, and liberal Protestant traditions as well, have placed less emphasis on biblical inerrancy, and been more ready to accommodate the way historical-textual criticism details the historical embeddedness of scripture, with sometimes-surprising conclusions about contexts, authors, and theologies. As it turned out, Dan Brown was about as ignorant of this scholarship as some fundamentalists are.

Recollecting the Blood of the Lamb

> It is typical of my unregenerate soul that I can only
> see this as a marvelous theme for a novel.
>
> Anthony Burgess, reviewing *Holy Blood, Holy Grail*

The Da Vinci Code shares with *The Crying of Lot 49* and *Mumbo Jumbo* the premise that, as the latter puts it, "beneath or behind all political and cultural warfare lies a struggle between secret societies" (18), societies whose historical machinations and purposes must be uncovered by the protagonists. The three novels are exercises in the consolation of paranoia, to recall Jameson's apt phrase from chapter 5. *The Da Vinci Code* and *The Crying of Lot 49* share a sense of secularized disenchantment, with questions of religious identification and faith operating in a world where gods no longer walk—in contrast to *Mumbo Jumbo*, where the loas still ride their horses if one does not feed them properly. While Pynchon and Reed treat humorously the mythic conspiracy plots they etch out—though both their works have a serious theme as well—Brown appears wholly devoted to the conspiratorial and theological backdrop of his novel, with the plot functioning as the fictional mode for revealing real forces.[2]

The Da Vinci Code's conspiracy is uncovered during the novel's lengthy expositions, and it rests on two historical claims—one about the ancient world and Christian origins, and one about a secret society operating from early Christianity to the present—taken from a 1982 bestseller, *Holy Blood, Holy Grail*, by Michael Baigent, Richard Leigh, and Henry Lincoln (published in the United States as *The Holy Blood and the Holy Grail*). *The Da Vinci Code* was so derivative of this pop history that the authors sued Brown, unsuccessfully, for copyright infringement.[3] Joining the ancient and modern timelines, as in Reed, are the Knights Templar, who withhold a secret from the world. The novel's claim about Christian origins is that the mortal Jesus married Mary Magdalene, and that she bore a daughter after he was crucified. Mary and the child, the legend goes, travelled to France, where some of their descendants still live—including, it turns out by the novel's end, the French cryptologist paired with Langdon, Sophie Neveu.[4] The patriarchal church, meanwhile, concealed this truth, replacing Jesus's purpose in constructing his church through his wife Mary (representing, we suppose, the sacred feminine) with male power and a set of traditions and writings that devalued Mary in particular, and women and sexuality generally. The church makes "the Grail" into a matter of Jesus's blood rather than his bloodline.

Intriguingly, *The Da Vinci Code* "corrects" Christianity by establishing the importance of Jesus's bloodline rather than his blood, or to adapt Werner

Sollers's terms, changing the truth about Christianity from being a matter of "consent" to a matter of "descent." Just as (we saw) white authors
such as Kingsolver and Robinson adopt intensely multicultural tropes when
working through the question of religious identity in the contemporary
period, so too does Dan Brown in one sense multiculturalize the questions involved. Ishmael Reed and Gloria Anzaldúa imagine that beneath
the pagan-Christian historical struggle lies a palimpsest of a deeper Christian debt to pagan gods. This is true for Reed both with the Vodou loa,
the African-originated deities pictorially represented by Catholic saints, but
also with the Wallflower Order's secret worship of a black idol and, even
before that, the rivalry between Osiris and Set that in his mythic telling was
the origin of monotheism. Similarly, Anzaldúa portrays folk Catholicism
as concealing the true Aztec origin of Our Lady of Guadalupe, herself a
survivor of a previous polytheist struggle between a fertility pantheon and a
war-and-empire-building pantheon. The truth about these pagan gods was
historically suppressed by the Catholic Church, Reed and Anzaldúa and
Brown contend, in a movement that repressed human sexuality (especially in
Reed and Anzaldúa); for Anzaldúa and Brown more particularly, the patriarchal church conducts a war against what Brown calls the "sacred feminine,"
represented by a previously vibrant "goddess." Though each author crafts a
slightly different shape for this pagan-Christian struggle, the mythic pagan
history becomes the focus of what is to be reclaimed. *The Da Vinci Code* is
a kind of white American adoption of, and response to, the multicultural
mythography of *Mumbo Jumbo* and *Borderlands*.[5]

The search for proper religious identity is the endgame, in one sense,
of *The Da Vinci Code*, just as it is for Reed and Anzaldúa. The project of
recovering the pagan past entails a proper realignment of religious identity; as with Reed and Anzaldúa, and multiculturalism in general, religious
identification becomes a matter of descent rather than consent. Brown thus
follows their lead in using the figure of "blood" to describe the necessity
of aligning one's religious commitment to those of one's ancestors. But he
also supersedes them: whereas for Reed and Anzaldúa "blood" figures the
necessity of discovering one's ancestral gods, for Brown it figures the discovery that one's ancestor actually was a god—sort of. Thus Sophie, finally
discovering her long-lost brother, senses "the blood coursing through his
veins . . . the blood she now understood they shared" (580) as "the most
direct surviving" descendants of Jesus and Mary (581).[6] Responding to one
character's declaration about the Church's patriarchal cover-up that "the
greatest story ever told is, in fact, the greatest story ever *sold*" (350), Richard
Rambuss has observed of the novel's resolutely heterosexual mythology and

plot that it is also the "straightest story ever told." I suggest that *The Da Vinci Code* is likewise among the whitest stories every told, a novel without racial history and indeed without race. While it shares a key trope of multicultural religious fiction—the historical pagan-Christian struggle, the preference for the former, the need to realign religious commitments—it is not haunted, as Robinson's *Gilead* is, by a nonwhite presence, nor is it committed, as Kingsolver's *Poisonwood Bible* is, to an ethos of cultural pluralism and relativism. Instead, *The Da Vinci Code*'s seemingly multicultural plot of discovering one's ancestral religious identity turns on the postmodern expertise of reading signs and clues.

That reading depends in part on a notion of expertise. The novel shares with Reed and Anzaldúa a backbone of research, and similarly invites its readers into its research in the way that Reed's bibliography or Anzaldúa's endnotes do, mentioning several sources, including *Holy Blood, Holy Grail* (332), and anagrammatically hiding reference to that pop history's authors in Leigh Teabing's name. Reed's humor and postmodern form, however, warn the reader that his mythology is both tongue-in-cheek and seriously intentioned. Anzaldúa, on the other hand, is as humorless as Brown, but her research sources are as academic as they are speculative: while not necessarily representative of a consensus view, in other words, they are evidence-based and published in peer-reviewed anthropological journals or are anthropological textbooks. What really sets Brown apart from Reed and Anzaldúa in terms of their creative texts' frames of research, I wish to argue in the following pages, is that Brown makes academic expertise and evaluation of evidence central to his novel's plot and theme. PaPa LaBas and Oedipa are metaphysical detectives, but they are not experts in the conspiracies they uncover, and their authors are far too playful for us to take seriously—or only seriously—the metaphysical plots they uncover. As for Brown, critics of the novel who reviewed the numerous television interviews he gave following the novel's publication see his intentions as entirely serious (see, e.g., Lacy 82; Mexal 1087). There are no irony signals in *The Da Vinci Code* that would, in the manner of *The Crying of Lot 49* or *Mumbo Jumbo*, alert the reader to parody, humor, or the self-conscious tall tale.

I want to explore the religious ramifications of the novel's historical claims, beginning with a brief account of the secret society—brief partly because it has been addressed extensively by historians, and partly because it is less religiously interesting than the claims about Jesus and his family. As Norris J. Lacy confirms, what emerged after the novel's publication was "a thriving cottage industry: debunking the theories and revealing the errors in Brown's book" (81), an "industry of more than ninety books on the subject of all the things Brown got factually wrong" (Nelson 99). Rather than extensively rehearse those debunkings, I outline them and then turn to the more relevant religious claims of the novel.

The novel's action is sparked by the murder of the four "sénéchaux" of the secret Priory of Sion, whose identities have somehow been discovered. One of them is the curator at the Louvre, and he sets out the clues and riddles that eventually lead his granddaughter Sophie and Langdon to the secret of the Grail. "The Priory of Sion," Brown tells us on the "FACT" page that prefaces the novel, "a European secret society founded in 1099—is a real organization. In 1975 Paris's Bibliothèque Nationale discovered parchments known as *Les Dossiers Secrets*, identifying numerous members of the Priory of Sion, including Sir Isaac Newton, Botticelli, Victor Hugo, and Leonardo da Vinci" (1). As it turned out, however, the Priory of Sion was the object of an elaborate hoax begun years earlier by a French citizen who believed he was the descendent of the Merovingian dynasty of French kings, which ruled between the fifth and eighth centuries CE. As historians Bill Putnam and John Edwin Wood explain, Pierre Plantard "created a whole series of documents including elaborate genealogical tables that purported to trace his ancestry back to" Dagobert II (19); one of the documents contained a reference to a fabricated "Priory of Sion" dating to the twelfth century, and listed a table of grandmasters including da Vinci and Newton (20). But Plantard's deception was just a second layer "of false historical accretions" (19): an enterprising hotelier who bought Rennes-le-Château in the 1950s cultivated rumors that a turn-of-the-century priest who became mysteriously wealthy had uncovered the thirteenth-century treasure of the wife of Louis VIII on those grounds, rumored to include the documents that Plantard later fabricated and planted in the Bibliothèque Nationale.

Plantard's hoax was the product of much research; his addition of a fictional Plantard line onto the existing Merovingian family tree was enough to fool the amateur historians of *Holy Blood, Holy Grail*, who were researching the legend of Mary's arrival in France when they came across the documents. Their innovation was to connect the fictional Priory to their idée fixe of the marriage between Mary and Jesus and their descendants' survival in France. While Plantard admitted the hoax in 1993 (Nelson 99), this fact appears to have been unknown to Brown, who treats the Priory and other fabricated documents and events wholly seriously. While some critics have wondered whether Brown might be just pretending to believe his novel's elaborate mythology as he laughs "all the way to the bank" (Lacy 89), most conclude that "in interviews and in print, he has appeared too earnest and confident, too convinced, too much a Grail evangelist" to make his sincerity suspicious

(89). "Brown's knowledge of church history, art history, and Western esoteric societies has the stretched-thin feel of an undergraduate term paper," Victoria Nelson writes (97), but the novel and post-publication statements suggest Brown has mobilized that knowledge very much in earnest.

Part of our fascination with historical secrets rests with the way novelists join known history and existing mysteries to speculations and outright fictions. *The Crying of Lot 49* invites readers to pursue its textual clues, mimicking Oedipa's detective work by discovering that some of its references are to real people and events (Narcissus was a Bishop of Jerusalem in the second century) even as others are outright fiction (there is no Tristero). The Knights Templar really existed during the Crusades, to use another example, and they really were quartered, in 1120, on the Temple Mount in Jerusalem, which the Templars believed were above the ancient ruins of Solomon's Temple, destroyed in 587 BCE, and they really did emerge from being an impoverished order of knights (with their emblem being two knights riding on a single horse, suggesting their lack of resources) to being a wealthy and powerful order. Their order was dissolved almost two centuries later on what appear to be trumped-up charges of heresy and idolatry, particularly to an idol of "Baphomet." Thus, in *Mumbo Jumbo*, Reed spins these historical facts into the idea that an African-originated pagan god was hidden in the depths of Solomon's Temple, and that the Templars—a.k.a. the Wallflower Order—continue to worship this deity in secret, "He who made us and has not left us" (17). For Reed, the amusing episode suggests the serious symbolism that Western monotheism depends on an incompletely suppressed, non-Western, pagan polytheism.

In *The Da Vinci Code*, on the other hand, what the Templars discover is nothing less than a cache of secret documents outlining the truth about Jesus and Mary—a discovery whose control gives them enormous wealth and the power to blackmail the Vatican until they are largely destroyed in a counterstrike. "Nobody knows for sure" what the Templars found, Langdon explains to Sophie, "but the one thing on which all academics agree is this: The Knights discovered *something* down there in the ruins . . . something that made them wealthy and powerful beyond anyone's wildest imagination" (208). The novel proceeds to disclose that discovery in great detail, and the doctrinal core of the novel is an almost fifty-page exposition in which Langdon and the British Grail historian Leigh Teabing (whose name alludes to two of the *Holy Blood, Holy Grail* authors) explain the Catholic Church's cover-up and outline what the novel understands is the true, concealed theology about Jesus and Mary and their surviving bloodline. This story of biological instead of apostolic succession entails several nontraditional claims.

First, Teabing contends that Jesus's "life was recorded by thousands of followers across the land." As he explains, "More than *eighty* gospels were considered for the New Testament, and yet only a relative few were chosen for inclusion—Matthew, Mark, Luke, and John among them" (303).

Second, the secret Priory documents are rumored to include "the legendary *'Q' Document*—a manuscript that even the Vatican admits they believe exists. Allegedly, it is a book of Jesus' teachings, possibly written in His own hand." Teabing explains the possible existence of Jesus's authorship of Q by asking, "Why wouldn't Jesus have kept a chronicle of His ministry? Most people did in those days" (336).

Third, these earlier documents attest to the fact that Jesus was mortal, not divine, and that "Jesus was viewed by His followers as a mortal prophet . . . a great and powerful man, but a *man* nonetheless" (306).

Fourth, Jesus was married to Mary Magdalene, who was "of royal descent" (like Jesus himself), and had a child with her (327). "The marriage of Jesus and Mary Magdalene is part of the historical record," Teabing explains; and anyway, "the social decorum during that time virtually forbade a Jewish man to be unmarried. According to Jewish custom, celibacy was condemned." The fact that the Bible doesn't mention Jesus's marriage is evidence of the marriage, Teabing reports: "If Jesus were not married, at least one of the Bible's gospels would have mentioned it and offered some explanation for His unnatural state of bachelorhood" (322).

Fifth, Mary as the Grail "represents the sacred feminine and the goddess, which of course has now been lost, virtually eliminated by the Church" (313). The Grail, Langdon explains, "is symbolic of the lost goddess" because "when Christianity came along, the old pagan religions did not die easily" (313). Mary was not so much divine as symbolic of the lost pagan goddess that was not totally vanquished.

Sixth, the central truths of Jesus's humanness and his marriage to Mary are stories told in "the earliest Christian records" (322), which include "the Nag Hammadi and Dead Sea Scrolls" (322). "The Dead Sea Scrolls," Teabing tells Sophie, "were found in the 1950s hidden in a cave near Qumran in the Judean desert. And, of course, the Coptic Scrolls in 1945 at Nag Hammadi. In addition to telling the true Grail story, these documents speak of Christ's ministry in very human terms" (308). Similarly, the "Sangreal documents include tens of thousands of pages of information" that attest to these two truths—"thousands of pages of unaltered, pre-Constantine documents, written by the early followers of Jesus, revering Him as a wholly human teacher and prophet" (336).

Seventh, as suggested by the quotation above, "The Bible, as we know it today, was collated by the pagan Roman emperor Constantine the Great"

(304) to meld warring factions of Christians and pagans into a unified empire. To do so, he "upgraded Jesus' status" from mortal to divine (307), a process affirmed when "Jesus's establishment as 'the Son of God' was officially proposed and voted on by the Council of Nicaea" (306) called together for this purpose. "Constantine," Teabing contends, "commissioned and financed a new Bible, which omitted those gospels that spoke of Christ's *human* traits and embellished those gospels that made Him godlike. The earlier gospels were outlawed, gathered up, and burned" (307).

Eighth, these "earlier gospels" and written accounts of Jesus were purposefully preserved by the Priory after Constantine's revision, and other earlier Christian records survived in the form of recently found documents among the Dead Sea Scrolls and Nag Hammadi library.

Ninth, the secret kept by the Priory is the subject of a truce between it and the Church. The Priory holds "persuasive scientific evidence . . . that the Church's version of the Christ story is inaccurate, and that the greatest story ever told is, in fact, the greatest story ever *sold*" (350). But that truce is temporary, according to Teabing, who suggests that "part of the Priory history has always included a plan to unveil the secret. With the arrival of a specific date in history, the brotherhood plans to break the silence and carry out its ultimate triumph by unveiling the Sangreal documents to the world and shouting the true story of Jesus Christ from the mountaintops" (350). Teabing looks forward to this new and final revelation the Church wants concealed: thus, the reader is led to believe, the truce has been broken in a sudden Vatican bid to seize the Priory's documents and slay their four highest leaders. "The Church," following astrological signs, Langdon says, "calls this transitional period the End of Days" (351). It is the early days of the beginning of the twenty-first century, and "many Grail historians," Teabing explains, "believe that *if* the Priory is indeed planning to release this truth, *this* point in history would be a symbolically apt time" (352). The rest of the action in the novel turns on whether Sophie and Langdon can uncover and preserve this secret from the clutches of the Church before Silas can beat them to it.

All of these nine historical details are wrong. In fact, some of them are laughably, forehead-smackingly wrong. Teabing, for instance, describes the Dead Sea Scrolls as including Christian documents—and gospels about Jesus—but they are not Christian at all and they say nothing of Jesus. They are actually a library of writings of an apocalyptic Jewish sect composed between the third century BCE and the first century CE and hidden around the time of the First Jewish-Roman War (66–73 CE). They are of immense historical value for the study of ancient Judaism and early Christianity, offering insight into historical, religious, and intellectual contexts, but they are not Christian documents. Teabing's (and consequently, Brown's) lumping together of these two different caches of ancient documents is sloppy in the extreme. To be sure, *The Da Vinci Code*, with its quest for ancient documents, is very much premised on the two great twentieth-century discoveries of ancient documents at Qumran (in the West Bank, where the Dead Sea Scrolls were discovered and excavated by 1956) and Nag Hammadi (in upper Egypt, discovered in 1945), and the very true idea that new discoveries of ancient apocalyptic Jewish and Gnostic Christian texts can richly illuminate and even challenge our understanding of ancient religions. But *The Da Vinci Code*'s errors about history and ancient texts also suggest what it means to think about and fictionally treat religion during the conservative Christian resurgence.

Brown's Postmodern Bible Study

> It is the end of skepticism.
>
> Don DeLillo, *White Noise*

I would like to argue that *The Da Vinci Code* should be understood as a postmodern attack on conservative Protestant understandings of the Bible. Its postmodernism lies not in its form, which is marked by a ploddingly conventional style and structure; indeed, its only formally interesting facet is the narrator's brief ruse of actively misleading the reader into thinking that Teabing and "the Teacher"—who has been anonymously directing Silas's search for the Grail—are two different people, with the latter murdering the former (505–06). While the novel's historicism makes it a candidate for the postmodern in Jameson's terms—"as an attempt to think the present historically in an age that has forgotten how to think historically in the first place" (*Postmodernism* ix)—the particular shape of Brown's attempt to think historically is best understood as the Lyotardian levelling of the expert playing field. *The Da Vinci Code*'s wholesale adoption of the postmodern historical and textual argument of *Holy Blood, Holy Grail* makes it historiographic in a sense, but the novel lacks the metafictional component that might make it postmodern in Linda Hutcheon's definition.[7] Rather, *The Da Vinci Code*'s postmodernism is analogous to Intelligent Design: it levels the playing field of expertise, partly by treating the methods and knowledge of the historical-critical method of Bible criticism as a set of expert language games that can be engaged precisely by treating them as games. As with Intelligent Design, this postmodern higher criticism was not so much aimed at actual Bible scholars—though it rhetorically holds out the hope of convincing actual experts of its startling discoveries—as it is aimed at a lay audience who do not have the historical and textual training to understand just how wrong its sensationalist utterances are. Brown adopts this postmodern scholarship and novelistically pursues its critique of conservative Protestant certainties about the history, authority, origins, and content of the Bible.

The postmodern Bible scholarship language games that *The Da Vinci Code* plays are clarified when measured against the modern, expert consensus among mainstream Bible scholars. A good representative of this group is New Testament scholar Bart D. Ehrman, whose 2004 *Truth and Fiction in "The Da Vinci Code"* was part of the "industry" that responded to Brown's bestseller. (This book is a good start for readers looking for a brief, accessible, and authoritative overview of Brown's errors about ancient Christians and the New Testament.) One of the biggest mistakes is the idea that there were "thousands" of eyewitness-written accounts of Jesus's life, eventually producing more than eighty gospels. In fact, there are no eyewitness accounts of Jesus's life. The four gospels in the New Testament were composed between thirty to sixty years after Jesus's death, and were written not by eyewitnesses (let alone disciples), but by authors who based their work on circulating oral traditions and, probably, some written documents. Other "gospels"—that is, early written accounts of Jesus's life—do exist, and "there are at least a couple of dozen that we know about" (Ehrman, *Truth* 49), but certainly not eighty. As we saw in chapter 5, Q is a hypothetical document—it is the best explanation for the concurrence of passages between Luke and Matthew that are not in Mark—but there is no known extant copy, and no scholarship contends it was written by Jesus himself. Most critical scholars think Jesus was very probably illiterate, like (almost?) all of his earliest followers. The idea that Jesus himself and "thousands" of his lifetime followers wrote accounts is simply ignorant of the fact that most people in first-century Palestine could not read or write (99).

One of Teabing's oddest charges is that the Church concealed earlier eyewitness accounts in favor of the theology of the gospels Constantine included in the New Testament. As with other contentions, this is almost totally incorrect. The Dead Sea Scrolls, as noted, contain no Christian documents and the mostly Gnostic Nag Hammadi material does contain rival gospels, but these are judged by critical Bible scholars to have been written later than the canonical gospels, not earlier. One of the earliest of these writings, and among the most important, is the Coptic Gospel of Thomas, which consists, like the hypothetical Q, of merely a list of the sayings of Jesus, many of them very close to sayings in the four canonical gospels. Scholars believe this manuscript was probably composed in the early mid second century, later than the last canonical gospel of John, although it "may include some traditions even *older* than the gospels of the New Testament" (Pagels xvii; see also Ehrman, *New* 180–82). More important, the Coptic Gospel of Thomas, like other Gnostic Nag Hammadi texts, portrays a Jesus who was less human and more divine, not more human and less divine, as Teabing asserts. As we saw in chapter 7, most Gnostic Christianity (to the extent that it can be summarized as a system of thought) was based on the premise that the material world was created by an evil god, and that Jesus was the mortal container for the immortal spirit of Christ, a messenger come to provide the *gnosis*, or secret understanding, that might allow those with perception to see the truth and thereby escape the material realm. The Gnostic gospels are not earlier, eyewitness accounts that humanized Jesus, as Teabing contends, but later accounts that removed Jesus further from mundane human life. Teabing's library has a copy of Pagels's *The Gnostic Gospels* (Brown 322), but, I surmise, that book was read far more carefully by Cormac McCarthy than it was by Teabing, Brown, or the authors of *Holy Blood, Holy Grail*.

Teabing and Brown likewise totally misrepresent the construction of the Bible, attributing to Constantine a primary role. "The historical reality," Ehrman writes,

> is that the emperor Constantine had nothing to do with the formation of the canon of scripture: he did not choose which books to include or exclude, and he did not order the destruction of the Gospels that were left out of the canon (there were no imperial book burnings). The formation of the New Testament was instead a long and drawn-out process that began centuries before Constantine and did not conclude until long after he was dead. (*Truth* 74)

Constantine's role in the development of Christianity—besides the Edict of Milan in 313 CE announcing religious tolerance as the official policy of the Roman Empire—was to call the Council of Nicaea in 325, not, as Brown's Teabing asserts, to make Jesus divine, but to come to a consensus as to *how* he was divine. "From the very beginning," Ehrman summarizes, "—as far back as we have Christian writings (long before Constantine)—it became commonplace to understand that Jesus was in some sense divine. But there was always a stumbling block, because most Christians understood as well that Jesus was also human" (17). Constantine's role was to call for Christian bishops to arrive at a Christological consensus—a discussion in which he himself did not partake.

The final set of historical errors submitted by Teabing and Brown revolve around the purported marriage between Jesus and Mary, as well as the purported gynocentrism of the early, true Church. In order to counter such claims, Ehrman offers a brief primer on the historical method—a fact that will become important to my argument. "It is difficult," he says, "for critical historians (or anyone) to reconstruct what actually happened in the past for the simple reason that the events of history can never be *proven*" (xxi). Seeing history as "a matter of probabilities," Ehrman suggests that "the best way to try to reconstruct the past is by using our sources critically" (xxi). For mainstream Bible scholars, that means examining our earliest and best sources critically for "the historical Jesus"—which are primarily the books of the New Testament, since there are not earlier, better, eyewitness accounts as Teabing suggests—"to see if they are reliable or not" (xxii). As described briefly in chapter 5, historians have developed a critical methodology for figuring out which sources are likely more reliable and which less—including multiple independent attestation, earlier is better, cutting "against the grain" (124), and being aware of social contexts. Using such criteria, there is no good evidence for a marital and/or sexual relation between Jesus and Mary. Teabing suggests that the supposed earlier and truer Gospel of Philip uses "companion" to describe Mary's relation to Jesus, and that "as any Aramaic scholar will tell you, the word *companion*, in those days, literally meant *spouse*" (Brown 323). But as Ehrman corrects, the Gospel of Philip is in Coptic, not Aramaic, and the word in question is the Greek loan word *koinōnos*, which "in fact means not 'spouse' (or 'lover') but 'companion' (it is commonly used of friends and associates)" (*Truth* 143–44).

The critical historian trying to reconstruct what really happened, in other words, needs evidence and reasons for the reconstruction, and only ultimately can say what more probably happened, especially with ancient history using ancient and imperfect sources. Did Jesus and Mary marry and have children? It's possible. But it's also possible Jesus was a space alien. The problem with both these hypotheses is that evidence for them is almost nonexistent. Thus, as Ehrman describes historical methodology, "knowing about Jesus is not simply guesswork, on the one hand, or a matter of coming up with an imaginative idea, on the other hand." He continues:

> It is always easy for someone—anyone!—to come up with a speculative or sensationalist claim about Jesus: Jesus was married! Jesus had babies! Jesus was a magician! Jesus was a Marxist! Jesus was an armed revolutionary! Jesus was gay! And I am not denying that people are perfectly within their rights to make any claim they want about Jesus, whether sensationalist or cautious. But if historians are to accept such claims, they need to look at the *evidence*. The only reliable evidence we have comes from our earliest sources, and we can neither simply take

these at face value nor just read between the lines in order to make the sources say what we want them to say. They have to be used critically, following established criteria and historical principles. (138)

Ehrman concedes, "It is true that there have occasionally been historical scholars (as opposed to novelists or 'independent researchers') who have claimed that it is likely that Jesus was married" (153)—footnoting William E. Phipps's *Was Jesus Married: The Distortion of Sexuality in the Christian Tradition* (UP of America, 1986), which was the source for *The Holy Blood and the Holy Grail*'s contention that Jesus as a rabbi would have been "virtually certain" to be married (348) and that "the word 'companion' is to be translated as 'spouse'" (404). But, Ehrman goes on to say, "the vast majority of scholars of the New Testament and early Christianity have reached just the opposite conclusion" (153). Thus, Ehrman concludes on this point, "in *none* of our early Christian sources is there any reference to Jesus' marriage or to his wife. . . . List every ancient source we have for the historical Jesus, and in none of them is there mention of Jesus being married" (153).

Ehrman's account of the critical-historical method and the almost total but nonetheless incomplete consensus on this question of Jesus's marriage (as well as his dismissal of "independent researchers," surely an allusion to the *Holy Blood, Holy Grail* authors), resonates with the fact that *The Da Vinci Code* is very much bound up with questions of expertise and authoritative knowledge. As with other researcher characters in contemporary American fiction—Reed's Papa LaBas, Pynchon's Oedipa, Sagan's Ellie, and McCarthy's judge—what allows one to perceive the concealed religious message is expertise in reading relevant signs and clues. Thus, it is useful to consider the Priory to be somewhat like Pynchon's Tristero or Reed's Wallflower Order, as secret societies at work through history, and which, in the case of Pynchon and Brown, are structured around a legendary title to royalty. But in Brown, the postmodernism of Pynchon and Reed comes full circle epistemologically: the research previously put to playful, humorous use in Pynchon and Reed becomes wholly serious for Brown. It is the end of skepticism (as DeLillo's Jack Gladney thinks in the epigraph above), with Brown himself as the culmination of this postmodern trope.

At the center of the novel's postmodernism is the collapse of expertise. Brown seems unaware of mainstream historians' rejection of *Holy Blood, Holy Grail*, the source of most of his errors.[8] The novel acknowledges the existence of elite expertise at the secular university: it's at such places, Brown imagines, that not very widely known knowledge about ancient religions and texts is established, and the novel uses this aura of academic credentials, with Langdon a "Professor of Religious Symbology" at "Harvard University" (8). But, just as the protagonist is a professor of an academic field that does not exist,[9] so too is there little sense of what the credentials are supposed to represent: training in relevant ancient languages, expert evaluation, and research published in peer-reviewed journals. The novel, indeed, does not comprehend how academic, peer-reviewed publishing is different from any other publishing enterprise. Langdon recalls meeting with "Prominent New York editor Jonas Faukman" who hesitates about Langdon's manuscript on the Grail: "if I agree to publish an idea like this, I'll have people picketing outside my office for months" (as if this would be bad for book sales). He continues, "Besides, it will kill your reputation. You're a Harvard historian, for God's sake, not a pop schlockmeister looking for a quick buck. Where could you possibly find enough credible evidence to support a theory like this?" (213–14). At this point, "with a quiet smile," Langdon produces "a bibliography of over fifty titles—books by well-known historians, some contemporary, some centuries old—many of them academic bestsellers. All the book titles suggested the same premise Langdon had just proposed" (214). Besides the odd point that the bibliography of evidence for its claims is provided as a supplement to (and not within) the actual manuscript, there seems to be only a rudimentary sense of the question of research context.

By now, this analysis may sound somewhat elitist—perhaps like Ehrman's casual dismissal of "independent researchers." But my point is not to insist on the unearned respect and privileges of academic researchers and publishing methods. It is rather that *The Da Vinci Code* turns on the prestige of academic authority, however insufficiently it understands the rules of (and historical reasons for) that authority. It matters that Langdon is an academic because through him Brown inoculates his readers against skepticism to the novel's historical claims. The reader frequently hears Langdon's expressions of skepticism and derision toward conspiracy theory, which help allay suspicion that the whole history outlined by the novel is surprisingly interesting, if not surprisingly well-written, fiction. Thus, the novel tells us, "For academics, the Templars' history was a precarious world where fact, lore, and misinformation had become so intertwined that extracting a pristine truth was almost impossible. Nowadays, Langdon hesitated even to mention the Knights Templar while lecturing because it invariably led to a barrage of convoluted inquiries into assorted conspiracy theories" (207). "*Everyone loves a conspiracy*," the novel with Langdon as focalizer says at one point (221): and indeed, it repeatedly expresses skepticism to conspiracy theories and crazy ideas throughout (see, e.g., 321). As Timothy Beal notes,

> part of what makes this alter-history of Christianity believable to so many readers is not only Brown's prefatory claim (reiterated in interviews) to historical accuracy, but also the fact that all this material is placed in the mouths of scholars who, though fictional, are identified with actual institutions of higher education and research. Moreover, the good professors often begin with actual names, dates, texts, and kernels of scholarly historical consensus before their tales spin off into wild speculation and outright fabula.

If our proxy Langdon, the academic skeptic who derides conspiracy theory, becomes convinced by these strange ideas, then the reader is permitted to be convinced as well. The reader is positioned like Sophie: a bright, eager student absorbing the brilliant and esoteric connections offered by the lecturers Teabing and Langdon.

In its mimicry of the expert evaluation of evidence, *The Da Vinci Code* counts as a postmodern language game that levels the playing field of academic expertise about what we can reasonably know of ancient Christian and Jewish history. It is a fictional form of the postmodern knowledge found in *Holy Blood, Holy Grail*, as well as other source books mentioned such as Margaret Starbird's *The Woman with the Alabaster Jar: Mary Magdalene and the Holy Grail* (1993) and *The Goddess in the Gospels: Reclaiming the Sacred Feminine* (1998). (The subtitle of the latter apparently supplied Brown with his signal phrase.[10]) When the *Holy Blood, Holy Grail* authors released a revised edition in 1996, three years after Plantard had admitted that the Priory of Sion was his hoax, they described how their historical thesis had withstood attacks. They suggested of one Catholic bishop's charge of seventy-nine "errors of fact" that, aside from four small mistakes (putting Ephesus in Greece instead of Asia Minor, for example), the others "proved not to be errors of fact at all, but errors of faith—or, more specifically, issues of contention and interpretation still being debated by scholars—and we had 'erred' only to the extent that we deviated from established tradition" (6). Some interpretations, the bishop warned, do not "have the support of most scholars," which the authors gloss as "meaning, of course, the orthodox scholars whom he found most congenial" (6). One begins to see the picture here of what Beal calls the "scholarly historical consensus" being redescribed as an "orthodox" "tradition" upheld merely by "faith"—thus placing the authors in the position of a brave Galileo challenging benighted ideology with better evidence.

As seen from the review of the way Brown gets much of his New Testament scholarship wrong, both *The Da Vinci Code* and the pseudo-scholarship on which it is based are riddled with errors. My point is not that we must always slavishly adhere to the expert consensus in matters of Bible scholarship, biology, or any other field. There will sometimes be startling challenges to expert consensuses that start out as voices in the wilderness but that, over time, become the new accepted understanding—as was true of our understanding of the Bible's authorship after many decades of work by historical-critical scholars. The question, rather, is which strange ideas (as with evolution or questions of Bible authorship) stand the test of time under the scrutiny of experts who evaluate the claims and evidence and eventually come to embrace the changed paradigm. This is an idealized vision of the formation of modern knowledge, of course, but in general form it is the basis for many advances in human understanding. *The Da Vinci Code* and the pop history from which it is derived, on the other hand, level the playing field of expert authority, which they treat as collapsed and hollow systems of faith vulnerable to alternative stories that are just as good and true.

Fundamentalist Hermeneutics

> Western Christian reading of the Bible in the days before the rise of historical criticism in the eighteenth century was usually strongly realistic, i.e. at once literal and historical, and not only doctrinal or edifying. The words and sentences meant what they said, and because they did so they accurately described real events and real truths that were rightly put only in those terms and no others. Other ways of reading portions of the Bible, for example, in a spiritual or allegorical sense, were permissible, but they must not offend against a literal reading of those parts which seemed most obviously to demand it.
>
> Hans W. Frei, *The Eclipse of Biblical Narrative*

There are no conservative Protestants in *The Da Vinci Code*. In one flashback, Silas hallucinates Jesus saying to him *"you are born again"* (75), but this phrase's key constituency of evangelical Protestantism is missing from Brown's novel. Nonetheless, its attack on the historical accuracy and authority of the Bible held a graver risk for conservative Protestants than for Catholics or liberal Protestants, both of which had come to terms with some of the findings of the historical criticism (to the extent that they know about them). While its "faux Catholic" plot involving the Catholic Church and Opus Dei, and its art and architecture setting are European-focused, the theological issue central to its story seems designed with an American Protestant audience in mind. If we remember that Christian fundamentalism was a reaction to modern Bible scholarship in particular, this dimension of the novel comes into focus. The central findings of the historical-critical method on the New Testament—that its construction was historical, that there were rival gospels, and so on—is the scandal to fundamentalists, and in this sense the novel is responding to conservative Christian resurgent concerns.

As Timothy Beal suggests, *The Da Vinci Code* is

> a modern-day apocryphal Gospel. . . . It has emerged as the latest addition to the New Testament apocrypha, that extracanonical body of literature about Jesus and early Christianity that is excluded from the New Testament. It is an alter-Gospel.

This twenty-first-century Gospel according to Dan offers a rival account of Jesus's life and meaning, placing itself alongside the apocryphal gospels (particularly those found among the Nag Hammadi texts) that it uses to fictionally extrapolate a marriage between Jesus and Mary. What makes it an attack on conservative Protestantism in particular is the way it challenges biblical authority by attempting to expose it as partial, historically constructed, based on power politics, and crafted to conceal the truth about Jesus. What makes that attack postmodern is how it undercuts the scholarly consensus (that, for instance, the four Gospels included in the New Testament actually are among the earliest and best witnesses to the "historical Jesus") by suggesting that this consensus is a faith position no better than its alternative story of marriage, betrayal and deceit. As Teabing nicely summarizes, "The Sangreal documents simply tell the *other* side of the Christ story. In the end, which side of the story you believe becomes a matter of faith and personal exploration" (336).

The problem with Brown's postmodern attack on the authority of the Bible in conservative Protestantism is that much of the basis for fundamentalist hermeneutics was itself already postmodern: it was systematically producing rival bodies of knowledge about the Bible's authoring and composition that mimicked the methods and rational approach of mainstream criticism. In this sense, I wish to distinguish between the antimodernism of Christian fundamentalism when it first emerged—itself based on long-standing traditional resistance to the higher historical criticism emerging in Europe (primarily Germany) in the nineteenth century and earlier—from the postmodernism of fundamentalist scholarship of the present. Postmodern Christian Bible scholarship uses some of the methods, diction, approaches and rationales of modern historical criticism to arrive at conclusions that are at odds with the consensuses of that historical scholarship—to arrive, that is, at a premodern understanding of biblical meaning of the kind outlined by Hans Frei in the epigraph above. A few examples will suffice.

The influential *General Introduction to the Bible: Revised and Expanded* by Norman L. Geisler and William E. Nix (Moody Bible Institute, revised edition, 1986) begins the way many Bible textbooks begin, with a descriptive list of our best, most ancient manuscripts and codices, and addresses questions of variation, translation, authorship, cultural setting, and so on. The authors sometimes accept the logic and conclusions of mainstream Bible critics, as when they conclude that the story of Jesus and the woman caught in adultery (mentioned in chapter 5) is a later addition not attested in the earliest manuscripts of the gospel of John (485). They likewise lean toward seeing the "long" ending of Mark (which gives an account of Jesus's post-resurrection appearance to his disciples) as a later addition to the original gospel (488). Thus, when assessing these questions of manuscript variations, they work within the established scholarly principles of multiple attestations, earlier is better, and so on. But, in keeping with modern scholarship's generation of principles through which historians hope to arrive as close as possible to what was probably originally written (since none of the original manuscripts survive, and we have only copies of copies of copies . . .), they generate a new principle to guide scholarly work: where the biblical text itself asserts its status as eyewitness or proclaims a particular author of a book or epistle, such assertions are not to be questioned or rejected. This forms the limit of natural, rationalistic inquiry beyond which fundamentalist hermeneutics will not go.

A fuller articulation of this principle of scholarship is developed in J. Barton Payne's "Higher Criticism and Biblical Inerrancy," one of the essays in Geisler's collection *Inerrancy* (Zondervan, 1979). On the authorship of 2 Peter—the source of an ambiguous epigraph for Sagan's *Contact*, as we've seen—Payne writes,

> Suffice it to note that this book does not simply claim to be the words of 'Peter, . . . apostle of Jesus Christ' (1:1) and allude to the writer's personal experiences with Jesus (1:12–14). It explicitly bases the authority of its teaching on the reality of its author's having been one of the three human eyewitnesses to Christ's transfiguration (1:16–18). One's choice between Petrine authenticity and pseudepigraphic fraud rests once again on the limits that are recognized as legitimate for criticism of the inerrant Word of God. (106)

Because the text itself announces its apostolic authorship, in other words, this fact constitutes a hermeneutic principle that should guide the scholar's work.

Such principles form the basis of proper scholarship, Payne says: "the truly scientific approach to biblical criticism is the way of obedience—indeed, of total obedience—to the witness of Jesus Christ" (95–96). The scholar's added value, he argues, is to historically contextualize (within limits) the Bible's authorship, but not to question or evaluate its claims. Thus,

> the form-critical study of Deuteronomy as a 1400 B.C. Hittite type of suzerainty testament has done much both for the understanding of the book and for its authentication to this very period. But once theory moves away from description into evaluation and begins to adopt a negative stance toward the data that it is supposed to be explaining—by seeking to sift out the erroneous from the valid, the false from the true, and the superstitious from the divine—at that moment it has gone beyond its tether and placed itself in opposition to the standards of Jesus. (96)

The posited distinction is between the legitimate comparison of variants to "recover" "the text of Matthew's autograph" in 29:20 (i.e., does it have "Amen" at the end or not?), and the "illegitimate negative higher criticism" that "raise[s] questions against the reliability of Matthew's autography" (97). Scholars who don't accept these limits to inquiry have succumbed to "the peculiar attraction of the built-in 'occupational hazard' of pride" (109).

This postmodern scholarship runs into some problems in terms of history and method. Geisler and Nix claim, "The whole New Testament was written between A.D. 40 and 70" (441n25), a dating within one generation of Jesus's death, but that varies widely from the expert consensus that, while some books were written relatively early (some of the Pauline epistles date from the 50s), the gospels themselves were composed between 60 and 95 CE, and some of the later pseudographical epistles (like 2 Peter, for example) appear to date into the second century. Because this postmodern Bible scholarship defends the Church fathers' early tradition of apostolic authorship—by the actual disciples Matthew and John, as well as Mark, an associate of Peter, and Luke, a companion of Paul (but not "companion" in *The Da Vinci Code* sense)—it runs into particular problems on dating and with the extensive correspondence among the three "synoptic" gospels. As reviewed in chapter 5, modern scholarship understands those common features to be the result of the priority of Mark's gospel, and the fact that Luke and Matthew had access to Mark, as well as another, probably written, source, called Q.

The problem with this account from a fundamentalist point of view is that the notion that some writers copied from others opens up a can of worms for apostolic authorship and authority. Why would Jesus's disciple Matthew, an eyewitness, copy material from Mark, who was not an eyewitness?

While different historians using good records might use the same words for Jesus's actual speeches, it is highly unlikely that the different gospel writers independently came to identically word the gospels' diegesis. Consequently, Geisler and Nix write,

> Source criticism in the New Testament over the past century has focused on the so-called "Synoptic Problem," since it relates to difficulties surrounding attempts to devise a scheme of literary dependence to account for the combinations of similarities and dissimilarities among the synoptic gospels (Matthew, Mark, and Luke). Theories that one source, Q or *Quelle* (Ger. "Source"), was used by the three evangelists, who wrote in various sequences with the second depending on the first and the third on the other two. These theories were typical forerunners of the *Two-Source theory* advanced by B. H. Streeter, which asserted the priority of Mark and eventually gained wide acceptance among New Testament scholars. Streeter's arguments have been questioned, and his thesis has been challenged by others. (436)

The sense that what is in fact the expert consensus has been "questioned" and "challenged" is underlined in a footnote, where they cite other inerrantist scholars' assertions that the two-source theory "is inadequate and that the synoptic gospels arose in relatively independent circumstances" and that "the times, places, and circumstances of each gospel were sufficiently scattered to constitute them as independent witnesses to the life of Jesus" (437n11). As the language here of "independent witnesses" and "independent circumstances" attests, postmodern hermeneutics adopts higher criticism's preference for independent witnesses when trying to attest to the likelihood of a historical event so as to answer the problem of the synoptic gospels and Markan priority by turning the tables and implying that they somehow independently have come upon the same wording, a sign of their shared historical accuracy about Jesus. Inerrantist scholars are highly self-reflective about their rejection of Markan priority and the modern consensus answer to the synoptic problem, seeing as their consequences the devaluing of the "authority as God's Word" and the reason for mainstream churches' loss of membership (Derickson 100, 102).[11]

The goal of this postmodern, fundamentalist hermeneutics is not really to overturn the modern scholarly consensus, but rather to make it permissible—intellectually respectable—to view the Bible the way they do, as inerrant. Accordingly, it aims to produce and cultivate an uncertainty as to the consensus. Ultimately, its goal is to make the question a matter of faith: no one really know the truth about the authorship, and so a faith decision is permitted—indeed, demanded. The playing field is levelled by telling a story as good as the modern scholarly consensus. The parallel is obvious to the field of Intelligent Design and creation science, neither of which is trying to overturn the evolutionary consensus or is really directing its utterances toward an expert academic audience. That parallel is recognized by inerrantists themselves:

> When science told us creation was impossible and the world was billions of years old, theologians came up with theistic evolution as their means of being accepted, at least in part, by the academy. Why? They were too cowardly to confess that God knew what He was talking about in Genesis 1–11. . . . But does science really have the answers? Macro-evolution has been demonstrated to be absolutely impossible at the cell level by [Intelligent Design author] Michael Behe, who only put in writing what scientists knew for years and kept quiet about. Why? The academy, controlled by evolutionists, could not live with truth that completely invalidated their philosophical underpinnings, which were necessary to maintain a denial of God's existence. Are we not seeing the same thing happen in the area of biblical studies? Are not too many of our numbers adopting discredited theories, created by unbelievers in their rejection of God's revelation, and allowing them to degrade a correct handling of Scripture? (Derickson 102–03)

For Derickson, mainstream scientists and historical-critical scholars deny evidence from biology and the Bible because they cling to their secular, atheistic fantasies. What this Christian postmodernism ignores, of course, is the asymmetry of the situation: there are Christian and atheist scholars who accept evolution and the findings of historical-critical methods, but no nonconservative theist or atheist scholars who repudiate evolution and the historical-critical findings—an asymmetry suggestive of the highly motivated reasoning of the latter.[12] What marks the conservative Christian resurgence in the contemporary period is its postmodern network of hundreds of biology and Bible professors at conservative Christian institutions of higher learning who are committed to resisting evolution and modern Bible scholarship, plus a network of institutions, journals, conferences, and presses dedicated to saving their students (and America) from the deleterious effects of modern knowledge.

To be sure, many fundamentalist and conservative evangelical Bible scholars excel in philology and the relevant ancient language expertise (Greek, Aramaic, Hebrew, Coptic, Latin), sharing these tools of the trade with mainstream scholars and thus, as it were, speaking the language(s) of the scholarship. Both evolutionary biology and Bible scholarship focus on interpreting ancient records—the former field likes to discover new fossils, the latter new manuscripts. However, biologists can see the mechanisms of evolution at work in organisms today; this additional empirical validation of evolutionary theory does not exist by analogy with historians of ancient religions and texts, who are left with the task of arguing over what is more likely to have happened, and what less. For this reason I see the conservative Christian challenges to evolution as more cynically Lyotardian in their collapsing of expert authority than the conservative Christian challenges to mainstream Bible scholarship. Nonetheless, I term these networks Christian postmodernism because they remain institutionally outside of the mainstream expert consensuses even as they use some of their rhetoric and methods—significantly more so for Intelligent Designers than for inerrantist Bible scholars.

The existence of mainstream consensuses does not mean research has stopped, of course: as with evolution, profound questions and problems remain to be solved as best they can on the available evidence and, as always, the hope that more evidence will come to light in the form of further discoveries of ancient manuscripts. But even new work intended to be paradigm-shifting scholarship remains comfortably within the methods and assumptions of the historical-critical method. Shelly Matthews, for example, has recently distinguished between the "historical-critical paradigm" and a newer body of scholarship she calls a "rhetorical-ethical paradigm" (xi)—contrasting both with "the dogmatic-theological paradigm" (xii) of inerrantist scholarship. But this new work in mainstream Bible scholarship, examining textual traces and silences in the context of differently socially situated reading audiences (recognizable questions and methods to those in literary studies), is nonetheless working within the conclusions and historical principles of the modern, mainstream historical-critical consensus, as opposed to the dogmatic-theological paradigm of what I am calling fundamentalist, postmodernist hermeneutics.[13]

What emerged following the publication of *The Da Vinci Code* could thus be thought of as a battle of rival postmodernisms—or, better, an intra-postmodern battle over the origin and authorship of the New Testament. Like their mainstream consensus colleagues (e.g., Ehrman and Beal), fundamentalist apologists criticized the shaky postmodern foundation of Brown's novel; unlike them, they did so by offering in its place a postmodernism of their own that clustered around a few crucial ideas: eyewitness, apostolic authorship, early dating, the denial of pseudegraphia in the New Testament, inerrancy and divine inspiration, and hence, the minimization of the human role in the historical construction of the Bible. Thus, argued Hank Hanegraaf and Paul L. Maier in *The Da Vinci Code: Fact or Fiction?* (Tyndale, 2004), "the reliability of the Gospel accounts is confirmed through the eyewitness credentials of the authors," including the canonical gospels but also 1 John and 2 Peter, which they take to be authored by the apostles John and Peter (44), but which the mainstream historical-critical consensus sees as pseudographic (with more certainty about 2 Peter; see, e.g., Ehrman, *New* 394). Erwin W. Lutzer likewise argued in *The Da Vinci Deception* (Tyndale, 2004), in contrast to Brown's purported earlier, eyewitness gospels, for "the canonical Gospels, written by eyewitnesses" (36), including in this defense of apostolic authorship the usual notion that Luke, the companion of Paul, must have been doing research for his gospel (46). Similarly, *The Da Vinci Code Controversy: 10 Facts You Should Know*, by Michael J. Easley and John F. Ankerberg (Moody, 2006), argued against Brown's claims to earlier eyewitness gospels by likewise confirming apostolic authorship of the four gospels according to the usual scheme (15), citing Geisler as an authority regarding canonicity and inspiration (17, 21). Indeed, Geisler and Nix's classic remained the go-to authority for many of the conservative Christian responses that took place in print and across the Internet.[14] Thus, one writer at a Christian website whose mission was to contest the novel's "alter-Gospel" (as Beal put it) but also evangelize, reasonably argues that when "we examine the claims of Christianity, we must look at the historical support for those claims," but then goes on to cite Geisler and Nix's dubious dating that "all twenty seven books [of the New Testament] were written, copied, and began to be disseminated among the churches before the end of the first century" (Esposito). In arguing for the canonical gospels "written by eyewitnesses and completed before AD 70," Lutzer likewise prefers this nonconsensus early dating, though he admits "the Gospel of John might have been as late as AD 95" (36). Crucial for all fundamentalist critiques of Brown was the idea of the eyewitness, apostolic origin of the New Testament in which there are never pseudographical claims to authorship—as there are in the false Gnostic gospels that supposedly ground *The Da Vinci Code*. "That this Word of God would use deception is unthinkable," Lutzer emphasizes (35).

To be sure, what I'm calling Christian postmodern hermeneutics existed on a spectrum with conservative scholarship rather than as an entirely distinct entity. Conservative scholar Darrell L. Bock's *Breaking the Da Vinci Code: Answers to the Questions Everyone's Asking* (Nelson, 2004) implies mainstream dating but waffles on apostolic authorship (117–18), suggesting that while the latter is still under discussion, "most accept that these Gospels were rooted in groups that had contact with these apostles" (117). This preserves the scheme wherein Paul, and the eyewitnesses Peter, Matthew and John, go their separate ways bearing their good news and their communities eventually write down these distinct oral traditions. Unmentioned is the problem of why Matthean and Lukan communities are copying part of Mark's gospel, or finding a resource in Q (i.e., what the explanation for the "synoptic problem" could be in this scheme).[15] Bock's angle suggests how one might try to retain as much traditional understanding while conceding as little as possible.[16] To be fair, the historical basis for many of the claims made by conservative (and even postmodern) Christian apologist contesters of *The Da Vinci Code* (in book reviews, essays, and in websites like the one cited above) was better than the error-filled pop history transmitted from *Holy Blood, Holy Grail* to Brown. In this sense, they were not equal postmodernisms, or equally postmodern in levelling the playing field and taking up language games.

But their overall shared disregard for expert knowledge is really what makes *The Da Vinci Code* such an odd novel to contest conservative Protestant notions of biblical authority. Postmodernism could not successfully critique fundamentalism because the latter had already adapted postmodern strategies. To Teabing's insistence that there were suppressed earlier written "eyewitness" accounts of Jesus's life, inerrantists simply replied that we already have earlier written "eyewitness" accounts—the canonical gospels themselves. Though some believe that postmodernism is opposed to conservative Christian orthodoxy—as when Douthat charges the revisionists with producing a "postmodern Jesus" (*Bad* 176)—I am arguing instead that while this is true in some manifestations (i.e., *The Da Vinci Code*), on another, deeper level, postmodernism and conservative Christian belief were unlikely allies, not enemies. The real antagonism lay not between *The Da Vinci Code* and conservative Protestant hermeneutics, but between fundamentalism and its old, indeed originary foe, modern Bible scholarship. Though it gets most of the relevant details wrong, *The Da Vinci Code* was premised on a few facts of New Testament history that produce theological anxiety, especially for conservative believers in inerrancy. There *were* rival gospels. The New Testament canon *was* constructed in part to contest beliefs that orthodox Christianity came to identify as heretical, in a process wherein non-prior orthodoxy itself became constituted. The gospels are *not* eyewitness accounts of Jesus's life; in fact, if any were ever written, none has survived. We don't have the original "autographs" of the New Testament books (or Old Testament books)—what we have are copies of copies of copies. There are, if we listen carefully, rival theological beliefs represented in the Bible. There are contradictions, and fraudulent claims to authorship.

The strangeness of the situation—of Brown adopting poor scholarship in order to build a case against biblical tradition—is that in a not insignificant way, the news was already bad enough from a traditionalist point of view. One doesn't have to make up sensationalist pseudo-historical claims about Jesus because the challenge to traditional Christian theology by the historical-critical method by the beginning of the twenty-first century was already considerable. The consensus portrait of Jesus that has emerged is that Jesus thought of himself as an apocalyptic Jewish prophet whose message was the imminent cosmic battle in which God's good forces would rout those of evil—a battle that would take place within the lifetime of his listeners (see, e.g., Ehrman, *New* 203–32). That battle never occurred.[17] In contrast to the four New Testament gospels being a unified, univocal portrait, the gospel writers have importantly different pictures of Jesus, with the earliest account (in Mark) not seeing Jesus as God, an apparently later theological innovation (as in the opening of John). Indeed, concludes mainstream New Testament scholar James D. G. Dunn in his classic *Christology in the Making*, "there is no indication that Jesus thought or spoke of himself as having pre-existed with God prior to his birth or appearance on earth. Such self-assertions appear only in the latest form of the canonical Gospel tradition [i.e., in John but not the three earlier, synoptic gospels] and presuppose substantial developments in christological thinking which cannot be traced back to Jesus himself" (254). As modern Bible scholarship appears to show, what Jesus thought would happen, and who he thought he was, are significantly different than the orthodox Christian theology that developed.

That difference may explain why Douthat takes *The Da Vinci Code* as an opportunity in *Bad Religion* for his diatribe against scholarship that questions Christian orthodoxy, lumping Brown together with Ehrman and Pagels. For Douthat, "revisionist writers" (160) like Ehrman and Pagels have supplied popular writers like Brown with dubious, heretical ideas: "Over the last three decades, the idea of a 'real Jesus,' hidden for millennia and only now revealed, has probably been the religious intelligentsia's greatest contribution to the culture of American Christianity. From its academic core the quest has rippled outward, influencing high art and lowbrow entertainment, novelists and nonfiction writers, believers and atheists and everyone in between" (162). Douthat distinguishes the purported "New Testament revisionism" (174) of Ehrman and Pagels from scholars who say things he approves of and whom he calls "New Testament scholar[s]" (169, 166) like Bruce Metzger—who was, in fact, Ehrman's teacher and who is his coauthor.[18] Douthat says that revisionist scholars like Ehrman occasionally concede basic truths such as that the Gnostic Gospels appear to be dated later than the canonical gospels (167), but in fact this information is regularly supplied by Ehrman, including in his basic textbook (*New Testament* 181), and that mainstream dating is likewise confirmed in Pagels.[19] Douthat also ignores the fact that Ehrman wrote an entire book refuting the bad historical claims of *The Da Vinci Code* (in 2004, well before Douthat's 2012 diatribe), and incorrectly states, based on an apparent reading of Ehrman's "bestselling books" (161), that how Ehrman "lost his faith completely when he went to graduate school and realized that actual human beings might have been involved in the composition of the gospels, is almost a parody of a fundamentalist cautionary tale" (179). In fact, Ehrman recounts his story of losing inerrantist beliefs through his training in the historical-critical method, but his journey from "evangelical Christianity to agnosticism" (*Jesus* 273) was not because "I came to realize that the Bible was a human book, or that Christianity was a human religion" (277). It was, rather, the problem of suffering (278). Ultimately, Douthat seems to consider legitimate scholarship anything that does not disrupt orthodoxy, and illegitimate, publicity-seeking revisionism any ideas or evidence that challenge orthodox, traditional beliefs—a strategic division that suggests that the danger the historical-critical method poses to Christian belief is not ultimately confined to fundamentalism.

Twentieth-century archeological-textual discoveries of the kind that forms the premise for *The Da Vinci Code* have advanced our knowledge of ancient religious history. The Dead Sea Scrolls, while not mentioning Jesus, have helped fill in the portrait of the Jewish apocalypticism in which Jesus, like John the Baptist, took part. Likewise, the Nag Hammadi texts have, especially in their portrait of Christian Gnosticism, helped establish the diversity of ideas about Jesus among his early followers. They help illuminate how the development of Christian orthodoxy was historical, like the texts themselves.

Nor have such disenchanting advances in our understanding of ancient religions been confined to the New Testament. Almost rivaling the magnitude of the Dead Sea Scrolls and Nag Hammadi texts was the 1929 archeological excavation of Ugarit, an ancient city in contemporary Syria. The finding included numerous clay tablets about ancient Canaanite myths, including stories about the Canaanite gods El and Baal, "an extraordinary discovery [that] was one of the most important of the twentieth century for illuminating the larger context in which the Hebrew Bible was written. In these texts, the Canaanites speak for themselves" (Coogan 82). Such stories have reinforced the already developing picture of the Hebrew Bible as having multiple authors and sources, not all of which are always in theological agreement. Though we have far fewer ancient documents of the Hebrew Bible than the New Testament to work with (and no originals, it goes without saying), modern historical-critical scholarship has been able to sketch a portrait of the Hebrew Bible's multiple authors—and its multiple gods. We now understand, for instance, that the famous (and slightly contradictory) two accounts of creation in Genesis were not only written by two different authors, but feature two different creator gods, El and Yahweh. The Hebrew Bible, read in light of this scholarship, tells the story of the merging of the Canaanite high god El from the north with the southern storm god Yahweh. Some of the oldest portions of the Hebrew Bible retain a prior, mythical quality, before Yahweh became the one true God—traces of his storm-god qualities and his vanquishing of the primal waters during creation that linger in the text (e.g., Ps 29, 89). The El-Yahweh relationship in the south, before they merged, looked considerably like the El-Baal relationship in the north, and Yahweh's defeat of his rival Baal (also a storm-god) in the Hebrew Bible (see 1 Kings 18:21–40) seems to confirm the idea that it tells the story of the emergence of monotheism, through monolatry, out of a more ancient Israelite polytheism with deep ties to Canaanite religion. The lingering traces of ancient Israelite polytheism can still be seen textually today in the Hebrew Bible.[20]

While parts of this too-brief review might come as surprising news to some religious readers, they shouldn't, writes Bart Ehrman. "None of the information presented here," he says near the end of *Jesus, Interrupted*, "is news to scholars or their students, many of whom have attended top-level seminaries and divinity schools . . . The historical-critical approach to the New Testament is taught in all these schools. . . . the basic views that I've sketched here are widely known, widely taught, and widely accepted among New Testament scholars and their students, including the students who graduate and go on to pastor churches" (271). Nonetheless, Ehrman continues, this knowledge is generally not conveyed by pastors to their congregations, who prefer "approaching the Bible devotionally rather than historical-critically" (272). Perhaps they don't know where to start, having themselves been taught theology and historical criticism in different, generally nonintersecting sets of classes, Ehrman muses. He does not believe that knowledge of the historical method—being informed of the consensus of modern Bible scholarship—would lead to "a crisis of faith, or even the loss of faith" among parishioners (272). Although Ehrman, representative of the modern critical consensus on the New Testament, cannot hold with the postmodern, fundamentalist tenet that "God is the ultimate Author of the Bible, even though He employed human prophets and apostles to write down what He revealed to them" (Archer 67), he concludes that knowing the facts about the historical authorship of biblical "revelation" does not doom faith.

God's Policy of Revelation

> An omniscient and omnipotent God who does
> not even take care that His intentions shall be
> understood by His creatures—could He be a God
> of goodness? A God, who, for thousands of years,
> has permitted innumerable doubts and scruples to
> continue unchecked as if they were of no importance
> in the salvation of mankind, and who, nevertheless,
> announces the most dreadful consequences for any one
> who mistakes his truth? Would he not be a cruel god
> if, being himself in possession of the truth, he could
> calmly contemplate mankind, in a state of miserable
> torment, worrying its mind as to what was truth?
>
> Friedrich Nietzsche, *Morgenröte / Dawn of the Day*

I would like to conclude this chapter, however, with the suggestion that the fundamentalist rejection of modern Bible scholarship—and its creation of a rival postmodern ecosystem of inerrantist academic expertise—has occurred for understandable theological reasons. As with the problem of evolution, conservative Christian theology apprehends the danger of conceding the findings of the historical-critical method. Strikingly, it is a danger that *The Da Vinci Code* feels in its own way—as does, even, Sagan's *Contact*. Indeed, both these novels conclude, surprisingly, with an approval of the Christian theology of revelation and its premise of necessary secrecy. We recall that the plot of *The Da Vinci Code* turns on whether the secret about Jesus and Mary will be revealed. Teabing has argued that the Priory kept secret its explosive knowledge for centuries, but has plans to "break the silence" by "unveiling . . . the true story of Jesus Christ" (350). While the Priory is waiting for "a time when the world is ready to handle the truth" (387), Teabing desires the public disclosure of the documents and the truth they contain (382). As we discover, he is the one who has masterminded the pursuit of the Grail documents, including the murder of the Priory leaders. By the end of the novel, Teabing has been arrested, Langdon and Sophie have uncovered the truth, and Sophie has been reunited with her grandmother and long-lost brother, the Priory having separated the siblings because they "represented the most direct surviving royal bloodline and therefore were carefully guarded by the Priory" (581). But Teabing's notion of full public disclosure of the truth, it turns out, has never been part of the plan because, Sophie's grandmother explains, "It is the mystery and wonderment that serve our souls, not the Grail itself. The beauty of the Grail lies in her ethereal nature" (584). The story of the Grail, Mary Magdalene, is already told in "art, music, and books" (584).

One might think that the revelation of these extremely important documents—including, possibly, a Q written by Jesus himself—would be something the world deserved to know. But the novel ends with the sense that it is not so much the truth that sets us free as the idea that being kept in the dark is an advantage for the spiritual "mystery and wonderment" that *not* knowing can produce. In the final scene, Langdon arrives at just such faith himself, falling to his knees "with a sudden upwelling of reverence" at the inverted pyramid of the Louvre beneath which, he has come to believe, Mary's bones have found a final resting place (597). We approach here Hungerford's sense of faith in faith itself: underlining the importance of not knowing, the importance of the truth remaining hidden, the novel tellingly has Teabing become the villain in its plot twist. "The Truth. Mankind deserves to know that Truth," he pleads, reasonably, we might think (537). But we know Teabing is the villain at this point because, in this liberal, post-9/11 novel of religion, his question to Langdon and Sophie, "Are you with me, or against me?" (541) echoes George W. Bush's stark geopolitical definition shortly after the terror-ist attacks, "Either you are with us, or you are with the terrorists."[21] (Presi-dent Bush, in turn, was echoing who he called [in 1999] his favorite political philosopher, Jesus: "Whoever is not with me is against me" [Matt 12:30].) Aligning the desire for disclosing the "Truth" with the villainous Teabing, and imagining instead human ignorance of truth as the precondition for spiritual wonder and faith, *The Da Vinci Code* paradoxically upholds the core Christian theological tenet that God must hide himself from us, offering ambiguous knowledge of him only through indirect, historically embedded revelation.

We see a similar, and similarly strange, approval of God's policy of revela-tion in Carl Sagan's *Contact*. As I argue in chapter 6, Sagan seems to suggest an equivalency between science and religion, to show their shared sense of reasoned wonder at the mystery of creation. That synthesis culminates in an acceptance of the shared policy of revelation: Ellie's testimony of a personal experience she has no evidence for must be taken on faith by others; simul-taneously, the aliens have withdrawn, the Message has stopped, the Machine appears to have not worked, and the aliens have closed the metro to further trips. On the one hand, Sagan seems to suggest that the Earth's dangerous geopolitics are settled by the receipt of the Message: knowing that we're not alone helps us mature and avoid our species' self-destruction, with the prom-ise in a distant future of joining the community of aliens (a symbolic echo of the community of angels in heaven). In this reading, by the end of the novel, even though the specifics of Ellie's experience are secret, there is still the planetary sense that we're not alone.

But on the other hand, in straining to achieve the parallel between sci-ence and faith, *Contact* brings into focus the ethics of superior beings who choose to communicate only to a select few at a specific historical moment: in other words, the moral question of the God / aliens who absent themselves. The aliens intervene by sending a Message once—a singular Revelation—and then withdraw. The planet has been touched by a message from the heavens, but now we must work out our own salvation in fear and trembling, without help, or even without moral precepts or instructions. This interpretation seems confirmed by the novel's final suggestion of a message found in pi, the "Author's Signature" that attests to the presence of a Creator. It is, however, an Author for whom individuals don't count: only advanced mathematicians of advanced civilizations will see pi's message. Nor does it circumvent the problem of indirect address: only advanced mathematicians and computer scientists—a new gnostic cabal—will be able to verify this Message from God for the rest of us, who will have to believe them or not. Just as the theology of evolution seems to make sense only on the species level, so too this theology of revelation, as Sagan exemplifies it and as thoughtful Christian theology does too, discount the individual, especially those historic individuals who lived before the revelations or in non-Christian societies. (Theology has had to develop complicated theories about the fate of individuals who had no opportunity to hear the gospel.) *Contact* and *The Da Vinci Code* begin as novels seeking to contest the conservative theology of the Christian resurgence, but they end up approving of its core structure, God's policy of revelation.

I suggest Christian fundamentalism senses the theological danger of conceding the findings of the historical-critical method because it apprehends the consequences for the policy of revelation, that God chooses to communicate to us indirectly through a series of ancient documents. The ethics of that policy are troubling, and become more so once we begin to see, in the case of Christianity, that the surviving documents may reflect human origins as much as divine revelation. We don't have clear historical records of one of the most consequential lives lived on this planet, but testimonies built on previous oral traditions that sometimes invented stories. The central character himself may have thought differently about who he was and what would shortly occur than did the religion built up around him in the centuries following his death. The texts themselves and the process of choosing which to include were implicated from the start in arguments about right thinking and right belief. The authors of the books, not surprisingly, seem not to have had the goal of recording precise historical transcripts for readers two thousand years later, but with more immediate rhetorical considerations that saw them massaging existing oral traditions and making up suitable speeches for a setting decades past. For God to place importance on individuals' faith decisions about what must seem in summary to be an unnecessarily uncertain set of propositions is cause for theological anxiety; better to return to surer ground by bringing us closer to historical origin and purity through assert-ing apostolic authorship, divine dictation, and early authoring. Christian postmodernism avoids many of the theological problems generated by the historical-critical method because it returns us to a more authoritative Bible tradition, understanding that this good God would not have clouded his rev-elation and its transmission with so much uncertainty.

God's policy of revelation, like his policy of using evolution, entails sig-nificant problems of theodicy. Human history (and prehistory) suggest we need more help than sending in ancient times occasional prophets or a sav-ior whose words and identities are not conveyed with sufficient clarity and reliability. The theological problem with revelation (for the resurgence, and elsewhere) is that we humans are very good at making mistakes: at commit-ting violence and atrocities, at deluding ourselves with false ideologies, of othering groups of people, sometimes with murderous results, of insisting on own self-righteousness at the expense of others, at convincing ourselves why we are not responsible for our fellow humans' well-being, at making up reasons why we should dominate and use another person, or groups of people. In terms of mistakes and errors, we've got the ground covered: we don't need any help. What we need from God is a way out of our errors, not a reinforcement of them through revelation, or, worse, a source of new ones. The problem with God's policy of revelation is compounded by the existence of rival testaments to God's word within monotheism alone: even clarifying which holy book was correct would have been a help, especially given the fact that allegiances to the different books have sometimes been the historical occasions for considerable human violence and suffering.

In *Blood Meridian*, the judge asks the good question, "If God meant to interfere in the degeneracy of mankind would he not have done so by now?" (153). In one sense, theology faces as its first task the construction of a reasonable alibi for God. Why isn't he here, now, to make his will clear, to tell us who we are, and how we should live? Thinking about life in God's presence rather than in his absence is admittedly a kind of event horizon beyond which life becomes difficult to imagine. But while it may be dif-ficult to imagine human life near the presence of God, Christian writers such as Dante and C. S. Lewis have done so for hundreds of years. Indeed, the premise of the Judeo-Christian tradition is that humans in our natural state are in close communion with the good Creator who made us. The fact that we're not in that natural state requires explanation—one that puts the blame on us, not God. Besides the theodicy problems posed by evolution, this is the other reason to want to retain the Genesis story, insofar as it helps answer the theodicy problems posed by revelation: there is a reason God has disappeared, acknowledging that our separation is not our natural condition. Christian theology's powerful answer to its primary problem—where is God, and why is he absent?—was the theological innovation that human free will only works in his absence. Our free will depends, in other words, on not knowing if there is a God, and if there is, what his will is. But this answer, that God has crafted a law about how free will works within which he must operate, may not satisfy the problem of theodicy it is partly meant to solve.

We begin to see the theological problems for a God who has the traditional, orthodox qualities in Christian theology of omnipotence, omniscience, and benevolence to choose the policy of revelation to announce himself—just as, we saw, for this same God to choose natural selection as his method for the origin of the tremendous variety of life. Liberal theology has found itself backing away from some of the qualities of the traditional God in response; these make up some of the "nova" that, Charles Taylor explains, now make up our field of potential belief positions. Fundamentalism, I submit, is one of these nova; apprehending real theological dangers, it has engaged in a century-long struggle to avoid the truths of evolution and the historical-critical method. In this combat postmodernism is not yet one more threat to be beaten back, but a resource to be embraced in its struggle against modern knowledge. This theological tradition's struggle against elite knowledge forms the backbone of the conservative Christian resurgence since the 1970s, and the theological implications of these ideas have been unavoidable for the American literature that has sought to respond to the social and political empowerment of the Christian Right in recent years.

Conclusion
Politics, Literature, Method

On December 7, 2005, Harold Pinter delivered a remarkable lecture as he accepted the Nobel Prize for Literature. It began,

> In 1958 I wrote the following:
> "There are no hard distinctions between what is real and what is unreal, nor between what is true and what is false. A thing is not necessarily either true or false; it can be both true and false."
>
> I believe that these assertions still make sense and do still apply to the exploration of reality through art. So as a writer I stand by them but as a citizen I cannot. As a citizen I must ask: What is true? What is false? (1)

It was a remarkable distinction between the realms of art and the real by an early British postmodern experimenter, entailing the practical repudiation of his edgy postmodern doctrine of an almost half-century before. The need for this new distinction, or clarification of the limits of the postmodern, was triggered by the second Iraq war, as Pinter went on to explain:

> As every single person here knows, the justification for the invasion of Iraq was that Saddam Hussein possessed a highly dangerous body of weapons of mass destruction, some of which could be fired in 45 minutes, bringing about appalling devastation. We were assured that

was true. It was not true. We were told that Iraq had a relationship with Al Qaeda and shared responsibility for the atrocity in New York of September 11th 2001. We were assured that this was true. It was not true. We were told that Iraq threatened the security of the world. We were assured it was true. It was not true. (3)

How was it that the blurring of the distinction between fiction and reality had become the tool not of postmodern aesthetic subversion but of power and war? How did it happen that the indistinction between "what is real and what is unreal"—almost an early formulation of what would become, in Jean Baudrillard's hands, the theory of the postmodern simulacra—could be a tactic not only of avant-garde art, but for bringing the United States to war against a country unrelated to the events of 9/11?

Politics

Pinter's charge that President Bush's administration had crafted a "vast tapestry of lies" along these lines seemed harsh (3). While most Americans in 2004 believed that Iraq had Weapons of Mass Destruction[1] (a fact that played no small role in the Presidential election), by 2008 the Senate Intelligence Committee's report on the use of intelligence leading up to the war had established "how much the Bush administration knowingly twisted and hyped intelligence to justify that invasion," reported a *New York Times* editorial looking at its conclusions. "The report shows," the editorial suggests, "that there was no intelligence to support the two most frightening claims Mr. Bush and his vice president used to sell the war: that Iraq was actively developing nuclear weapons and had longstanding ties to terrorist groups. It seems clear that the president and his team knew that that was not true, or should have known it—if they had not ignored dissenting views and telegraphed what answers they were looking for" (Truth). The summary is reluctant to say that Bush and administration officials lied, partly because it had no access to other people's mental intentions. Lying has to be accompanied by the intent to deceive, which is not possible if someone has first convinced himself.

Pinter's distinction between truth-telling and lying could not, perhaps, capture the complex sifting and crafting of information during the buildup to the war. That more complex relation between language and the real was suggested most baldly in journalist Ron Suskind's story, told during the 2004 presidential campaign, of a summer 2002 interview with a "senior adviser to Bush" (since revealed to be Karl Rove). As Suskind famously recounted it,

The aide said that guys like me were "in what we call the reality-based community," which he defined as people who "believe that solutions emerge from your judicious study of discernible reality." I nodded and murmured something about enlightenment principles and empiricism. He cut me off. "That's not the way the world really works anymore," he continued. "We're an empire now, and when we act, we create our own reality. And while you're studying that reality—judiciously, as you will—we'll act again, creating other new realities, which you can study too, and that's how things will sort out. We're history's actors . . . and you, all of you, will be left to just study what we do." (Suskind)

It was a fairly strong declaration of Baudrillardian postmodernism: journalists might try to discover and then report preexisting facts, but some in the administration understood the relation between representation and the real to be more malleable. Representation need not follow after, and be based on, the real, but might, in the postmodern condition, be part of the act of "creating other new realities." Baudrillard had called this the precession of the simulacra—the sign that comes before the real, serving, indeed, as a model for its production.

Faith is a complex phenomenon. It involves not only, or not especially, belief in things unseen, but also, at times, processes of harmonization and confidence, the active cognitive search for visible signs of the deeper truths we intuit. I have suggested that the Bush presidency was the apex, thus far, of the conservative Christian resurgence. As D. Michael Lindsay argues in the sympathetic *Faith in the Halls of Power: How Evangelicals Joined the American Elite*, "When it comes to actual policy decisions, the most powerful evangelical voices come from those working inside an administration. This is the difference a presidential appointment can make and explains, in part, why the Carter administration had a much less evangelical tenor than that of George W. Bush." Further, "Bush has surrounded himself with more evangelicals than any other U.S. president in the last fifty years" (26) even though "evangelicals are still a minority on the senior staff" (27).[2] Indeed, Rove was not a born-again Christian; nor were the architects of the war, Vice President Dick Cheney and Secretary of Defense Donald Rumsfeld. Cheney and Rumsfeld participated in faithlike processes of harmonization and mental sifting, however, with both setting up mechanisms to "stovepipe" raw intelligence directly into offices they controlled rather than go through the usual vetting and critical evaluation of fresh intelligence by experts across America's several intelligence agencies (Hersh). I would like to suggest that such practices of eschewing expert opinion during the search for the answers one wants found a ready home in the Bush administration for a reason: the presidency had as its hallmark, like the conservative Christian resurgence from which it came, the active crafting of the real through faith practices long honed in the religious tradition out of which it emerged. It is not just that George W. Bush had a political platform that contained policy ideas informed by conservative Christian traditions. Rather, the novelty of his administration was the way in which the specific doctrinal content informing all manner of policies during these years, including positions on homosexuality,[3] abortion,[4] sex education,[5] evolution, foreign policy in the Middle East,[6] climate change,[7] economic policy,[8] voter fraud, and so on, was accompanied by hostility to expert evaluation and evidence-weighing. There is a reason, in other words, why what conservative *New York Times* columnist David Brooks called the "alternative-reality right" has emerged in recent decades: it partly emerged from, and certainly overlaps with, the faith practices of the conservative Christian resurgence. In a Venn diagram of the Republican Party, the Christian Right and the alternative-reality right would largely, but not totally, overlap.

We are all vulnerable to motivated reasoning, in which we select details and facts that confirm our established views, and have difficulty even registering information that undercuts our previous mental conclusions.[9] Sartre's famous counsel to "think against oneself" is difficult for everyone. I emphasize (again) that it is not religion in general that leads naturally to the anti-intellectualism that characterizes contemporary American conservatism.[10] Rather, the historically specific strains of religion that produced the Christian Right helped train movement conservatism (and today's Republican Party) in the "habits of mind" that conceive expert evaluation as liberal moves in a larger discursive set of postmodern language games. This was true because fundamentalism's originary struggle was its rejection of secular elite conclusions about evolution and Bible authorship associated with institutions like universities. Conservative Christians cultivated a skepticism about the neutrality of such elites, but also developed rival forms of expertise in creation science, Intelligent Design, and various forms of fundamentalist Bible hermeneutics. It should come as no surprise that the skepticism and the countermethods of the Christian Right seeped into other ways of responding to elite assertions—most particularly about supply-side economics, abstinence-only sex education, climate-change denial, the Founders' purpose to build a Christian nation without slavery, and so on. While not all religion produces these forms of know-nothingism, New Atheist assertions notwithstanding, today's conservatism is dominated by the "alternative-reality right" that emerged from a contingent historical circumstance whose intellectual characteristic was (if I may adapt the nonevangelical William F. Buckley's famous formulation) to stand athwart human knowledge and yell "Stop."

The political and social consequences of the conservative Christian resurgence have arguably been very bad for America. Disputing the science of evolution and the conclusions of the historical-critical method is of small immediate consequence. But the supreme moral self-confidence and antagonism to contrary evidence and expertise that characterize the resurgence, crystalized in today's Republican Party, have brought us the second Iraq war with all its human and financial costs. Its antipathy to science may only have dire consequences for several thousand people, teens who missed key information during their abstinence-only sex education, but its rejection of climate-change science may result in catastrophe for millions more. There is, as economists say, an "opportunity cost" of the road not taken in terms of economic policy that might have alleviated the Great Recession and allowed millions of young people to pursue the normal course of careers rather than postponing family and life decisions due to Republican refusals to endorse mainstream, textbook economic solutions that might have, as Paul Krugman's book put it, *End This Recession Now!* The Republican Party's scorched-earth opposition to the Obama presidency is due in part to the apocalyptic, Manichean strain that the resurgence has brought to politics, in which legislative compromise is seen as capitulation. Its purported efforts to "repeal and replace" the Affordable Care Act have crashed into the awkward reality that the conservative solution for healthcare was already Obamacare: that is, government subsidization of health insurance provided by private companies and purchased by individuals, together with a mandate. The anti-tax, small-government policies of the Republican Party (often embraced by centrist Democrats in the last few decades) have encouraged the vast rise in wealth and income inequality recently demonstrated by Thomas Picketty's *Capital in the Twenty-First Century*, as an extremely small sliver of the population takes home (and then builds on through investment) a larger and larger portion of national wealth, even as middle- and working-class real incomes stagnate.

As Putnam and Campbell show, Americans are more partisan now than they have been in decades; there are no longer conservative Democrats and liberal Republicans in Congress who in previous decades engineered legislative compromises. But as the bipartisan team of Thomas E. Mann and Norman J. Ornstein argued in *It's Even Worse Than It Looks: How the American Constitutional System Collided With the New Politics of Extremism* (2012), the reasons for that increase in partisanship lie mostly with the Republican Party:

However awkward it may be for the traditional press and nonpartisan analysts to acknowledge, one of the two major parties, the Republican Party, has become an insurgent outlier—ideologically extreme; contemptuous of the inherited social and economic policy regime; scornful of compromise; unpersuaded by conventional understanding of facts, evidence and science; and dismissive of the legitimacy of its political opposition. When one party moves this far from the center of American politics, it is extremely difficult to enact policies responsive to the country's most pressing challenges. (xiv)

That scorched-earth opposition brought the country to the brink of defaulting on its debt in 2013, as Republicans tried the new tactic of holding the national economy hostage to extract policy concessions.

To be sure, and as I have argued, American conservatism today is an alliance of several groups, and not all these problems can be laid at the feet of the conservative Christian resurgence. But the current Republican Party's apocalypticism, its hostility to facts and evidence that contradict its ideological positions, and its resistance to traditional political compromise have deep wells in the conservative Christian traditions out of which it partly grew. The (at times) not very latent role of white resentment and racism that form the emotional core of the Party likewise has deep roots in the Christian segregationism out of which it grew, and in the Christian slavery before that; conservatives, especially religious conservatives, have never squarely faced that history.[11] The class warfare practiced by today's Republican Party—its hostility to even mild redistributionist policies through taxation, which might subsidize healthcare (even through private companies), extend Social Security to help bring seniors out of poverty, and finance better-quality and more-affordable education that would enable more class mobility—is likewise the continuation of conservative Christianity's support for power rather than the relatively powerless, the rich rather than the poor, the healthy rather than the sick. The Tea Party is the concentrated essence of these Republican priorities: Tea Party–identified Republicans are even whiter, more racially resentful, more small-government-oriented, and more Christian, than their Republican compatriots. While some observers in 2015 wondered if the Tea Party's time had passed,[12] from another point of view we could reasonably say that it has already won: Tea Party views have further radicalized the Republican Party, and Republican politicians who resist adopting Tea Party policies (and even, sometimes, when they do) risk primary challenges from even more extreme Tea Party–aligned politicians—as happened, in 2014, even to ousted Republican House leader Eric Cantor, who had previously engineered Republican obstructionism and hostage-taking. If the Tea Party is on its way to disappearing, that may be only because it has assimilated the Republican Party to its emotional core of white Christian resentment and small-government anger. A Ted Cruz presidency might complete this task.

It is difficult to say where this will all end, as *Gilead*'s narrator wonders about the new radio evangelism. Some Christians in this unholy alliance might wonder what they think they get out of it. In return for white resentment and racism, anti-immigrant and anti-healthcare policies, class warfare in favor of the rich and powerful against the poor, hatred of homosexuals and gay rights, vastly imbalanced Israeli-Palestinian policies, a know-nothingism on climate change that endangers the planet and future generations, cultivated, learned ignorance of science and other bodies of human knowledge, and the motivated reasoning that brought us the hugely costly second Iraq war, they receive just one reasonable thing: a pro-life position. Christians accepting this deal get just one thing that could reasonably be construed as ethical—the opposition to abortion under all circumstances and at all times. Some Christians have obviously already eschewed this deal, seeing it as a rotten one; as I note in the introduction, a full quarter of self-described evangelicals did not vote for President Bush in 2004, and many more liberal Protestants and Catholics likewise were never part of this coalition. Indeed, some former members have repudiated the deal, including Frank Schaeffer, who in retrospect has called some Christian Right leaders "anti-American religious revolutionaries" (*Crazy* 298), people who "would later use their power in ways that would have made my father throw up" (299). He notes that "after 9/11, the public got a glimpse of the anti-American self-righteous venom that was always just under the surface of the evangelical right. Pat Robertson, Jerry Falwell, and others declared that the attack on America was a punishment from God" (299). Frank Schaeffer repents of the resurgence that he, with his father, helped to establish: "To our lasting discredit, Dad and I didn't go public with our real opinions of the religious-right leaders we were in bed with" (300).

Will other, more moderate evangelicals begin to question this deal as well? It's difficult to tell. As Greeley and Hout assert, denomination (which tends to be inherited from one's family) constrains belief: in this sense, political policies and identities, like the religious ones to which they are strongly connected, are not freely and separately chosen after intentional acts of deliberation—and to the extent this is true, the Republican alliance may endure. On the other hand, as Putnam and Campbell's data show, some positions do "evolve," as did Obama's and many other Americans' on homosexual marriage. They may likewise weaken in other areas. A 2014 Pew US Religious Landscape Study showed a significant rise in the religiously unaffiliated "nones," from 16.1 to

almost 22.8 percent of the population between 2007 and 2014.[13] This continued "rise of the nones" seemed to come largely at the expense of Catholics
(down 3.1 percent to 20.8 percent) and mainline Protestants (down 3.4 percent to 14.7 percent), contributing to an overall decline of 7.8 percent of the
population describing themselves as Christian (down to 70.6 percent in 2014).
But the share of evangelicals dropped only 0.9 percent (to 25.4 percent), even
as its absolute numbers increased (from about 59.8 million to 62.2 million
people); in contrast to Catholics and mainline Protestants, who are losing
members due to "switching" (what I have called conversion in this book),
evangelical Protestants are gaining more members through switching than
they lose. While a full discussion of these changing demographics is beyond
the scope (and expertise) of this book, the new data appear to confirm Putnam
and Campbell's earlier thesis that the political sorting that produced the "God
gap" is continuing apace: the middle is hollowing out, with the nones voting
largely Democratic and the evangelicals voting largely Republican, and indeed
continuing to crucially influence its policy platforms and nomination processes. In any case, the social and political muscle of the conservative Christian
resurgence—wishfully termed "one momentarily influential fringe" by Marilynne Robinson in 2005 (*Death* 262)—has become deep and powerful over the
last forty years. It will continue to evolve but it is far from being a spent force.

Literature

This book has concentrated on, broadly speaking, liberal literary critiques
of the conservative Christian resurgence and the Christianization of the
Republican Party for the simple reason that, as Michael Kimmage argues in
his illuminating essay "The Plight of Conservative Literature," "the American right . . . is among the most underrepresented entities in American
literature" (950). Indeed, Kimmage observes,

> In America, the literary world has leaned toward the left. The world
> of conservatives, [William F.] Buckley's world, acquired great power at
> the political center in the years after 1968, without generating much
> of a literary culture. Twentieth-century America produced no major
> right-wing novelist—no Dostoevsky, no Céline, no Solzhenitsyn.
> America's novelists are typically uncomfortable with established politi-
> cal power and especially uncomfortable if that power is tied to the
> Republican Party. (948–49)

Kimmage contrasts the absence of conservative literary fiction with the
conservative interest in "championing literature, such as the canonical texts

fought over in the 1980s and 1990s, literature as a tributary of Western culture, to be protected from the Marxism, the feminism, or the postmodern relativism of the English professors." (We might think here of George Will's observation, regarding Lynne Cheney's tenure as chair of the National Endowment for the Humanities during the George H. W. Bush administration even as her husband was Secretary of Defense, that "in this low-visibility, high intensity war, Lynne Cheney is secretary of domestic defense. The foreign adversaries her husband, Dick, must keep at bay are less dangerous, in the long run, than the domestic forces with which she must deal" [72].) But the "challenge, for conservatives," Kimmage argues, "has been to sponsor literature as a living branch of contemporary culture. The conservative emphasis on precedent and experience, the anti-utopian cast of the conservative mind, leads conservative authors to autobiography, to a nonfiction reckoning with the dilemmas of history, politics, and the self. The literary imagination thrives on the left, where utopia has long been at home" (949).

Noting the exceptions of Saul Bellow's *Mr. Sammler's Planet* and Tom Wolfe, as well as popular literature by Ayn Rand and "Tim LaHaye and Jerry Jenkins's Left Behind novels (1995–2007), which are certainly Christian in tone, [but] are narrowly conservative, expressing the conservatism of an evangelical minority more than anything like a national conservatism" (952), Kimmage contends that Leftism has a centuries-long history to work with in literature, whereas the American conservative movement, born in the 1950s, has no past to be similarly mined for the "conservative novel" (953). One is reminded on this point of the Obama-voting Marilynne Robinson, who, while expressing reservations about modernity and secular humanism, may not be comprehensible as part of a movement conservative literary tradition, especially given her nostalgia for the moral clarity of antebellum Midwest abolitionism. Thus it has been left to this largely liberal American literary tradition to register and respond to conservative Christian resurgence since the 1970s, even as other popular fictions—like William Paul Young's *The Shack*, or the *Left Behind* series—can be understood as the resurgence's populist literary arm.[14]

This imbalance may suggest part of the answer to Paul Elie's recent question about what seemed to him the puzzling absence of contemporary "fiction about the quandaries of Christian belief"—noting that the successors to Flannery O'Connor are "thin on the ground" and asking "Where has the novel of belief gone?" "If any patch of our culture can be said to be post-Christian, it is literature," he writes, which is "a strange development": "Strange because the current upheavals in American Christianity—involving sex, politics, money and diversity—cry out for dramatic treatment." Overall,

Elie finds a distressing absence in contemporary American literature: "Belief as upbringing, belief as social fact, belief as a species of American weirdness: our literary fiction has all of these things. All that is missing is the believer." As noted in chapter 3, Elie contrasted *Gilead*'s "wise, tender reverence against the bellicose cymbal-clanging of George W. Bush's White House," a contrast reflecting how Robinson's 2004 novel was a liberal Christian repudiation of the conservative Christian resurgence to which it is indirectly addressed. But other works of fiction suggest that it wasn't so much that the novel of belief had disappeared as that it reemerged in terms informed by the logics of multiculturalism and postmodernism, disguised through our widely accepted secularization thesis in Herbergian cultural identities and thematized as the esoteric training required to read the traces of ambiguous, sacred writing.

I have termed as "Christian postmodernism" the contemporary procedures wherein resurgent conservative Christians have not just yelled "Stop," but have used think-tanks, religious networks, and Christian colleges, universities, and publishing houses to mimic the modern modes of knowledge and expertise in order to craft uncertainty as to the consensuses of modern knowledge. As Crystal Downing puts it, postmodernism can serve faith by crafting uncertainty about what we know, and how we know it. That this process is not intrinsic to all religion is shown in the two primary examples in this book, wherein the asymmetry of expertise is telling. Many Christians accept the science of evolution (represented by *Dover* trial witnesses Kenneth Miller and John Haught), but there are no non-Christians (or, more broadly, nontheists) pursuing creation science or Intelligent Design. Similarly, many Christian scholars (such as Bruce Metzger) accept, with their nonreligious colleagues (such as Bart Ehrman), the mainstream consensus on the dating and authorship of the New Testament, but no non-Christian scholars hew to the fundamentalist line about eyewitness gospels and apostolic authorship. My term "Christian postmodernism" is intended to help us think through the way the resurgence and postmodernism were entangled in the contemporary period, and to forestall the easy assumption (found, we have seen, in Hardt and Negri) that fundamentalism and postmodernism must naturally be oppositional.

Similarly, my term "Christian multiculturalism" allows us to see with fresh eyes the surprising convergence between conservative Christianity and multiculturalism's understanding of religious identities. That convergence was vividly on display at the *Dover* trial, where the Intelligent Design attorney for the school board defendants (from the conservative Catholic Thomas More Law Center, working pro bono) suggested that "the courts are trying to cleanse America of religion, to remove Christianity from the public square.

It's really a cleansing, a kind of genocide. . . . This case is about changing that. Our hope is to get to the Supreme Court from here and, hopefully, change the law. Stop the genocide" (quoted in Humes 228). In a significant way, this formulation aptly captures the confluence of postmodernism, multiculturalism, and the resurgence. As his language of "cleansing" suggests, this breathtaking analogy takes its reference more from the murderous so-called ethnic cleansings in the Balkans in the 1990s than from the central European Holocaust of the 1940s. Christians are not being prevented from taking communion or celebrating Easter, or forced to convert to secular humanism, but rather, according to the lawyer, they are being prohibited from teaching specific theological ideas about God's particular method of creation in public classrooms. In his analogy, this has the same effect as killing Christians who hold those beliefs. Apart from showing the continued importance of matters of belief (in addition to, and as, religious practice) for many Christians in the resurgence, this formulation captures how religious beliefs are not so much matters of disagreement as of identity. There can be no argument about which ideas are true, in this formulation, because one's ideas are simply a function of who one is. In this cultural model of religious identity, the language of genocide seals in—racially—the inherited characteristics of the group. As in canonical multicultural American literature such as *Mumbo Jumbo, Borderlands / La Frontera, Ceremony, House Made of Dawn, The Plot Against America, The Poisonwood Bible,* and *Gilead,* multicultural religion is removed from the realm of universal ideas about the true and good—ideas that might be disagreed over, negotiated, or reconciled.

Of course, when evolution is taught in the classroom no one is actually being killed (though conservative Christians such as Francis Schaeffer argue that the naturalism intrinsic to science encourages abortions because we view fetuses as soulless matter—see, e.g., 235). Nonetheless, the analogy to genocide underlines the heritable, familial quality of most people's religious faith. Somewhat like the religious imaginary in Roth and Robinson, the risk that the Intelligent Design lawyer sees is actually one of cultural assimilation of Christian youth into mainstream, secular America, one that will be accomplished by the teaching of the origin of species through natural selection. It is no accident that the site of this struggle is the public school classroom, where familial cultural narratives can come into conflict with established science. The huge growth in the Christian homeschooling movement, while initially a reaction in part to desegregation decisions, should be understood as the ongoing Christian attempt to prevent their children's cultural assimilation into secular society, an assimilation hastened by exposure to evolution, sex education, gay-positive curricula, climate-change science, and so on.

In this resurgent account of the Dover trial, then, religion is both postmodern (in that it rejects modern scientific expertise, opting instead for alternative Lyotardian "moves" within the language game of biology) and multicultural (in that faith is understood as the victim of ethnic disrespect, even hatred).

Thus, to answer Tracy Fessenden's excellent question—"what's *American* about postsecular claims made in, around, or on behalf of American literature" ("Problem" 165)—in a slightly different register, I suggest that the nodes of entanglement I have named as Christian multiculturalism and Christian postmodernism could have happened nowhere else. Christian multicultur- alism depended on and took inspiration from developments in American multiculturalism whose genealogy lay in a particular twentieth-century his- tory of American race relations, social-science discourse, and judicial trans- formation. Christian postmodernism, meanwhile, grew out of particularly American habits of fundamentalist thought characterized by hostility to intellectual elites, tendencies toward paranoia and conspiracy, and an ecosys- tem of counterexperts embedded in institutions (academic, media, church) purposed for combatting elite knowledge and the secularism it seemed to entail. The most globally prominent creationist is the Australian Ken Ham, but his prominence has emerged because of his American location as the head of the movement's most famous museum—the Creation Museum in Kentucky—the base from which, in 2014, he debated Bill Nye the science guy and decried Neil deGrasse Tyson's reboot of Sagan's *Cosmos* series for its focus on evolution, age of the universe, and warnings about climate change. Christian postmodernism, like Christian multiculturalism, might resonate in other (especially English-speaking) countries, but their developments were made possible only because of the specifically American conservative Chris- tian resurgence and its genealogies in American history, institutions, religious contexts, and discursive practices.

In retrospect, the alliance between the conservative Christian resurgence and the postmodern should not have been surprising. Given the secularity of the modern, its grand narratives of human enlightenment and advance- ment through reason and science, and the liberation of the human spirit from a dark past characterized by ignorance and religion, we should have expected that postmodernism's indictment of the weaknesses and blindnesses of this mode—its unarticulated assumptions, its hidden teleology, its ends in violence—would find resonance with a movement that had been an early victim of modernity. While secular postmodernists might understand their indeterminacies as naturally hostile to the certainties and literalisms culti- vated by theological conservatives, it appears that way only from within the modern, or what Charles Taylor calls "the immanent frame" (542); what postmodernism made indeterminate and epistemologically and ontologically plural were modern conclusions and ways of knowing, which fundamentalists had long regarded as the problem.

Although I have employed Lyotard's theory chiefly as a way of illuminating Christian postmodernism, my explanation concords with some other articulations of the postmodern condition. Resurgent revisions of American history, rewriting the nation as the sacred mission of evangelical founders (as I review in chapter 3) could be understood as symptoms of Jameson's diagnosis of the postmodern as characterizing the attempt to do history but no longer knowing how. Jean Baudrillard's emphasis on the precession of the simulacra evocatively suggests the Reagan and Bush II eras of reality-generation through powerful representational models. Likewise, Bruno Latour's rumination "Why Has Critique Run Out of Steam?" insightfully investigates the conundrum that

> entire Ph.D. programs are still running to make sure that good American kids are learning the hard way that facts are made up, that there is no such thing as natural, unmediated, unbiased access to truth, that we are always prisoners of language, that we always speak from a particular standpoint, and so on, while dangerous extremists are using the very same argument of social construction to destroy hard-won evidence that could save our lives. (227)

His condemnation of the consequent "artificially maintained controversies" is as valid for questions of evolution as it is for his example of climate change science (227). Like Pinter sensing the strangely shifted political terrain of the postmodern, Latour argues for a change of course: "My argument is that a certain form of critical spirit has sent us down the wrong path, encouraging us to fight the wrong enemies and, worst of all, to be considered as friends by the wrong sort of allies because of a little mistake in the definition of its main target. The question was never to get *away* from facts but *closer* to them, not fighting empiricism but, on the contrary, renewing empiricism" (231).

Crucially, rendering consensus knowledge indeterminate and uncertain reopens a respectable place for faith because, in this view, the moderns are just as faith-based as the religious traditions they eschewed in their founding moment. The opportunity that postmodernism opens for theological conservatives was readily remarked by some, like Downing: having to make a leap of faith, to believe in something amidst the world's uncertainties and indeterminacies, as postmodernism tells us we must do and in fact, whether we know it or not, we always already have done, is not an idea that took conservative Christians by surprise. I have chosen as a text indicating the problems with a postmodern critique of conservative faith Dan Brown's *The Da Vinci Code* not because, we have seen, it is formally postmodern or aesthetically interesting. Its postmodernism, rather, lies in its scholarly apparatus and its conclusions. Indeed, I am not aware of any formally postmodern American fiction that takes the conservative Christian resurgence and its cultural politics as an opportunity for fiction, or as a critical target. That no such book exists is part of the strange coincidence that I have tried to name here: it is as though the resurgent Christianity was not recognizable by the postmodern masters, or not fictionally interesting, perhaps because its postmodernism was somewhat incomprehensible but unsettlingly familiar.[15] Even a more literary novel such as Atwood's *The Handmaid's Tale*, seen by some critics as trying to challenge fundamentalist certainties about language on which biblical literalism rests by cultivating a postmodern sense of the ambiguity, restlessness, and instability of interpretation (see, e.g., Myhal; Caminero-Santangelo), understands that, however strong that postmodern uncertainty is, it is not, ultimately, the thing that will really subvert the religious fundamentalism of Gilead, the totalitarian Christian state which, it is hinted (e.g., 82, 300), eventually succumbs for military and economic reasons, not ones of epistemological instability or postmodern uncertainty. As *The Crying of Lot 49* teaches us, postmodern uncertainty is the invitation to faith, not its obstacle.

Christian postmodernism and Christian multiculturalism make American literature's response to the conservative Christian resurgence complicated and confusing because they locate its entanglements with our postwar paradigms of literary innovation. A generation of inaugural multicultural writers—Reed and Anzaldúa, Walker and Momaday, Silko and Acosta, Chin and Morrison—had imagined religious difference as a key component of their new cultural pluralism; strangely, they agreed with resurgent Christians about the Christian identity of the nation and the need to return to ancestral religious traditions. As American fiction addressed the resurgence in indirect, roundabout ways, writers discovered a kind of limit to the cultural paradigm because the logic of cultural relativism, in Kingsolver, and the rereading of religious conversion as forms of cultural assimilation, as in Robinson and Roth, could not really equip writers to deal with the universal claims of the resurgence. Confusingly, the resurgence oscillated on a dual register of the universal and the cultural, sometimes speaking in one mode and at other times speaking and practicing in another.

Pynchon, meanwhile, sensed the spiritual geography of the emerging alliance, as well as how the ontological pluralism it cultivated allowed for new avenues of postmodern belief. Nature and history encoded kinds of sacred writing requiring certain expert modes of reading, some of our contemporary writers saw, and the thematization of expert reading was often an indirect way of addressing the conservative Christian resurgence's inaugural quarrels with the science of evolution, as McCarthy and Sagan perceived, and with the historical-critical method, as Pynchon and Brown developed. Christian postmodernism develops counterexpert bodies of knowledge in the fields of reading nature and texts. As the fictions of McCarthy, Sagan and Brown reflect, there are good reasons of theodicy for why conservative theology tries hard to evade modern discoveries, which seem to many to push back the possibilities for the classical Christian notion of God's character.

Method

The political flashpoints for the conservative Christian resurgence—evolution, abortion, climate change, sex education, homosexuality, and so on—are not the results of simple ignorance, misinformation, or lack of education. Indeed, social scientists studying the reception of new information in highly charged areas of dispute have shown that "the divide over belief in evolution between more and less religious people is *wider* among people who otherwise show familiarity with math and science."[16] Resistance to facts—the mental filtering and harmonization that all humans do—has become particularly sharpened for this conservative constituency; it is a studied, purposeful aversion to elite knowledge reminiscent of Sacvan Bercovitch's conclusion about Huckleberry Finn's innocence, "that Huck is innocent insofar as innocence means ineducatability" (116). But scientific naturalism and the historical-critical method are interpretively tied to larger evils in the conservative Christian worldview, evils that make it extremely difficult for many conservative Christians to hear arguments and evidence in their favor. Triggered by the "cultural crisis" of World War One, 1920s fundamentalism took its inspiration from the twelve-volume set *The Fundamentals* (1910–1915), which derided the "speculative hypotheses" of higher biblical criticism and evolution—to both of which were attributed the sources of German warmongering (Marsden 121, 148–49). Conservative Christian history often understands the Holocaust as resulting from the naturalistic science of evolution, just as the murderous regime of the Stalinist Soviet Union is understood as the predictable result of atheistic communism. Francis Schaeffer, for example, draws a line of causation from Darwin to racism and Nazism (151). Nor is this link confined to conservative Christians: Marilynne Robinson ties the rise of Nazism to Darwin and his contemporary Herbert Spencer, wondering, "Why do these innocent scientific ideas veer so predictably toward ugliness and evil?" (*Death* 56). The Intelligent Design lawyer's linking of evolution to genocide did not come out of nowhere; once one believes that evolution, and scientific naturalism more generally, leads to genocide, the Holocaust, abortion and euthanasia, it is difficult to have a dispassionate discussion of the evidence for even seemingly unrelated things like climate change.

Historians, literary critics, and religious studies scholars face a profound problem of method. We saw a facet of this problem of method in chapter 3's discussion of slavery. Douglass's phrase "Christian slavery" was meant to provoke Northern abolitionists (many of whom were evangelical Christians), but it raised the thorny issue of the extent to which abolitionism or slavery could be thought of as resulting from, or reinforced by, religion. Most contemporary Christians find the idea of Christian slavery impossible, assuming (if they recognize them at all) that Southerners who claimed religious sanction for their practices must have been hypocrites or self-deluded enemies of true faith. Indeed, my argument in chapter 3 is that Robinson's exploration of the Christian relation to slavery stops decidedly short of recognizing the way in which Christianity seemed to animate not just the abolitionism she rightly admires, but the owners of other human beings who argued vehemently for the justice of their system, and were willing to die for it in the Civil War. Schaeffer, LaHaye, and other contemporary Christian apologists of a more conservative ilk skirt the question. As I suggested in examining the scholarship supported by the Lilly Endowment, liberal academic scholarship generally emphasizes the religious practices and belief traditions of the disempowered rather than the religious traditions of the rich, powerful, and oppressive.

We thus face a methodological problem of symmetrical bias when studying religion. As historian David A. Hollinger reflected about his participation in a Lilly Seminar, "there is a tendency to credit religion in general and Christianity in particular with producing and sustaining a host of valuable aspects of contemporary culture, title to which might well be reclaimed, or at least respectfully shared, by other parties. At work here is a familiar dynamic in the struggle for possession of cultural capital." Drawing on Pierre Bourdieu's important concept, he continues, "Ideas the value of which is recognized in a large social arena will be claimed by particular groups as their own contribution. One of the means by which groups achieve, maintain, or lose relative power in a multi-group arena is to be identified or not identified with highly valued items in the common cultural inventory. What endows an item with the capacity to function as cultural capital is the prestige it enjoys among many groups" (114). Christian historians, and religiously motivated religious studies scholars more generally, have a tendency to want to claim credit for good historical influences such as abolitionism and opposition to Nazism, while simultaneously disowning the bad things: thus was Orsi's warning, as we saw in chapter 3, that the new "lived religion" scholarship (which he helped form and theorize and which, we saw, was supported by the moderate Christian Lilly Endowment) was tending to "overlook religion's complicity in sustaining structures and patterns of alienation and domination" ("Everyday" 15). Partly for this reason, we have lots of good historical work on Christian abolitionism, but not so much on Christian proslavery ideology and practice.

This problem of bias is only somewhat less true of "secular humanism": the humanists—those who identify as the intellectual descendants of the Enlightenment, for example—want to disown slavery and the Holocaust, which Christian apologists pin on atheism, materialism, and evolution. Each side (both of which, I recognize, are actually made up of a wide range of belief and unbelief positions) want to own the good things and disown the bad, making it very difficult to disentangle questions of influence and articulation when it comes to social and political evils. Not only does each side wish to own as "cultural capital" those accomplishments, ideas, practices, or events that are held in high prestige, but, conversely, each wants to disown their opposites, which we might call cultural excrement. Cultural excrement is that which one doesn't want to be smeared with—slavery, the Holocaust, genocides and ethnic cleansings, the French reign of terror, concentration camps and death camps, revolutionary upheavals with huge costs in human lives, murderous social transformations, and so on—what you run away from, what you deny comes from your culture. Just as Christians today might deny that, for example, proslavery ideology and practice was "really" Christian, so too might secular humanists contest the idea that a "true" Enlightenment, properly understood, would lead to terror or death camps. This problem of bias is built into contemporary discussions of religion.

How to solve it? A more rigorously descriptive historiography, a more empirical practice of doing history, might provide a way around this problem. Lived religion's goal (as yet unmet, I would argue) of being "radically" phenomenological, of paying greater attention to ordinary, everyday religious practice and religious belief, holds promise. But an obstacle is that such rigorous description and attention to the phenomenological cannot generally happen without being already filtered through our presuppositions and biases about what religion is and how it functions. It's not easy just to look at the data and distill our theories and interpretations from it; our presuppositions about religion act as barriers to the reception of data in the first place (in addition to then coloring our interpretations of the data that get through our filters). These assumptions generally go unarticulated, even to ourselves.

A remarkable exception to our generally unarticulated assumptions is George Marsden's classic history *Fundamentalism and American Culture*, whose Afterword strikingly illuminates the question of the Christian historian's subject position vis-à-vis his scholarly field. "The awareness that God acts in history in ways that we can only know in the context of our culturally determined experience should be central to a Christian understanding of history," he writes. The problem is that "The history of Christianity reveals a perplexing mixture of divine and human factors," making the historian's task difficult. He continues, in a remarkable passage that is worth quoting in full:

> The present work, an analysis of cultural influences on religious belief, is a study of things visible. As such it must necessarily reflect more than a little sympathy with the modern mode of explanation in terms of natural historical causation. Yet it would be a mistake to assume that such sympathy is incompatible with, or even antagonistic to, a view of history in which God as revealed in scripture is the dominant force, and in which other unseen spiritual forces are contending. I find that a Christian view of history is clarified if one considers reality as more or less like the world portrayed in the works of J.R.R. Tolkien. We live in the midst of contests between great and mysterious spiritual forces, which we understand only imperfectly and whose true dimensions we only occasionally glimpse. Yet, frail as we are, we do play a role in this history, on the side either of the powers of light or of the powers of darkness. It is crucially important then, that, by God's grace, we keep our wits about us and discern the vast difference between the real forces for good and the powers of darkness disguised as angels of light.

Such a larger vision is, I think, the proper context for understanding the historian's modest task of trying to identify the formative cultural elements that have either properly shaped or distorted our understanding of God and his revelation. Since God's work appears to us in historical circumstances where imperfect humans are major agents, the actions of the Holy Spirit in the church are always intertwined with culturally conditioned factors. The theologian's task is to try to establish from scripture criteria for determining what in the history of the church is truly the work of the Spirit. The Christian historian takes an opposite, although complementary, approach. While he must keep in mind certain theological criteria, he may refrain from explicit judgment on what is properly Christian while he concentrates on observable cultural forces. (259–60)

It is worth making a couple of points about this surprising passage. The first is that its bias toward a normative view of Christianity makes it very difficult to see history clearly. In Marsden's view, true Christianity is always good because behind it lies "the powers of light," and, indeed, God himself. Where Christianity seems to cause harm or be aligned with evil and oppression—as with Douglass's Christian slavery—it is the result of "the powers of darkness disguised as the angels of light." Though Marsden tries to separate this admittedly theological assumption from the scholarly mode of "natural historical causation," it is not difficult to see that the theological assumptions about true and false Christianity will color the historiographic questions of how the religion influenced both sides of the slavery debate, to use the current example. Such assumptions cause Marsden to downplay the histories of Christian slavery and Christian segregation as the ancestors of the Religious Right (see, e.g., 237 and 324n14). In his normative view, these would not really have been Christian in origin: they would have been the result of "culturally conditioned factors" that "distorted our understanding of God and his revelation," people working for "the powers of darkness [while] disguised as angels of light."

I have identified similar assumptions in the liberal Christian writer Marilynne Robinson and the progressive Christian literary theorist Terry Eagleton, and suggested that a similar reluctance to take Christians (like the proslavery Richard Furman) at their word is behind much of the Lilly-supported "lived religion" scholarship that, Orsi concedes, tends not to look at the destructive elements of Christianity. We find another example of the urge to look away in Putnam and Campbell's otherwise rightly lauded *American Grace*: while commenting on President Lincoln's observation that "both sides read the same Bible and pray to the same God, and each invokes His aid against the other" (quoted 375), they write, somewhat bewilderingly, "Lincoln's words, however, obscure an important point about the way religion relates to politics, since they imply a symmetry between the religious justifications of pro- and antislavery advocates. Actually, white Southerners would have been pro-slavery without religion; while white Northerners likely would have been antislavery only because of religion" (375–76). They provide no reason or evidence for this interpretation; the implication seems to be that, because of economic need, the Southerners would have been proslavery without any religious influence (thus religion is not to blame for proslavery forces), whereas Northerners, who didn't have slaves, wouldn't have cared one way or the other about slavery

(thus religion does get the credit for antislavery forces). This is a good example of the way abolitionism functions as cultural capital while slavery functions as cultural excrement: Putnam and Campbell are saying that economic
temptation corrupted Southern religion, whereas, since there were no economic temptations for Northerners, their opposition could only have been
due to the benign influence of religion. The unspoken assumption here is
that any moral good must have an origin in religion: there could no more be a
nonreligious ethical impulse—say, recognition of the suffering of and injustice
toward one's fellow humans—that motivated some Northerners than there
could be a noneconomic religious impulse that motivated some Southerners.

The second point to make about Marsden's Afterword is its, to put it
bluntly, shocking invocation of Tolkien's fantasy fiction, to which we are
invited to compare our own world as imbricated in "great and mysterious
spiritual forces." This is one of the major historians of American religion
recommending as a model someone who had a profoundly ahistorical conception of history. The supernaturalism Marsden invites us to understand
as the deeper current of human history is an invitation to bring one's presuppositions about supernatural entities to bear on our history, ones that
will return us to a particular, normative notion of God. It is difficult to see
what advantages the supernaturalizing of human history along these lines
would bring. Indeed, the supernaturalization of conflict, of the kind in Tolkien's world that Marsden recommends to us, has itself been part of the evil
apparatus that Christians have sometimes visited upon their antagonists. As
Sacvan Bercovitch has shown, Puritans believed that God used indigenous
peoples as His tool to punish and correct Puritan communities in the New
World (see also Fessenden, *Culture* 53). As the agent of such a supernatural,
pedagogical force, the Puritans' Indians were, like Tolkien's orcs, without
history or agency themselves.[17] What could possibly be gleaned from Tolkien's supernatural picture to help us better understand the evil developments
and histories of fascism, or slavery, or genocides, especially since it draws us
away from earthly explanations of culture, society, politics and economics,
and into a transcendent world where a normative Christian theology still
holds sway, as it obviously does for Tolkien? Once we bring our expectations
of supernatural, superhuman characters and their moral qualities to bear on
human history, we have opened the path to greater mystification, not better
understanding. Indeed, the preference for understanding the 9/11 murderers
as the embodiment of "evil," to the extent that it was understood super-
naturally, closed off possible political analysis of Al Qaeda's motivations. But
one didn't have to approve of Al Qaeda's methods to see that it was worth
wondering what their political beliefs and objectives were, beyond just being

evildoers. The normative theology that governed Tolkien and his fictional world, I submit, will not help us do a better, more comprehensive and historically phenomenological study of religion.

Marsden is not alone in bringing normative theology to bear on his academic subject matter. Those who read Charles Taylor's magnificent and massive *A Secular Age* to the end may be a little surprised to find its argument in the last two hundred pages or so turn increasingly to a Christian apologetics grounded in a similar normative theology. Thus, regarding Taylor's line about the rise of fascism in Europe that "There was no place left for the morality of Christianity, and certainly not of liberalism; the ultimate goal was to make something great out of one's life" (418), Michael Lackey comments, "For those who have read the writings of Hitler and many prominent Nazis, Taylor's claim simply infuriates, for . . . Hitler announced that his political party regards 'Christianity as the foundation of our national morality' and that 'the Government of the Reich . . . regards Christianity as the unshakable foundation of the morals and moral code of the nation'" (335). As Lackey argues, "Taylor believes that there is such a thing as true Christianity, and given the way Hitler and the Nazis behaved, he concludes that they were not Christian, as he defines the term" (335). Lackey's point is apt; the core of Christianity for Taylor (and others) is agape, the love of the other even at the expense of the self. It is difficult to reconcile that core with the Holocaust's murderous genocide, with the suffering of millions of African American slaves, or with the instrumentalized killings and displacements of indigenous peoples in the Americas. Accordingly, Taylor and others see such claims to Christianity, if they are registered at all, as cynical insincerity (returning us thereby to DeLillo's nun's pretense theory of faith), gross ideological manipulation, or grandiose self-delusion.

But they need not be. Christians in the past, as now, understand that agape has a shape in practice. The Christian slavery that Richard Furman practiced and theologized, for instance, was embedded in a larger Christian framework of patriarchy and paternalism, in which one's care for one's wife, one's children, one's servants, and one's slaves did not entail social equality, political power, unlimited freedom, or dispossession of property. Douglass, in fact, notes several good and kind slaveholders—although he remarks on the pernicious moral effects of the peculiar institution on them (37, 39–40, 71)—and Morrison makes one such couple central to the most famous slavery novel of the contemporary period. Furman, in fact, urged Christian slaveholders to offer religious instruction for their slaves, "For though they are slaves, they are also men; and are with ourselves accountable creatures; having immortal souls, and being destined to future eternal reward." He likewise warns the masters against "unreasonable, rigorous services" or "cruel punishment," for neither has "a scriptural nor a moral right"[18]—though this last part is not quite true, given Douglass's Auld's propensity to quote Jesus's line that "He that knoweth his master's will, and doeth it not, shall be beaten with many stripes" (53). At the other end of the spectrum, even the benign and inoffensive evangelical *The Purpose Driven Life*, by Rick Warren—"the best-selling hardcover book in American publishing history" (D Williams 276)—recommends a particular shape for agape, emphasizing "loving other believers . . . belonging and learning to love the family of God" (59). Warren would surely recognize Jesus's teaching to love thy neighbor as thyself; my point is merely that, as this hugely popular resurgent author shows, Christians often prioritize agape in practice. As then, so now.

At the end of *A Secular Age*, Taylor commends a reading of the parable of the Good Samaritan, a story that "can be seen as one of [the] original building blocks out of which our modern universalist moral consciousness has been built" (738). In philosopher Ivan Illich's view, Taylor says, this story is intended to teach not a new set of moral rules (i.e., the extension of our moral responsibility to those outside our group), but rather "a new kind of community" (738), a "network" (739) of people who respond to wounded others on the basis of agape, which he says "moves outward from the guts" (741). In Illich's reading, Taylor says, once we institutionalize the care of others through rules and purposed organization (first in the church, then in a secularized state), we miss the lessons of contingency and gut reaction of the original parable. This is a moving and inspired reading; I commend it as well. But other Christians in other historical moments have had other understandings of this parable, told by Jesus to answer the question posed to him, "who is my neighbor?" who must be loved as myself (see Luke 10:29). Furman, like millions of other Southern Christians, understood agape as working within a social order that included property rights; they understood that it made them responsible for the physical and spiritual care of their property, but that agape was focused through a particular, peculiar institution. Furman's Christian agape is different from Taylor's Christian agape. I think we can all agree that the latter's is much preferable. But so agreeing does not make Furman's practice and theory un-Christian.

Taylor's normative Christianity—and he is not alone—centers around New Testament agape, but also the potential for transformation or transcendence beyond immanent human fulfilment, and the ordering of one's own disordered life. But it is easy to see that, at other moments and times in history, the practice of agape has been circumscribed by one's own racial or national group, and the will to order one's own life has entailed violently ordering the lives of others. Taylor's cores of Christianity—agape, transformation and transcendence, ordering—have themselves had widely different shapings by actual historical Christians, some of which have resulted in forms of Christian violence and evil. These possibilities are built into God's policy of revelation, the consequences of God's choice (if it was a choice) to remain hidden, speaking indirectly in ambiguous and ancient records.

Taylor's concepts of agape, transcendence, and ordering are governed by his sense of what he calls "God's pedagogy" (772)—the slow and winding history wherein God's benevolent will toward humans is slowly unpacked for us under his tutelage. God's pedagogy is one way of answering the question from *Blood Meridian* whose words animate the title of this study, "If God meant to interfere in the degeneracy of mankind would he not have done so by now?" (153): the pedagogy of God is indeed a kind of ongoing intervention. As with Marsden's unseen cosmic forces, the supernatural frame is the invisible but necessary backdrop for normative Christian theology that can only be mistakenly associated with cultural excrement by fallible human agents. I take this to be the real problem of method for those of us studying religion in the fields of history, literature, and religious studies today: behind the common scholarly assumption that religion is naturally benevolent (that is, unless twisted for bad purposes) is actually a set of supernatural assumptions about the ongoing activity of the classical God. It is right for Christians to have an intra-Christian debate about proper practice and theory (as Stowe and Douglass were doing with the likes of Furman), and those arguments may invoke claims about God's pedagogy or the actions of "great and unseen spiritual forces." But taking implicit sides in such intra-Christian debates cannot be the method of the historian or the literary critic, and we must likewise avoid speculating about the motives and influences of unseen supernatural entities.

Taylor has put to rest the "master narrative" of secularization as "a recession of religion in the face of science, technology and rationality" (573–74). The inaccuracy of the secularization thesis is quite spectacularly on display in the United States, as I hope I have been able to show with the conservative Christian resurgence. My argument has been not that the two bodies of modern knowledge emerging since the nineteenth century—evolution and the historical-critical method—are, as Taylor likewise denies, "proofs" against the existence of God (366). Rather, it is that they have necessitated for many a rethinking of Christian theology. That rethinking results in (we might say) evolving or changing notions of God and the transcendent, even as the resurgence remains a deep current of faith that refuses to undertake such revaluations, a powerful current that has generally responded to the two bodies of knowledge by denying their validity. Adherents should continue to argue for or against these revaluations, and for what might count as the preferred core(s) of faith. But scholars suspending such normative expectations about Christian theology and practice can begin to see, among other phenomena, the unexpected and wholly strange coemergence of the conservative Christian resurgence alongside the multicultural and the postmodern in the contemporary period. These strange nodes of entanglement I have called Christian multiculturalism and Christian postmodernism can be part of a refreshed effort to recognize the "super-nova" of enduring and new faith positions and to try to examine the facts as best we can arrive at them. We are still in the middle of the conservative Christian resurgence, with few signs that the God gap is closing, and, with Marilynne Robinson's preacher, we must wonder where it will end. But we need not be left behind as we watch the resurgence come to renewed power—or trail off. Alert to the American strangeness of Christian multiculturalism and Christian postmodernism, we can seek to decipher its signs and clues in the literature and culture of our time.

NOTES

Introduction

1. http://www.pewforum.org/2013/03/26/us-christians-views-on-the-return-of-christ/. The more recent 2010 poll numbers seemed congruent with American belief in the 1980s: a 1983 Gallup poll (quoted in Wojcik 7) showed that 62 percent of Americans had "no doubts" that Jesus would return, while a 1991 International Social Survey showed Americans holding high levels of belief in heaven (91%), hell (82%), miracles (77%), and the devil (78%) (quoted in Greeley and Hout 24).

2. The original twelve-part series was published between 1995 and 2004; a three part prequel arrived between 2005–06, and a sequel in 2007, so there are actually sixteen novels in the *Left Behind* series. This does not include the forty-novel *Left Behind: The Kids* adolescent series.

3. The nun's experience may also reflect the fact that non-Hispanic Catholicism has indeed been in decline for decades (Putnam and Campbell 300–06).

4. See Kruse for a complementary genealogy of the Christian Right in which a coalition between corporate leaders and conservative Christians hostile to the New Deal nurtured the patriotic notion of "one nation under God" during the Cold War and eventually aligned with Republican Party politicians.

5. Who were these conservative Christians? Scholars use different terms to define the shape and strength of this recent conservative religious affiliation. When describing the "coalition of the religious [that] began to come together" during the first aftershock as a "political movement," Putnam and Campbell use the term "Religious Right" (389). They use the term "evangelical" to describe its key constituent group, defining it by denomination and contrasting it with "mainline Protestantism," also defined by denomination (602–03n16), and note that this evangelicalism generally shares fundamentalism's biblical literalism, traditional family and gender values, and millennial expectations about the Second Coming (89). Sociologists Andrew Greeley and Michael Hout use the term "Conservative Christians," also defined by denomination against "Mainline Protestant" and (as with Putnam and Campbell) against the historically distinct religious tradition of African American Protestantism (8). They eschew the terms "evangelical" and "fundamentalist" as "a pair of misleading labels" (11). Their identifier "Conservative Christians" includes conservative Catholics and is broader than their "Conservative Protestant" (189n2). Cultural anthropologist Susan Harding uses "born again" and "Bible-believing" to refer to fundamentalists, Pentecostals, charismatics, and those evangelicals "who mobilized politically and culturally in the 1980s" (xvi); she traces in particular the emergence in the 1970s and 1980s of the alliance between post-separatist fundamentalists like Jerry

Falwell (who would found the Moral Majority in 1979) and conservative evangelicals such as Francis Schaeffer (130), a tracing sensitive to the continued presence of "separatist" (i.e., those not prioritizing direct political engagement) fundamentalists such as Bob Jones Jr. (10, 149). Historian of American fundamentalism George M. Marsden likewise uses the phrase "Religious Right" to include "cultural conservatives from other heritages such as Roman Catholics and Mormons. The Protestant part of this coalition has often been referred to, especially by those who do not appreciate the internal divisions within conversionist Christianity, as simply 'evangelical,' or sometimes as simply 'fundamentalist.' It would be more accurate to say that the Religious Right as a political movement has attracted many [previously] separatist fundamentalists and 'fundamentalistic' evangelicals" (234–35). Historian Daniel K. Williams uses "Christian Right" as an umbrella term for the alliance that developed alongside and then within the Republican Party; his work is especially useful for its examination of the particular political issues, actors, and elections behind the developing religious-political polarization that Putnam and Campbell describe.

These categories are imprecise and not monolithic, and they tend to hide the considerable diversity of American political orientations, as well as religious practice and belief. For example, only 73 percent of white "evangelicals" voted for evangelical president George W. Bush in the 2004 election (Putnam and Campbell 283), which means a very significant portion of white evangelicals had not been "sorted" into conservative Republican voting patterns. (But see D. Michael Lindsay, who reports Bush as having 87 percent of the evangelical vote in 2004 [24]; this may be an error, or, more likely, a different definition of "evangelical.") Not only are there liberal Christians in "mainline Protestant," African American, and Catholic churches, then, but there are also Democratic-voting "evangelical" Christians. Nonetheless, Putnam and Campbell confirm that the difference in religiosity between the two parties is real (371), a God gap with significant and continuing consequences for the issues activated during the culture wars.

6. Many of the details about Bachmann in this sketch are from Ryan Lizza's *New Yorker* portrait.

7. For more details, see the *New York Times* story at http://www.nytimes.com/2013/07/03/world/africa/bush-a-fond-presence-in-africa-for-work-during-and-since-his-presidency.html?pagewanted=all.

8. See Brooks. Conservative Christians are less likely to believe in scientific evidence either that the earth is warming or that this is the result of human causes (http://www.pewforum.org/Science-and-Bioethics/Religious-Groups-Views-on-Global-Warming.aspx). They are also less likely to be in favor of policy that mitigates climate change, a fact that David C. Barker and David H. Bearce attribute to their high belief that the Second Coming of Christ will occur by 2050 (268).

9. See http://www.people-press.org/2015/04/07/a-deep-dive-into-party-affiliation/.

10. See also 860–61, where Shirley Neuman situates *The Handmaid's Tale* in terms of the co-development of the "New Right" and Falwell's Moral Majority, noting in particular the emerging hostility to feminism.

11. Taylor continues by noting that this Fourth Great Awakening "is surprisingly consistent with the revivals of the eighteenth and nineteenth centuries," except that it is "a *global* phenomenon occurring in many different countries and in virtually all

established religious traditions" (258). As attractive as the term is, however, "Fourth Great Awakening" is not generally used by contemporary sociologists or historians of religion to describe the upswing in conservative religious energy since the 1970s, partly because much of that demographic increase was due to larger families among conservative Protestants and partly because it did not include enough conversions from "none" or liberal to conservative denominations to qualify as a "revival" in the tradition of the recognized three Great Awakenings in US history.

1. Multiculturalism, Secularization, Resurgence

1. The tone from Boyle and his colleague William Sloane Coffin Jr., from whom we do hear a speech, is more priestly and philosophical than evangelical, with Coffin defending the right of humanists to have ethics without religion, and hence eligibility to be conscientious objectors (72).

2. See my *Genealogy* 184–209 for Morrison's multicultural break from the assimilationist civil rights consensus.

3. See Douglas, *Genealogy*, chapter 8.

4. See Douglas, *Genealogy*, chapters 1 and 8, for more on Hurston's anthropology and its shaping of Reed's literary vision.

5. Intriguingly, a good portion of this sura deals with Jesus, who is the immediate context for the verse's argument that he should not be understood to be divinely associated with God. The verse reads in full, "Those who say, 'God is the Messiah, son of Mary,' have defied God. The Messiah himself said, 'Children of Israel, worship God, my Lord and your Lord.' If anyone associates others with God, God will forbid him from the Garden, and Hell will be his home. No one will help such evildoers" (5:72).

6. This is Reed's wink: Earline is embarking on Hurston's anthropological career, which did indeed benefit future artists like Reed thirty to forty years later.

7. In *Paradise*, Morrison turns her attention to Christian fundamentalism, but of an African American strain that was notably outside of the alliance developed by the Religious Right; thus, while the novel is keenly attentive to religious experience, as McClure and others have shown, she is not attending to the conservative Christian resurgence as such. McClure's study of Morrison's novel, examining the Exodus tradition in African American Christianity, shows that the "postsecular" in Morrison is as much a multicultural reclamation (and critical examination) of a cultural religious tradition as it is a postmodern "creolizing [of] the cosmos" (*Partial* 106).

8. This white creation story parallels the invention of whites by a black scientist in (early) Nation of Islam formulations.

9. See, e.g., Silko and Arnold 166–67.

10. See Douglas, "Flawed," for an examination of the theological ramifications of *House Made of Dawn*.

11. See Douglas, *Genealogy*, chapter 7.

12. Thus, while modern disenchantment is often understood as oppositional to Christianity, the two can in other moments join forces against "primitive," pagan, or shamanistic religious traditions that are excluded from the partially secularized civil religion regime outlined by Bellah and Herberg.

13. In his excellent account of their literary and publishing alliance, Christopher Shinn writes, "The partnership of Reed and Chin has led in a substantial way to

the rise of the Asian American movement itself in the 1970s, yet this connection has largely been understudied by most literary scholars and has not been elaborated upon in any sort of meaningful way, with a few notable exceptions, for almost thirty years" (68). Shinn shows how "Reed and Chin have indeed revolutionized the U.S. literary canon" (77), and my argument's purpose is to show how overtly religious this revolutionary multicultural alliance was.

14. See my *Genealogy*, conclusion, for an account of Kingston's non-authoritative anti-ethnography.

15. Benjamin Tong, a Chinese American sociologist contemporaneous to Chin, provided in the 1970s not only an account of Confucian difference and cultural survival, but one that also, à la Anzaldúa, contained a history of a prior power and class struggle that explained the specific historical formation of the kind of Confucianism arriving with the first Chinese American immigrants. Chin and Tong refer to one another in their writings of this decade, and Tong received thanks from the *Aiiieeeee!* editors ("Preface" xxii). As David Li has noted, Tong's preference (like Chin's) was the model of "African American rebellion" rather than "Jewish assimilation" (23).

16. A 2010 American Literature Association meeting had her speaking, with African American author Charles Johnson, at a panel on "Buddhism and Life Writing."

17. Thus see Bellah (*Religion in Human Evolution* 399–480), who locates in Confucius and Plato axial transitions analogous to those in ancient Israel's prophets and ancient India's Vedic and Buddhist traditions.

2. *The Poisonwood Bible*'s Multicultural Graft

1. See, for example, Kakutani, Klinkenborg, Lezard, and Thomas. See Siegel for a nonreligious dissenting critique; see Byfield and Byfield, Stafford, and Zoba for critical Christian appraisals; and Bromberg for a positive Christian evaluation.

2. See Lofton's chapter "Reading Religiously" for an excellent account of religion and Oprah's Book Club.

3. Scholarship addressing the novel's critique of neocolonialism includes the works in this book's bibliography by Demory, Dunch, Jacobs, Jacobson, Jussawalla, Koza, Kunz, Meillon, Meire, Novy, Ognibene, Purcell, Roos, Strehle, Varela-Zapata, Weese, White, and York. Those seeing Nathan as a stick figure include Born.

4. See, for example, Purcell 96.

5. Leah refers to "the parable of the one mustard seed falling on a barren place, and the other one on good soil" (39). This conflates two different parables, that of the mustard seed and that of the sower. See Mark 4:3–9 and 4:30–32.

6. That is, according to Boyarin, a Judaism of late antiquity that developed "in the environment of a Pauline Christianity" from the second century onward (2), and which became mainstream for diasporic Jews in the centuries following the destruction of the Temple in 70 CE.

7. See the Pew Research Center's "Tolerance and Tension: Islam and Christianity in Sub-Saharan Africa," Pew Research Religion and Public Life Project, 15 Apr. 2010, Web. http://www.pewforum.org/2010/04/15/executive-summary-islam-and-christianity-in-sub-saharan-africa. Accessed August 20, 2015.

8. See chapter 3 of the Pew Research Center study referenced above, "Traditional African Religious Beliefs and Practices," 33–35 PDF file.

9. See chapter 5 of the Pew Research Center study referenced above, "Religion and Society," 48–57. PDF file.

10. See George; Dawit and Mekuria; James; and Lewis.

11. Thus Kingsolver finds herself caught in the trap outlined by Vincent Pecora, who in *Secularization and Cultural Criticism* cites female genital mutilation as precisely one of those fault lines along which current theoretical arguments about universalism are taking place. Echoing the critique of Walker by Grewal and Kaplan, the human rights discourse animating Western critiques of the practice has been questioned by those such as Talal Asad, who, Pecora reports, argues that the purported universalism of that Western critique is itself a remnant of Christian cultural belief. "If we accept Asad's reasoning completely," Pecora notes, the discourse of human rights becomes "no more than a projection of secularized Christian nation-states. . . . That is, particular religious beliefs have supplied substantive norms that are then elaborated, self-interestedly, as 'universal'" (42). He continues:

> Asad notes that Western intellectuals decry female genital mutilation in Africa (practiced both within and outside Islamic areas) as a violation of human rights, though no one says anything about what Asad calls "the custom of male genital mutilation"—that is, circumcision—in the Judeo-Christian West . . . . The outrage in the West over female genital mutilation rests for him primarily on a culturally specific belief, which he traces to Christianity's views about bodily integrity and suffering, that individuals have a right to sexual pleasure as part of their human-rights inheritance. (42)

While the parallel between the two "circumcisions" is highly dubious, as Pecora notes, Asad's argument nonetheless captures one side of the enduring argument about the ground for universalist ethics. Walker's reception suggests the reason for Kingsolver's hesitancy as she faces the genuine conundrum, outlined by both Pecora and Boyarin, of how universalism might make an ethical argument that is true for others, while simultaneously respecting those others' cultural differences. I am situating Kingsolver's difficulties here as resulting from what Fessenden calls "the task of recovering a history of cooperation between movements to expand women's freedoms, on the one hand, and movements to consolidate Anglo-Saxon domination, on the other hand," a task that entails "a call to redress that history by disentangling feminism from imperialism in the present, as far as possible" (162).

12. See Barbara Kingsolver: The Authorized Site, 2012, Web. http://www.king solver.com/faq/previous-books.html#35. Accessed May 11, 2015. As Kingsolver explained about Nathan on her fan website:

> Did I do justice to his faith? I would call his faith "deeply misguided Christianity, combined with mental illness," and yes, I think I pegged it. But many other spiritual traditions are also represented here. I have no antagonism toward generous-hearted Christianity, or missionaries, and I took some care to show that. My favorite character is Brother Fowles, a Christian who does beautiful things with the notion of mission. At one point in the novel he says, "There are Christians, and there are Christians." Nathan Price and the Jesus-like Fowles are utterly different men who use the same name for opposite brands of faith and works.

As she here suggests, Fowles represents an entirely different orientation for what Christianity can be, and often is: a social gospel–oriented mission focused on poverty and health.

Kingsolver's own religious views seem to confirm a literary alliance with the multi-cultural pagan Alice Walker. In her foreword to *The Poisonwood Bible* she carefully notes that, while she did spend some time in the Belgian Congo during childhood (which was otherwise spent mostly in rural Kentucky), her parents were not missionaries but medical workers, "different in every way" (x) from the religious Prices. An intriguing parallel between Kingsolver and Fowles suggests their shared sense of wonder at the natural world. As Fowles ruminates to Leah before his debate with Nathan, "When I want to take God at his word exactly, I take a peep out the window at His Creation. Because *that*, darling, He makes fresh for us every day, without a lot of dubious middle managers" (248)—the latter a reference to the problematic status of culturally embedded and translated scripture. In an essay on the dangers of genetically modified crops published four years after *The Poisonwood Bible*, meanwhile, Kingsolver recalls watching a hummingbird build her nest outside her window and responding with a similar sense of reverence and awe:

> If you had been standing with me at my kitchen sink to witness all this, you would likely have breathed softly, as I did, "My God." The spectacular perfection of that nest, that tiny tongue, that beak calibrated perfectly to the length of the tubular red flowers from which she sucks nectar and takes away pollen to commit the essential act of copulation for the plant that feeds her—every piece of this thing and all of it, my God. You might be expressing your reverence for the details of a world created in seven days, 4,004 years ago (according to some biblical calculations), by a divine being approximately human in shape. Or you might be revering the details of a world created by a billion years of natural selection acting utterly without fail on every single life-form, one life at a time. (*Small Wonder* 95)

"I'm a scientist," she concludes at the end of the essay, "who thinks it wise to enter the doors of creation not with a lion tamer's whip and chair, but with the reverence humankind has traditionally summoned for entering places of worship: a temple, a mosque, or a cathedral. A sacred grove, as ancient as time" (108). Purcell's distinction here is apt: whereas St. Francis was a panentheist (nature is in God, but God is also beyond nature), Fowles and Kingsolver are pantheists (the divine is synonymous with and co-extensive with nature); indeed, Kingsolver seems to have self-identified as a "pantheist" in response to an author questionnaire (see Snodgrass 15; Purcell 98). By the end of the novel, Adah has come to believe that voodoo is "the earth's oldest religion," and that as voodoo-practitioners, our oldest human ancestors "worshipped everything living and everything dead" (528). Kingsolver and Alice Walker would likely agree. (My thanks to Mikka Jacobsen for pointing out the parallel window scenes in Kingsolver's novel and essay.)

13. "High cultural pluralism" for Mark McGurl "combines the routine operation of modernist autopoetics with a rhetorical performance of cultural group membership preeminently . . . marked as ethnic" (56). I retain the broader term multiculturalism—which is marked by both cultural pluralism but also cultural relativism—in this study partly because I want to retain the "accretions from the

so-called 'culture wars' of the 1980s and 90s" McGurl wishes to separate out from high cultural pluralism but which are an important aspect of my account of how that multiculturalism developed alongside and entangled with the conservative Christian resurgence. The other, more important reason I retain the term multiculturalism is because I believe that tracing contemporary multiculturalism back to the pluralism of Randolph Bourne, Alain Locke, Horace Kallen, and before them William James, as McGurl does (56–57) in his otherwise excellent study, is problematic. As I show in *A Genealogy of Literary Multiculturalism*, contemporary multiculturalists in the late 1960s and into the 1970s were not reading Bourne, Locke, Kallen, or James; the more compelling line of influence for both pluralism and relativism—and indeed the model of what minority "culture" was—lay in a return to anthropology, chiefly Boasian anthropology through Zora Neale Hurston, but also through Americo Paredes and anthropologists of Native American groups. Thus, if my hypothesis is correct that Kingsolver had her eye on Alice Walker's work and its reception as she composed *The Poisonwood Bible*, it provides some confirmation for why and how Kingsolver should be understood in this lineage of multiculturalism. Walker edited and introduced Hurston's *I Love Myself When I Am Laughing*, which included an excerpt from Hurston's autobiography describing the palace of skulls at Abomey. The palace serves the same lesson of cultural relativism for Hurston as it does for Kingsolver.

14. For a classic account of the secularization thesis, see Stark.

15. See Leonard et. al.

16. Thus, according to one recent interpreter of the book, when Job realizes that his question about God's justice has been displaced by God's sermon about His power, he replies to God, with irony, "Word of you had reached my ears, / but now that my eyes have seen you, / I shudder with sorrow for mortal clay" (Miles 325; see Coogan 478). As Bart Ehrman points out in *God's Problem*, there are competing theological explanations for suffering in Job (as in the Bible generally), and a later author has evidently tried to frame the poet's disquisition on suffering with a narrative that has God "rewarding" Job by the end of the book with even more stuff—animals and children—than he had before all his troubles started. Michael Coogan suggests, "Job was something like a hypertext, a work in progress revised by writers and translators at different times" and that "some of the changes may have been motivated by theological concerns" (474).

3. Christian Multiculturalism and Unlearned History in Marilynne Robinson's *Gilead*

1. I recognize the considerable scholarship attesting to Twain's respect for Jim's humanity and agency; nonetheless, such treatments tend unconvincingly to see Huck's assertion that he'll go to hell to help save Jim as "the climax of the novel, though it goes on for another dozen chapters" (Prusak 14). These readings downplay the ending of *Huckleberry Finn*, in which the supposedly humanized Jim is the object of Huck and Tom's adolescent fictional play; its classic critique is that by Leo Marx. Perhaps the best account that might save the moral seriousness of the novel is Sacvan Bercovitch's reading of Twain's misanthropic irony, such that Twain himself treats Jim with respect, but critiques Huck's treatment of him at the end, and thus the readers as well, insofar as we accept the premise of the final chapters and believe in Huck's integrity

and moral development. Likewise, noting the timing of the novel's canonicity, Jonathan Arac argues that "Cold War liberal American culture seemed to find in *Huckleberry Finn* a century-old solution to the race problems that had newly reemerged on the national agenda. Twain's solution would permit an imaginary national first person to trust that, like Huck, in 'our' hearts 'we' had always been right" (20).

2. In Douglass's 1857 speech "West India Emancipation" he said, "Hence, my friends, every mother who, like Margaret Garner, plunges a knife into the bosom of her infant to save it from the hell of our Christian Slavery, should be held and honored as a benefactress" (22). I use Douglass's phrase "Christian slavery" to characterize that set of practices and beliefs, especially during the intense hardening of positions between 1830 and 1860, as opposed to its more widely studied antagonist, Christian abolitionism.

3. See Donald B. Gibson, who suggests that the "sanitizing" appendix was written to defend Douglass against charges of "doubt and apostasy," in recognition that the otherwise occasional "submerged expressions of apostasy and doubt among slaves and black freemen in the antebellum South" were not so submerged in Douglass's *Narrative* (86–87). For a rival view, see Carson. See Douglass's *My Bondage and My Freedom* (*Autobiographies* 231) for his account of his teenage salvation experience.

4. Douglass gives two different dates (1832 and 1833) for the Methodist tent revival meeting at different points in his account.

5. See Douglass's *My Bondage* (*Autobiographies* 249–55) for a more detailed account of Auld's conversion.

6. See Gibson 89 for other examples of ex-slave testimony that Christian slaveholders were among the most dreaded.

7. See Douglass's *Life and Times of Frederick Douglass* (*Autobiographies* 697, 723) for proslavery Christians making this argument.

8. See Furman, paragraph 8.

9. See Furman, paragraphs 10 and 11.

10. When I taught at Furman University (which is named after Richard Furman, though it has long disowned its namesake's signatory contribution to US history), I one day went to its library's special collections to request a copy of Furman's 1823 pamphlet. The chief librarian somewhat nervously inquired as to my purpose and was relieved when I explained I intended to use it for course material on literature and race. It turned out that there had recently been an inquirer about and enthusiast for Furman in the local community who agreed with the apology's theological arguments. It is difficult to tell how widespread this lingering support may be; it is an embarrassing opinion obviously not to be voiced publicly. In 2012 it was revealed that Republican member of the Arkansas House of Representatives Loy Mauch had written repeated letters to a local newspaper over the previous decade voicing arguments of the kind made by Furman almost two centuries before. In 2009 he wrote, "If slavery were so God-awful, why didn't Jesus or Paul condemn it, why was it in the Constitution and why wasn't there a war before 1861? The South has always stood by the Constitution and limited government. When one attacks the Confederate Battle Flag, he is certainly denouncing these principles of government as well as Christianity" (quoted in http://www.arktimes.com/ArkansasBlog/archives/2012/10/06/loy-mauch-update-the-republican-rep-is-on-record-on-slavery-too). Arkansas Republicans distanced themselves from this view; Mauch was defeated in November 2012.

11. In this same essay Robinson comments, "The rhetorical battles that preceded the Civil War were waged in the language of Scripture, splitting the churches, so even those bonds between interests and loyalties and regions were strained or severed" (142). This is the closest she comes to recognizing the existence of Christian slavery.

12. In my view, Wiebke Omnus entirely misses the point of Robinson's views on history when attributing to her the postmodern sense that "historical truth is not absolute" (422) in narrating her novel from the "subjective" (413) perspective of Ames. Omnus concludes, "*Gilead* illustrates Robinson's understanding of history as dependent upon the point of view of the historian" (416).

13. On the Christian wisdom of the novel, see Anglican Archbishop Rowan Williams's address to the Conference on Christianity and Literature ("Native Speakers").

14. Furman does not mention Noah's curse on Ham in his apology, but it was a cornerstone of other biblical defenses of slavery—as with Josiah Priest's *Bible Defence of Slavery* (1851). In emphasizing Ham's curse, Priest joined the newer racial science to his exposition of the biblical record, recasting the kind of arguments Furman was making about Paul's support of and Jesus's silence on slavery in terms of the curse on Ham's descendants, now understood as racialized Africans.

15. The precise historical reference here is probably to the baseball-player-turned-revivalist-preacher Billy Sunday, who cheerfully admitted in 1903 that he "knew less about theology than a jackrabbit knew about ping pong" (http://www.mc.cc.md.us/Departments/hpolscrv/bsunday.html; see also Marsden 130). Sunday occasionally used radio near the end of his career in the 1930s, but he "never could make the leap" to radio and leave the "revival trail" behind (Bruns 298). The point here would be that, as Ames looks at the proto-resurgence in 1956, it is fundamentalists of Sunday's ilk—theatrical, anti-intellectual, populist—who are achieving mass audiences through radio ministries.

16. My *Genealogy of Literary Multiculturalism* develops these examples in detail.

17. On multiculturalism and identity generally, see also Michaels's *Our America: Nativism, Modernism, and Pluralism* and *The Trouble with Diversity: How We Learned to Love Identity and Ignore Inequality.*

18. I am bracketing here another possible reason for evading Christian slavery: that it provokes possibly lethal questions of theodicy. Gibson writes that Douglass "saw that both proslavery and antislavery forces where [*sic*] busy using God for their own purposes, and that if God is responsible for whatever deliverance occurs, then He is also responsible for whatever deliverance does not occur" (94). See also Jacobs 186 for her careful suspension of such questions.

19. Their recognizably shared resources in, and research into, American slave narratives is likely why *The New York Times* asked Atwood to review Morrison's novel: http://www.nytimes.com/books/98/01/11/home/8212.html.

20. *Home* (2008) makes central the subplot of Jack's apostasy and possible return. Told from the general perspective of Jack's sister Glory, it develops Jack's character and background. *Home* changes little of the dynamic I am naming, although it does bring into focus a little more Jack's problem of not being able to tell his father that he has an African American partner and mixed-race child. The novel is critical of Jack's father's (and Ames's) parochial suspicion of and opposition to the nascent non-violent civil rights demonstrations (97, 155–56, 204, 217). Since the article version

of the first half of this chapter was published (see Douglas, "Christian Multicultural-ism"), Jonathan Lear's persuasive review of both novels, "Not at Home in Gilead," appeared in *Raritan*. Noting that "Jack is the only person in Gilead who evidently feels compassion for the plight of black people in 1950s America" (40), Lear presents the most plausibly sympathetic reading of the novels, seeing Jack as their "Christian hero" (47) instead of Ames, who is the subject of almost all the reverent criticism on the two works. *Lila* (2014), the third in the sequence, gives the backstory of Ames's young wife in Depression-era poverty; it is a story of difficult and surprising grace that leaves behind the Africanist presence characterizing the previous two novels.

21. But see D. Williams 247–48, who attributes to the Bush campaign a miscal-culation in visiting the separatist, fundamentalist school, given its policy of lingering Christian segregation.

22. For lived religion and religious studies scholarship on practice, see Hall; Orsi, *Between*; Orsi, "Everyday"; Maffly-Kipp, Schmidt, and Valeri; and Griffith.

23. As will be obvious from this nutshell description of the move toward practice in the "lived religion" scholarship, it emerges in continuity from the general anthro-pological requirement for the social scientist and participant observer, seen already in Hurston, to suspend the metaphysical truth claims of the religion now studied as a culture. Thus, in Geertz's chief example from his famous 1966 essay (perhaps characteristically, this anthropology of religion shies away from the monotheisms and takes its chief examples from shamanistic and pagan cultures), he discusses how the observers of a Balinese religious performance become participants in the sym-bolic fusion of the everyday real world and the metaphysical order which the deities Rangda and Barong represent. Rangda and Barong are "genuine realities" as the vil-lagers "come to know them" during the communal performance, suggests Geertz, and thus "To ask, as I once did, a man who had *been* Rangda whether he thinks she is real is to leave oneself open to the suspicion of idiocy" (118). Geertz leaves this sense of idiocy productively ambiguous: to the villager, Geertz might be an idiot for two different reasons ("of course she is real—did you not just see me instantiate her memory and essence during the performance?" or "of course she is not real—did you not just see me put on and take off this mask during this communal tale?"), but to the anthropologist, he may be an idiot for violating the suspension of disbelief that is the anthropologist's professional stance. On the other hand, this stance is something of an enabling ruse. Geertz the anthropologist knows Rangda does not exist as a real supernatural force, and his Western readers know too, and with this unspoken shared knowledge—this wink—we treat this Balinese religious ritual for what it really is: a (likely unfamiliar) cultural practice. Once we understand religions as cultures and not as the universal systems that some of them claim to be, the cultural relativism bequeathed to multiculturalism from Boasian anthropology asks us to bracket their metaphysical statements.

24. *Gilead* thus shares an interesting and strange parallel to another classic of American fiction from the Noughties (2000s), Cormac McCarthy's *The Road*, in which a dying father also struggles with the problem of how best to prepare his young son whom he will soon leave behind.

25. Another good example emerges from Solomon Northup's *Twelve Years a Slave* (1853). "There never was a more kind, noble, candid, Christian man than William Ford," Northup recollects about one of his former masters: "he was a model master,

walking uprightly, according to the light of his understanding, and fortunate was the slave who came to his possession. Were all men such as he, Slavery would be deprived of more than half its bitterness" (57). This portrait of the practice of Christian slavery would have to be balanced by the portrait of a later owner: "Like William Ford, his brother-in-law, Tanner was in the habit of reading the Bible to his slaves on the Sabbath, but in a somewhat different spirit. He was an impressive commentator on the New-Testament," Northup observes drily: "When he came to the 47th verse, he looked deliberately around him, and continued—'And that servant which knew his lord's *will*,'—here he paused, looking around more deliberately than before, and again proceeded—'which knew his lord's *will*, and *prepared* not himself'—here was another pause—'*prepared* not himself, neither did *according* to his will, shall be beaten with many *stripes*'" (82). "'That nigger that don't take care—that don't obey his lord—that's his master—d'ye see?—'" continued the exegete, "'that '*ere* nigger shall be beaten with many stripes. Now, 'many' signifies a *great* many—forty, a hundred, a hundred and fifty lashes. *That's* Scripter!'" (83).

26. See www.lillyendowment.org/religion.html for a description of the Lilly Endowment's aims and the projects it supports.

27. On Lilly's support of "evangelical scholars," see Lindsay (81). As John Schmalzbauer and Kathleen Mahoney note, the "new evangelical historiography" across the social sciences and humanities is marked not just by growing attention to questions of religion, but by growing religious identification of scholars, especially literary critics and historians (4): "By bringing religious academics . . . into conversation with secular intellectuals . . . the Lilly seminar helped legitimate the reintegration of faith and knowledge in American higher education" (16).

28. But to state the obvious, many of the beliefs Eagleton describes as New Atheist "secular fantasies" of Christianity—belief in God's existence, that he created the universe, that we have souls, that God cares about sin, that hell exists—are widespread among American Christians, as Greeley and Hout demonstrate. While Christian belief is quite various, these are not minority beliefs: eighty-two percent of fundamentalist and evangelical Christians believe in hell, as do sixty-two percent of "mainline" Protestant Christians (Greeley and Hout 24). The importance of traditional belief is even more marked for the resurgence:

> Conservative Protestants, as might be expected, are strongly orthodox in their beliefs. Regarding some beliefs, for example, in God's existence or life after death, there is little difference among the three Protestant groups we are studying. More than nine out of ten believe in God and more than four out of five believe in life after death. Even so, there are some discernable shades of belief. Conservative and Afro-American Protestants are more likely to express their belief in God without doubt (83 percent and 81 percent, respectively) than Mainline Protestants (60 percent), while Afro-American Protestants are less sure about the afterlife (81 percent) than Conservatives (87 percent believe) and Mainline Protestants (86 percent believe). (23)

Thus, even though the resurgence is marked by the importance of belief, belief can be varied in sometimes surprising ways—and so Eagleton might find himself aligned with the not-insignificant minority of one in ten American Christians who do not believe in God.

29. For how early Christianity formed through struggles about doctrine, see Ehrman, *Lost Christianities.*

30. Indeed, it is not only Christian-identified critics that make this move. In his otherwise illuminating essay on *Gilead* and *Home,* Jonathan Lear, who says he is not Christian (52), asserts that "the social world refuses Jack because it is enmeshed in an illusion of Christian life: for example, an outlook that requires 'Negroes' to worship at their own church. Here is the heart of the illusion: the day-to-day acceptance of the thought that 'separate but Christian' is a viable expression of Christian worship" (45). The normative view of religion as benevolent in its natural state unless twisted by social conditions or ideologies extends beyond religious practitioners.

4. Recapitulation and Religious Indifference in *The Plot Against America*

1. See, for example, Kingston, "Cultural," where she rejects the way critics and readers read her fictionalized memoir *The Woman Warrior* for its supposed cultural information about the Chinese American community, writing, "Why must I represent someone other than myself?" (63).

2. The parallels between the Lindbergh and Bush presidencies, and the American emergencies in 1940 and 2004, were the subject of an article by Steven Kellman that stated, "Roth's best-selling novel was widely read, obliquely, as if the plot against America it portrayed were really Bush's consolidation and abuse of power at the beginning of the twenty-first century. Roth's Lindbergh, not unlike Bush, is a Republican interloper who glides into office offering little sense of where he stands" (113). *Plot,* Kellman argued, was indeed about the "issues of patriotism, faith, and security that roiled and divided the nation in 2004. . . . *The Plot Against America* is a secular American Jew's nightmare about the ascendancy of fervent Christians who define American identity in terms that exclude the Roths of Weequahic" (116). David Gates suggested that "Roth doesn't oversell any parallels between his imaginary 1940s and the real present. But anybody who feels hopeless at the ascendancy of today's Christian right may feel a chill" (56). The *Sunday Times* declared, "On the face of it, Roth's latest story has nothing to do with conspiracy theories or the terrorist attack on the twin towers," but that nonetheless the novel "casts the post-September 11 era in a chilling new light" (Anon). Paul Berman suggested that "'The Plot Against America' is not an allegorical tract about the present age, with each scene or character corresponding to events of our own time. I think that in composing his novel, Roth has simply run his eye across the modern horizon, and gathered in the sights, and rearranged them in a 1940's kaleidoscope" (6). Gabriel Brownstein suggested that "references to George W. Bush's America are impossible to miss" in *The Plot Against America,* including the government's breaches of American constitutional rights, tax breaks during American emergency, and the perpetual state of fear instilled in citizens. Kellman also documented how many reviewers at the time read this as "a mirror of contemporary concerns" (117). He, like Douthat, raised the possibility that Roth may be disingenuous in his disavowal, noting that this is a writer who has "long delighted in playing texts against countertexts, lives against counterlives" (122), a possibility that Dan Shiffman also suggests (62–63). Gurumurthy Neelakantan called the novel "unmistakably a reaction" to 9/11 (128), and argued further that "Roth's novel merits scrutiny against the background of

rising Christian fundamentalism and the Holocaust denial of the zealous revisionists in contemporary America as elsewhere" (129). Myles Weber, from a different political angle, suggested, "The salient point is this: Roth, in a novel published four weeks before a U.S. presidential election that was bound to turn on national defense issues, chose to draw the public's attention to the mass atrocities that might have resulted from the deferment of a brutal military campaign" (208). Jonathan Yardley stated, "That Roth has written *The Plot Against America* in some respects as a parable for our times seems to me inescapably and rather regrettably true" (3).

3. As Greil Marcus demonstrates, Roth's literary model is Sinclair Lewis's 1935 *It Can't Happen Here*, a novel about the growing threat of American fascism and the election of a pro-fascist American president (89–100); as Marcus points out, Roth reminds us of the precursor by having Mayor La Guardia eulogize Walter Winchell with the words, "It can't happen here? My friends, it *is* happening here" (*Plot* 305).

4. For more on how the ideology of the Third Reich constructed difference as racial rather than strictly religious, see Hutton and Smedley 287–90. For an analysis of the earlier religious distinction, see Ehrman, *Jesus, Interrupted* 242–45.

5. This conventional understanding of the essentially secular nature of Nazi race ideology has recently been challenged and is increasingly untenable. Michael Lackey cites the work of Doris L. Bergen (*The Twisted Cross: The German Christian Movement in the Third Reich*), Richard Steigmann-Gall (*The Holy Reich: Nazi Conceptions of Christianity, 1919–1945*), and Susannah Heschel (*The Aryan Jesus: Christian Theologians and the Bible in Nazi Germany*) as part of this challenge, and argues himself in *The Modernist God State: A Literary Study of the Nazis' Christian Reich* that Nazi racial ideology was undergirded by Kantian Christian idealism that construed "Jewish materialism" as "a theological signifier" (261). In Lackey's compelling and evidence-based argument, many Nazis understood their nation-state to have "true Christianity" as its basis (232). In this reading, the point is that to the extent that "scientific" or biological racism justified oppression and murderous violence, it arrived late on the scene as a supplement to an already-sanctioned religious concept—a point as true in Germany in the 1930s as it was in the United States in the 1840s. This fact does not change the argument that Nazi ideology foreclosed the possibility of Jewish conversion or assimilation, in contrast to the counterfactual Lindbergh presidency, as we shall see. In any case, Roth is unlikely to be familiar with this new historical scholarship examining the religious dimensions of what Lackey calls "the Nazis' Christian Reich" (223) and is better understood as participating in the secularization thesis that still dominates our understanding of the twentieth century. See Lackey 37–84.

6. The following argument about sociological theory and its influences comes from *Genealogy*, particularly chapters 2–4.

7. For an analysis of the occasional biological troping of learned cultural difference among these authors, see Douglas, *Genealogy*, chapters 6–9.

8. My claim here is not that Roth is necessarily familiar with these multicultural novels (though he may be), but rather that the historical allusions in his novel suggest he is aware of the developing midcentury "liberal consensus" that turned previously racialized minorities into groups marked instead by cultural difference, and of the policy changes—Japanese American resettlement, African American desegregation, and Native American Relocation—that were enabled by this paradigm shift.

These became points of departure for canonical, inaugural multicultural novels by authors such as Morrison and Momaday.

9. See O'Callaghan 608 and Gerber 102–09 for a contrary view on such public debates.

10. These terms—*converso, marrano,* and *anusim*—are not unproblematic, as Freedman notes (211).

11. But see Freedman 209–50, who notes that this reading of the origins of the racial worldview (as Smedley's title has it) is contested by other historians, although he agrees that this was the "aboriginal moment" of "proto-race and proto-ethnicity" (220).

12. On the novel's patriotism, see Shiffman.

13. In addition to seeing the series as using anti-Semitic stereotypes, Sherryll Mleynek suggests that the authors are ethically irresponsible for writing, in a post-Holocaust context, a series that imagines "Jewish erasure" both by conversion and then by Armageddon: there are no Jews left by the end of book 12 because only those who convert to Christianity have survived.

14. See Freedman in general for his superb analysis of the *Left Behind* series' "remarkable creation of an American antisemitism without Jews" (159).

15. Coughlin claimed he began his radio broadcasts in response to a Ku Klux Klan cross-burning on his Detroit parish grounds, but his biographer finds no evidence of the event and believes it to be a fabrication (see D. Warren 17–19).

16. Roth may have the last laugh, however, with Earl's misunderstanding of Christian doctrine because, as Daniel Boyarin notes in *The Jewish Gospels: The Story of the Jewish Christ,* "The lines between exalted angels and gods get harder and harder to draw and see" (166n27) as one delves into Jewish apocalyptic pre-Christian theology. Thus, according to Boyarin, the Christian doctrine of God the Father and God the Son may have emerged from apocalyptic Jewish imagery of a co-rulership in Heaven shared by the elder "Ancient of Days" and a younger "son of man" that we find in Daniel 7. This remnant of ditheism may have, in turn, emerged from the suppressed ancient Hebrew polytheism still present in the Hebrew Bible, as is seen in particular in the way in which the Ancient of Days/son of man relation seems to be an evolution of the El/Baal and El/Yahweh relationships discernable in what Hebrew Bible scholars see as some of the work's oldest passages (44–45). As Boyarin explains,

> The general outlines of a theology of a young God subordinated to an old God are present in the throne vision of Daniel 7, however much the author of Daniel labored to suppress this. In place of the notions of 'El and YHVH as the two Gods of Israel, the pattern of an older god and a younger one—a god of wise judgment and a god of war and punishment—has been transferred from older forms of Israelite/Canaanite religion to new forms. Here, the older god is now entirely named by the tetragrammaton YHVH (and his supremacy is not in question), while the functions of the younger god have been in part taken by supreme angels or other sorts of divine beings, Redeemer figures, at least in the 'official' religion of the biblical text. Once YHVH absorbs 'El, the younger god has no name of his own but presumably is identified at different times with the archangels or other versions of the Great Angel, Michael, as well as with Enoch, Christ, and later Meṭaṭron as well. (51)

It's not impossible, in other words, that Roth's Earl is inadvertently correct in see-ing the theological space of the head of the angels as the site of Jesus's interpellation.

17. Michaels recalls a Berkeley dinner party early in his career at which "the wife of a senior colleague . . . started talking about how the Jews were ruining the English Department"—to which he answered, "I'm Jewish" (*Trouble* 34). As he elaborates in his conclusion to *The Trouble With Diversity* (speaking of himself in the third person), "Walter Benn Michaels is not only upper middle class, he is also Jewish. God only knows what he means when he writes this, but, since he doesn't believe in God, it doesn't mean he believes in or practices Judaism. And it also doesn't mean he believes in the existence of a Jewish race or of a Jewish culture that could be somehow defined without reference to either race or religion" (197). His nonreligious, non-racial, noncultural Jewish identity is a riddle that Roth would recognize.

18. Schaeffer's continued fundamentalism, I believe, is captured by his simulta-neously inerrantist and literalist views of the Bible—even though these are slightly downplayed in *How Should We Then Live?*, which is aimed at a dual Christian and non-Christian audience. Schaeffer speaks of "the historic space-time Fall" (87), for instance, which first seems a little ambiguous, but later describes death as "abnor-mal," suggesting that it "did not exist as God made the world" (128). His reference to "the historic Fall" (134) and his commencing of the "Chronological Index" at 3500 BCE (259)—comfortably within Bishop Ussher's calculations—suggest that he reads the Genesis creation stories as factually accurate descriptions. When he later defines evolution as "chance alone" and "solely by time plus chance" (150), one senses that the misdescription is purposefully incorrect: surely this Christian intellectual who can grasp and convey in mostly passable if broad brush strokes dif-ferent artistic, theological, and philosophical movements could come to an acceptable understanding of the process of natural selection and why natural selection is not just random chance. Schaeffer also argues, "Statistical studies indicate that pure chance (randomness) could not have produced the biological complexity in the world out of chaos, in any amount of time so far suggested" (148), citing a mathematician also mentioned by the Institute for Creation Research. In terms of that other great nineteenth-century challenge to traditional Christian theology—the development of the historical critical method of investigating biblical texts—Schaeffer is simi-larly recalcitrant and less elusive. He rejects as part of secularizing humanism Albert Schweitzer's *The Quest for the Historical Jesus* (1906) and its preference for excluding questions of the supernatural from the analysis of what the historical Jesus is more likely to have done and said. Those who accept such methods are doomed to retreat into theological liberalism, Schaeffer believes: thus "Karl Barth held until the end of his life the 'higher critical' views of the Bible which the nineteenth-century liberal theologians held, and thus he viewed the Bible as having many mistakes" (176). The higher critical method, by abandoning biblical inerrantism, undermines the Bible as a source of absolutes and makes impossible "applying the Bible's values in a historic situation, in either morals or law" (177). Indeed, Schaeffer warns against the kind of relativism that undermines the worldview of a Christian who accepts the findings of the higher criticism. As he puts it in the final "Special Note" which "is primar-ily for Christians," his readers should not "try to keep hold of the value system, the meaning system, and the 'religious matters' given in the Bible, while playing down what the Bible affirms about the cosmos, history, and specific commands in morals.

We are following our own form of existential methodology if we put what the Bible says about the cosmos, history, and absolute commands in morals in the realm of the culturally oriented" (255). The Bible must continue to be read as a historical, factual, and inerrant record in order for it to provide the absolute values for Christians to use as they reengage the world. (See also Frank Schaeffer, *Crazy* 308–09).

19. "Under Roman law, the offspring of slave women assumed the status of their mothers, except when the mother had been free and married at the time of conception or, from the second century AD, if she had in fact been free at any moment during pregnancy" (Scheidel 306). Schaeffer's slipperiness here is purposeful: "slavery based on race" is meant to conceal the fact that it wasn't one's race that made one a slave (there were free people of African descent in the colonies and then in the States) but the slave status of one's mother—a situation as true for the ancient biblical world as it was for American slavery.

20. As Ryan explained about welfare programs opposed by the Republican Party, "We don't want to turn the safety net into a hammock that lulls able-bodied people to lives of dependency and complacency, that drains them of their will and their incentive to make the most of their lives." As Paul Krugman remarked about Ryan's hammock theory, "There are actually two assertions here. First, antipoverty programs breed complacency; that is, they discourage work. Second, complacency—the failure of the poor to work as much as they should—is what perpetuates poverty" (http://www.nytimes.com/2014/03/07/opinion/krugman-the-hammock-fallacy. html). As Kevin M. Kruse demonstrates in *One Nation Under God: How Corporate America Invented Christian America*, one genealogy of the Christian Right lay in the cooperative efforts by pro-business leaders and conservative Christians against the New Deal, a coalition that illuminates a continuity between the fictional Lindbergh and historical Bush presidencies that many critics saw at the heart of Roth's *The Plot Against America.*

21. Recalls Schaeffer's son Frank, "Dad used to be somewhat dismissive of Jack [Kemp] in private. 'I like Jack, but he has a bee in his bonnet,' Dad said. This was what Dad called Jack's supply-side economic theories" (285)—the hypotheses that George H. W. Bush once characterized as "voodoo economics" but that would come to form the centerpiece of Republican economic policy for decades.

22. According to Frank Schaeffer, he argued his father into its inclusion. As Frank describes their argument in his semi-apostate memoir *Crazy for God*: "'I don't want to be identified with some Catholic issue. I'm not putting my reputation on the line for them!' Dad shouted" (266), to which Frank raged back, "*Fucking coward! You're always talking about the 'dehumanization of man': now, here is your best example!*" (267).

23. This is not to say that the Christian Right was without fringe elements that envisioned a Christian nation beyond Schaeffer's or LaHaye's imaginings. Indeed, in the 1980s and 90s "Rousas John Rushdoony's Christian Reconstructionist movement . . . called for a sweeping overhaul of society and a replacement of American constitutional measures with the revival of Old Testament law" (D Williams 225). Related policies included "the reinstitution of slavelike indentured servitude and a restoration of the death penalty for homosexuals, adulterers, and 'Sabbath-breakers'" (225), as well as replacing income tax with church tithing and reducing the federal government to the "protection of property rights" (226). This program approaches

Atwood's vision, though "Rushdoony's claim of 20 million Reconstructionists was highly exaggerated" (226). The movement's adherents were also known as "Theonomists" and "Dominionists," explains Frank Schaeffer: "people who believed in taking 'dominion' over society and the world in the name of Jesus [and who] believed in restoring American law to its strictest Puritan origins. They wanted to make America into a modern-day Calvin's Reformation Geneva. They were our version of the Taliban" (*Crazy* 333). This was a fringe element outside what we might call the mainstream Christian Right (which is not to say the fringe and the center never overlapped or shared themes). Schaeffer Sr. "regarded Rushdoony as clinically insane" (333).

24. See the account at http://news.virginia.edu/content/history-scholar-prayer-did-not-come-george-washington.

25. Linking civil religion back to the religious disposition of the Founders—that is, a providential Deism in which design is the crucial, but relatively disenchanted, property of the universe, and Lockean disembedded individuals come together, pursuing their own aims, thereby mutually benefitting one another (C. Taylor 447)—illuminates the resurgent rejection of civil religion. The alliance between the Religious Right and neoliberalism has meant that it does not so much want to do away with the Lockean structure of free individuals working for their own ends, thereby indirectly serving the community. Rather, it is that the Right, as we see in LaHaye and Schaeffer, attaches this notion of free market individuals back to a body with a theological purpose, and back to a sense of personal relation to God in a reenchanted world: reenchanted in the sense that God is not only present in the mechanism he has created and in the individuals he has set free to work for themselves, mutually benefitting one another, but is also present for the individual as one who answers prayers and has a specific intentionality for and agency on behalf of the nation.

26. As we shall see on the issue of evolution, textbook publishers' need to appease the extremely large market of Texas "rather strongly inclines educational publishers to tailor their products to fit the standards dictated by the Lone Star State," with the consequence that resurgent-led Texas schoolboards have an outsized effect on national textbook contents in terms of their efforts "to bring Jesus into American history" (Shorto).

5. Thomas Pynchon's Prophecy

1. See Fessenden, "The Problem of the Postsecular," for a different critique of the term: that the postsecular seems to prize an undefined but homogenous sacred "whoosh," and that the postsecular constructs a monolithic religious past (162). She argues that critics need to give rich contextualizations or risk affirming a Matthew Arnold–like secularization strategy replacing religion by literature, which she sees Hungerford and McClure as part of (164); that we should avoid constructing a good religion (spirituality) / bad religion (backwards faith) dichotomy (165); and that we need to name the American character of the postsecular (165). I return to this last question in my conclusion.

2. That Pynchon has his eye on a specifically American history of receding belief may be hinted at when a lawyer character is urged to do something "Darrowlike, spectacular" (43), thus alluding to Clarence Darrow's work as the defense attorney for John Scopes.

3. As Lackey shows, Eliot partook in "a strategic agenda, which was crafted by a religiously committed segment of the society, to Christianize people in the West at the level of the subconscious. We see this specific approach most clearly in the secret and just recently published writings of the Moot, an organization of prominent intellectuals" that included Eliot (90).

4. As later critics would argue when classifying Pynchon's novel as a "metaphysical detective story" (e.g., Sweeney 188; see also Merivale and Sweeney's taxonomy [18]), the possibility of undercutting detective conventions is contained within the genre itself. Thus the novel, "with its heroine named after the first detective of them all" (123), Mendelson says, echoes the problem faced by Oedipus, who "begins his search for the solution of a problem . . . as a detached observer, only to discover how deeply implicated he is in what he finds" (118). As Mendelson notes, the problem of belief is analogous to the problem of reading, of interpretation (138)—thus returning us to Pynchon's generic choice of the detective story.

5. Hitchens's account of Bible scholarship is sloppy and not to be trusted. For example, he erroneously attributes Q as a source for John, and suggests the later Gnostic gospels date as early as the canonical gospels (112).

6. It is not, for example, in the Codex Vaticanus (Metzger 223), one of the oldest extant manuscripts of the Greek Bible found in the collection of the Vatican Library—like Pynchon's fictional Wharfinger parodic edition. A good nonspecialist introduction to these historical-critical methods is Bart Ehrman's *Did Jesus Exist?: The Historical Argument for Jesus of Nazareth*.

7. Notes James Nohrnberg of the Jesus-Tristero parallel, "The content of revelation in the New Testament is necessarily esoteric, for faith is the evidence of things unseen. As Pynchon's reference to it suggests, the Bible records not the search for the 'historical Jesus' . . . but rather the signs of Jesus's spiritual power. But these were experienced in the corporate life of the primitive Christian community. The existence of the historical Tristero raises analogous problems of verification, since its existence is chiefly manifested in the signs of hieroglyphs employed by the various 'communions' that communicate through its offices and that are formed under its signs" (154).

8. Hofstadter borrows the phrase "pseudo-conservative" from Theodor Adorno to name the way in which these members "believe themselves to be conservatives and usually employ the rhetoric of conservatism" but "show signs of a serious and restless dissatisfaction with American life, traditions, and institutions" (43). He argues that Goldwater was not really conservative because his movement did not aim to conserve but rather wanted a sharp break with the recent past. The Goldwater movement prized hardcore "economic individualism" and other conservative truths but eschewed the traditional defense of "a tissue of institutions" on which society depends (94), and which typically marks conservatism. In other words, as Hofstadter's editor Sean Wilentz suggests, the phrase "pseudo-conservative" is useful insofar as it names "a strain of right-wing radicals who sought to deny their radicalism" (Foreword xvii). Wilentz suggests that the "permanent force" articulated in the Goldwater campaign culminated in "the most radical right-wing presidency in modern times, under the guise of conservatism" in George W. Bush (xxv): "The Manichean political psychology of the pseudo-conservative radicals fully converged with anti-intellectualism and cultural politics in the administration of

George W. Bush, along with what Hofstadter had detected as an inverted bolshevism based on stealth, supreme self-confidence, and the will to power" (xxviii).

9. See also McClure, who traces Pynchon's ontological pluralism in *Gravity's Rainbow* to William James (*Partial* 34–35).

6. Science and Religion in Carl Sagan's *Contact*

1. See the video at https://www.youtube.com/watch?v=ld4X9NQdnog at 26:15.

2. See Jones for an oral history of the question; see Davies 116–39 for its broader context.

3. A short, cogent explanation of the variables in the Drake Equation can be found in Sagan, *Varieties* 109–23.

4. On the religious ramifications of discovering extraterrestrial intelligence, see Davies 178–95.

5. Describing the implications of recent discoveries, *The New York Times* wrote in 2013, "Astronomers reported that there could be as many as 40 billion habitable Earth-size planets in the galaxy, based on a new analysis of data from NASA's Kepler spacecraft." http://www.nytimes.com/2013/11/05/science/cosmic-census-finds-billions-of-planets-that-could-be-like-earth.html?_r=2&.

6. Billy Jo Rankin, Jr.'s name may allude to that of the politically influential fundamentalist Billy James Hargis, who was one of those of whom Hofstadter wrote in 1965, "Fundamentalist leaders play a part in right-wing organizations far out of proportion to the strength of fundamentalism in the population at large"—including Hargis "of the Christian Crusade, which flourishes in the Southwest" (74), the area in which Oedipa makes her discoveries. Hargis was a John Bircher, opponent of desegregation, and supporter of Joe McCarthy and Barry Goldwater.

7. As Thomas Lessl argues, evolution for Sagan could also be understood in terms of "a world hypothesis or root metaphor" (177): in *Cosmos*, "Cosmic evolution, beginning with the 'Big Bang,' begets chemical evolution, which begets biological evolution, which begets human evolution, which begets scientific evolution. In such a progressive time spectrum, science is clearly made to stand at the pinnacle of history" (178).

8. See Moore et. al., who note that in 1960 "*The Flintstones*, television's first prime-time animated series, debuts on ABC. The show, which portrayed a 'modern stone-age family' of humans who lived with dinosaurs, saber-toothed tigers, wooly mammoths, and other extinct animals, lasted 166 episodes and indoctrinated millions of children and adults with the notion that humans lived contemporaneously with dinosaurs. This claim was repeatedly rejected by biologists, geologists, and other scientists, but has remained a foundation of young-earth creationism (e.g., that dinosaurs and humans were created on the sixth day of creation). Indeed, the Creation Museum, operated by the antievolution organization Answers in Genesis, includes dioramas depicting humans living with dinosaurs. In 2002, NSF reported in its *Science and Technology Indicators* that 48% of Americans believe that humans and dinosaurs lived at the same time" (238–39).

9. See Harding, chapter 8, for a good discussion of creationism and the Museum of Earth and Life History at Falwell's Liberty University; see Larson, *Summer of the*

Gods for a historical account of the *Scopes* trial; see Larson, *Trial and Error* for the larger twentieth-century legal history of creationism. For primary documents, see Whitcomb and Morris; and H. Morris, *History*.

10. Though, as Forrest and Gross point out, there are still many young-earth creationists among ID theorists—"ID is much more conventional in its creationist views than most people realize" (275). Indeed, in *Creationism's Trojan Horse*, Forrest and Gross establish the genealogy of the Intelligent Design movement from both young-earth and old-earth creationism in the decades before the 1990s; thus, Intelligent Design should be understood as part of the Christian social and political resurgence, especially since many of the thinkers and writers associated with the movement, as well as the funding sources of the Discovery Institute, were involved with other intellectual strains in that resurgence, such as the identification of America as a Christian nation, and the "wedge" strategy against scientific materialism. Cementing its status as a culture wars think-tank, the Discovery Institute has recently branched out to oppose climate change science (see, e.g., Luskin, the Discovery Institute's "research coordinator").

11. In *Intelligent Design*, Dembski explains of Sagan's novel that the prime numbers of the extraterrestrial message are a nonrandom pattern indicating intelligence (128–30). He uses this again in *The Design Revolution* as an example of science looking for, and finding, a pattern of intelligent design in nature (34–35). Phillip Johnson also cites the novel approvingly in terms of the science of searching for designs in "The Intelligent Design Movement" (30–31). SETI researchers have yet to hear anything indicating intelligence; pi has been calculated to 10 trillion decimal places, and still no message (http://io9.com/5904812/the-first-4000000-digits-of-pi-visualized-in-a-single-image).

12. For a detailed account of the Dover trial, see Humes; a detailed discussion of Intelligent Design can be found in the superb Forrest and Gross.

13. Another excellent example is the new "law" on information and entropy that Dembski imagines himself to have constructed: the "Law of Conservation of Information," in which "complex specified information cannot be created by natural processes, because by his newly discovered law, information is conserved in natural processes" (Forrest and Gross 138–39). As Forrest and Gross show, Dembski mistakes the math involved; they conclude, "Misunderstanding or misuse of the Second Law of Thermodynamics has been a creationist hallmark for nearly a century" (140).

14. Both the Institute for Creation Research and Intelligent Design originally envisioned themselves as having active research programs. The ICR formed archeological expeditions to try to find Noah's Ark on Mount Ararat in 1972 and 1983 (H. Morris 253), and Intelligent Designers, in an early white paper strategy document, envisioned a program of scientific research followed by public outreach. But the latter aspect of the program—that is, engagement in the culture wars—quickly outstripped the nonexistent research program, which is why several ID proponents felt the movement was not ready for the Dover court case. The appetite to engage in the larger culture war obviated the necessary preparation: as the leaked Discovery Institute "wedge strategy" document in 1999 revealed, Intelligent Design was seen internally by some of its proponents to be part of a larger strategy "'To defeat scientific materialism and its destructive moral, cultural, and political legacies' and 'to replace materialistic explanations with the theistic understanding that nature and

human beings are created by God'" (Humes 75–76). See Humes 356–57n3 for an excerpt of the Wedge document.

15. The way this played out in the news coverage was that Intelligent Design was a serious intellectual movement whose claims were being wrongly ignored by science. Only the exhaustive neutral analysis through expert witnesses and weighing actual evidence in *Dover* allowed Intelligent Design's cover to be blown. The question of whether Intelligent Design and other creationist authors believe their discourse is an interesting one mostly beyond the purview of this chapter, if only because of the difficulty of ascertaining the mental states of other people. Sartre's "bad faith" is one description of their psychic structure—which surely must vary among individuals— that preserves an element of (prior) self-deception. Forrest and Gross's devastating portrait in *Creationism's Trojan Horse*, on the other hand, sees Intelligent Design much more cynically, with its purveyors knowingly perpetrating fraud in a public relations campaign on a mostly scientifically naïve public. The recycling of old utterances— without addressing the critiques that have been publically and exhaustively mounted against them—suggests this picture might be right, at least with some practitioners. A slightly more sympathetic portrait of creation science spokesman Henry Morris appears in Miller, who had a private talk with his opponent in a hotel cafeteria the morning after their public debate; Miller expected a "charlatan," but discovered someone who sincerely believes science will one day arrive at the truths revelation already holds (173).

16. InterVarsity Press is the publishing arm of Inter Varsity Christian Fellowship, one of the moderate to conservative evangelical Christian student groups on North American college campuses. It has British roots and a C. S. Lewis tradition of apologetics.

17. For instance, in the film the bomber who destroys the American Machine is a fanatical Christian preacher, and her father's funeral is an opportunity for Ellie to disregard a priest's inadequate consolations. Most important, perhaps, is that there is no hidden message in pi and no switched step-fathers.

7. Evolution and Theodicy in *Blood Meridian*

1. An earlier version of this chapter appeared in *Religion & Literature* 45.2 (Summer 2013).

2. This character appears to have been inspired by a Baptist preacher in Nacogdoches c. 1838–1840 called R. G. Green, known for "drunkenness" and "to have become a moral wreck, resulting, it was said, from some sort of domestic trouble" (quoted in Sepich 13).

3. These scandals include, most notably, that of Oklahoma preacher Billy James Hargis, who was possibly Sagan's model for Billy Jo Rankin, Jr., we have seen, and who was forced to resign in 1974 from the presidency of the American Christian College, which he had founded, for having sex with male and female students, and the famed child preacher Marjoe Gortner, who as an adult in 1972 made a documentary film about how evangelists manipulate their audiences.

4. See M. Taylor 258. As I note in the introduction, historians of religion and social scientists agree that there has been a conservative Christian resurgence in recent decades, but the term "Fourth Great Awakening" is generally eschewed (Tolson).

5. In this chapter I reframe the questions of theodicy I provisionally raised in "The Flawed Design: American Imperialism in N. Scott Momaday's *House Made of Dawn* and Cormac McCarthy's *Blood Meridian*." Where that essay, through a comparative reading of the two novels, examined their fictional attention to American imperialism in the Southwest and the history of violence it recorded, this chapter historicizes McCarthy's novel with the question of its treatment of religion, and in particular that of the problem of suffering intrinsic to evolution, within the context of the contemporary conservative Christian resurgence.

6. As an example of the imperfection of the Gnostic reading, both Daugherty and Mundik take at face value the judge's charge, decades later, that the kid "alone reserved in your soul some corner of clemency for the heathen" (312)—even though it is difficult to imagine what that clemency could possibly have been, since the kid has partaken in every murderous slaughter performed by the Glanton gang, as Hungerford notes. To believe this idea we are perhaps forced to imagine that the kid was just pretending to shoot this whole time, or maybe just that he had qualms as he shot away. See Hungerford 93.

7. See Coogan 430–32 for the interpretation that apocalypticism was a theological innovation responding to prophetic discourse's inability to account for God's unresponsiveness, and Ehrman, *Lost Gospel* 119–20.

8. There are yet other influences on the Gnostic worldview: Ehrman suggests, for instance, that the radical dualism of Gnostic theology may reflect some influence by Platonism in the Hellenistic world (119).

9. See Wallach for a good examination of the temporal frame of "deep time" in McCarthy's work, including *Blood Meridian*. In what follows, I read allusions to prehistory less as metaphors that work to "deflate" human self-importance and contextualize characters' ethical behavior than as references that specify the historical theological controversies about biological evolution both in the time of the novel's setting and in the time of its composition (Wallach 105–6).

10. As it still does: see *Institute for Creation Research*, "God's Invisible Things."

11. Hoyle was actually describing the probability of life originating, not natural selection (see 18–19), but he may have used the metaphor elsewhere to characterize natural selection (see, e.g., http://www.nytimes.com/2007/10/28/weekinreview/28johnson.html?_r=0).

12. Indeed, attentive to the geography and history of this religious opposition to evolution, McCarthy includes a reference to the *Scopes* trial in his 1979 novel *Suttree*, in which the title character converses with the "old tattered barrister" John Randolph Neal, who was the chief counsel for John Scopes years before (366). My thanks to the anonymous reviewer of the article version of a portion of this chapter for pointing this episode out.

13. Lincoln 113. See also Kushner, and Flood.

14. For the date of 1975, see Shannon; for the later date, see also Lincoln 8–9.

15. Kushner 48. The Santa Fe Institute is known among other things for its focus on "Complexity Science," a rigorous interdisciplinary field that stands in contrast to the supposed "irreducible complexity" of Intelligent Design.

16. Stephen Jay Gould's popular scientific articles in the early 1980s may have been among McCarthy's influences, including "Nonmoral Nature" (on the implications of parasites for nineteenth century natural theology) and a trio of articles on

scientific creationism ("Evolution as Fact and Theory," "A Visit to Dayton," and "Moon, Mann, and Otto"). These were all published in *Natural History Magazine* except for "Evolution as Fact and Theory," which appeared in *Discover*; all were collected in *Hen's Teeth and Horse's Toes* (Norton, 1983). The first of the three latter pieces argues against creationism, partly because Gould acknowledges that his work on "punctuated equilibrium" had been distorted by creationists to make their case (259); the second is a cultural history and journalistic account of touring the town made famous by the *Scopes* trial; the third is Gould's reflections as an expert witness, in December 1981, during "the first legal test upon the new wave of creationist bills that mandate equal time or 'balanced treatment' for evolution and a thinly disguised version of the Book of Genesis read literally, but masquerading under the nonsense phrase 'creation science'" (280). Gould was a popular science writer and authority (like Sagan) who was directly involved with the new resurgent legal challenges to teaching evolution.

17. "The physical world, as a divine creative act, provides a window into the life and mind of God, who created it," writes Intelligent Design theorist William Dembski: "Creation elucidates the Creator" (*End* 142, 143).

18. I thus agree with Dana Phillips's argument that "For McCarthy, the history of the West is natural history," with the clarification that I am contending that *Blood Meridian* reads human history in general, not just that of the West, in continuity with natural history—as seen, for instance, in the epigraph about Homo sapiens scalping, cited above. Indeed, Phillips acknowledges that longer lineage when he nicely puts it, "We might periodize him [McCarthy] with some confidence, then, as a writer not of the 'modern' or 'postmodern' eras but of the Holocene, with a strong historical interest in the late Pleistocene and even earlier epochs" (453, 452).

19. The randomness is a problem only insofar as some theists accepting evolution expect a teleology within it, that evolution was heading toward us. But as Stephen Jay Gould argues, if we were able to "rewind the tape" of evolution (*Wonderful* 50), we would not expect it to go the same way again. The system is not intrinsically heading toward us, and if it were possible to repeat the experiment, as it were, we would not expect the results to include humans—thus suggesting how contingent rather than directed the "design" process was. (An alternative view, based on the evolutionary principle of convergence, is found in Simon Conway Morris, *Crucible of Creation*, which suggests that evolution would have arrived at some form of higher intelligence.) Additionally, the design process of random mutation plus natural selection is hugely inefficient: it is only true statistically, over eons, that natural selection will privilege the more capable. There often will have been many contingent circumstances in which, for one arbitrary reason or another, the better adapted organism (or species) just got unlucky and did not survive to pass on its genetic heritage. Mass extinctions are just such indications of evolutionary history by "lottery" (Gould, *Wonderful* 47, 306–7).

20. This conception of the problem of theodicy is different from Gould's focus in "Nonmoral Nature" on the caterpillars who get eaten from the inside out, while alive but paralyzed, by the many wasp species that use this practice for hatching their larvae. Gould suggests that "the greatest challenge to [our nineteenth-century forebears'] concept of a benevolent deity was not simple predation—but slow death by parasitic ingestion" (33) and concludes with the argument that, as the title suggests,

nature is not moral in the sense that a lesson can be distilled from how nature works; these are human terms and we misread if we try to understand nature in ethical terms. He ends with Darwin's "personal bewilderment about such deep issues as the problem of evil"—that it is fruitless to try to join the two questions of science and ethics—and states that "evolution cannot teach any ethical theory at all" (44); in other words, these are (as Gould put it elsewhere) non-overlapping magesteria that have little to do with, or say about, each other. But my contention is that, notwithstanding his brief dismissal of predation as a problem for "the concept of a benevolent deity," ethics comes into play once we begin to imagine, with McCarthy, a creator who chooses evolution as a method for his creation. The question is not whether "nature" is "moral" (we can concede with Gould that it is not) but what its mechanisms say about the moral character of the systems designer.

21. Hoesch, "Fossil Record," n.p. Intriguingly, Hoesch ties this problematic theodicy of evolution to what he imagines is "the growing rise of Gnosticism": that at least the Gnostics understand the incompatibility of a good God with a theistic, old-earth acceptance of evolution. See also ICR, "Sin" and J. Morris, "Evolution" for overviews of creation science's contention that systemic death could not have been introduced by the biblical God.

22. This ICR theology is consistent with young-earth creationism's earlier critique of evolution. The Genesis Flood links evolution to Communism (443–44), and suggests that because evolution requires death before the Fall of Adam, it is impossible. As Whitcomb and Morris write, evolution "assumes that uncounted billions of animals had experienced natural or violent deaths before the Fall of Adam; that many important kinds of animals had long since become extinct by the time God created Adam to have dominion over every living creature; and that long ages before the Edenic curse giant flesh-eating monsters like Tyrannosaurus Rex roamed the earth, slashing their victims with ferocious dagger-like teeth and claws" (454–55). Because carnivores didn't exist before the Fall (461), evolution, they reason, couldn't be correct: "Does the Book of Genesis, honestly studied in the light of the New Testament, allow for a reign of tooth and claw and death and destruction before the Fall of Adam?" (455). The logic here suggests the historical development of modern creationism: the 1961 Genesis Flood is for a pre-Epperson audience urging it to resist modern thought by pointing out the problems with evolution for a literal reading of the Bible, which it assumes, like its audience, is correct. The post-Edwards, post-Dover ICR website, however, suggests the different argumentative strategy of trying to undercut the already widespread and publically taught paradigm of evolution by stressing the theological problems that result from it, and recommending its rejection and biblical literalism as an antidote.

23. For a Christian account of evolution that does not take the question of theodicy seriously ("Like beauty, the brutality of life is in the eye of the beholder"), see Miller 246.

24. Such as Kenneth Weiss and Anne Buchanan's The Mermaid's Tale: Four Billion Years of Cooperation in the Making of Living Things.

25. An earlier contender for the key mechanism of evolution proposed by Jean-Baptiste Lamarck would have provided a much better theodicy than natural selection. Lamarck famously suggested that organisms adapted to their environment by passing on acquired characteristics to their descendants: thus the giraffe's long neck

results from a long line of individual giraffes who, generation after generation, grew their necks by stretching to reach leaves, and passing that acquired gene for longer necks to their offspring. This scheme included a role for the effort and agency of the individual organism, and thus the possibility of ethical evaluation: as Peter Bowler remarks, "Lamarckism could be seen as the kind of mechanism that a benevolent God would have chosen to ensure a comfortable life within an ever-changing world" (227). As Bowler's *Evolution: The History of an Idea* suggests, attempts to give a designer a necessary role have been connected since Darwin's time to growing anxiety that "it was impossible to argue for the existence of a benevolent God from a mechanism as selfish and wasteful as natural selection" (224). While Lamarckianism preserved a role for the agency and value of the individual organism, other attempts to save a benevolent God in natural selection—such as emphasizing the development of altruism, or the intrinsic value of evolution's "goal" in humans—tend to justify the problematic process in terms of valuable ends; in so doing, their theodicies make sense only at the species level, where individuals don't count. This theology might save Sagan's dispassionate Deistic designer, but it doesn't save the traditional good God of Christianity.

26. Dembski offers what might be thought of as an Intelligent Design theodicy of evolution in *The End of Christianity*, in which he proposes the novel idea that God made creation good, but that an ancestral human community (the equivalent of Adam and Eve) committed an original sin that brought evil into the world. God applied this retroactively to creation, thereby enabling the death and suffering involved in natural selection, which was the fashion whereby the human community evolved in the first place. In this way, the pain and suffering involved in evolution are both the consequence of *and* the condition for human agency: humans evolved through a system that they themselves triggered. This theodicy of time travel paradox—what happens if you go back in time and kill your own grandfather?—has deservedly not gained much traction as far as I can tell.

27. Cormac McCarthy Papers, Collection 91, Box 39, Folder 8.

8. The Postmodern Gospel According to Dan

1. The National Organization for Albinism and Hypopigmentation was not amused, protesting Brown's novel (www.albinism.org/popcult/film.htm) as being in a tradition of "overwhelmingly negative" portrayals begun, indeed, with Melville (http://www.albinism.org/popcult/classic.htm).

2. On the novel's mode of "historical realism," see Mexal (1092).

3. Notes Nelson, "The awkward point for a lawsuit is that Brown took their ersatz scholarship at face value as historically true, and a historical fact cannot be plagiarized, only transmitted" (99).

4. I follow the novel's practice of referring to the male characters Langdon and Teabing by their surnames, but Sophie by her first name. It is an oddly infantilizing gesture in a novel seeking to affirm the "the sacred feminine," but it may in part be due to the fact that Sophie's name itself becomes important symbolically (it means wisdom) and practically (it is used by her grandfather as one of the code-words leading to the Grail secret). Silas, the Opus Dei monk in pursuit of the Grail, is also referred to by his first name.

5. Brown need not have, and probably hasn't, read Reed and Anzaldúa; my claim here, rather, is that we can read Brown's turn to a pagan backstory as part of a larger cultural search for what gets left behind and repressed in Christianity. As Charles Taylor puts it, "Much of our deep past cannot simply be laid aside, not just because of our 'weakness', but because there is something genuinely important and valuable in it. Recognizing this fact, in our present culture, usually means being anti-Christian, embracing some of the values of 'paganism', or 'polytheism'" (771).

6. But, as one statistician of descent population patterns contended of *The Da Vinci Code*, "If anyone living today is descended from Jesus, so are most of us on the planet." See www.slate.com/articles/health_and_science/science/2006/03/why_were_all_jesus_children.html.

7. *The Da Vinci Code* is predicated on an element of historiographic awareness: Teabing's pithy suggestion that the "greatest story ever told is . . . the greatest story ever *sold*" holds a kernel of awareness of history as narrative, as a rhetorical situation with an audience. But Hutcheon argues that "among the consequences of the post-modern desire to denaturalize history is a new self-consciousness about the distinc-tion between the brute *events* of the past and the historical *facts* we construct out of them. Facts are events to which we have given meaning" (*Politics* 57). She further qualifies that "in historiographic metafiction the very process of turning events into facts through the interpretation of archival evidence is shown to be a process of turning the traces of the past (our only access to those events today [found in things like "its documents, the testimony of witnesses, and other archival materials" (58)]) into historical representation" (57). *The Da Vinci Code* is a caricature of this interest in historiography, being premised on an "event" whose archival trace was an actual hoax. Its postmodernism tilts toward the sloppy rather than the genuine probing and attendant anxiety about our relation to the past that we find in the more sophisticated (and playful) postmodernism of Reed's *Mumbo Jumbo*, E. L. Doctorow's *The Book of Daniel*, Kingston's *China Men*, and Art Spiegelman's *Maus*, texts whose metafiction (absent from Brown) underline the meaning-making subject who narrativizes the "brute events" into "historical facts," turning the screw of historiographic questions.

8. On Jesus's probable marriage, see *Holy Blood* 347–49; on the Nag Hammadi gospels (erroneously called "scrolls," as in Brown) as eyewitness accounts, see 403; on the Gnostic gospels' historical veracity, see 405; on the Gnostic gospels suggesting Jesus was more human than divine, see 406; on the Council of Nicaea's vote that Jesus was divine, not a mortal prophet, see 388; on Constantine's role in forming Christian orthodoxy and suppressing heresy, see 388; on the historical priority of some Gnostic gospels, see 389–90.

9. Religious studies professor Timothy Beal tells the story of a student arriving in his office one day to explain "in hushed tones, that he wanted to leave his bio-engineering major and pursue the study of 'religious symbology.'" After puncturing that particular dream, Beal continues, "Always the evangelist for the major if not for the novel, I hastened to highlight the drama inherent in the study of religion—exotic ideas, unfamiliar rites, lies my youth minister told me. His eyes began to glaze. It was clear that Professor Langdon wouldn't be caught dead in our Department."

10. Starbird is a Catholic independent scholar who, she says, set out to refute *Holy Blood, Holy Grail*, but who became convinced of its claims instead (http://www.margaretstarbird.net/).

11. See Derickson in general for a good overview of the problem of Markan priority for inerrantist belief, and the resulting preference for upholding the church fathers' traditional attribution of apostolic authorship to the four gospels, even though the gospel writers do not name themselves.

12. Some conservative Muslims contest evolution as well. Most famous in the West is Adnan Oktar's extravagantly produced three-volume *Atlas of Creation*, sent unsolicited to scientists and libraries in the West in 2006 and 2007, arguing that evolution was (as Intelligent Designers were also putting it during this time) "a theory in crisis." See http://www.nytimes.com/2007/07/17/science/17book.html.

13. As Matthews recognizes, "the rhetorical-ethical and historical-critical paradigms need not be understood as mutually exclusive" (xi). Thus, The rhetorical-ethical paradigm's focus on questions of rhetoric and persuasion, the role of readers in "activating" a biblical text's meaning, the imitation in (to use Matthews's study text) Acts of previous scenes or plots based on well-known classical sources, and attention to the way ancient historians often composed stories or speeches based on what should have happened or been said rather than with our modern eye to historical, journalistic reporting of accurate detail, are ideas that a scholar versed in the historical-critical method could accept, but that those in the dogmatic-theological paradigm cannot. In other words, even modern scholars seeking to figure out what really happened in Acts and what Paul really said in Athens would have to recognize the way in which ancient historians often wrote according to their retrospective sense of what should have been said at the time rather than with the modern historian's eye to discover exact words: that they are "literary compositions rather than historical transcripts" (13).

14. A Google search of "'The Da Vinci Code' Geisler Nix" produces 55,000 hits, for example; adding "General Introduction to the Bible" lowers it to 11,900 (July 2014).

15. Fundamentalist hermeneutics for this reason prefers Matthean to Markan priority (see Derickson).

16. Bock also hits back against liberal interpretations by Pagels and Karen King that are sympathetic with Gnosticism—both the idea that there are suppressed alternative Christian communities that might have valuable things to say to us, and the idea that women had a larger role in the earliest communities that became gradually suppressed.

17. Thus, the bewildered Rayford, trying to make sense of the rapture in *Left Behind*, turns to the end of the Bible and reads of Jesus saying "Yes, I am coming quickly" (124). He reflects,

> if the Bible was as old as it seemed, what did "quickly" mean? It must not have meant soon, unless it was from the perspective of someone with a long view of history. Maybe Jesus meant that when he came, he would do it quickly. (124)

The preferred academic translation (NRSV) has "Surely I am coming soon" (Rev 22:20), but Rayford, reflecting the views of his fundamentalist authors, imagines that Jesus must have meant his return would be quickly in the sense of "with haste" rather than soon as in the sense of "imminently."

18. Indeed, as Metzger and Ehrman note in their coauthored *Text of the New Testament* (4th ed.), early Christological controversies are likely behind the some

ancient manuscript alterations (285–86). The notion that theology affected manuscript transmission and authorship—rather than the reverse idea in which pristine, preexisting theology is directly transcribed by authors in biblical texts—is part of mainstream scholarship, not historical revisionism as Douthat believes.

19. Like other mainstream NT scholars, Pagels thinks the Gospel of Thomas "although compiled c. 140, may include some traditions even *older* than the gospels of the New Testament" (xvii), thus placing the authorship of the canonical gospels earlier than the authorship of the Nag Hammadi text (see 24, 71).

20. As Robert Bellah's important *Religion in Human Evolution: From the Paleolithic to the Axial Age* summarizes recent scholarship (citing Mark S. Smith in particular),

> For decades the idea of religious distinctiveness in early Israel has steadily eroded. Yahweh, it seems, is not the original God of Israel, but a latecomer, arriving from, of all places, Edom, and generally identified with the south: not only Edom but Midian, Paran, Seir, and Sinai (Judges 5:4; Habakkuk 3:3; Psalm 68:8, 17). The original God of Israel was El, not Yahweh, as is evident in the patriarchal narratives: the name Isra-el means "El rules," not "Yahweh rules"—that would be Isra-yahu. Or maybe not El, the personal name of the old urban Canaanite high god, but el, the generic West Semitic term for god, spirit, or ancestor. Perhaps in Genesis 32, Jacob at the ford of the Jabbok was wrestling with a tribal "powerful being," not the transcendent God, nor the convenient later resolution of the problem, an angel. (287–88)

He continues, "Probably in premonarchical and certainly in early monarchical Israel something of archaic polytheism was present. Most unsettling has been the discovery that El's consort Asherah was inherited by Yahweh when El and Yahweh were merged . . . . The existence of a Mrs. God, so unseemly to Jewish and Christian orthodoxy, has become widely, though not universally, accepted" (289). Daniel Boyarin suggests that the Christian doctrine of the Trinity may have emerged from the remnant of just such ancient Israelite polytheisms, as in the relation between elder god "Ancient of Days" and the young god "the son of Man," itself modelled on the El-Yahweh / El-Baal relation. One begins to understand how impatience with the ambiguous, lingering polytheisms of Judaism and Christianity could give rise to Islam's insistence that "There is no god but God."

21. http://georgewbush-whitehouse.archives.gov/news/releases/2001/09/20010920-8.html. Westminster Abbey's "newest addition—a large, walk-through metal detector" may likewise suggest the post-9/11 atmosphere of heightened security (Brown 517).

Conclusion

1. In a February 2004 poll, 61 percent of Americans believed that "Iraq did have weapons of mass destruction that have not been found," compared to a prewar poll in December 2002 in which 89 percent of the public believed "Iraq currently does . . . have weapons of mass destruction—meaning chemical, biological or nuclear weapons" (http://abcnews.go.com/images/pdf/948a1BushKerry&WMDs.pdf, 16). By 2012, 62 percent of Republicans and 14 percent of Democrats continued to believe that "Iraq had weapons of mass destruction when the United States invaded in

2003" (http://www.dartmouth.edu/~benv/files/poll%20responses%20by%20party
%20ID.pdf, Q63).

2. See Lindsay for a list of the many evangelicals in the administration, and the
report that "Additionally, I found dozens of appointees at slightly lower levels who
share the president's style of evangelical faith. And whereas in previous administrations six to ten White House staffers would regularly attend Bible study, today's
White House Christian Fellowship is attended by fifteen to a hundred people.
Similar Bible study groups honeycomb the administration, across numerous federal
departments and agencies" (26).

3. The administration's opposition to recognizing same-sex marriages or civil
unions was rooted in conservative Christian antipathy to homosexuality, though
it stopped well short of including homosexuals among the "the pagans, and the
abortionists, and the feminists, and the gays and the lesbians," on whom Jerry Falwell pinned the 9/11 attacks, with Pat Robertson concurring (http://www.nytimes.
com/2001/09/15/us/after-attacks-finding-fault-falwell-s-finger-pointing-inap
propriate-bush-says.html), as God's punishment of America. Notes Daniel Williams,
Bush's views on homosexual rights were "more moderate . . . than most leaders of
the Christian Right" (256). The development of counterexpertise in this area has
to do with the notion of "conversion therapy" to change one's sexual orientation,
therapy that mainstream psychology sees as misguided and harmful. As Putnam and
Campbell note, American public opinion on homosexuality and same-sex marriage
has changed rapidly in the twenty-first century among young and old (568–69), as
was reflected, perhaps, in the Supreme Court's legalization of same-sex marriage in
June of 2015; homosexuality and same-sex marriage are bound to become a legacy
issue for only the most conservative Christians.

4. Abortion was, we have seen, a generative moment in the conservative Christian
resurgence. Putnam and Campbell report that, compared to homosexuality, public
opinion on abortion is not moving (408, 554). Most Americans fall into a middle
spectrum on abortion rights, favoring the right to an abortion in the first trimester
(though not as a routine method of birth control) but, outside of a grave likely birth
defect or a threat to the mother's life, not a right to an abortion in the ninth month
(http://www.washingtonpost.com/blogs/the-fix/wp/2013/04/12/if-gay-marriage-
and-pot-are-now-ok-why-not-abortion/?hpid=z3). Supreme Court Justice Ruth
Bader Ginsberg has recently mused that *Roe v. Wade* was too broad and too radical in its
judgment, noting the way it triggered a conservative backlash (http://www.politico.
com/story/2013/05/ruth-bader-ginsburg-roe-v-wade-abortion-91218.html).

5. One of the Bush administration's early acts was to take information about
condoms and safe sex off the National Institutes of Health's website, as part of its
overall resurgent policy of promoting abstinence-only sex education—thus giving
Perrotta the topic for his fiction. As in other areas, the policy of abstinence-only sex
education relies on postmodern counterexperts who contest scientific findings about
the efficacy of sex education programs, including those done by the Centers for
Disease Control and Prevention (see http://www.ucsusa.org/scientific_integrity/
abuses_of_science/abstinence-only-education.html). Many observers in the 2012
election cycle were surprised to see contraception emerge as a contested issue among
some Republican contenders, especially the question of whether, under "Obamacare," employers might be mandated to provide birth control coverage to employees.

6. On the influence of the Christian Right on US foreign policy, especially in the Middle East and Israel, see Kiracofe. As he summarizes, "The new state of Israel [founded in 1948] appeared to Christian Zionists as a momentous fulfillment of prophecy and a critical advancement of the apocalyptic End Times clock" (118) predicted by premillennial dispensationalist theology, which is dominant among fundamentalists and shared by many conservative Protestants. That anticipation was heightened with the 1967 Six Day War and Israel's "reunification of the divided Jerusalem" (121) as well as the annexing of the West Bank and Gaza; Christian Zionists today generally oppose a land-for-peace deal, support the Israeli settler movement, and envision the establishment of "greater Israel." The larger membership and implications of Christian Zionism is suggested by Catholic Republican presidential nominee Newt Gingrich's 2011 assertion that Palestinians are an "invented" people without the same rights to a homeland as Israelis (http://www.theguardian.com/world/2011/dec/10/palestinians-invented-people-newt-gingrich).

7. Climate change was yet another area in which it was easy to imagine a different political alignment of religious conservatives, perhaps one involving a commitment to the stewardship of the planet envisioned in Genesis when God gives humans dominion over the earth, and on the importance of intergenerational responsibility and covenants. Conservative Christians are less likely to believe in the science of climate change, and that humans are the chief cause of global warming. One reason for this alignment is the fact that, as Barker and Bearce argue, conservative Christians have a high level of belief that the Second Coming of Christ will occur by 2050 (268). Another is the learned, systemic distrust of scientific elites in the conservative Christian resurgence: the scientists who are peddling climate change, they reason, are the same ones who gave us evolution, and their universities are the same ones who gave us the historical-critical method in Bible scholarship.

8. The alliance between the Religious Right and supply-side economics (which aims at encouraging economic growth through lower taxes on producers of goods rather than emphasizing consumer demand) is another seemingly unusual, historically contingent convergence. Indeed, as Kevin M. Kruse's recent *One Nation Under God: How Corporate America Invented Christian America* wonderfully illuminates, in the 1930s corporate America "enlisted conservative clergymen" to "defeat the state power its architects feared most—not the Soviet regime in Moscow, but Franklin D. Roosevelt's New Deal administration in Washington" (xiv). In charting this history of "Christian libertarianism" (xiv), Kruse locates the antecedent of the Cold War alliance against atheistic communism—one that became increasingly partisan, as the connection between Billy Graham and the Nixon White House suggests (242)—and reveals its connection with post–Cold War anti-redistributionist policies. What George H. W. Bush derided as "voodoo economics" when in a nominating contest with Ronald Reagan in 1980 soon became mainstream Republican policy as the alliance with the Religious Right was also taking form. This was the economic doctrine that Francis Schaeffer had misgivings about when he groused that Jack Kemp had a "bee in his bonnet." This alliance was famously lampooned by Al Franken's cartoon "The Gospel of Supply Side Jesus" (recently animated here: http://www.youtube.com/watch?v=Gc-LJ_3VbUA).

What helps make sense of this alliance is the way in which economic activity is seen through a moral lens. In his "Pseudo-Conservatism Revisited—1965,"

Hofstadter notes "the moralistic quality of . . . economic ideas" in the new conservative movement—that previously there was an aspect of social reformism to conservative Christianity, now replaced by the view of the economy as "a vast apparatus of moral discipline, of rewards for virtue and industry and punishments for vice and indolence" (81)—an analysis richly prescient for the development of supply-side economics and the arguments in the wake of the financial crisis and the Great Recession (2007–2009). Thus, Hofstadter says, "The modern economy . . . seems reckless and immoral, even when it happens to work. In the intellectual synthesis of contemporary ultra-conservatism, the impulses of Protestant asceticism can thus be drawn upon to support business self-interest and the beautiful mathematical models of neo-classical economics" (81–82).

Besides the question of pro-business Christian theory (on which see the superb Moreton), Hofstadter's point helps explain why supply-side economics became a good fit for the Christian resurgence: it was a return of the Puritan idea that sanctification is evidence of justification; similarly, calls to return to the gold standard (which often accompanied supply-siderism) echoed religious anxiety about indeterminate signification seen in literalist Bible interpretation and Constitutional originalism. Keynesian deficit spending (the conventional solution to lack of consumer demand during a recession) was likewise seen in moral terms as being non-thrifty (90). As the economic arguments unfolded during the Great Recession, government deficit spending was often likened to household spending: government needed to get its budget in order, just as households do. The analogy was poor, as economist Paul Krugman kept pointing out—what households issue their own currency?—but it suggests the moralistic framework within which economic policy was being discussed on the Right. This line of thinking also suggests part of the reason why the Tea Party movement became a strangely logical reaction to the financial crisis. What might have been a progressive, leftist critique against the privatization of profit and the publicizing of risk and debt and against rising inequality (the financial industry that caused the economy to crash quickly resumed huge bonuses while millions of people remained un- or under-employed), and in favor of redistributionist policies actually became a moral drama about government overspending and overreach, complete with its own postmodern history fabrication (that the crisis was caused by government debt; that government programs under President Obama had dramatically proliferated).

As Krugman repeatedly noted, conservative economics came to see the economy as a "morality play" in which agents were rewarded or punished according to their decisions. As he also charged, supply-side and austerity policies were supported by a counterexpert apparatus that eschewed standard economic models and that engaged in deception (http://krugman.blogs.nytimes.com/2013/09/24/whats-it-all-about-then/), especially disguising as fiscal conservatism what was actually small-government ideology. (On mainstream economists' consensus on the effectiveness of stimulus in reducing unemployment, see http://www.igmchicago.org/igm-economic-experts-panel/poll-results?SurveyID=SV_5bfARfqluG9VYrP). The financial crisis, in other words, was not a problem to be solved but became an opportunity for conservatives to push back against the welfare state. That Krugman the modern Keynesian may be positioned against postmodern conservative economics is suggested by his comment, "The bottom line is that although I have political views—and wear them on my sleeve!—I'm not so postmodern as to believe that all truth is political. Some economic doctrines work, others don't. And my doctrine seems, objectively, non-politically, to have been working better than the other guys'" (http://krugman.blogs.nytimes.com/2013/05/01/not-everything-is-political/). Krugman's point was that a few economists were allowing their conservative views on the ideal size of government to affect their economic analysis, which led to erroneous predictions about inflation and interest rates while in a liquidity trap: "They're letting their views about how the world works be dictated by their vision of the kind of society they want; they're politicizing their economic analysis. And that's why they keep getting everything wrong."

The influence of Ayn Rand is considerable (for instance, on erstwhile vice-presidential candidate Paul Ryan, considered to be the economic policy expert among Congressional Republicans, who declared in 2009 that "we are right now living in an Ayn Rand novel" [https://www.youtube.com/watch?v=WmW19uoyuO8]). The appearance of paradox, given Rand's outspoken atheism, is resolved once one understands the way conservatives of different stripes consider the economic sphere to be the site where moral consequences play out—thus Ryan's "hammock theory" of welfare.

Recent research (albeit partisan), linked Tea Party small-government ideology to another spoke of the conservative alliance—white resentment. For many Tea Party supporters, the falsely imagined growth of government programs under an African American president, coupled with the desire for immigration reform (including pathways to citizenship) was a Democratic attempt to create legions of welfare-dependent nonwhite voters who would be reliable Democrats in future elections. See http://www.democracycorps.com/attachments/article/954/dcor%20rpp%20fg%20memo%20100313%20final.pdf.

9. See, e.g., http://www.nytimes.com/2009/09/08/science/08tier.html?_r=1, which suggests, "With our rational faculties muted, sometimes the unwelcome evidence doesn't even register, and sometimes we use marvelous logic to get around the facts." It continues,

> In one study, Republicans who blamed Saddam Hussein for the attacks of Sept. 11, 2001, were presented with strong counterevidence, including a statement from President George W. Bush absolving Hussein. But most of the people in the study went on blaming Hussein anyway, as the researchers report in the current issue of *Sociological Inquiry*. Some of the people ignored or rejected the counterevidence; some "counterargued" that Hussein was evil enough to do it; some flatly said they were entitled to counterfactual opinions. And some came up with an especially creative form of motivated reasoning that the psychologists labeled "inferred justification": because the United States went to war against Hussein, the reasoning went, it must therefore have been provoked by his attack on Sept. 11.

10. On the contrary, some veins of evangelical Protestantism can carry a particular tool set of prayerful introspection for seeking out self-deception. A moving episode in David Foster Wallace's unfinished novel *The Pale King* suggests just such a non-simple struggle for self-knowledge amidst self-deception as two teenage / young adult evangelical characters struggle with the moral question of what to do about their unplanned pregnancy (38–45).

11. Indeed, the racial politics of the Republican Party—vividly on display in fall of 2015 as presidential candidate Donald Trump played to the nativism of the Republican base—prevent it from demographically wider alliances with African American evangelicals and Hispanic Catholics, some of whom share their conservative Christian beliefs about abortion and homosexuality.

12. See, e.g., Michael Lind's suggestion that "Thanks to a shift in generational values among Millennials, social conservatism is experiencing a rapid, terminal decline" (http://thebreakthrough.org/index.php/journal/past-issues/issue-4/the-coming-realignment), and reports of the coming "New New Left" (http://www.thedailybeast.com/articles/2013/09/12/the-rise-of-the-new-new-left.html).

13. Pew Research Center, May 12, 2015, "America's Changing Religious Landscape." http://www.pewforum.org/2015/05/12/americas-changing-religious-landscape/.

14. This parallel literary world was ignored by the secular mainstream at a cost, Frank Schaeffer suggests: "The *Times* 'best-seller' list was misleading. Evangelical books were often outselling the *Times*' best-sellers. But the paper did not bother to count sales in religious bookstores. The people hurt most weren't evangelical authors (our books sold anyway); rather, the losers were Democratic Party leaders and other liberal readers of the 'paper of record' who were blindsided by subsequent events. The *Times*' readers were not given a heads-up about what was going on 'out there'" (*Crazy* 286–87).

15. See, for instance, Hutcheon's classic account *A Poetics of Postmodernism*: "Historiographic metafiction suggests that truth and falsity may indeed not be the right terms in which to discuss fiction . . . Postmodern novels like [Julian Barnes's] *Flaubert's Parrot*, [Timothy Findley's] *Famous Last Words*, and [John Fowles's] *A Maggot* openly assert that there are only *truths* in the plural, and never one Truth; and there is rarely falseness *per se*, just others' truths" (109). One senses the difficulty such postmodern formalism would have using these tools to confront the conservative Christian resurgence; hence Pinter's recantation.

16. Brendan Nyhan continues, reviewing a study by Dan Kahan,

> more people know what scientists think about high-profile scientific controversies than polls suggest; they just aren't willing to endorse the consensus when it contradicts their political or religious views. This finding helps us understand why my colleagues and I have found that factual and scientific evidence is often ineffective at reducing misperceptions and can even backfire on issues like weapons of mass destruction, health care reform and vaccines. With science as with politics, identity often trumps the facts. (http://www.nytimes.com/2014/07/06/upshot/when-beliefs-and-facts-collide.html?_r=0)

See also http://www.bloombergview.com/articles/2014-03-31/why-political-partisans-don-t-like-facts, which attributes to "cultural cognition" the reason many Republicans don't accept science's fact claims on climate change, even as many Democrats don't accept science's fact claims on Genetically Modified foods.

17. As may be well known, Tolkien created an incredibly elaborate historical, cultural, and even linguistic fictional world for his good guys, the elves and humans of Middle-earth. But in Tolkien's world, the broad population of the dark side has no subjectivity and indeed no history. When Sauron tries to bring the peoples of Middle-earth to their knees in *The Lord of the Rings*, he is the embodiment of pure,

supernatural evil, the chief servant of Melkor, who functions in Tolkien's extended fictional universe (as elaborated in *The Silmarillion*) as the equivalent of Satan, the chief of the angels who rebels against the creator God, Eru Ilúvatar. While Sauron, the embodiment of supernatural evil, has some legendary backstory, and is thus a subject with diabolic motivation, the many evil creatures who serve him are not: they are beings outside of history, without history. How do the orcs live? What is their heritage? What are their economic and social arrangements? Do the orcs or goblins have cultural and artistic traditions? Are there any political disagreements or differences within orc societies? We have no idea, because Tolkien was utterly uninterested in such questions. The orcs and goblins are races without history, culture, society or economics, precisely because they simply and only embody evil. Critics have rightly ascribed to Tolkien a racializing, indeed racist view of elf-orc relations (see, e.g., Werber), a structuring of fantasy races that he has passed on to an entire genre, now extended from books to films and games, that he was instrumental in founding. Tolkien, in other words, doesn't just naturalize elf-orc hostility (it's in their blood), but supernaturalizes it by placing it within the framework of the cosmic battle between the departed Eru Ilúvatar and the Melkor-inspired Sauron.

18. See Furman, paragraphs 21 and 24.

WORKS CITED

Abrahams, Israel, Jacob Haberman, and Charles Manekin. "Belief." *Encyclopaedia Judaica*. Ed. Michael Berenbaum and Fred Skolnik. 2nd ed. Vol. 3. Detroit: Macmillan Reference USA, 2007. 290–94. *Gale Virtual Reference Library*. Web. 26 May 2011.

Acosta, Oscar Zeta. *The Autobiography of a Brown Buffalo*. 1972. New York: Vintage Books, 1989. Print.

———. *Revolt of the Cockroach People*. 1973. New York: Vintage, 1989. Print.

African Pollinator Initiative. "Crops, Browse, and Pollinators in Africa: An Initial Stock-Taking." Nairobi: African Pollinator Initiative Secretariat, 2004. Web.

Allison, Dorothy. *Bastard Out of Carolina*. New York: Plume, 1993. Print.

Alpern, Stanley B. "The European Introduction of Crops into West Africa in Precolonial Times. *History in Africa* 19 (1992): 13–43. Web. *JSTOR*.

Anzaldúa, Gloria. *Borderlands / La Frontera: The New Mestiza*. 1987. 2nd ed. San Francisco: Aunt Lute Books, 1999. Print.

Arac, Jonathan. *"Huckleberry Finn" as Idol and Target*. Madison: U of Wisconsin P, 1997. Print.

Archer, Gleason L. "Alleged Errors and Discrepancies in the Original Manuscripts of the Bible." Geisler 57–82. Print.

Armstrong, Karen. *The Battle for God: A History of Fundamentalism*. New York: Ballantine, 2001. Print.

Asad, Talal. *Genealogies of Religion: Discipline and Reasons of Power in Christianity and Islam*. Baltimore: Johns Hopkins UP, 1993. Print.

Atwood, Margaret. *The Handmaid's Tale*. 1985. New York: Anchor, 1998. Print.

———. "An Interview with Margaret Atwood on Her Novel *The Handmaid's Tale*." *The Handmaid's Tale*. 1985. New York: Anchor, 1998. 317–21. Print.

Austenfeld, Anne Marie. "The Revelatory Narrative Circle in Barbara Kingsolver's *The Poisonwood Bible*." *Journal of Narrative Theory* 36.2 (2006): 293–305. Web. *Project Muse*. 17 May 2011.

Badiou, Alain. *Saint Paul: The Foundation of Universalism*. Trans. Ray Brassier. Redwood City, CA: Stanford UP, 2003. Print.

Baigent, Michael, Richard Leigh, and Henry Lincoln. *Holy Blood, Holy Grail*. 1982. Rev. ed. London: Arrow, 1996. Print.

Barker, David C., and David H. Bearce. "End-Times Theology, the Shadow of the Future, and Public Resistance to Addressing Global Climate Change." *Political Research Quarterly* 66 (June 2013): 267–279. Print.

Barth, John. "The Literature of Exhaustion." *Atlantic Monthly* August 1967: 29–34. Print.

Barton, Nicholas H, Derek E. G. Briggs, Jonathan A. Eisen, David B. Goldstein, and

Nipam H. Patel. *Evolution*. Cold Spring Harbor, NY: Cold Spring Harbor Laboratory Press, 2007. Print.

Baudrillard, Jean. *Simulacra and Simulation*. Trans. Sheila Faria Glaser. Ann Arbor: U of Michigan P, 1994. Print.

Beal, Timothy K. "Romancing the 'Code'." *Chronicle of Higher Education* 9 June 2006: B14. Web. http://chronicle.com/article/Romancing-the-Code-/31037.

Behe, Michael J. *Darwin's Black Box: The Biochemical Challenge to Evolution*. New York: Free Press, 1996. Print.

Bellah, Robert. "Civil Religion in America." *Daedalus* 91.1 (1967): 1–21. Web. http://www.robertbellah.com/articles_5.htm.

———. *Religion in Human Evolution: From the Paleolithic to the Axial Age*. Cambridge, MA: Belknap / Harvard UP, 2011. Print.

Benford, Gregory. "Theology and the Interstellar Subway." Rev. of *Contact*, by Carl Sagan. *New York Times* 3 Nov. 1985: 12. Print.

Bercovitch, Sacvan. "Deadpan Huck: Or, What's Funny about Interpretation." *The Kenyon Review* 24: 3/4 (Summer–Autumn 2002): 90–134. Print.

Bergen, Doris L. *The Twisted Cross: The German Christian Movement in the Third Reich*. Chapel Hill: U of North Carolina P, 1996. Print.

Berman, Paul. "What If It Happened Here?" Rev. of *The Plot Against America*, by Philip Roth. *New York Times Book Review* 3 Oct. 2004: 1+. Web. 17 Feb. 2011.

Bloom, Harold. "Introduction." In Cormac McCarthy, *Blood Meridian*, vii–xv. New York: Modern Library, 2010. Print.

Bock, Darrell L. *Breaking the Da Vinci Code: Answers to the Questions Everyone's Asking*. Nashville: Nelson, 2004. Print.

———. "Christian Analysis of Da Vinci Code: What Dan Brown Did Not Tell You— Three Major Errors Plus a Few More." *TheTruthAboutDaVinci.com*. 2009. Web.

Born, Brad. "Kingsolver's Gospel for Africa: (Western White Female) Heart of Goodness." *Mennonite Life* 56.1 (2001). Web.

Bowler, Peter J. *Evolution: The History of an Idea*. Rev. ed. Berkeley: U of California P, 1989. Print.

Boyarin, Daniel. *The Jewish Gospels: The Story of the Jewish Christ*. New York: The New Press, 2012. Print.

———. *A Radical Jew: Paul and the Politics of Identity*. Berkeley: U of California P, 1994. Print.

Brekus, Catherine. "Writing as a Protestant Practice: Devotional Diaries in Early New England. Maffly-Kipp et al. 19–34. Print.

Bromberg, Judith. "A Complex Novel about Faith, Family and Dysfunction." Rev. of *The Poisonwood Bible*, by Barbara Kingsolver. *National Catholic Reporter* 19 Mar. 1999. Web.

Brooks, David. "President Rick Perry?" *New York Times* 25 August 2011. Web.

Brown, Dan. *The Da Vinci Code*. New York: Anchor, 2003. Print.

Brownstein, Gabriel. "The *Plot* Sickens." Rev. of *The Plot Against America*, by Philip Roth. *Villagevoice.com*. 27 Sept. 2004. Web. 17 Feb. 2011.

Bruns, Roger. *Preacher: Billy Sunday and Big-Time American Evangelism*. Champaign: U of Illinois P, 1992. Print.

Buckley, William F., Jr. "Our Mission Statement." *National Review* 19 Nov. 1955. Web. http://www.nationalreview.com/article/223549/our-mission-statement-william-f-buckley-jr.

Buell, Lawrence. "Religion on the American Mind." *American Literary History* 19:1 (Spring 2007): 32–55. Print.

Burgess, Anthony. "A Mystic Drop Too Much." Rev. of *The Holy Blood and the Holy Grail* by Michael Baigent, Richard Leigh, and Henry Lincoln. *The Observer* (London) 17 Jan 1982: 31. Print.

Busby, Mark. "Rolling the Stone, Sisyphus, and the Epilogue of *Blood Meridian*." *Southwestern American Literature* 36.3 (Summer 2011): 87–95. Print.

Byfield, Ted, and Virginia Byfield. "The Evil Missionary." Rev. of *The Poisonwood Bible*, by Barbara Kingsolver. *Alberta Report* 26.7 (1999). *EBSCO Host*. Web.

Caminero-Santangelo, Marta. "Moving Beyond 'The Blank White Spaces': Atwood's Gilead, Postmodernism, and Strategic Resistance." *Studies in Canadian Literature* 19:1 (1994). Web.

Canfield, Douglas. *Mavericks on the Border: The Early Southwest in Historical Fiction and Film.* Louisville: UP of Kentucky, 2000. Print.

Carson, Sharon. "Shaking the Foundation: Liberation Theology in *Narrative of the Life of Frederick Douglass*." *Religion and Literature* 24.2 (1992): 19–34. Print.

Casanova, José. *Public Religions in the Modern World.* Chicago: U of Chicago P, 1994. Print.

Chafets, Zev. "The Huckabee Factor." *New York Times* 12 Dec. 2007. Web. http://www.nytimes.com/2007/12/12/magazine/16huckabee.html?pagewanted=2.

Chamberlain, Samuel. *My Confession: Recollections of a Rogue.* Ed. William H. Goetzmann. Unexpurgated and Annotated Edition. Austin: Texas State Historical Association, 1996. Print.

Chappell, David L. "Religious Ideas of the Segregationists." *Journal of American Studies* 32 (1998): 237–62. Print.

Chin, Frank. "Come All Ye Asian American Writers of the Real and the Fake." *The Big Aiiieeeee!: An Anthology of Chinese American and Japanese American Literature.* Ed. Jeffery Paul Chan, Frank Chin, Lawson Fusao Inada, and Shawn Wong. New York: Meridian, 1991. 1–92. Print.

———. "This Is Not an Autobiography." *Genre* 18:2 (Summer 1985): 109–30. Print.

Chin, Frank, and Jeffery Paul Chan. "Racist Love." *Seeing Through Shuck.* Ed. Richard Kostelanetz. New York: Ballantine Books, 1972. 65–79. Print.

Chin, Frank, Jeffery Paul Chan, Lawson Fusao Inada, and Shawn Hsu Wong, eds. *Aiiieeeee!: An Anthology of Asian American Writers.* 1974. New York: Mentor, 1991. Print.

Coetzee, J. M. "What Philip Knew." Rev. of *The Plot Against America*, by Philip Roth. *New York Review of Books* 18 Nov. 2004. Web. 14 Aug. 2013.

Coogan, Michael D. *The Old Testament: A Historical and Literary Introduction to the Hebrew Scriptures.* 2nd ed. New York: Oxford UP, 2011. Print.

Cormac McCarthy Papers. Southwestern Writers Collection. The Wittliff Collections. Texas State University, San Marcos.

Crouch, Stanley. "Roth's Historical Sin." *Salon.* 11 Oct 2004. Web. 26 May 2011.

Darwin, Charles. *On the Origin of Species by Means of Natural Selection, or, The Preservation of Favored Races in the Struggle for Life.* London: John Murray, 1859. Print.

Daugherty, Leo. "Gravers False and True: *Blood Meridian* as Gnostic Tragedy." *The Southern Quarterly: A Journal of the Arts in the South* 30.4 (1992): 122–33. Print.

Davies, Paul. *The Eerie Silence: Renewing Our Search for Alien Intelligence.* Boston: Houghton Mifflin, 2010. Print.

Davis, Percival, and Dean H. Kenyon. *Of Pandas and People: The Central Question of Biological Origins.* 2nd ed. Dallas: Haughton Publishing, 1993. Print.

Dawit, Seble, and Salem Mekuria. "The West Just Doesn't Get It." *New York Times* 7 Dec 1993. Web. *Infoweb.*

Dawkins, Richard. *The Blind Watchmaker: Why the Evidence of Evolution Reveals a Universe Without Design.* New York: Norton, 1987. Print.

DeLillo, Don. *White Noise.* 1985. New York: Penguin, 2009. Print.

Dembski, William A. *The Design Revolution: Answering the Toughest Questions About Intelligent Design.* Downers Grove, IL: InterVarsity, 2004. Print.

———. *The End of Christianity: Finding a Good God in an Evil World.* Nashville: B&H Publishing, 2009. Print.

———. *Intelligent Design: The Bridge Between Science & Theology.* Downers Grove, IL: InterVarsity, 2002. Print.

Demory, Pamela H. "Into the Heart of Light: Barbara Kingsolver Rereads *Heart of Darkness.*" *Conradiana* 34.3 (2002): 181–93. Web. *Literature Online.* 24 May 2011.

Denton, Michael. *Evolution: A Theory in Crisis.* Chevy Chase, MD: Adler & Adler, 2002. Print.

Deresiewicz, William. "Homing Patterns: Marilynne Robinson's Fiction." *Nation* 13 Oct. 2008: 25–30. Print.

Derickson, Gary W. "Matthean Priority/Authorship and Evangelicalism's Boundary." *The Master's Seminary Journal* 14:1 (Spring 2003): 87–103. Web. http://www.tms.edu/tmsj/tmsj14e.pdf.

Dick, Philip K. *The Man in the High Castle.* New York: Vintage, 1962. Print.

Discovery Institute. "Frequently Asked Questions." Web. http://www.discovery.org/id/faqs. Accessed 14 May 2015.

Domina, Lynn. "Liturgies, Rituals, Ceremonies: The Conjunction of Roman Catholic and Native American Religious Traditions in N. Scott Momaday's *House Made of Dawn.*" *Paintbrush: A Journal of Contemporary Multicultural Literature* 21 (1994): 7–27. Print.

Douglas, Christopher. "Christian Multiculturalism and Unlearned History in Marilynne Robinson's *Gilead.*" *Novel* 44.3 (2011): 333–53. Print.

———. "The Flawed Design: American Imperialism in N. Scott Momaday's *House Made of Dawn* and Cormac McCarthy's *Blood Meridian.*" *Critique* 45.1 (Fall 2003): 3–24. Print.

———. *A Genealogy of Literary Multiculturalism.* Ithaca, NY: Cornell UP, 2009. Print.

Douglass, Frederick. *Autobiographies.* 1845, 1855, 1881. New York: Library of America, 1994. Print.

———. "West India Emancipation." *Two Speeches by Frederick Douglass; West India Emancipation And the Dred Scott Decision.* Rochester, NY: C. P. Dewey, 1857. Web. http://www.loc.gov/resource/mfd.21039/#seq-1. 8 May 2014.

Douthat, Ross. *Bad Religion: How We Became a Nation of Heretics.* New York: Free Press, 2012. Print.

———. "Dan Brown's America." *The New York Times.* Web. 18 May 2009.

———. "It Didn't Happen Here." Rev. of *The Plot Against America,* by Philip Roth. *Policy Review* 129 (2005): 73–8. Web. *EBSCO.* 17 Feb. 2011.

Downing, Crystal L. *How Postmodernism Serves (My) Faith: Questioning Truth in Language, Philosophy and Art.* Downers Grove, IL: InterVarsity, 2006. Print.

Drinnon, Richard. *Keeper of Concentration Camps: Dillon S. Myer and American Racism.* Los Angeles: U of California P, 1987. Print.

Dunch, Ryan. "Beyond Cultural Imperialism: Cultural Theory, Christian Missions, and Global Modernity." *History and Theory* 41.3 (2002): 301–25. Web. *JSTOR.* 19 May 2011.

Dunn, James D. G. *Christology in the Making: An Inquiry into the Origins of the Doctrine of the Incarnation.* London: SCM Press, 1980. Print.

Eagleton, Terry. *Reason, Faith and Revolution: Reflections on the God Debate.* New Haven: Yale UP, 2009. Print.

Easley, Michael J., and John F. Ankerberg. *The Da Vinci Code Controversy: 10 Facts You Should Know.* Chicago: Moody, 2006. Print.

Eddins, Dwight. *The Gnostic Pynchon.* Bloomington: Indiana UP, 1990. Print.

Ehrman, Bart. *Did Jesus Exist?: The Historical Argument for Jesus of Nazareth.* New York: HarperOne, 2012. Print.

——. *God's Problem: How the Bible Fails to Answer Our Most Important Question—Why We Suffer.* New York: HarperCollins, 2008. Print.

——. *Jesus, Interrupted: Revealing the Hidden Contradictions in the Bible (and Why We Don't Know About Them).* New York: HarperOne, 2010. Print.

——. *Lost Christianities: the Battle for Scripture and the Faiths We Never Knew.* New York: Oxford UP, 2003. Print.

——. *The Lost Gospel of Judas Iscariot: A New Look at Betrayer and Betrayed.* New York: Oxford UP, 2006. Print.

——. *Truth and Fiction in* The Da Vinci Code. Oxford, U.K.: Oxford UP, 2004. Print.

Eighmy, John Lee. *Churches in Cultural Captivity: A History of the Social Attitudes of Southern Baptists.* Knoxville: U of Tennessee P, 1987. Print.

Elie, Paul. "Has Fiction Lost Its Faith?" *New York Times* 19 Dec. 2012. Web. http://www.nytimes.com/2012/12/23/books/review/has-fiction-lost-its-faith.html?pagewanted=all.

Eliot, T. S. "East Coker." *The Complete Poems and Plays.* New York: Harcourt, Brace, 1952. Print. 123–29.

——. "The Waste Land." *The Complete Poems and Plays.* New York: Harcourt, Brace, 1952. Print. 37–55.

Esposito, Lenny. "Arguments from Silence." Web. http://www.thetruthaboutdavinci.com/arguments-from-silence.html. 3 Oct. 2015.

Faust, Drew Gilpin, ed. *The Ideology of Slavery: Proslavery Thought in the Antebellum South, 1830–1860.* Baton Rouge: Louisiana State UP, 1981. Print.

Fessenden, Tracy. *Culture and Redemption: Religion, the Secular, and American Literature.* Princeton, NJ: Princeton UP, 2007. Print.

——. "The Problem of the Postsecular." *American Literary History* 26:1 (2014): 154–67. Print.

Flood, Alison. "Cormac McCarthy's Parallel Career Revealed—as a Scientific Copy Editor!" *The Guardian* 21 Feb. 2012. Print.

Fontenot, Chester J. "Ishmael Reed and the Politics of Aesthetics, or Shake Hands and Come Out Conjuring." *Black American Literature Forum* 12.1 (Spring 1978): 20–23. Print.

Forrest, Barbara, and Paul R. Gross. *Creationism's Trojan Horse: The Wedge of Intelligent Design.* Oxford, U.K.: Oxford UP, 2005. Print.

Freedman, Jonathan. *Klezmer America: Jewishness, Ethnicity, Modernity.* New York: Columbia UP, 2008. Print.

Frei, Hans W. *The Eclipse of Biblical Narrative: A Study in Eighteenth and Nineteenth Century Hermeneutics.* New Haven, CT: Yale UP, 1974. Print.

Furman, Richard. "Exposition of the Views of the Baptists, Relative to the Coloured Population in the United States." 2nd ed. 1823. Charleston: A. E. Miller, 1838. Web. http://history.Furman.edu/~benson/docs/rcd-fmn1.htm. 20 May 2015.

Gates, David. "It Can't Happen Here." Rev. of *The Plot Against America*, by Philip Roth. *Newsweek* 20 Sept. 2004: 56. Web. 10 May 2011.

Gates, Henry Louis Jr. "Forty Acres and a Gap in Wealth." *New York Times* 18 Nov. 2007. Web. http://www.nytimes.com/2007/11/18/opinion/18gates.html.

Geertz, Clifford. "Religion as a Cultural System." *The Interpretation of Cultures.* New York: Basic, 1973. 87–125. Print.

Geisler, Norman L., ed. *Inerrancy.* Grand Rapids, MI: Zondervan, 1979. Print.

Geisler, Norman L., and William E. Nix. *General Introduction to the Bible: Revised and Expanded.* Chicago: Moody Bible Institute, 1986. Print.

George, Olakunle. "Alice Walker's Africa: Globalization and the Province of Fiction." *Comparative Literature* 53.4 (2001): 354–72.

Gerber, Jane S. *The Jews of Spain: A History of the Sephardic Experience.* New York: Simon and Schuster, 1992. Print.

Gibson, Donald B. "Faith, Doubt, and Apostasy: Evidence of Things Unseen in Frederick Douglass's *Narrative.*" *Frederick Douglass: New Literary and Historical Essays.* Ed. Eric J. Sundquist. Cambridge, U.K.: Cambridge UP, 1990. 84–117. Print.

Giddings, Paula. "'Alice Walker's Appeal': An Interview with Paula Giddings from *Essence* (1992)." *The World Has Changed: Conversations with Alice Walker.* Ed. Rudolph P. Byrd. New York: New Press, 2010. 86–92. Print.

"God's Invisible Things." Web. *Institute for Creation Research.* 2 May 2013.

Goodstein, Laurie. "Defenders of Christianity Rebut *The Da Vinci Code.*" *The New York Times* 27 Apr. 2004. Web.

Gould, Stephen J. *Hen's Teeth and Horse's Toes.* New York: Norton, 1983. Print.

——. *Wonderful Life: The Burgess Shale and the Nature of History.* Norton, 1989. Print.

Graham, P. H., and P. Ranalli. "Common Bean (*Phaseolus vulgaris* L.)." *Field Crops Research* 53 (1997): 131–46. Web. *ScienceDirect.*

Greeley, Andrew, and Michael Hout. *The Truth about Conservative Christians: What They Think and What They Believe.* Chicago: U of Chicago P, 2006. Print.

Grewal, Inderpal, and Caren Kaplan. "Warrior Marks: Global Womanism's Neo-Colonial Discourse in a Multicultural Context." *Camera Obscura* 39 (1996): 4–33. Print.

Griffith, R. Marie. *God's Daughters: Evangelical Women and the Power of Submission.* Berkeley: U of California P, 1997. Print.

Hagen, John D. Jr. "The Real Story of the Council of Nicea." *America* 5 June 2006. Web.

Hall, David D., ed. *Lived Religion in America: Toward a History of Practice.* Princeton, NJ: Princeton UP, 1997. Print.

Hamilton, Michael, and Johanna Yngvason. "Patrons of the Evangelical Mind." *Christianity Today* 8 July 2002: 42–47. Print.

Hanegraaf, Hank, and Paul L. Maier. *The Da Vinci Code: Fact or Fiction?* Carol Stream, IL: Tyndale, 2004. Print.

Harding, Susan Friend. *The Book of Jerry Falwell: Fundamentalist Language and Politics.* Princeton, NJ: Princeton UP, 2001. Print.

Hardt, Michael, and Antonio Negri. *Empire.* Cambridge, MA: Harvard UP, 2000. Print.

HarperCollins Study Bible: New Revised Standard Version. 1989. Ed. Wayne A. Meeks, Jouette M. Bassler, Werner E. Lemke, Susan Niditch, and Eileen M. Schuller. New York: Division of Christian Education of the National Council of the Churches of Christ in the U.S.A., 1993. Print.

Hartshorne, Charles. *Omnipotence and Other Theological Mistakes.* State U of New York P, 1984. Print.

Haught, John F. *God After Darwin: A Theology of Evolution.* 2nd ed. Westview Press, 2008. Print.

Hemingway, Ernest. "A Clean, Well-Lighted Place." *The Short Stories of Ernest Hemingway.* New York: Charles Scribner's Sons, 1966. 379–83. Print.

——. *The Sun Also Rises.* 1926. New York: Scribner, 2006. Print.

Herberg, Will. *Protestant-Catholic-Jew: An Essay in American Religious Sociology.* 1955. Rev. ed. New York: Anchor, 1960. Print.

Hersh, Seymour M. "The Stovepipe." *Annals of National Security.* 27 Oct. 2003. Web.

Heschel, Susannah. *The Aryan Jesus: Christian Theologians and the Bible in Nazi Germany.* Princeton, NJ: Princeton UP, 2008. Print.

Hitchens, Christopher. *God is Not Great: How Religion Poisons Everything.* Toronto: McClelland & Steward, 2007. Print.

Hoesch, William A. "The Fossil Record: Commending the Gnostics." Web. *Institute for Creation Research.* 19 May 2015.

Hofstadter, Richard. *The Paranoid Style in American Politics.* New York: Vintage, 2008. Print.

Hollinger, David A. *Cosmopolitanism and Solidarity: Studies In Ethnoracial, Religious, and Professional Affiliation in the United States.* Madison: U of Wisconsin P, 2006. Print.

Hoyle, Fred. *The Intelligent Universe.* London: Michael Joseph, 1983. Print.

Humes, Edward. *Monkey Girl: Evolution, Education, Religion, and the Battle for America's Soul.* New York: Harper Perennial, 2007. Print.

Hungerford, Amy. *Postmodern Belief: American Literature and Religion Since 1960.* Princeton, NJ: Princeton UP, 2010. Print.

Hurston, Zora Neale. 1927. "The Florida Expedition." Franz Boas Papers, American Philosophical Society.

——. *Tell My Horse: Voodoo and Life in Haiti and Jamaica.* 1938. New York: Harper & Row, 1990. Print.

Hurtado, Larry. "Ungodly Errors: Scholarly Gripes about *The Da Vinci Code*'s Jesus." *Slate* 22 May 2006. Web.

Hutcheon, Linda. *A Poetics of Postmodernism: History, Theory, Fiction.* New York: Routledge, 1988. Print.

——. *The Politics of Postmodernism.* New York: Routledge, 1989. Print.

Hutton, Christopher M. *Race and the Third Reich.* Cambridge, U.K.: Polity, 2005. Print.

Jacobs, Harriet. *Incidents in the Life of a Slave Girl.* 1861. New York: Oxford UP, 1988. Print.

Jacobs, J. U. "Translating the 'Heart of Darkness': Cross-Cultural Discourse in the Contemporary Congo Book." *Current Writing* 14.2 (2002): 104–17. Print.

Jacobson, Jacob J. "Imagined Geographies." *Seeds of Change: Critical Essays on Barbara Kingsolver.* Ed. Priscilla Leder. Knoxville: U of Tennessee P, 2010. 175–98. Print.

James, Stanlie M. "Shades of Othering: Reflections on Female Circumcision/Genital Mutilation." *Signs* 23.4 (1998): 1031–48. Print.

Jameson, Fredric. Foreword. In Lyotard vii–xxi. Print.

———. *Postmodernism: or, the Cultural Logic of Late Capitalism.* Durham, NC: Duke UP, 1991. Print.

———. "Reviews." Rev. of *The Names,* by Don DeLillo, and *Richard A.,* by Sol Yurick. *Minnesota Review* 22 (Spring 1984): 116–22. Print.

Johnson, Phillip. *Darwin on Trial.* Downers Grove, IL: InterVarsity, 1993. Print.

———. "The Intelligent Design Movement: Challenging the Modernist Monopoly on Science." *Signs of Intelligence: Understanding Intelligent Design.* Ed. William Dembski and James Kushiner. Grand Rapids, MI: Baker Book House, 2001. 25–41. Print.

Johnson, Stephen. "An Overview of Plant-Pollinator Relationships in Southern Africa." *International Journal of Tropical Insect Science* 24.1 (2004): 45–54. Web. *ScienceDirect.*

Johnson, Stephen, and Kim E. Steiner. "Generalization versus Specialization in Plant Pollination Systems." *Trends in Ecological Evolution* 15: 190–93. Web. *Elsevier.*

Jones, Eric M. "'Where is Everybody?': An Account of Fermi's Question." Web. http://www.fas.org/sgp/othergov/doe/lanl/la-10311-ms.pdf.

Jussawalla, Feroza. "Reading and Teaching Barbara Kingsolver's *Poisonwood Bible* as Postcolonial." *Revista alicantina de estudios ingleses* 16 (2003): 165–75. Web. http://hdl.handle.net/10045/1280. 23 May 2011.

Kakutani, Michiko. "No Ice Cream Cones in a Heart of Darkness." Rev. of *The Poisonwood Bible,* by Barbara Kingsolver. *The New York Times* 16 Oct. 1999. Web.

Kaplan, David A. "Is It Torture or Tradition?" *Newsweek* 20 Dec. 1993: 124. Print.

Kaufmann, Michael. "The Religious, the Secular, and Literary Studies: Rethinking the Secularization Narrative in Histories of the Profession." *New Literary History* 38.4 (Autumn 2007): 607–28. Print.

Kellman, Steven G. "It *Is* Happening Here: *The Plot Against America* and the Political Moment." *Philip Roth Studies* 4.2 (2008): 113–23. Web. *Project Muse.* 17 Feb. 2011. Print.

Kim, Elaine. *Asian American Literature: An Introduction to the Writings and Their Social Context.* Philadelphia: Temple UP, 1982. Print.

Kimmage, Michael. "The Plight of Conservative Literature." *A New Literary History of America.* Ed. Greil Marcus and Werner Sollors. Cambridge, MA: Harvard UP, 2009. 948–53. Print.

Kingsolver, Barbara. *The Poisonwood Bible.* New York: HarperPerennial, 1998. Print.

———. *Small Wonder.* Illus. by Paul Mirocha. New York: HarperCollins, 2002. Print.

Kingston, Maxine Hong. *China Men.* New York: Vintage, 1980. Print.

———. "Cultural Mis-readings by American Reviewers." *Asian and Western Writers in Dialogue: New Cultural Identities.* Ed. Guy Amirthanayagam. London: Macmillan, 1982. 55–65. Print.

Kiracofe, Clifford A. *Dark Crusade: Christian Zionism and U.S. Foreign Policy.* New York: I. B. Tauris, 2009. Print.

Kirk, Stephanie. "Gender and the Writing of Piety in New Spain." *American Literary History* 26.1 (Spring 2014): 6–27. Print.

Klinkenborg, Verlyn. "Going Native." Rev. of *The Poisonwood Bible,* by Barbara Kingsolver. *The New York Times* 18 Oct. 1999. Web.

Koza, K. A. "The Africa of Two Western Women Writers: Barbara Kingsolver and Margaret Laurence." *Critique* 44.3 (2003): 284–94. Web. *Academic Search Complete.* 17 May 2011.

Krugman, Paul. *End This Recession Now!* New York: Norton, 2013. Print.

Kunz, Diane. "White Men in Africa: On Barbara Kingsolver's *The Poisonwood Bible*." *Novel History: Historians and Novelists Confront America's Past (and Each Other).* Ed. Mark C. Carnes. New York: Simon and Schuster, 2001. 285–97. Print.

Kushner, David. "Cormac McCarthy's Apocalypse." *Rolling Stone* 27 Dec 2007: 43–53. Print.

Lackey, Michael. *The Modernist God State: A Literary Study of the Nazis' Christian Reich.* New York: Continuum, 2012. Print.

Lacy, Norris J. "*The Da Vinci Code*: Dan Brown and the Grail That Never Was." *Arthuriana* 14.3 (2004): 81–93. Print.

LaHaye, Tim. *Faith of Our Founding Fathers.* Brentwood, TN: Wolgemuth & Hyatt, 1987. Print.

LaHaye, Tim and Jerry Jenkins. *Glorious Appearing: The End of Days.* Wheaton, IL: Tyndale, 2004. Print.

———. *The Indwelling: The Beast Takes Possession.* Wheaton, IL: Tyndale House, 2000. Print.

———. *Left Behind: A Novel of the Earth's Last Days.* Large Print edition. Thorndike, ME: Thorndike Press, 2000. Print.

———. *Tribulation Force: The Continuing Drama of Those Left Behind.* Wheaton, IL: Tyndale, 1996. Print.

Larson, Edward J. *Summer for the Gods: The Scopes Trial and America's Continuing Debate over Science and Religion.* Cambridge, MA: Harvard UP, 1997. Print.

———. *Trial and Error: The American Controversy over Creation and Evolution.* 3rd ed. New York: Oxford UP, 2002. Print.

Latour, Bruno. "Why Has Critique Run out of Steam? From Matters of Fact to Matters of Concern." *Critical Inquiry* 30 (Winter 2004): 225–48. Print.

Lear, Jonathan. "Not at Home in Gilead." *Raritan* 32.1 (2013): 34–52. Print.

Leonard, Karen I., Alex Stepick, Manuel A. Vasquez, and Jennifer Holdaway. *Immigrant Faiths: Transforming Religious Life in America.* New York: Altamira, 2005. Print.

Lepore, Jill. *The Whites of Their Eyes: The Tea Party's Revolution and the Battle over American History.* Princeton, NJ: Princeton UP, 2010. Print.

Lessl, Thomas M. "Science and the Sacred Cosmos: The Ideological Rhetoric of Carl Sagan." *Quarterly Journal of Speech* 71.2 (1985): 175–87. Print.

Lewis, Hope. "Between Irua and 'Female Genital Mutilation': Feminist Human Rights and the Cultural Divide." *Harvard Human Rights Journal* 8.1 (1995): 1–55. Print.

Lezard, Nicholas. "Believe in Evil: Nicholas Lezard on the Curse of the Congo." Rev. of *The Poisonwood Bible*, by Barbara Kingsolver. *The Guardian* 8 Jan. 2000. Web.

Li, David Leiwei. *Imagining the Nation: Asian American Literature and Cultural Consent.* Stanford, CA: Stanford UP, 1998. Print.

Lincoln, Kenneth. *Cormac McCarthy: American Canticles.* New York: Palgrave, 2009. Print.

Lindsay, D. Michael. *Faith in the Halls of Power: How Evangelicals Joined the American Elite.* New York: Oxford UP, 2007. Print.

Lizza, Ryan. "Leap of Faith: The Making of a Republican Front-Runner." *The New Yorker* 15 Aug 2011: 54–63. Print.

Lockwood, Robert P. "The Five Most Influential Anti-Catholic Books." *Catholic Answers Magazine* (formerly *This Rock Magazine*) May 2007. Web.

Lofton, Kathryn. *Oprah: The Gospel of an Icon.* Berkeley: U of California P, 2011. Print.

Luskin, Casey. "Nation's Schools Targeted with Mythical Alarmist 'Consensus' Program." Web. http://news.heartland.org/newspaper-article/2014/07/10/nations-schools-targeted-mythical-alarmist-consensus-program. 23 July 2014.

Lutzer, Erwin W. *The Da Vinci Deception.* Wheaton, IL: Tyndale House, 2004. Print.

Lynch, Cecelia. "Dogma, Praxis, and Religious Perspectives on Multiculturalism." *Millennium: Journal of International Studies* 29.3 (2000): 741–59. Web. *Sage.* 17 May 2011.

Lyotard, Jean-François. *The Postmodern Condition.* Trans. Geoff Bennington and Brian Massumi. Minneapolis: U of Minnesota P, 1984. Print.

Maffly-Kipp, Laurie F., Leigh E. Schmidt, and Mark Valeri, eds. *Practicing Protestants: Histories of Christian Life in America, 1630–1965.* Baltimore: Johns Hopkins UP, 2006. Print.

Maier, Paul L. "The Da Vinci Code." *Christian Research Journal* 27 (2004). Web. 10 June 2009.

Mailer, Norman. *Armies of the Night: History as a Novel, the Novel as History.* New York: Plume, 1994. Print.

Mann, Thomas E., and Norman J. Ornstein. *It's Even Worse Than It Looks: How the American Constitutional System Collided with the New Politics of Extremism.* New York: Basic, 2012. Print.

Marcus, Greil. *The Shape of Things to Come: Prophecy and the American Voice.* New York: Picador, 2007. Print.

Marsden, George M. *Fundamentalism and American Culture.* 2nd ed. Oxford, U.K.: Oxford UP, 2006. Print.

Marx, Leo. "Mr. Eliot, Mr. Trilling, and *Huckleberry Finn*." *American Scholar* 22 (1953): 423–40. Print.

Matthews, Shelly. *The Acts of the Apostles: Taming the Tongues of Fire.* Sheffield, U.K.: Sheffield Phoenix, 2013. Print.

McCarthy, Cormac. *Blood Meridian: or the Evening Redness in the West.* New York: Vintage, 1992. Print.

——. *Blood Meridian* draft. Cormac McCarthy Papers, Collection 91, Box 38, Folder 3.

——. *Suttree.* New York: Vintage, 1979. Print.

——. *The Road.* New York: Alfred A. Knopf, 2006. Print.

McClure, John. *Partial Faiths: Postsecular Fiction in the Age of Pynchon and Morrison.* Athens: U of Georgia P, 2007. Print.

——. "Postmodern/Post-Secular: Contemporary Fiction and Spirituality." *Modern Fiction Studies* 41.1 (1995): 141–63. Print.

McGee, Patrick. *Ishmael Reed and the Ends of Race.* New York: St. Martin's, 1997. Print.

McGurl, Mark. *The Program Era: Postwar Fiction and the Rise of Creative Writing.* Harvard U P, 2009. Print.

McHale, Brian. *Postmodernist Fiction.* New York: Routledge, 1987. Print.

McNally, Michael D. "Honoring Elders: Practices of Sagacity and Deference in Ojibwe Christianity." Maffly-Lipp et al. 77–99. Print.

Meillon, Bénédicte. "Aimé Césaire's *Une Saison au Congo* and Barbara Kingsolver's *The Poisonwood Bible* in the Light of Postcolonialism." *Anglophonia* 21 (2007): 197–211. Print.

Meire, Héloïse. "Women, A Dark Continent? *The Poisonwood Bible* as a Feminist Response to Conrad's *Heart of Darkness.*" *Seeds of Change: Critical Essays on Barbara Kingsolver.* Ed. Priscilla Leder. Knoxville: U of Tennessee P, 2010. 71–86. Print.

Mendelson, Edward. "The Sacred, the Profane, and *The Crying of Lot 49.*" *Pynchon: A Collection of Critical Essays.* Ed. Edward Mendelson. Englewood Cliffs, N.J.: Prentice-Hall, 1978. 112–46. Print.

Merivale, Patricia, and Susan Elizabeth Sweeney. "The Game's Afoot: On the Trail of the Metaphysical Detective Story." *Detecting Texts: The Metaphysical Detective Story from Poe to Postmodernism.* Ed. Patricia Merivale and Susan Elizabeth Sweeney. Philadelphia: U of Pennsylvania P, 1999. 1–24. Print.

Metzger, Bruce M. *The Text of the New Testament: Its Transmission, Corruption, and Restoration.* Oxford, U.K.: Oxford U P, 1964. Print.

Metzger, Bruce M., and Bart D. Ehrman. *The Text of the New Testament: Its Transmission, Corruption, and Restoration.* 4th ed. New York: Oxford U P, 2005. Print.

Mexal, Stephen J. "Realism, Narrative History, and the Production of the Bestseller: *The Da Vinci Code* and the Virtual Public Sphere." *The Journal of Popular Culture* 44.5 (2011): 1085–1101. Print.

Michaels, Walter Benn. *Our America: Nativism, Modernism, and Pluralism.* Durham, NC: Duke U P, 1995. Print.

——. "Plots Against America: Neoliberalism and Antiracism." *American Literary History* 18.2 (2006): 288–302. Print.

——. *The Shape of the Signifier: 1967 to the End of History.* Princeton, NJ: Princeton U P, 2004. Print.

——. *The Trouble with Diversity: How We Learned to Love Identity and Ignore Inequality.* New York: Holt, 2006. Print.

Miles, Jack. *God: A Biography*. New York: Alfred A. Knopf, 1995. Print.

Miller, Kenneth R. *Finding Darwin's God: A Scientist's Search for Common Ground Between God and Evolution*. New York: Harper Perennial, 1999. Print.

Mleynek, Sherryll. "The Rhetoric of the 'Jewish Problem' in the *Left Behind* Novels." *Literature & Theology* 19.4 (2005): 367–83. Print.

Modern, John Lardas. "How to Read Literature, Win Friends, Influence People, and Write about American Religion." *American Literary History* 26.1 (Spring 2014): 191–203. Print.

Momaday, N. Scott. *House Made of Dawn*. 1968. New York: Perennial Classics, 1999. Print.

Moore, Randy, Mark Decker, and Sehoya Cotner. *Chronology of the Evolution-Creationism Controversy*. Santa Barbara, CA: Greenwood, 2010. Print.

Moreton, Bethany. *To Serve God and Wal-Mart: the Making of Christian Free Enterprise*. Cambridge, MA: Harvard UP, 2009. Print.

Morris, Henry. *History of Modern Creationism*. San Diego: Master, 1984. Print.

Morris, John. "Evolution and the Wages of Sin." Web. *Institute for Creation Research*. 2 May 2013.

Morris, Simon Conway. *The Crucible of Creation: The Burgess Shale and the Rise of Animals*. Oxford, U.K.: Oxford UP, 1998. Print.

Morrison, Toni. *Beloved*. 1987. New York: Vintage, 2004. Print.

——. *The Bluest Eye*. 1970. New York: Plume, 1993. Print.

——. "The Pain of Being Black." Interview by Bonnie Angelo. *Time* 22 May 1989: 120–22. Print.

——. *Playing in the Dark: Whiteness and the Literary Imagination*. New York: Vintage, 1992. Print.

——. "Unspeakable Things Unspoken." *Within the Circle: An Anthology of African American Literary Criticism from the Harlem Renaissance to the Present*. Ed. Angelyn Mitchell. Durham, NC: Duke UP, 1994. 368–98. Print.

Mundik, Petra. "Striking the Fire Out of the Rock: Gnostic Theology in Cormac McCarthy's *Blood Meridian*." *South Central Review* 26.3 (2009): 72–97. Print.

Myhal, Bob. "Boundaries, Centers, and Circles: The Postmodern Geometry of *The Handmaid's Tale*." *Lit: Literature Interpretation Theory* 6:3–4 (1995): 213–31. Print.

Neelakantan, Gurumurthy. "Philip Roth's Nostalgia for the *Yiddishkayt* and the New Deal Idealisms in *The Plot Against America*." *Philip Roth Studies* 4.2 (2008): 125–36. Web. *Project Muse*. 17 Feb. 2011.

Nelson, Victoria. "Faux Catholic: A Gothic Subgenre from Monk Lewis to Dan Brown." *Boundary 2* 34.3 (2007): 87–107. Print.

Neuman, Shirley. "'Just a Backlash': Margaret Atwood, Feminism, and 'The Handmaid's Tale.' *University of Toronto Quarterly* 75.3 (Summer 2006): 857–68. Print.

Newman, Marc T. "The Land of Faery as Cosmic Cheat: A Lewisian Analysis of Robert Zemekis' *Contact*." *Journal of Religion and Popular Culture* 22.1 (2010): 1–23. Web.

Nicholls, Peter. "Carl Sagan's Messages from the Milky Way." Rev. of *Contact*, by Carl Sagan. *The Washington Post Book World* 13 Oct 1985: 6. Print.

Nietzsche, Friedrich. *Morgenröte / The Dawn of Day*. Trans. John McFarland Kennedy. New York: Macmillan, 1911. Web. http://www.gutenberg.org/files/39955/39955-pdf.pdf. 3 Oct. 2015.

Nohrnberg, James. "Pynchon's Paraclete." *Pynchon: A Collection of Critical Essays*. Ed. Edward Mendelson. Englewood Cliffs, N.J.: Prentice-Hall, 1978. 147–61. Print.

Noll, Mark A. *The Scandal of the Evangelical Mind*. Grand Rapids, MI: Eerdmans, 1994. Print.

Northup, Solomon. *Twelve Years a Slave*. 1853. New York: Penguin, 2012. Print.

Novy, Marianne. "Barbara Kingsolver's *Poisonwood Bible* in Dialogue with Shakespeare." *Shakespeare Jahrbuch* 137 (2001): 66–74. Print.

Numbers, Ronald L. *The Creationists: From Scientific Creationism to Intelligent Design*. Expanded Edition. Cambridge, MA: Harvard UP, 2006. Print.

O'Callaghan, Joseph. *A History of Medieval Spain*. Ithaca, NY: Cornell UP, 1975. Print.

Ognibene, Elaine R. "The Missionary Position: Barbara Kingsolver's *The Poisonwood Bible*." *College Literature* 30.3 (2003): 19–36. Web. *JSTOR*. 17 May 2011.

Okada, John. *No-No Boy*. Seattle: U of Washington P, 1976. Print.

Omi, Michael, and Howard Winant. *Racial Formation in the United States from the 1960s to the 1980s*. New York: Routledge, 1986. Print.

Omnus, Wiebke. "History Remembered: Religion, Violence, and 'the War Against Slavery.'" *English Language and Literature* 58.3 (2012): 413–25. Print.

Orsi, Robert A. *Between Heaven and Earth: The Religious Worlds People Make and the Scholars Who Study Them*. Princeton, NJ: Princeton UP, 2005. Print.

———. "Everyday Miracles: The Study of Lived Religion." Hall 3–21. Print.

Ostrander, Rick. "The Practice of Prayer in a Modern Age: Liberals, Fundamentalists, and Prayer in the Early Twentieth Century." Maffly-Kipp 177–95. Print.

Pagels, Elaine. *The Gnostic Gospels*. New York: Vintage, 1989. Print.

Paley, William, Matthew D. Eddy, ed., and David Knight, ed. *Natural Theology: Or Evidence of the Existence and Attributes of the Deity, Collected from the Appearances of Nature*. 1802. Oxford, U.K.: Oxford UP, 2006. Print.

Paradis, Kenneth. "Typological Realism in Contemporary Evangelical Fiction: Tragedy, Eternity, and *The Shack*." *English Studies in Canada* 37.1 (2011): 107–33. Print.

Payne, J. Barton. "Higher Criticism and Biblical Inerrancy." Geisler 85–113. Print.

Pecora, Vincent P. *Secularization and Cultural Criticism: Religion, Nation, & Modernity*. Chicago: U of Chicago P, 2006. Print.

Perrotta, Tim. *The Abstinence Teacher*. New York: St. Martin's, 2007. Print.

———. "Tom Perrotta's Culture Wars." Interview. *The Abstinence Teacher*. New York: St. Martin's, 2007. 362–68. Print.

"Philip Roth: Literary Hit Man with a 9/11 Bullet in His Gun." *Sunday Times* [London] 19 Sept. 2004: 15. Web. 17 Feb. 2011.

Phillips, Dana. "History and the Ugly Facts of Cormac McCarthy's *Blood Meridian*." *American Literature* 68.2 (1996): 433–60. Print.

Phipps, William E. *Was Jesus Married?: The Distortion of Sexuality in the Christian Tradition*. New York: Harper, 1970. Print.

Picketty, Thomas. *Capital in the Twenty-First Century*. Trans. Arthur Goldhammer. Cambridge, MA: Harvard U P, 2014. Print.

Pierce, Kenneth M. "Putting Darwin Back in the Dock." *Time* 16 March 1981: 80–82. Print.

Pinter, Harold. "Nobel Lecture: Art, Truth & Politics." *Nobelprize.org*. Nobel Media AB 2013. Web. http://www.nobelprize.org/nobel_prizes/literature/laureates/2005/pinter-lecture-e.html. 24 Jun 2014.

Plath, Sylvia. *The Bell Jar*. New York: Faber, 1963. Print.

Plumer, Eric Antone. *The Catholic Church and American Culture: Why the Claims of Dan Brown Struck a Chord*. Scranton, PA: U of Scranton P, 2009. Print.

Posnock, Ross. *Philip Roth's Rude Truth: The Art of Immaturity*. Princeton, NJ: Princeton U P, 2006. Print.

Poundstone, William. *Carl Sagan: A Life in the Cosmos*. New York: Henry Holt, 1999. Print.

Priest, Josiah. *Bible Defence of Slavery: or, The Origin, History, and Fortunes of the Negro Race, as Deduced from History, Both Sacred and Profane, Their Natural Relations—Moral, Mental, and Physical—to the Other Races of Mankind, Compared and Illustrated—Their Future Destiny Predicted, etc*. Louisville, KY: J. F. Brennan, 1851. Print.

Prusak, Bernard G. "When Words Fail Us: Reexamining the Conscience of *Huckleberry Finn*." *The Journal of Aesthetic Education* 45.4 (Winter 2011): 1–22. Print.

Purcell, William F. "The Gospel According to Barbara Kingsolver." *Logos: A Journal of Catholic Thought & Culture* 12.1 (2009): 93–116. Web. *Academic Search Complete*. 17 May 2011.

Putnam, Bill, and John Edwin Wood. "Unravelling the Da Vinci Code." *History Today* 55.1 (2005): 18–20. Print.

Putnam, Robert D., and David E. Campbell. *American Grace: How Religion Divides and Unites Us*. New York: Simon and Schuster, 2012. Print.

Pynchon, Thomas. *The Crying of Lot 49*. 1966. New York: Harper Perennial, 2006. Print.

——. "Entropy." *The Norton Anthology of American Literature*. Shorter 8th ed. Ed. Nina Baym et al. New York: Norton, 2013. 2668–78. Print.

——. *Gravity's Rainbow*. New York: Penguin, 1973. Print.

Quinton, Anthony. "A Master Impersonator's Epitome of the 1980s: This Rabbit Will Run and Run." Rev. of *Rabbit is Rich*, by John Updike. *Times* [London, England] 14 Jan. 1982: 8. Web. *The Times Digital Archive*. 28 Apr. 2014.

Quran. Trans. M.A.S. Abdel Haleem. Oxford, U.K.: Oxford U P, 2004. Web. http://asadullahali.files.wordpress.com/2010/09/the_quran.pdf. 28 Apr. 2014.

Rambuss, Richard. "The Straightest Story Ever Told." *GLQ: A Journal of Lesbian and Gay Studies* 17.4 (2011): 543–73. Print.

Reed, Ishmael. *Mumbo Jumbo*. New York: Simon and Schuster, 1972. Print.

——. *Yellow Back Radio Broke-Down*. 1969. Normal, IL: Dalkey Archive Press, 2000. Print.

Regier, Ami. "Replacing the Hero with the Reader: Public Story Structure in *The Poisonwood Bible*." *Mennonite Life* 56.1 (2001). Web. http://www.bethelks.edu/mennonitelife/2001mar/regier_pf.php.

Rich, Frank. "President Lindbergh in 2004." *New York Times* 23 Sept. 2004. Web. 2 Feb. 2011.

Rich, Motoko. "A Writer's Search for the Sex in Abstinence." *New York Times* 14 Oct. 2007. Web. http://www.nytimes.com/2007/10/14/books/14rich.html? pagewanted=2&_r=0.

Robinson, Marilynne. *The Death of Adam: Essays on Modern Thought.* 1998. New York: Picador, 2005. Print.

———. *Gilead.* Toronto: HarperCollins, 2004. Print.

———. *Home.* Toronto: HarperCollins, 2008. Print.

———. "Hysterical Scientism: The Ecstasy of Richard Dawkins." *Harper's Magazine* 29 Nov. 2006: 83–88. Print.

———. *Lila.* Toronto: HarperCollins, 2014. Print.

Roos, Henriette. "The Sins of Our Fathers: The Missionary in Some Modern English Novels on the Congo." *Tydskrif vir Letterkunde* 46.1 (2009): 58–78. Web. *Scientific Electronic Library Online South Africa.* http://www.scielo.org.za/pdf/tvl/v46n1/v46n1a05.pdf. 23 May 2011.

Roth, Philip. *American Pastoral.* New York: Vintage, 1997. Print.

———. "The Conversion of the Jews." *Goodbye, Columbus and Five Short Stories.* New York: Vintage, 1993. 137–58. Print.

———. *The Counterlife.* New York: Vintage, 1996. Print.

———. "Defender of the Faith." *Goodbye, Columbus and Five Short Stories.* New York: Vintage, 1993. 159–200. Print.

———. *The Facts: A Novelist's Autobiography.* Toronto: Collins, 1988. Print.

———. *The Plot Against America.* New York: Vintage, 2005. Print.

———. *Portnoy's Complaint.* New York: Vintage, 1994. Print.

———. "The Story Behind 'The Plot Against America.'" *New York Times* 19 Sept. 2004. Web. 2 Feb. 2011.

Rothberg, Michael. "Against Zero-Sum Logic: A Response to Walter Benn Michaels." *American Literary History* 18.2 (2006): 303–11. Print.

Rubin-Dorsky, Jeffrey. "Philip Roth and American Jewish Identity: The Question of Authenticity." *American Literary History* 13.1 (2001): 79–107. Print.

Rushdy, Ashraf H. A. "Daughters Signifyin(g) History: The Example of Toni Morrison's *Beloved.*" *American Literature* 64 (1992): 567–97. Print.

Sadlek, Gregory M. "Robert Zemeckis's *Contact* as a Late-Twentieth Century *Paradiso.*" *Journal of Religion and Film* 5.2 (October 2001). Online.

Sagan, Carl. *Contact.* New York: Simon and Schuster, 1985. Print.

———. *Conversations with Carl Sagan.* Ed. Tom Head. Jackson: UP of Mississippi, 2006. Print.

———. *The Varieties of Scientific Experience: A Personal View of the Search for God.* Ed. Ann Druyan. New York: Penguin, 2006. Print.

Schaeffer, Francis A. *How Should We Then Live?: The Rise and Decline of Western Thought and Culture.* Old Tappan, NJ: Fleming H. Revell, 1976. Print.

Schaeffer, Frank. *Crazy for God.* Cambridge, MA: Da Capo, 2007. Print.

———. *Portofino.* New York: Macmillan, 1992. Print.

———. *Why I am an Atheist Who Believes in God.* Salisbury, MA: Regina Orthodox Press, 2014. Print.

Scheidel, Walter. "The Roman Slave Supply." *The Cambridge World History of Slavery.* Vol. 1: *The Ancient Mediterranean World.* Ed. Keith Bradley and Paul Cartledge. Cambridge, U.K.: Cambridge UP, 2011. Web. *Cambridge Histories Online.* http://dx.doi.org.ezproxy.library.uvic.ca/10.1017/CHOL9780521840668. 5 March 2014.

Schmalzbauer, John, and Kathleen Mahoney. "Religion and Knowledge in the Post-Secular Academy." Web. *SSRC Working Papers.* http://blogs.ssrc.org/tif/wp-content/uploads/2009/09/post-secular-academy.pdf. 9 May 2014.

Sepich, John. *Notes on* Blood Meridian. Rev. ed. Austin: U of Texas P, 2008. Print.

Shannon, Noah Gallagher. "Cormac McCarthy Cuts to the Bone." *Slate* 5 Oct 2012. Web.

Shiffman, Dan. *"The Plot Against America* and History Post-9/11." *Philip Roth Studies* 5.1 (2009): 61–73. Print.

Shinn, Christopher. "The Art of War: Ishmael Reed and Frank Chin and the U.S. Black-Asian Alliance of Multicultural Satire." *African American Humor, Irony, and Satire: Ishmael Reed, Satirically Speaking.* Ed. Dana A. Williams. Newcastle, U.K.: Cambridge Scholars, 2007. Print.

Shoop, Casey. "Thomas Pynchon, Postmodernism, and the Rise of the New Right in California." *Contemporary Literature* 53.1 (2012): 51–86. Print.

Shorto, Russell. "How Christian Were the Founders?" *New York Times Sunday Magazine* 11 Feb 2010: MM32. Print.

Shy, Todd. "Religion and Marilynne Robinson." *Salmagundi* 155-56 (2007): 251–64. Print.

Siegel, Lee. "Sweet and Low." Rev. of *The Poisonwood Bible,* by Barbara Kingsolver. *The New Republic* 22 March 1999. Web.

Silko, Leslie Marmon. *Almanac of the Dead.* New York: Penguin Books, 1991. Print.

——. *Ceremony.* New York: Penguin Books, 1977. Print.

Silko, Leslie Marmon, and Ellen Arnold. *Conversations with Leslie Silko.* Jackson: UP of Mississippi, 2000. Print.

Silver, Daniel J. "God and Carl Sagan in Hollywood." *Commentary* (September 1997): 52–54. Print.

"Sin Caused Death." Web. *Institute for Creation Research.* 2 May 2013.

Sison, Antonio D. "Epiphany of the Throne-Chariot: Merkabah Mysticism and the Film *Contact." Journal of Religion and Film* 9.1 (2005). Web.

Smedley, Audrey. *Race in North America: Origin and Evolution of a Worldview.* 2nd ed. Boulder: Westview, 1999. Print.

Smith, H. Shelton. *In His Image, but . . . Racism in Southern Religion, 1780–1910.* Durham, NC: Duke UP, 1972. Print.

Smith, Roy Steinholl. "White Man's Burden: Recent Thought about Christian Practice." *Religious Studies Review* 21.3 (1995): 192–95. Print.

Snodgrass, Mary Ellen. *Barbara Kingsolver: A Literary Companion.* Jefferson, NC: McFarland, 2004. Print.

Spielvogel, Jackson. *Hitler and Germany: A History.* Englewood Cliffs, NJ: Prentice Hall, 1988. Print.

Stafford, Tim. "Books: Poisonous Gospel." Rev. of *The Poisonwood Bible,* by Barbara Kingsolver. *Christianity Today* 11 January 1999. Web.

Stark, Rodney. "Secularization, R.I.P." *Sociology of Religion* 60.3 (1999): 249–73. Print.

Steigmann-Gall, Richard. *The Holy Reich: Nazi Conceptions of Christianity, 1919–1945.* Cambridge, U.K.: Cambridge UP, 2003. Print.

Strehle, Susan. "Chosen People: American Exceptionalism in Kingsolver's *The Poisonwood Bible.*" *Critique* 49.4 (2008): 413–28. Web. *Academic Search Complete.* 17 May 2011.

Suskind, Ron. "Faith, Certainty and the Presidency of George W. Bush." *New York Times Magazine* 17 Oct. 2004. Web. http://www.nytimes.com/2004/10/17/magazine/faith-certainty-and-the-presidency-of-george-w-bush.html.

Sweeney, Susan Elizabeth. "The Metaphysical Detective Story." *Crime and Detective Fiction.* Ed. Rebecca Martin. Ipswich, MA: Grey House, 2013. 176–96. Print.

Taylor, Charles. *A Secular Age.* Cambridge, MA: Harvard UP, 2007. Print.

Taylor, Mark. *After God.* Chicago: U of Chicago P, 2007. Print.

Teilhard de Chardin, Pierre. *Christianity and Evolution.* Trans. René Hague. London: Collins, 1971. Print.

Thomas, Joan. "White Mischief: Culture Wars in the Congo." Rev. of *The Poisonwood Bible,* by Barbara Kingsolver. *The Toronto Globe and Mail* 14 Nov. 1998. Web.

Thompson, Bob. "At 'Home' with the Past: In Life and in Her Novels, Marilynne Robinson Looks Back to find Meaning." *Washington Post* 20 Oct. 2008. Web. http://www.washingtonpost.com/wp-dyn/content/article/2008/10/19/AR2008101902106_pf.html. 8 May 2011.

Tilson, Everett. *Segregation and the Bible.* New York: Abingdon, 1958. Print.

Tolson, Jay. "A New Great Awakening?" *U.S. News and World Report* blog. Web. 25 January 2008.

Tong, Benjamin. "The Ghetto of the Mind." *Amerasia Journal* 1.3 (1971): 1–31. Print.

"The Truth about the War." Editorial. *New York Times* 6 June 2008. Web. http://www.nytimes.com/2008/06/06/opinion/06fri1.html?pagewanted=all&_r=1&.

The Two-Way blog. "Creation Museum: Bill Nye Debate Sparked Funding 'Miracle.'" 1 March 2014. Web. http://www.npr.org/blogs/thetwo-way/2014/03/01/284397588/creation-museum-bill-nye-debate-sparked-funding-miracle.

Updike, John. *Rabbit Angstrom: The Four Novels: Rabbit, Run, Rabbit Redux, Rabbit is Rich, and Rabbit at Rest.* New York: Everyman's, 1995. Print.

Varela-Zapata, Jesus. "Staying on After the Empire: The Changing Role of Church Missions in Africa from Colonial to Post-Colonial Times." *Colonies, Missions, Cultures in the English Speaking World: General and Comparative Studies.* Ed. and intro. Gerhard Stilz. Tübingen: Stauffenburg; 2001. 99–110. Print.

Velie, Alan. "The Return of the Native: The Renaissance of Tribal Religions as Reflected in the Fiction of N. Scott Momaday." *Religion & Literature* 26.1 (1994): 135–45. Print.

Walker, Alice. *The Color Purple.* New York: Pocket Books, 1982. Print.

——. Foreword: "Zora Neale Hurston—A Cautionary Tale and a Partisan View." 1976. In *Zora Neale Hurston: A Literary Biography.* By Robert Hemenway. Urbana, IL: U of Chicago P, 1977. xi–xviii. Print.

———. *Possessing the Secret of Joy.* New York: Pocket Books, 1992. Print.

———. *The Same River Twice: Honoring the Difficult.* New York: Washington Square, 1996. Print.

Walker, Alice, and Pratibha Parmar. *Warrior Marks: Female Genital Mutilation and the Sexual Blinding of Women.* San Diego: Harcourt, 1993. Print.

Walker, Madeline. *The Trouble with Sauling Around: Conversion in Ethnic American Autobiography, 1965–2002.* Iowa City: U of Iowa P, 2011. Print.

Wall, James M. "Fluff and Substance." Rev. of *Contact. Christian Century* 30 July 1997. Web.

Wallace, David Foster. *The Pale King.* New York: Little, Brown, 2011. Print.

Wallach, Rick. "Cormac McCarthy's Metaphors of Antiquity and Deep Time." In *Cormac McCarthy: Uncharted Territories / Territoires Inconnus*, 105–13. Reims: Presses Universitaires de Reims, 2003. Print.

Warren, Donald. *Radio Priest: Charles Coughlin, the Father of Hate Radio.* New York: Free Press, 1996. Print.

Warren, Rick. *The Purpose Driven Life: What on Earth Am I Here For?* 2002. Expanded ed. Grand Rapids, MI: Zondervan, 2011. Print.

Waser N. M., L. Chittka, M. V. Price, N. M. Williams, and J. Ollerton. "Generalization in Pollination Systems, and Why It Matters." *Ecology* 77 (1996): 1043–60. Print.

Webb, George E. *The Evolution Controversy in America.* Lexington: UP of Kentucky, 2002. Print.

Weber, Myles. "Whose War Is This?" *New England Review* 27.4 (2006): 206–11. Web. *Project Muse.* 17 Feb. 2011.

Weese, Katherine J. "'The Eyes in the Trees': Transculturation and Magic Realism in Barbara Kingsolver's *The Poisonwood Bible.*" *Feminist Narrative and the Supernatural: The Function of Fantastic Devices in Seven Recent Novels.* Jefferson, NC: McFarland, 2008. 109–24. Print.

Weiss, Kenneth, and Anne Buchanan. *The Mermaid's Tale: Four Billion Years of Cooperation in the Making of Living Things.* Cambridge, MA: Harvard UP, 2009. Print.

Werber, Niels "Geo- and Biopolitics of Middle-Earth: a German Reading of Tolkien's *The Lord of the Rings.*" *New Literary History* 36 (2005): 227–46. Print.

Whitcomb, John C., and Henry M. Morris. *The Genesis Flood: The Biblical Record and Its Scientific Implications.* Phillipsburg, NJ: Presbyterian and Reformed Publishing, 1961. Print.

White, Jeanna Fuston. "The One-Eyed Preacher, His Crooked Daughter, and Villagers Waving Their Stumps: Barbara Kingsolver's Use of Disability in *The Poisonwood Bible.*" *South Central Review* 26.3 (2009): 131–46. Web. *Literature Online.* 19 May 2011.

Wideman, John Edgar. *The Homewood Books.* Pittsburgh: U of Pittsburgh P, 1992. Print.

Wilentz, Sean. *The Age of Reagan: A History 1974–2008.* New York: Harper Perennial, 2008. Print.

———. Foreword. Hofstadter xi–xxx. Print.

Will, George F. "Literary Politics." *Newsweek* 22 Apr. 1991: 72. Print.

Williams, Daniel K. *God's Own Party: The Making of the Christian Right.* Oxford, U.K.: Oxford UP, 2010. Print.

Williams, Rowan. "Native Speakers: Identity, Grace, and Homecoming." *Christianity and Literature* 61.1 (2011): 7–18. Print.

Wilson, E. O. "Evolution and Our Inner Conflict." *New York Times* 24 June 2012. Web. http://opinionator.blogs.nytimes.com/2012/06/24/evolution-and-our-inner-conflict/.

Wojcik, Daniel. *The End of the World as We Know It: Faith, Fatalism, and Apocalypse in America.* New York: New York UP, 1997. Print.

Wright, Richard. *Native Son.* 1940. New York: HarperCollins, 1998. Print.

Yardley, Jonathan. "Homeland Insecurity." Rev. of *The Plot Against America*, by Philip Roth. *Washngtonpost.com.* 3 Oct. 2004. Web. 17 Feb. 2011.

York, R. A. "Barbara Kingsolver's *The Poisonwood Bible.*" *The Extension of Life: Fiction and History in the American Novel.* Madison, NJ: Fairleigh Dickinson UP, 2003. 138–49. Print.

Young, William Paul. *The Shack: Where Tragedy Confronts Eternity.* Newbury Park, CA: Windblown Media, 2007. Print.

Zoba, Wendy Murray. "Missions Improbable." Rev. of *The Poisonwood Bible*, by Barbara Kingsolver. *Books & Culture: A Christian Review*, 1998. Web. 3 Oct. 2015.

INDEX